GREAT BRITAIN & I

TOURIST and MOTORING ATLAS / ATLAS ROUTIER et TOURISTIQUE
TOERISTISCHE WEGENATLAS / ATLANTE STRADALE e TURISTICO / ATLAS DE CARRETERAS y TURISTICO

Contents
Sommaire / Inhaltsübersicht / Inhoud / Sommario / Sumario

Inside front cover: key to map pages
Intérieur de couverture : tableau d'assemblage / Umschlaginnenseite: Übersicht / Binnenzijde van het omslag: overzichtskaart
-Copertina interna: quadro d'insieme / Portada interior: mapa índice

II - III

Channel Tunnel - Tunnel sous la Manche
Folkestone Terminal - Terminal de Calais (F)
Shipping Services
Liaisons maritimes / Schiffsverbindungen / Scheepvaartverbindingen / Collegamenti marittimi / Líneas marítimas

IV - XXI

Main road map
Grands axes routiers / Durchgangsstraßen / Grote verbindingswegen / Grandi arterie stradali / Carreteras principales
1 inch = 15.8 miles - 1:1 000 000 - 1 cm = 10 km

1 - 119

Key   **1**
Légende / Zeichenerklärung / Verklaring van de tekens / Legenda / Signos convencionales

Great Britain & Ireland   **2 - 119**
Grande-Bretagne & Irlande / Großbritannien & Irland / Groot-Brittannië & Ierland
Gran Bretagna & Irlanda / Gran Bretaña & Irlanda
1 inch = 4.75 miles - 1: 300 000 - 1 cm = 3 km

120 - 147

Index Great Britain   **120 - 138**
Index Grande-Bretagne / Register Großbritannien / Register Groot-Brittannië / Indice Gran Bretagna / Índice Gran Bretaña

Index Ireland   **139 - 147**
Index Irlande / Register Irland / Register Ierland / Indice Irlanda / Índice Irlanda

148 - 192

Key   **148**
Légende / Zeichenerklärung / Verklaring van de tekens / Legenda / Signos convencionales

Town plans Great Britain   **149 - 185**
Plans de ville Grande-Bretagne / Stadtpläne Großbritannien / Stadsplattegronden Groot-Brittannië
Piante di città Gran Bretagna / Planos de ciudades Gran Bretaña

Town plans Ireland   **186 - 191**
Plans de ville Irlande / Stadtpläne Irland / Stadsplattegronden Ierland / Piante di città Irlanda / Planos de ciudades Irlanda

Eochair / Allwedd / Comnarthai ar phleanna bailte / Symbolau ar gynlluniau'r trefi   **192**

Back of the guide: distances
En fin de volume : distances / Am Ende des Buches: Entfernungen / Achter in het boek: afstanden
Alla fine del volume: distanze / Al final del volumen: distancias

Channel Tunnel
Tunnel sous la Manche

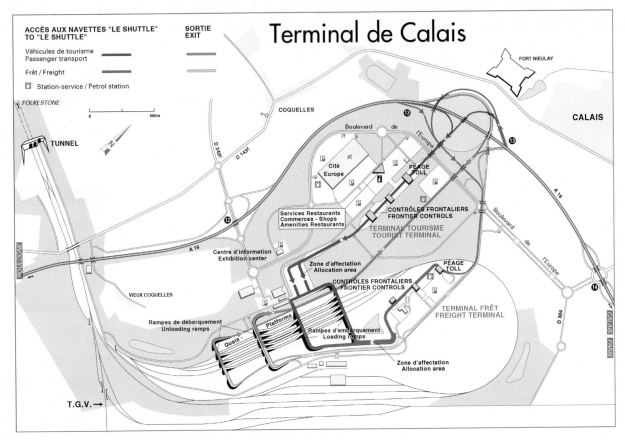

Terminal de Calais

ACCÈS AUX NAVETTES "LE SHUTTLE"
TO "LE SHUTTLE"

SORTIE
EXIT

Véhicules de tourisme
Passenger transport

Frêt / Freight

Station-service / Petrol station

FOLKESTONE

TUNNEL

500m

COQUELLES

FORT NIEULAY

CALAIS

Boulevard de l'Europe

Cité Europe

PÉAGE TOLL

CONTRÔLES FRONTALIERS
FRONTIER CONTROLS

Services Restaurants
Commerces - Shops
Amenities Restaurants

TERMINAL TOURISME
TOURIST TERMINAL

Boulevard de l'Europe

Centre d'information
Exhibition center

Zone d'affectation
Allocation area

CONTRÔLES FRONTALIERS
FRONTIER CONTROLS

PÉAGE TOLL

VIEUX COQUELLES

TERMINAL FRÊT
FREIGHT TERMINAL

Rampes de débarquement
Unloading ramps

Quais - Platforms

Rampes d'embarquement
Loading ramps

Zone d'affectation
Allocation area

T.G.V.

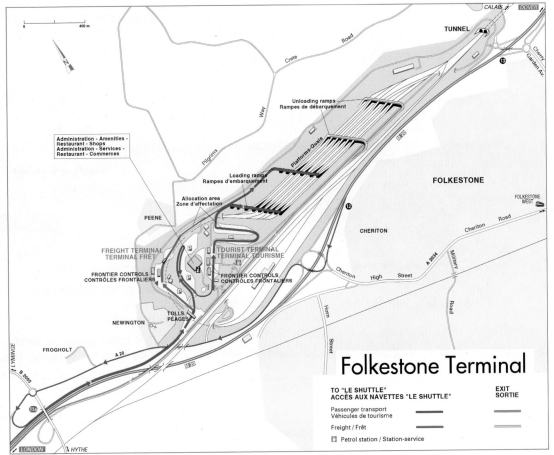

CALAIS   DOVER

TUNNEL

Road

Crete

Way

Pilgrims

Unloading ramps
Rampes de débarquement

Cherry   Garden Av.

Administration - Amenities -
Restaurant - Shops
Administration - Services -
Restaurant - Commerces

Platforms-Quais

FOLKESTONE

FOLKESTONE WEST

Loading ramps
Rampes d'embarquement

Allocation area
Zone d'affectation

PEENE

CHERITON

Cheriton   Road

FREIGHT TERMINAL
TERMINAL FRÊT

TOURIST TERMINAL
TERMINAL TOURISME

FRONTIER CONTROLS
CONTRÔLES FRONTALIERS

FRONTIER CONTROLS
CONTRÔLES FRONTALIERS

Cheriton   High   Street

TOLLS
PÉAGES

Horn   Street

Military   Road

NEWINGTON

FROGHOLT

A 20

LYMINGE   B 2065

LONDON   HYTHE

Folkestone Terminal

TO "LE SHUTTLE"
ACCÈS AUX NAVETTES "LE SHUTTLE"

EXIT
SORTIE

Passenger transport
Véhicules de tourisme

Freight / Frêt

Petrol station / Station-service

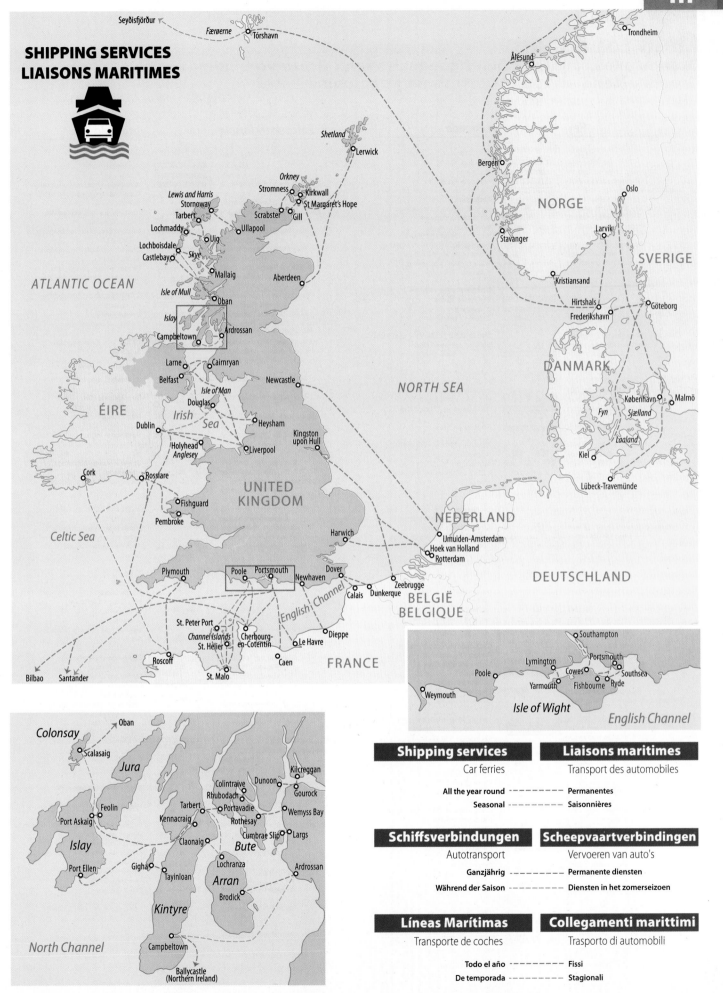

SHIPPING SERVICES
LIAISONS MARITIMES

ATLANTIC OCEAN

Seyðisfjörður
Færøerne
Tórshavn

Shetland
Lerwick

Orkney
Stromness Kirkwall
St Margaret's Hope
Scrabster Gill

Lewis and Harris
Stornoway
Tarbert
Lochmaddy Uig
Lochboisdale
Castlebay Skye
Mallaig
Isle of Mull
Oban
Islay
Campbeltown Ardrossan

Aberdeen

Larne Cairnryan
Belfast
Newcastle
Isle of Man
Douglas
ÉIRE Irish
Dublin Sea Heysham
Holyhead Kingston
Anglesey Liverpool upon Hull
Cork
Rosslare
UNITED
Fishguard KINGDOM
Pembroke

Celtic Sea
Harwich
Plymouth Poole Portsmouth
Newhaven Dover
St. Peter Port Zeebrugge
Channel Islands Calais Dunkerque
St. Hélier Cherbourg- Dieppe
en-Cotentin Le Havre BELGIË
Roscoff BELGIQUE
Bilbao Santander Caen FRANCE
St. Malo English Channel

NORGE
Trondheim
Ålesund
Bergen
Oslo
Stavanger Larvik
SVERIGE
Kristiansand
Hirtshals Göteborg
Frederikshavn
DANMARK
København Malmö
Fyn Sjælland
Laaland
Kiel
Lübeck-Travemünde
NEDERLAND
IJmuiden-Amsterdam
Hoek van Holland
Rotterdam
DEUTSCHLAND
NORTH SEA

Isle of Wight inset
Southampton
Lymington Portsmouth
Poole Cowes
Yarmouth Fishbourne Ryde Southsea
Weymouth Isle of Wight
English Channel

Scotland inset
Colonsay
Oban
Scalasaig
Jura
Kilcreggan
Colintraive Dunoon
Rhubodach Gourock
Tarbert Portavadie
Kennacraig Rothesay Wemyss Bay
Feolin Cumbrae Slip Largs
Port Askaig Claonaig Bute
Islay Lochranza
Port Ellen Gigha Ardrossan
Tayinloan Arran
Brodick
Kintyre
North Channel
Campbeltown
Ballycastle
(Northern Ireland)

III

Shipping services	**Liaisons maritimes**
Car ferries	Transport des automobiles
All the year round -------	Permanentes
Seasonal --- ---	Saisonnières

Schiffsverbindungen	**Scheepvaartverbindingen**
Autotransport	Vervoeren van auto's
Ganzjährig -------	Permanente diensten
Während der Saison --- ---	Diensten in het zomerseizoen

Líneas Marítimas	**Collegamenti marittimi**
Transporte de coches	Trasporto di automobili
Todo el año -------	Fissi
De temporada --- ---	Stagionali

Main road map
Grands axes routiers / Durchgangsstraßen / Grote verbindingswegen
Grandi arterie stradali / Carreteras principales

Key	Légende	Zeichenerklärung	Legenda

Roads / Routes / Straßen / Strade

Motorway	Autoroute	Autobahn	Autostrada
Motorway: single carriageway	Route-auto	Autostraße	Strada-auto
Motorway (unclassified)	Autoroute et assimilée	Autobahn oder Schnellstraße	Autostrada, strada di tipo autostradale
Dual carriageway with motorway characteristics	Double chaussée de type autoroutier	Schnellstraße mit getrennten Fahrbahnen	Doppia carreggiata di tipo autostradale
Interchanges:	Échangeurs :	Anschlussstellen:	Svincoli:
complete, limited, not specified	complet, partiels, sans précision	Voll - bzw. Teilanschluss, ohne Angabe	completo, parziale, imprecisato
Interchange numbers	Numéros d'échangeurs	Anschlussstellennummern	Svincoli numerati
Recommended MICHELIN main itinerary	Itinéraire principal recommandé par MICHELIN	Von MICHELIN empfohlene Hauptverkehrsstraße	Itinerario principale raccomandato da MICHELIN
Recommended MICHELIN regional itinerary	Itinéraire régional ou de dégagement recommandé par MICHELIN	Von MICHELIN empfohlene Regionalstraße	Itinerario regionale raccomandato da MICHELIN
Road surfaced - unsurfaced	Route revêtue - non revêtue	Straße mit Belag - ohne Belag	Strada rivestita - non rivestita
Motorway/Road under construction	Autoroute - Route en construction	Autobahn/Straße im Bau	Autostrada - Strada in costruzione

Road widths / Largeur des routes / Straßenbreiten / Larghezza delle strade

Dual carriageway	Chaussées séparées	Getrennte Fahrbahnen	Carreggiate separate
2 wide lanes	2 voies larges	2 breite Fahrspuren	2 corsie larghe
2 lanes - 2 narrow lanes	2 voies - 2 voies étroites	2 Fahrspuren - 2 schmale Fahrspuren	2 corsie - 2 corsie strette

Distances / Straßenentfernungen / Distanze

Distances (total and intermediate)	Distances (totalisées et partielles)	Straßenentfernungen (Gesamt- und Teilentfernungen)	Distanze (totali e parziali)
On motorway in kilometers	Sur autoroute en kilomètres	Auf der Autobahn in Kilometern	Su autostrada in chilometri
Toll roads - Toll-free section	Section à péage - Section libre	Mautstrecke - Mautfreie Strecke	Tratto a pedaggio - Tratto esente da pedaggio
On road in kilometers	Sur route en kilomètres	Auf der Straße in Kilometern	Su strada in chilometri
On motorway (GB) in miles - in kilometers	Sur autoroute (GB) en miles - en kilomètres	Auf der Autobahn (GB) in Meilen - in Kilometern	Su autostrada (GB) in miglia - in chilometri
Toll roads - Toll-free section	Section à péage - Section libre	Mautstrecke - Mautfreie Strecke	Tratto a pedaggio - Tratto esente da pedaggio
On road in miles	Sur route en miles	Auf der Straße in Meilen	Su strada in miglia

Numbering - Signs / Numérotation - Signalisation / Nummerierung - Wegweisung / Numerazione - Segnaletica

European route - Motorway	Route européenne - Autoroute	Europastraße - Autobahn	Strada europea - Autostrada
Other roads	Autres routes	Sonstige Straßen	Altre strade
Destination on primary route network (Lancaster)	Localités jalonnant les itinéraires principaux	Richtungshinweis auf der empfohlenen Fernverkehrsstraße	Località delimitante gli itinerari principali

Safety Warnings / Alertes Sécurité / Sicherheitsalerts / Segnalazioni stradali

Snowbound, impassable road during the period shown	Enneigement : période probable de fermeture	Eingeschneite Straße: voraussichtl. Wintersperre	Innevamento: probabile periodo di chiusura
Pass and its height above sea level	Col et sa cote d'altitude	Pass mit Höhenangabe	Passo ed altitudine
Steep hill - Toll barrier	Forte déclivité - Barrière de péage	Starke Steigung - Mautstelle	Forte pendenza - Casello
Ford	Gué	Furt	Guado

Transportation / Transports / Verkehrsmittel / Trasporti

Airport	Aéroport	Flughafen	Aeroporto
Transportation of vehicles: year-round - seasonal	Transport des autos : permanent - saisonnier	Autotransport: ganzjährig - saisonbedingte Verbindung	Trasporto auto: tutto l'anno - stagionale
by boat	par bateau	per Schiff	su traghetto
by ferry	par bac	per Fähre	su chiatta
Ferry (passengers and cycles only)	Bac pour piétons et cycles	Fähre für Personen und Fahrräder	Traghetto per pedoni e biciclette
Motorail	Auto/Train	Autoreisezug	Auto/treno

Administration / Administration / Verwaltung / Amministrazione

Administrative district seat	Capitale de division administrative	Verwaltungshauptstadt	Capoluogo amministrativo
Parador / Pousada	Parador / Pousada	Parador / Pousada	Parador / Pousada
Administrative boundaries	Limites administratives	Verwaltungsgrenzen	Confini amministrativi
National boundary	Frontière	Staatsgrenze	Frontiera
Principal customs post	Douane principale	Hauptzollamt	Dogana principale
Secondary customs post	Douane avec restriction	Zollstation mit Einschränkungen	Dogana con limitazioni
Restricted area for foreigners / Military property	Zone interdite aux étrangers / Zone militaire	Sperrgebiet für Ausländer / Militärgebiet	Zona vietata agli stranieri / Zona militare

Sights / Lieux touristiques / Sehenswürdigkeiten / Mete e luoghi d'interesse

2- and 3-star MICHELIN Green Guide sites	Sites classés 2 et 3 étoiles par le Guide Vert MICHELIN	Sehenswürdigkeiten mit 2 und 3 Sternen im Grünen Reiseführer MICHELIN	Siti segnalati con 2 e 3 stelle dalla Guida Verde MICHELIN
Religious building	Édifice religieux	Sakral-Bau	Edificio religioso
Historic house, castle	Château	Schloss, Burg	Castello
Monastery	Monastère	Kloster	Monastero
Stave church	Église en bois debout	Stabkirche	Chiesa in legno di testa
Wooden church	Église en bois	Holzkirche	Chiesa in legno
Open air museum	Musée de plein air	Freilichtmuseum	Museo all'aperto
Antiquities	Site antique	Antike Fundstätte	Sito antico
Rock carving - Prehistoric monument	Gravure rupestre - Monument mégalithique	Felsbilder - Vorgeschichtliches Steindenkmal	Incisione rupestre - Monumento megalitico
Rune stone - Ruins	Pierre runique - Ruines	Runenstein - Ruine	Pietra runica - Rovine
Cave - Windmill	Grotte - Moulin à vent	Höhle - Windmühle	Grotta - Mulino a vento
Other places of interest	Autres curiosités	Sonstige Sehenswürdigkeit	Altri luoghi d'interesse
Scenic route	Parcours pittoresque	Landschaftlich schöne Strecke	Percorso pittoresco

Other signs / Signes divers / Sonstige Zeichen / Simboli vari

Recreation ground	Parc de loisirs	Erholungspark	Parco divertimenti
Dam - Waterfall	Barrage - Cascade	Staudamm - Wasserfall	Diga - Cascata
National park / Nature park	Parc national / Parc naturel	Nationalpark / Naturpark	Parco nazionale / Parco naturale

Signos Convencionales | Verklaring van de tekens

Carreteras | Wegen

Autopista	Autosnelweg
Carretera	Autoweg
Autopista, Autovía	Autosnelweg of gelijksoortige weg
Autovía	Gescheiden rijbanen van het type autosnelweg
Accesos:	Aansluitingen: volledig, gedeeltelijk,
completo, parcial, sin precisar	zonder aanduiding
Números de los accesos	Afritnummers
Itinerario principal recomendado por MICHELIN	Hoofdweg
Itinerario regional recomendado por MICHELIN	Regionale weg
Carretera asfaltada - sin asfaltar	Verharde weg - onverharde weg
Autopista - Carretera en construcción	Autosnelweg - Weg in aanleg

Ancho de las carreteras | Breedte van de wegen

Calzadas separadas	Gescheiden rijbanen
Dos carriles anchos	2 brede rijstroken
Dos carriles - Dos carriles estrechos	2 rijstroken - 2 smalle rijstroken

Distancias (totales y parciales) | Afstanden (totaal en gedeeltelijk)

En autopista en kilómetros	Op autosnelwegen in kilometers
Tramo de peaje - Tramo libre	Gedeelte met tol - Tolvrij gedeelte
En carretera en kilómetros	Op andere wegen in kilometers
En autopista (GB) en millas - en kilómetros	Op autosnelwegen (GB) in mijlen - in kilometers
Tramo de peaje - Tramo libre	Gedeelte met tol - Tolvrij gedeelte
En carretera en millas	Op andere wegen in mijlen

Numeración - Señalización | Wegnummers - Bewegwijzering

Carretera europea - Autopista	Europaweg - Autosnelweg
Otras carreteras	Andere wegen
Localidades situadas en los principales itinerarios	Plaatsen langs een hoofdweg met bewegwijzering

E 50 A3
25 28 103
Lancaster

Alertas Seguridad | Veiligheidswaarschuwingen

Nevada:	Sneeuw:
Período probable de cierre	vermoedelijke sluitingsperiode
Puerto y su altitud	Bergpas en hoogte boven de zeespiegel
Pendiente Pronunciada - Barrera de peaje	Steile helling - Tol
Vado	Wad

11-4
650

Transportes | Vervoer

Aeropuerto	Luchthaven
Transporte de coches:	Vervoer van auto's:
todo el año - de temporada	het hele jaar - tijdens het seizoen
por barco	per boot
por barcaza	per veerpont
Barcaza para el paso de peatones y vehículos dos ruedas	Veerpont voor voetgangers en fietsers
Auto-tren	Autotrein

Administración | Administratie

Capital de división administrativa	Hoofdplaats van administratief gebied
Parador / Pousada	Parador / Pousada
Limites administrativos	Administratieve grenzen
Frontera	Staatsgrens
Aduana principal	Hoofddouanekantoor
Aduana con restricciones	Douanekantoor met beperkte bevoegdheden
Zona prohibida a los extranjeros / Propiedad militar	Terrein verboden voor buitenlanders / Militair gebied

1 P R
P

Curiosidades | Bezienswaardigheden

STRASBOURG

Lugares clasificados con 2 y 3 estrellas por la Guía Verde MICHELIN	Locaties met 2 en 3 sterren volgens de Groene Gids van MICHELIN
Edificio religioso	Kerkelijk gebouw
Castillo	Kasteel
Monasterio	Klooster
Iglesia de madera	Stavkirke (houten kerk)
Iglesia de madera	Houten kerk
Museo al aire libre	Openluchtmuseum
Zona de vestigios antiguos	Overblijfsel uit de Oudheid
Grabado rupestre - Monumento megalítico	Rotstekening - Megaliet
Piedra rúnica - Ruinas	Runensteen - Ruïne
Cueva - Molino de viento	Grot - Molen
Otras curiosidades	Andere bezienswaardigheden
Recorrido pintoresco	Schilderachtig traject

Signos diversos | Diverse tekens

Zona recreativa	Recreatiepark
Presa - Cascada	Stuwdam - Waterval
Parque nacional / Parque natural	Nationaal park / Natuurpark

0 10 20 30 40 miles
0 10 20 30 40 50 60 km

Republic of Ireland: All distances and speed limits are signed in kilometres.

République d'Irlande: Les distances et les limitations de vitesse sont exprimées en kilomètres.

Irland: Alle Entfernungsangaben und Geschwindigkeitsbegrenzungen in km.

Ierland: Alle afstanden en maximumsnelheden zijn uitsluitend in kilometers aangegeven.

Repubblica d'Irlanda: Distanze e limiti di velocità sono espressi soltanto in chilometri.

República de Irlanda: Distancias y límites de velocidad están expresados sólo en kilómetros.

Key to 1:1 000 000 map pages
Légende des cartes au 1/1 000 000
Zeichenerklärung der Karten 1:1 000 000
Verklaring van de tekens voor kaarten met schaal 1:1 000 000
Legenda carte scala 1:1 000 000
Signos convencionales de los mapas a escala 1:1 000 000

ENGLAND

UNITARY AUTHORITIES

1	Bath and North East Somerset		43	North East Lincolnshire
	Bedford		44	North Lincolnshire
	Blackburn with Darwen		45	North Somerset
	Blackpool		46	North Yorkshire
	Bracknell Forest		47	Northamptonshire
	Brighton and Hove		48	Northumberland
7	Buckinghamshire		49	Nottinghamshire
8	Cambridgeshire			Nottingham
9	Central Bedfordshire		51	Oxfordshire
10	Cheshire East			Peterborough
11	Cheshire West and Chester			Plymouth
	City of Bristol			Portsmouth
13	Cornwall			Reading
14	Cumbria		56	Redcar and Cleveland
	Derby		57	Rutland
16	Derbyshire		58	Shropshire
17	Devon		59	Somerset
18	Dorset		60	South Gloucestershire
19	Durham		61	South Yorkshire
20	East Riding of Yorkshire			Southend-on-Sea
21	East Sussex		63	Staffordshire
22	Essex			Stockton-on-Tees
23	Gloucestershire			Stoke-on-Trent
	Greater London		66	Suffolk
	Greater Manchester		67	Surrey
26	Halton			Swindon
27	Hampshire		69	Telford and Wrekin
	Hartlepool		70	Thurrock
29	Herefordshire			Torbay
30	Hertfordshire		72	Tyne and Wear
31	Kent			Warrington
	Kingston-upon-Hull		74	Warwickshire
33	Lancashire		75	West Berkshire
	Leicester		76	West Midlands
35	Leicestershire		77	West Sussex
36	Lincolnshire		78	West Yorkshire
	Luton		79	Wiltshire
38	Medway			Windsor and Maidenhead
39	Merseyside			Wokingham
	Middlesbrough		82	Worcestershire
41	Milton Keynes			York
42	Norfolk			

SCOTLAND

UNITARY AUTHORITIES

1	Aberdeen City	17	Inverclyde
2	Aberdeenshire	18	Midlothian
3	Angus	19	Moray
4	Argyll and Bute	20	North Ayrshire
5	Clackmannanshire	21	North Lanarkshire
6	City of Edinburgh	22	Orkney Islands
7	City of Glasgow	23	Perth and Kinross
8	Dumfries and Galloway	24	Renfrewshire
9	Dundee City	25	Scottish Borders
10	East Ayrshire	26	Shetland Islands
11	East Dunbartonshire	27	South Ayrshire
12	East Lothian	28	South Lanarkshire
13	East Renfrewshire	29	Stirling
14	Falkirk	30	West Dunbartonshire
15	Fife	31	West Lothian
16	Highland	32	Na H-Eileanan Siar (Western Isles)

NORTHERN IRELAND

DISTRICT COUNCILS

1	Antrim and Newtownabbey	7	Fermanagh and Omagh
2	Ards and North Down	8	Lisburn and Castlereagh
3	Armagh, Banbridge and Craigavon	9	Mid and East Antrim
4	Belfast	10	Mid Ulster
5	Causeway Coast and Glens	11	Newry, Mourne and Down
6	Derry and Strabane		

WALES

UNITARY AUTHORITIES

1	Anglesey/Sir Fôn	12	Merthyr Tydfil/Merthyr Tudful
2	Blaenau Gwent	13	Monmouthshire/Sir Fynwy
3	Bridgend/Pen-y-bont ar Ogwr	14	Neath Port Talbot/Castell-nedd Phort Talbot
4	Caerphilly/Caerffili	15	Newport/Casnewydd
5	Cardiff/Caerdydd	16	Pembrokeshire/Sir Benfro
6	Carmarthenshire/Sir Gaerfyrddin	17	Powys
7	Ceredigion	18	Rhondda Cynon Taff/Rhondda Cynon Taf
8	Conwy	19	Swansea/Abertawe
9	Denbighshire/Sir Ddinbych	20	Torfaen/Tor-faen
10	Flintshire/Sir y Fflint	21	Vale of Glamorgan/Bro Morgannwg
11	Gwynedd	22	Wrexham/Wrecsam

32 = UNITARY AUTHORITIES

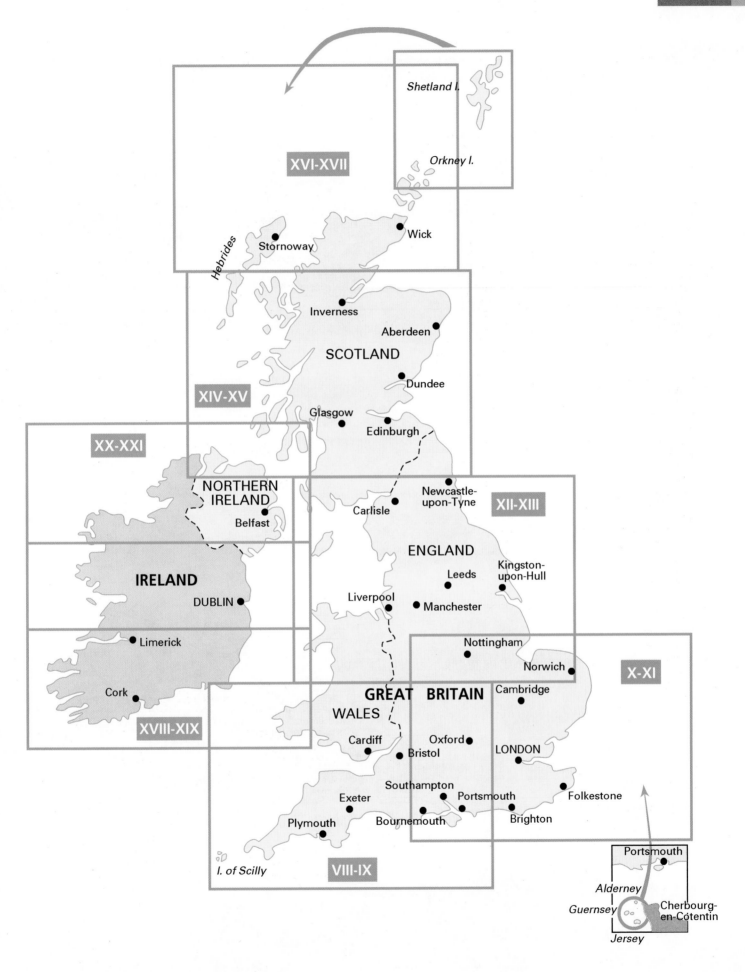

ST. GEORGE'S CHANNEL

e Harbour/
Ros Láir
Point

Saltee Islands

Strumble Head
Newport

Pembrokeshire Coast
National Park

St. David's Head
St. David's

St. Bride's Bay
Haverfordwest/Hwlffordd

Milford Haven/
Aberdaugleddau

Pembroke Dock
Pembroke A 4139
St. Govan's Head

Fishguard/
Abergwaun

Narberth
Whitland

Pembrokeshire
Coast National
Park

Neyland
Saundersfoot
Pendine

Tenby/
Dinbych-y-pysgod

Carmarthen Bay

Rhossili
Worms Head

Port-
Eynon

Cardigan
Newcastle
Emlyn
Crymmych

St. Clears

Kidwelly

Burry
Port

Llanelli

The Mumbles

Aberaeron
New Quay
Synod Inn
Aberporth

Llandysul

Carmarthen/
Caerfyrddin

Cross
Hands

Pontardulais

SWANSEA/
ABERTAWE

Port
Talbot

Porthcawl

Lampeter
Llandovery

Llandeilo

Ammanford
Pontardawe

Neath/
Castell Nedd

Maesteg

Bridgend/
Pen-y-bont

Elan Valley

Llanwrtyd
Wells

Black Mountain

Brecon
National

Merthyr

Aberdare/
Aberdar

BRISTOL CHANNEL

Lundy

Ilfracombe
Combe
Martin
Lynton Lynmouth
Porlock
Exmoor
National
Duns

Croyde
Braunton
Northam
Barnstaple
Simonsbath

Tarr
steps

South
Molton

Tiverton

Hartland Point

Clovelly
Bideford
Great
Torrington

Cliffs of
Morwenstow

Kilkhampton
Stratton
Bude

Holsworthy
Hatherleigh
Winkleigh

Crediton

Okehampton
High
Willhays

Moretonhampstead

EXETER

Tintagel

Camelford

Launceston

Lydford
Gorge

Dartmoor

National

Bovey
Tracey

Padstow
Wadebridge

Tavistock
Princetown
Park
Ashburton

Newton
Abbot

Bodmin
Callington
Buckland Abbey
Buckfastleigh

Newquay
Lostwithiel
Liskeard
Plympton
Saltash

PLYMOUTH

Totnes

Dartmouth

Fraddon
West
Looe
Torpoint
Plymstock

Truro
St. Austell
Fowey
Polperro

Newton
Ferrers

Modbury

Kingsbridge

Camborne
St. Ives
Redruth
Hayle
Penryn
St. Mawes

Tregony
Mevagissey

Trelissick Garden

Trewithen

Salcombe

Start Poi

St. Just
Penzance
Falmouth

St. Michael's Mount
Helston
Glendurgan
Garden

Land's End
Sennen
Mount's Bay
St. Keverne

Subtropical
Gardens

Tresco
St. Martin's
Isles of Scilly
St. Mary's

Lizard
Lizard Point

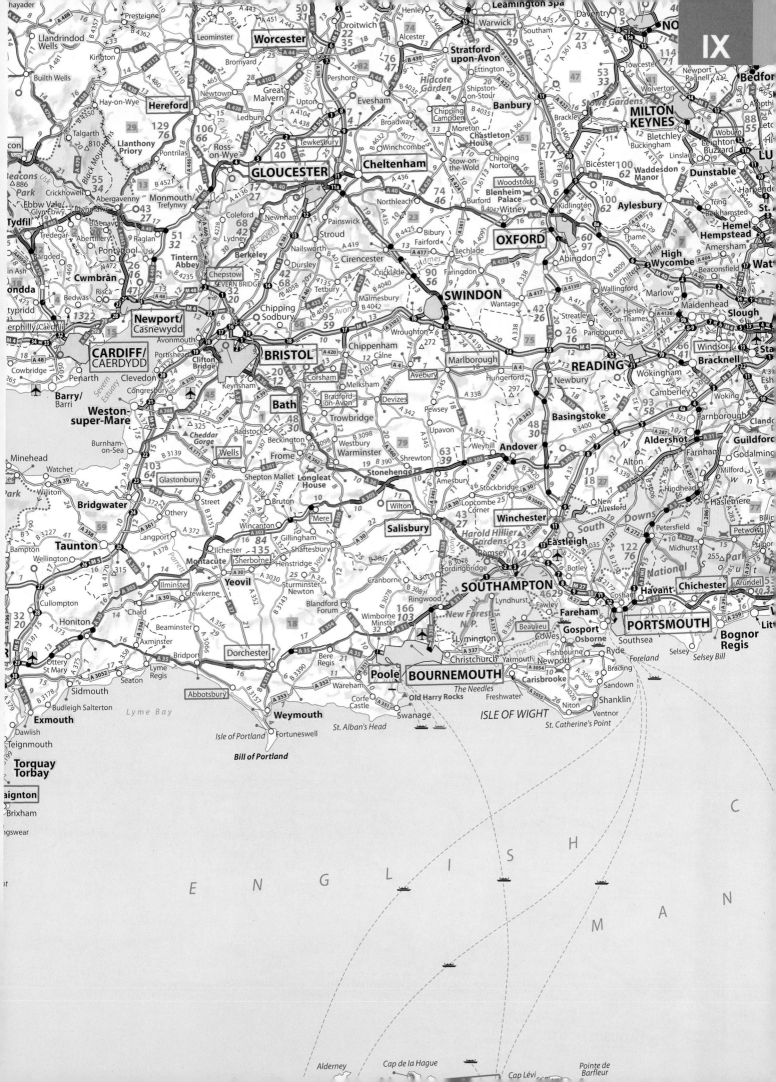

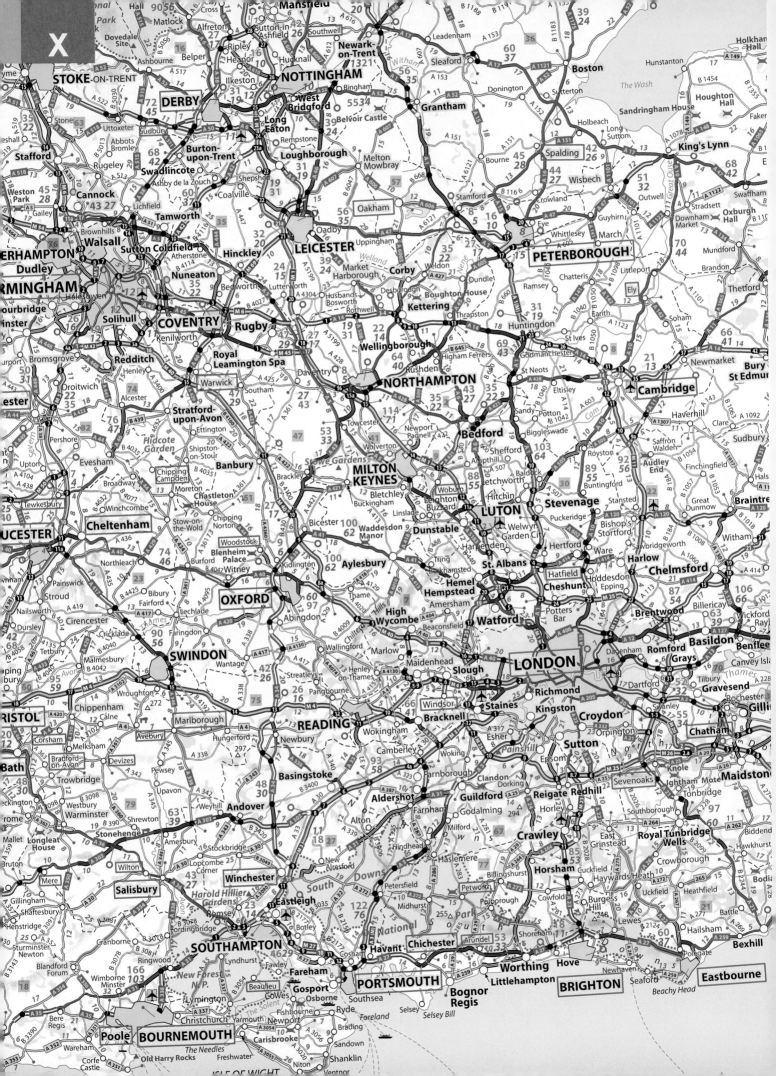

Wells-next-the-Sea • Blakeney • Sheringham • Cromer • Mundesley
Holt
A 149
Guist • Aylsham • North Walsham
Blickling Hall
St Dereham
Low Street
Acle
NORWICH • Great Yarmouth
Wymondham
Gorsleston-on-Sea
Watton • Attleborough
Lowestoft
Bungay • Beccles
Harleston • Southwold
Diss • Halesworth
Scole • Yoxford
Dennington • Leiston
Stowmarket • Saxmundham • Aldeburgh
Lavenham
IPSWICH
Hadleigh • Woodbridge
Felixstowe
Harwich
The Naze
Colchester • Walton-on-the-Naze • Frinton-on-Sea
Brightlingsea
West Mersea • **Clacton-on-Sea**
Maldon • Bradwell-on-Sea
Burnham-on-Crouch
Foulness Point
SOUTHEND-ON-SEA
Grain • Sheerness • *Isle of Sheppey*
Queenborough • Leysdown-on-Sea • Birchington • **Margate**
Herne Bay • *North Foreland*
gingham • Whitstable • Broadstairs
Sittingbourne • Faversham • **Canterbury** • Ramsgate
Sandwich
Deal
South Foreland
Ashford • **Dover**
Tenterden • Hythe • **Folkestone**
New Romney
Calais
Rye • Lydd • *Dungeness*
Winchelsea
Hastings
TUNNEL SOUS LA MANCHE / CHANNEL TUNNEL
STRAIT OF DOVER
PAS DE CALAIS
Cap Blanc Nez
Wissant • Terminal • Guînes
Cap Gris Nez • Ardres
Wimereux • Marquise
Boulogne-s-Mer
Hardelot-Plage • Samer • Desvres
Étaples
Le Touquet-Paris-Plage • **Montre**

MER DU
D ('S-GRA

Paimpol • *Île de Bréhat*
Pointe de l'Arcouest
St-Malo
Fort la Latte • **Dinard** • Paramé
Cap Fréhel • St-Lunaire • Rothéneuf • Cancale
Plouha • St-Quay-Portrieux • Sables-d'Or-les-Pins • St-Cast • St-Briac • St-Servan-sur-M. • *P.te du Grouin*
Étables-s-Mer • Binic • St-Jacut • **Le Mont-St-Mi**
Le Val-André • Erquy • Châteauneuf-d'Ille-et-Vilaine
Châtelaudren • Pléneuf-Val-André • Matignon • Ploubalay • Plancoët • Dol-de-Bretagne

Alderney
Cap de la Hague • **Cherbourg-en-Cotentin** • *Cap Lévi*
Baie d'Écalgrain
Nez de Jobourg
Beaumont-Hague
Les Pieux • Valognes
Guernsey
Bricquebec-en-Cotentin
St. Peter Port • *Sark* • St-Sauveur-le-Vicomte
Pezeries Point • *Icart Point* • Carteret
Barneville-Carteret
Port-Bail • La Haye-du-Puits
Jersey
Jersey zoo
Lessay
Gorey
St. Helier
St-Malo-de-la-Lande
Agon-Coutainville
Montmartin-s-Mer
Îles Chausey
Bréhal
Granville
St-Pair-s-Mer
Jullouville
Carolles

South Shields
SUNDERLAND
Jarrow
Gateshead
Washington
Seaham
Chester-le-Street
Houghton-le-Spring
Horden
Durham
Peterlee
Hartlepool
Spennymoor
Redcar
Marske-by-the-Sea
Sedgefield
Saltburn-by-the-Sea
Newton-Aycliffe
Billingham
Brotton
Stockton-on-Tees
Guisborough
Loftus
Whitby
Darlington
Eaglescliffe
MIDDLESBROUGH
Richmond
Cleveland Hills
North York Moors National Park
Northallerton
Scarborough
Scalby
Richmond
Bedale
Rievaulx Abbey
Helmsley
Pickering
Filey
Thirsk
Ripon
Easingwold
Malton
Norton
Bridlington
Flamborough Head
Pateley Bridge
Boroughbridge
Knaresborough
Driffield
Beeford
Harrogate
Wetwang
Wetherby
Harewood
Hornsea
Otley
Market Weighton
Bingley
Leven
LEEDS
Tadcaster
Beverley
Selby
Barlby
KINGSTON UPON HULL
Garforth
Castleford
Howden
Goole
Hedon
Withernsea
Halifax
Shaith
Patrington
Kilnsea
Dewsbury
Pontefract
Barton-upon-Humber
Spurn Head
Wakefield
Thorne
Crowle
Scunthorpe
Immingham Dock
Immingham
Huddersfield
Barnsley
Brigg
Grimsby
Cleethorpes
Doncaster
Epworth
Caistor
Conisbrough
Bentley
Stocksbridge
Rotherham
Bawtry
Market Rasen
Louth
Maltby
Mablethorpe
SHEFFIELD
Sutton-on-Sea
Chapel-en-le-Frith
Dronfield
Worksop
Retford
Gainsborough
Wragby
Staveley
Baslow
Castleton
Chatsworth House
Chesterfield
Tuxford
Lincoln
Horncastle
Partney
Alford
Bakewell
Hardwick Hall
Ollerton
Mansfield
Woodhall Spa
Spilsby
Skegness
Haddon Hall
Matlock
Clay Cross
Dovedale
Alfreton
Sutton-in-Ashfield
Southwell
Leadenham
Ashbourne
Belper
Ripley
Heanor
Hucknall
Newark-on-Trent
Sleaford
Boston
Holkham Hall
Wells-next-the-Sea
Blakeney
Sheringham
Holt
Hunstanton
Donington
Sutterton
Sandringham House
Houghton Hall
Blickling Hall
DERBY
Ilkeston
NOTTINGHAM
Bingham
Grantham
Fakenham
Guist
Aylsham
West Bridgford
Belvoir Castle
Holbeach
Long Sutton
King's Lynn
East Dereham
Burton-upon-Trent
Long Eaton
Spalding
Wisbech
Swaffham
Wymondham
Swadlincote
Loughborough
Shepshed
Melton Mowbray
Bourne
Oxburgh Hall
Watton
Ashby de la Zouch
Coalville
Stamford
Crowland
Outwell
Downham Market
Stradsett
Lichfield
Tamworth
Oakham
Oadby
Uppingham
Eye
Guyhirn
March
Whittlesey
Mundford
Brandon
Thetford
Sutton Coldfield
Hinckley
LEICESTER
Market Harborough
Corby
Weldon
PETERBOROUGH
Littleport
Ely
Diss
Nuneaton
Bedworth
Lutterworth
Husbands Bosworth
Desborough
Boughton House
Oundle
Ramsey
Chatteris
Kettering
Rothwell

Alness Invergordon Lossiemouth Buckie A942 Banff Macduff B9031 Fraserburgh
Cromarty Elgin Cullen A98 Loch of Strathbeg Rattray Head
Black Isle Fortrose Nairn Forres Fochabers Keith Turriff New Deer Mintlaw Peterhead
Tore Rothes Craigellachie Huntly Buchan Ness
Inverness Dufftown Dava Grantown-on-Spey Rhynie Mossat Oldmeldrum Ellon Cruden Bay Newburgh
Carrbridge Tomintoul Alford Inverurie Kintore
Aviemore Colnabaichin Craigievar Castle Crathes Castle ABERDEEN
Kingussie Cairn Gorm Cairngorm Mountains Ben Macdui Banchory
Carn Ban Newtonmore Craigievar Castle Stonehaven
Laggan Cairngorms National Park Braemar Balmoral Castle Inverbervie
Dalwhinnie Devil's Elbow Glas Maol Laurencekirk Marykirk
Pass of Drumochter The Pleasance Brechin Montrose
Blair Castle Blair Atholl S. Esk Kirriemuir Forfar Arbroath
Kinloch Rannoch Pitlochry Alyth Glamis Castle Glamis Carnoustie
Schiehallion Aberfeldy Dunkeld Blairgowrie Rattray Meigle Coupar Angus DUNDEE Monifieth
Ben Lawers Ben Chonzie Perth Newburgh Tayport Newport-on-Tay Buddon Ness
Killin Lochearnhead Crieff Auchterarder Leuchars St. Andrews Fife Ness
Ben Vorlich Callander Newburgh Auchtermuchty Cupar Crail
Doune Dunblane Kinross Falkland Anstruther Pittenweem
Bridge of Allan Dollar Lochgelly Glenrothes Leven Saint Monans Elie
Stirling Alloa Alva Dunfermline Methil Buckhaven
Kincardine Culross Cowdenbeath Kirkcaldy Firth of Forth
Denny Grangemouth Rosyth Burntisland North Berwick Dunbar
Kilsyth Bo'ness Inverkeithing Aberlady East Linton Cockburnspath
Kirkintilloch Falkirk Linlithgow S. Queensferry Prestonpans Leith Haddington St. Abb's Head
Cumbernauld Bathgate Hopetoun House Musselburgh Tranent Eyemouth
Armadale Livingston EDINBURGH Dalkeith Berwick-upon-Tweed
Clydebank Airdrie Whitburn Loanhead Penicuik RosslynChapel Duns
Coatbridge Motherwell West Linton Carnwath Lammermuir Hills Holy Island
Barrhead Hamilton Wishaw Carluke Lauder Greenlaw Belford Bamburgh Castle
East Kilbride Strathaven Lanark Peebles Galashiels Earlston Mellerstain Coldstream Wooler
Kilmarnock Biggar Innerleithen Melrose Abbey Dryburgh Kelso The Cheviot Alnwick
Galston Douglas Abington Broad Law Newtown St Boswells Selkirk Jedburgh Warkworth
Muirkirk Elvanfoot Hawick Carter Bar Northumberland National Park Rothbury Amble
Mauchline Sanquhar Moffat Beattie Otterburn Felton
Cumnock Drumlanrig castle Thornhill Kielder Resr. Ashington Newbiggin-by-the-Sea
New Cumnock Lochmaben Lockerbie Langholm Morpeth Blyth

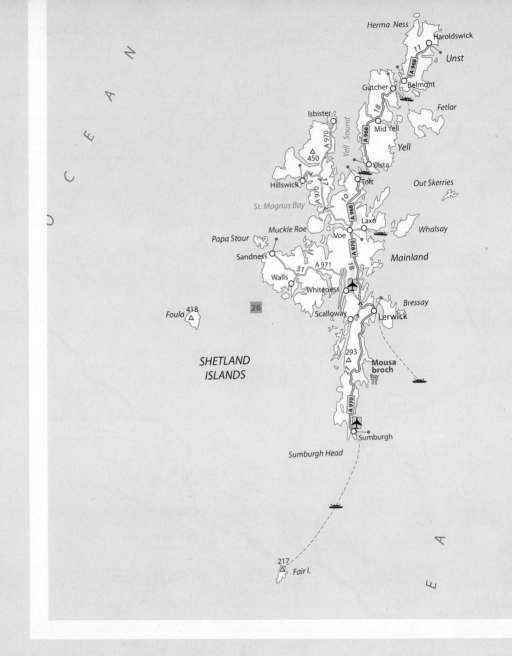

Herma Ness
Haroldswick
11
Unst
Gutcher Belmont
Fetlar
18
Isbister
A 970
Mid Yell
A 968
Yell
450
Ulsta
Out Skerries
Hillswick
10
Toft
A 970
St. Magnus Bay
Laxo
Muckle Roe
A 968
Papa Stour
Voe
Whalsay
Sandness
A 971
Mainland
31
Walls
A 970
Whiteness
Bressay
26
Scalloway
Lerwick
Foula 418
SHETLAND
ISLANDS
293
27
Mousa
broch
A 970
Sumburgh
Sumburgh Head
217
Fair I.

Butt of Lewis
Port of Ness
Kin
A 857
16
LEWIS
Barvas
A 857
Scourie
A 858
12
Eddrachillis
Carloway
292
Broad
Bay
THE MINCH
Flannan I.
Callanish
Standing
Stones
Stornoway
Portnaguran
A 858
Tiumpan Head
Garynahine
34
A 866
Eye Peninsula
574
Rubha Còigeach
Lochi
36
Kebock Head
A 859
NA H-EILEANAN
572
Hushinish
B 887
Clisham
Coigach
743
West Loch Tarbert
799
SIAR
Tarbert
Gruinard
Bay
Toe Head
A 859
24
Rubha Réidh
Laide
St. Kilda
32
29

ATLANTIC OCEAN

SHETLAND ISLANDS

Papa

Walls

Whiteness

Scal

Foula 418

26

Sumburgh H

217 Fair I.

22

Westray

North Ronaldsay

The North Sound

Pierowall

Kettletoft

Sanday

Westray Firth

Rousay

Eday

Stronsay

ORKNEY ISLANDS

Brough Head

Stronsay Firth

38

A 966

Skara Brae

Shapinsay

A 967

A 986

A 965

Mainland

Stromness

15

Kirkwall

Stenness

A 964

Skaill

20

Scapa Flow

A 961

10

Rora Head

479

A 961

Lyness

21

St Margaret's Hope

Hoy

South Ronaldsay

Pentland Firth

Burwick

Dunnet Head

Duncansby Head

Scrabster

Dunnet

A 836

Gills

John O' Groats

Cape Wrath

Whiten Head

Kyle of Tongue

Strathy Point

20

Castletown

A 99

Durness

A 836

Thurso

19

B 876

17

Noss Head

A 838

Bettyhill

Melvich

16

Roadside

34

21

Reiss

Loch Inchard

Coldbackie

A 836

27

290

A 882

24

Kinlochbervie

20

31

Tongue

B 871

Foinaven

927

Ben Hope

40

Syre

A 897

39

183

114

Wick

A 908

B 873

B 871

24

172

107

Laxford Bridge

A 836

Altnaharra

L. Naver

A 9

A 894

Kylestrome

39

Kinbrace

Morven

706

Latheron

Inchnadamph

A 838

Ben Klibreck

961

Ben Armine

713

17

998

A 837

Ben More Assynt

A 836

Loch Shin

A 897

20

Ledmore

Lairg

A 839

Helmsdale

49

27

14

A 9

18

A 837

31

11

21

Brora

Ullapool

A 839

Golspie

14

Bonar Bridge

A 949

Dornoch

Dornoch Firth

Aran Island

Gweebarra

Rossan Point — Glencolumbkille

R 263 — 27 — Killybeg

Bunglass Cliffs

Donegal

Bu Bun

Inishmurray

65
40

Rosses Point

Erris Head

Broad Haven

Ballycastle

Killala Bay

Easky

Slygo Bay

Strandhill

Belmullet — R 314 — Glenamoy — 379 — 19 — R 314 — 21 — R 297 — N 59

Inishkea — 19 — R 313 — Bangor — MAYO — Crossmolina — R 315 — Inishcrone — Mountains — 53 — 543 — Ballysadare

BlacksodBay — 32 — Oweniny — N 59 — 32 — R 316 — 11 — Ballina/ — SLIGO — 29 — N 17

670 — Ballycroy — 32 — 720 — 31 — R 312 — Béal an Átha — R 294 — 32 — 47 — 29 — Ballymo

Keel — R 319 — Nephin Beg Range — 698 — Nephin — 804 — Foxford — Tubbercurry — 11 — R 294 — Gorteen — 34

Achill Island — 521 — Mulrany — 18 — R 317 — Pontoon — N 26 — 40 — Charlestown — R 293 — 45

Corraun — Newport — Clew Bay — Castlebar/ — 39 — 24 — Swinford — N 5 — L Gara

Clare Island — R 311 — Caisleán an Bharraigh — Kiltimagh — R 320 — Ballaghaderreen — N 83 — Ca

Louisburgh — Westport/ — 18 — 11 — Manulla — R 324 — R 322 — 24 — Frenchpark — ROSC

Inishturk — R 335 — Croagh Patrick — 763 — R 330 — Ballintubber — R 331 — Ballyhaunis — Castlere

Inishbofin — Mweelrea Mts — Murrisk — 66 — 41 — Partry Mountains — 23 — Robe — Claremorris — 19 — N 60 — Ballym

Inishshark — Killary Harbour — 817 — 32 — 681 — Lough Mask — Ballinrobe — 63 — 39 — Clare — Dunmore — R 364 — Rosc

RinvylePt. — Letterfrack — 35 — Maumturk Mts — Leenane — R 336 — Clonbur — R 345 — Kilmaine — R 332 — Glennamaddy

The Twelve Pins — 728 — 701 — Connemara — 31 — Cong — R 334 — 50 — N 83 — N 328

Clifden — N 59 — 35 — Lough Corrib — Headford — Tuam/Tuaim — R 332 — Mount Bellew — R 359

Slyne Head — R 341 — 49 — 79 — Maam Cross — N 59 — Oughterard — 44 — 34 — 21 — 27 — 17 — 37 — R 363

Roundstone — R 340 — 21 — N 84 — M 17 — 19 — 45 — 28 — R 348 — M 6 — 31

Carna — Gortmore — GALWAY — Galway/ — 13 — 11 — Athenry — R 350

Kilkieran Bay — R 374 — 39 — R 336 — Gaillimh — Oranmore — 14 — 16 — Ballinas Béal na-Slua

Lettermullan — Gorumna Island — Spiddal — Barna — Galway Bay — 104 — 65 — 14 — 27 — Craughwell — Loughrea

Inishmore — Kilronan — BlackHead — 40 — Ardrahan — R 347

Dún Aonghasa — Inishmaan — Kinvarra — 13 — R 66 — 25

Aran Islands — Inisheer — Ballyvaughan — R 480 — 16 — R 353 — Gort — 45

Lisdoonvarna — R 67 — 29 — R 460 — R 478 — R 481

Key — Légende — Zeichenerklärung

Roads — Routes — Straßen

KEELE

Key	Légende	Zeichenerklärung
Motorway - Service areas	Autoroute - Aires de service	Autobahn - Tankstelle mit Raststätte
Dual carriageway with motorway characteristics	Double chaussée de type autoroutier	Schnellstraße mit getrennten Fahrbahnen
Interchanges: complete, limited	Échangeurs : complet, partiels	Anschlussstellen: Voll - bzw. Teilanschlussstellen
Interchange numbers	Numéros d'échangeurs	Anschlussstellennummern
International and national road network	Route de liaison internationale ou nationale	Internationale bzw. nationale Hauptverkehrsstraße
Interregional and less congested road	Route de liaison interrégionale ou de dégagement	Überregionale Verbindungsstraße oder Umleitungsstrecke
Road surfaced - unsurfaced	Route revêtue - non revêtue	Straße mit Belag - ohne Belag
Footpath - Waymarked footpath / Bridle path	Sentier - Sentier balisé/Allée cavalière	Pfad - Ausgeschilderter Weg / Reitpfad
Motorway / Road under construction	Autoroute - Route en construction	Autobahn - Straße im Bau
(when available: with scheduled opening date)	(le cas échéant : date de mise en service prévue)	(ggf. voraussichtliches Datum der Verkehrsfreigabe)

Road widths — Largeur des routes — Straßenbreiten

Key	Légende	Zeichenerklärung
Dual carriageway	Chaussées séparées	Getrennte Fahrbahnen
4 lanes - 2 wide lanes	4 voies - 2 voies larges	4 Fahrspuren - 2 breite Fahrspuren
2 lanes - 2 narrow lanes	2 voies - 2 voies étroites	2 Fahrspuren - 1 Fahrspur

Distances (total and intermediate) — Distances (totalisées et partielles) — Entfernungen (Gesamt- und Teilentfernungen)

24 39 — 14 10

Key	Légende	Zeichenerklärung
Toll roads on motorway	Section à péage sur autoroute	Mautstrecke auf der Autobahn
Toll-free section on motorway	Section libre sur autoroute	Mautfreie Strecke auf der Autobahn
in miles - en kilometers	en miles - en kilomètres	in Meilen - in Kilometern
on road	sur route	Auf der Straße

Numbering - Signs — Numérotation - Signalisation — Nummerierung - Wegweisung

M 5   A 38   N 20   N 31   A 190 B 629 R 561   YORK

Key	Légende	Zeichenerklärung
Motorway - GB: Primary route	Autoroute - GB : itinéraire principal (Primary route)	Autobahn - GB: Empfohlene Fernverkehrsstraße (Primary route)
IRL : National primary and secondary route	IRL : itinéraire principal (National primary et secondary route)	IRL: Empfohlene Fernverkehrsstraße (National primary und secondary route)
Other roads	Autres routes	Sonstige Straßen
Destination on primary route network	Localités jalonnant les itinéraires principaux	Richtungshinweis auf der empfohlenen Fernverkehrsstraße

Obstacles — Obstacles — Verkehrshindernisse

7-12%   +12%   11'9

Key	Légende	Zeichenerklärung
Roundabout - Pass and its height above sea level (meters)	Rond-point - Col et sa cote d'altitude (en mètres)	Verkehrsinsel - Pass mit Höhenangabe (in Meter)
Steep hill (ascent in direction of the arrow)	Forte déclivité (flèches dans le sens de la montée)	Starke Steigung (Steigung in Pfeilrichtung)
IRL: Difficult or dangerous section of road	IRL : Parcours difficile ou dangereux	IRL: Schwierige oder gefährliche Strecke
In Scotland: narrow road with passing places	En Écosse : route très étroite avec emplacements pour croisement	In Schottland: sehr schmale Straße mit Ausweichstellen (passing places)
Level crossing: railway passing, under road, over road	Passages de la route : à niveau, supérieur, inférieur	Bahnübergänge: schienengleich, Unterführung, Überführung
Prohibited road - Road subject to restrictions	Route interdite - Route réglementée	Gesperrte Straße - Straße mit Verkehrsbeschränkungen
Toll barrier - One way road (on major and regional roads)	Barrière de péage - Route à sens unique	Mautstelle - Einbahnstraße
Height limit under 15'6'' IRL, 16'6'' GB	Hauteur limitée au dessous de 15'6'' IRL, 16'6''GB	Beschränkung der Durchfahrtshöhe bis 15'6'' IRL, 16'6' GB
Load limit (under 16 t.)	Limites de charge (au-dessous de 16 t.)	Höchstbelastung (angegeben, wenn unter 16 t)

Transportation — Transports — Verkehrsmittel

15

Key	Légende	Zeichenerklärung
Railway - Passenger station	Voie ferrée - Gare	Bahnlinie - Bahnhof
Airport - Airfield	Aéroport - Aérodrome	Flughafen - Flugplatz
Transportation of vehicles: (seasonal services in red)	Transport des autos: (liaison saisonnière en rouge)	Autotransport: (rotes Zeichen: saisonbedingte Verbindung)
by boat	par bateau	per Schiff
by ferry (load limit in tons)	par bac (charge maximum en tonnes)	per Fähre (Höchstbelastung in t)
Ferry (passengers and cycles only)	Bac pour piétons et cycles	Fähre für Personen und Fahrräder

Accommodation - Administration — Hébergement - Administration — Unterkunft - Verwaltung

Key	Légende	Zeichenerklärung
Administrative boundaries	Limites administratives	Verwaltungshauptstadt
Scottish and Welsh borders	Limite de l'Écosse et du Pays de Galles	Grenze von Schottland und Wales
National boundary - Customs post	Frontière - Douane	Staatsgrenze - Zoll

Sport & Recreation Facilities — Sports - Loisirs — Sport - Freizeit

Key	Légende	Zeichenerklärung
Golf course - Horse racetrack	Golf - Hippodrome	Golfplatz - Pferderennbahn
Racing circuit - Pleasure boat harbour	Circuit automobile - Port de plaisance	Rennstrecke - Yachthafen
Caravan and camping sites	Camping, caravaning	Campingplatz
Waymarked footpath - Country park	Sentier balisé - Base ou parc de loisirs	Ausgeschilderter Weg - Freizeitanlage
Safari park, zoo - Bird sanctuary, refuge	Parc animalier, zoo - Réserve d'oiseaux	Tierpark, Zoo - Vogelschutzgebiet
IRL: Fishing - Greyhound track	IRL : Pêche - Cynodrome	IRL: Angeln - Windhundrennen
Tourist train	Train touristique	Museumseisenbahn
Funicular, cable car, chairlift	Funiculaire, téléphérique, télésiège	Standseilbahn, Seilbahn, Sessellift

Sights — Curiosités — Sehenswürdigkeiten

Rye (▲)   Ergol O

Key	Légende	Zeichenerklärung
Principal sights: see THE GREEN GUIDE	Principales curiosités : voir LE GUIDE VERT	Hauptsehenswürdigkeiten: siehe GRÜNER REISEFÜHRER
Towns or places of interest, Places to stay	Localités ou sites intéressants, lieux de séjour	Sehenswerte Orte, Ferienorte
Religious building - Historic house, castle	Édifice religieux - Château	Sakral-Bau - Schloss, Burg
Ruins - Prehistoric monument - Cave	Ruines - Monument mégalithique - Grotte	Ruine - Vorgeschichtliches Steindenkmal - Höhle
Garden, park - Other places of interest	Jardin, parc - Autres curiosités	Garten, Park - Sonstige Sehenswürdigkeit
IRL: Fort - Celtic cross - Round Tower	IRL : Fort - Croix celte - Tour ronde	IRL: Fort, Festung - Keltisches Kreuz - Rundturm
Panoramic view - Viewpoint - Scenic route	Panorama - Point de vue - Parcours pittoresque	Rundblick - Aussichtspunkt - Landschaftlich schöne Strecke

Other signs — Signes divers — Sonstige Zeichen

Key	Légende	Zeichenerklärung
Industrial cable way	Transporteur industriel aérien	Industrieschwebebahn
Telecommunications tower or mast - Lighthouse	Tour ou pylône de télécommunications - Phare	Funk-, Sendeturm - Leuchtturm
Power station - Quarry	Centrale électrique - Carrière	Kraftwerk - Steinbruch
Mine - Industrial activity	Mine - Industries	Bergwerk - Industrieanlagen
Refinery - Cliff	Raffinerie - Falaise	Raffinerie - Klippen
National forest park - National park	Parc forestier national - Parc national	Waldschutzgebiet - Nationalpark

Verklaring van de tekens

Wegen
KEELE

Autosnelweg - Serviceplaatsen
Gescheiden rijbanen van het type autosnelweg

Aansluitingen: volledig, gedeeltelijk
Afritnummers
Internationale of nationale verbindingsweg
Interregionale verbindingsweg
Verharde weg - Onverharde weg
Pad - Bewegwijzerd wandelpad / Ruiterpad
Autosnelweg in aanleg - weg in aanleg
(indien bekend: datum openstelling)

Breedte van de wegen
Gescheiden rijbanen
4 rijstroken - 2 brede rijstroken
2 rijstroken - 2 smalle rijstroken

Afstanden (totaal en gedeeltelijk)
Gedeelte met tol op autosnelwegen
Tolvrij gedeelte op autosnelwegen
in mijlen - in kilometers
op andere wegen

Wegnummers - Bewegwijzering
Autosnelweg - GB: Hoofdweg (Primary route)
IRL: Hoofdweg (National primary en secondary route)
Andere wegen
Plaatsen langs een autosnelweg of Primary route met bewegwijzering

Hindernissen
Rotonde - Bergpas en hoogte boven de zeespiegel (in meters)
Steile helling (pijlen in de richting van de helling)
IRL: Moeilijk of gevaarlijk traject
In Schotland: smalle weg met uitwijkplaatsen
Wegovergangen: gelijkvloers, overheen, onderdoor
Verboden weg - Beperkt opengestelde weg
Tol - Weg met eenrichtingsverkeer
Vrije hoogte indien lager dan 15' 6'' IRL, 16'6'' GB

Maximum draagvermogen (indien minder dan 16 t)

Vervoer
Spoorweg - Reizigersstation
Luchthaven - Vliegveld
Vervoer van auto's: (tijdens het seizoen: rood teken)
per boot
per veerpont (maximum draagvermogen in t.)
Veerpont voor voetgangers en fietsers

Verblijf - Administratie
Administratieve grenzen
Grens van Schotland en Wales

Staatsgrens - Douanekantoor

Sport - Recreatie
Golfterrein - Renbaan
Autocircuit - Jachthaven
Kampeerterrein (tent, caravan)
Sentiero segnalato - Recreatiepark
Safaripark, dierentuin - Vogelreservaat
IRL: Vissen - Hondenrenbaan
Toeristentreintje
Kabelspoor, kabelbaan, stoeltjeslift

Bezienswaardigheden
Belangrijkste bezienswaardigheden:
zie DE GROENE GIDS
Rye (▲)
Interessante steden of plaatsen, vakantieoorden
Ergol
Kerkelijk gebouw - Kasteel
Ruïne - Megaliet - Grot
Tuin, park - Andere bezienswaardigheden
IRL: Fort - Keltisch kruis - Ronde toren
Panorama - Uitzichtpunt - Schilderachtig traject

Diverse tekens
Kabelvrachtvervoer
Telecommunicatietoren of -mast - Vuurtoren
Elektriciteitscentrale - Steengroeve
Mijn - Industrie
Raffinaderij - Klif
Staatsbos - Nationaal park

Legenda

Strade
KEELE

Autostrada - Aree di servizio
Doppia carreggiata di tipo autostradale

Svincoli: completo, parziale
Svincoli numerati
Strada di collegamento internazionale o nazionale
Strada di collegamento interregionale o di disimpegno
Strada rivestita - non rivestita
Sentiero - Sentiero segnalato / Pista per cavalli
Autostrada, strada in costruzione
(data di apertura prevista)

Larghezza delle strade
Carreggiate separate
4 corsie - 2 corsie larghe
2 corsie - 2 corsie strette

Distanze (totali e parziali)
Tratto a pedaggio su autostrada
Tratto esente da pedaggio su autostrada
in migla - in chilometri
su strada

Numerazione - Segnaletica
Autostrada - GB: itinerario principale (Strada «Primary»)
IRL: itinerario principale (Strada «National primary» e «Secondary»)
Altre Strade
Località delimitante gli itinerari principali

Ostacoli
Rotonda - Passo ed altitudine (in metri)
Forte pendenza (salita nel senso della freccia)
IRL: Percorso difficile o pericoloso
In Scozia: Strada molto stretta con incrocio
Passaggi della strada: a livello, cavalcavia, sottopassaggio
Strada vietata - Strada a circolazione regolamentata
Casello - Strada a senso unico (su collegamenti principali e regionali)
Limite di altezza inferiore a 15'6'' IRL, 16'6''GB

Limite di portata (inferiore a 16 t.)

Trasporti
Ferrovia - Stazione viaggiatori
Aeroporto - Aerodromo
Trasporto auto: (stagionale in rosso)
su traghetto
su chiatta (carico massimo in t.)
Traghetto per pedoni e biciclette

Risorse alberghiere - Amministrazione
Confini amministrativi
Confine di Scozia e Galles

Frontiera - Dogana

Sport - Divertimento
Golf - Ippodromo
Circuito Automobilistico - Porto turistico
Campeggi, caravaning
Sentiero segnalato - Area o parco per attività ricreative
Parco con animali, zoo - Riserva ornitologica
IRL: Pesca - Cinodromo
Trenino turistico
Funicolare, funivia, seggiovia

Mete e luoghi d'interesse
Principali luoghi d'interesse,
vedere LA GUIDA VERDE
Rye (▲)
Località o siti interessanti, luoghi di soggiorno
Ergol
Edificio religioso - Castello
Rovine - Monumento megalitico - Grotta
Giardino, parco - Altri luoghi d'interesse
IRL: Forte - Croce celtica - Torre rotonda
Panorama - Vista - Percorso pittoresco

Simboli vari
Teleferica industriale
Torre o pilone per telecomunicazioni - Faro
Centrale elettrica - Cava
Miniera - Industrie
Raffineria - Falesia
Parco forestale nazionale - Parco nazionale

Signos convencionales

Carreteras
KEELE

Autopista - Áreas de servicio
Autovía

Enlaces: completo, parciales
Números de los accesos
Carretera de comunicación internacional o nacional
Carretera de comunicación interregional o alternativo
Carretera asfaltada - sin asfaltar
Sendero - Sendero señalizado / Camino de caballos
Autopista, carretera en construcción
(en su caso: fecha prevista de entrada en servicio)

Ancho de las carreteras
Calzadas separadas
Cuatro carriles - Dos carriles anchos
Dos carriles - Dos carriles estrechos

Distancias (totales y parciales)
Tramo de peaje en autopista
Tramo libre en autopista
en millas - en kilómetros
en carretera

Numeración - Señalización
Autopista - GB: Vía principal (Primary route)
IRL: Vía principal (National primary et secondary route)
Otras carreteras
Localidad en itinerario principal

Obstáculos
Rotonda - Puerto y su altitud (en métros)
Pendiente Pronunciada (las flechas indican el sentido del ascenso)
IRL: Recorrido difícil o peligroso
En escocia: carretera muy estrecha con ensanchamientos para poder cruzarse
Pasos de la carretera: a nivel, superior, inferior
Tramo prohibido - Carretera restringida
Barrera de peaje - Carretera de sentido único
Altura limitada (15'6'' IRL, 16'6''GB)

Limite de carga (inferior a 16 t)

Transportes
Línea férrea - Estación de viajeros
Aeropuerto - Aeródromo
Transporte de coches: (Enlace de temporada: signo rojo)
por barco
por barcaza (carga máxima en toneladas)
Barcaza para el paso de peatones y vehículos dos ruedas

Alojamiento - Administración
Limites administrativos
Limites de Escocia y del País de Gales

Frontera - Puesto de aduanas

Deportes - Ocio
Golf - Hipódromo
Circuito de velocidad - Puerto deportivo
Camping, caravaning
Sendero señalizado - Parque de ocio
Reserva de animales, zoo - Reserva de pájaros
IRL: Pêche - Cynodrome
Tren turístico
Funicular, Teleférico, telesilla

Curiosidades
Principales curiosidades:
ver LA GUÍA VERDE
Rye (▲)
Localidad o lugar interesante, lugar para quedarse
Ergol
Edificio religioso - Castillo
Ruinas - Monumento megalitico - Cueva
Jardín, parque - Curiosidades diversas
IRL: Fortaleza - Cruz celta - Torre redonda
Vista panorámica - Vista parcial - Recorrido pintoresco

Signos diversos
Transportador industrial aéreo
Emisor de Radiodifusión - Faro
Central eléctrica - Cantera
Mina - Industrias
Refinería - Acantilado
Parque forestal nacional - Parque nacional

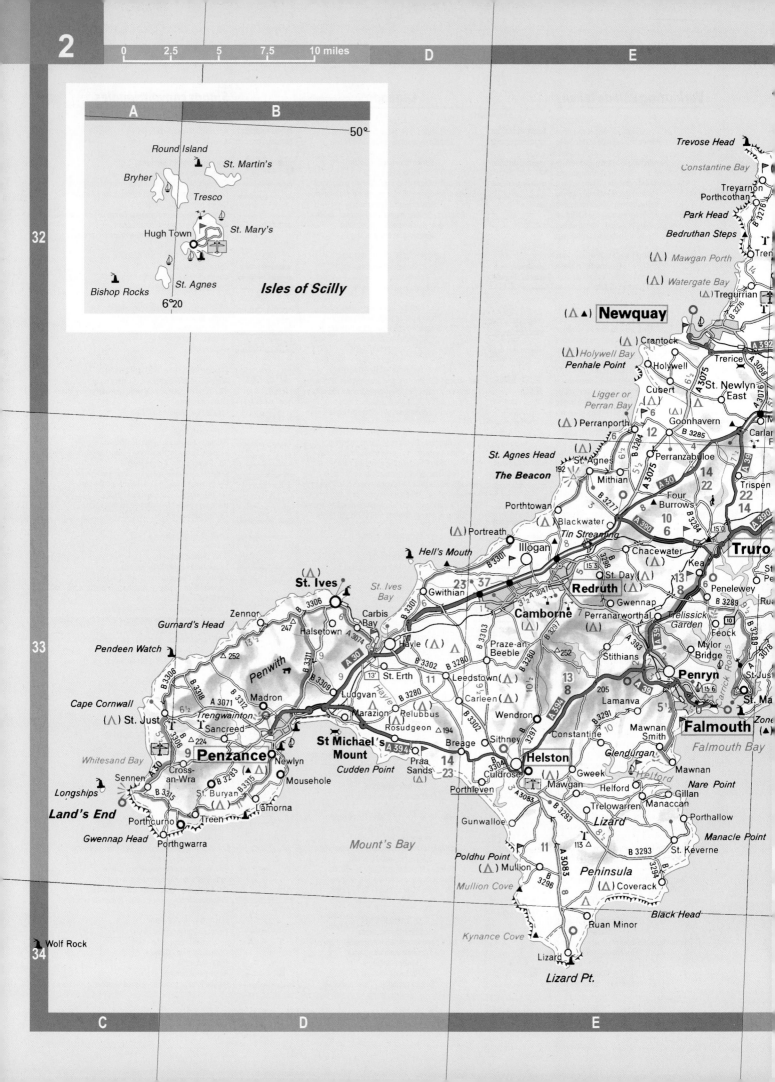

0   2.5   5   7.5   10 miles

Isles of Scilly

50°

Round Island

Bryher

St. Martin's

Tresco

Hugh Town   *St. Mary's*

Bishop Rocks   *St. Agnes*

6°20

Trevose Head

Constantine Bay

Treyarnon
Porthcothan

Park Head

Bedruthan Steps   Tren

(Λ) *Mawgan Porth*

(Λ) *Watergate Bay*

(Λ) Tregurrian

(Λ ▲) **Newquay**

(Λ) Crantock

(Λ) *Holywell Bay*   Holywell
Penhale Point

Trerice   St. Newlyn
East

Cubert

*Ligger or
Perran Bay*   Goonhavern   Carlar

(Λ) Perranporth   12   *B 3285*

(Λ)   Perranzabuloe   14
22

St. Agnes Head   St. Agnes   Trispen

The Beacon   192   Mithian   22
14

Four
Burrows   10   6

Porthtowan   Blackwater   *Tin Streaming*

(Λ) Portreath   Illogan   Chacewater   **Truro**
Kea

Hell's Mouth   *St. Ives
Bay*   St. Day (Λ)   13
8

(Λ)   Gwithian   23 • 37   **Redruth** (Λ)   Penelewey

St. Ives   Carbis
Bay   **Camborne**   Gwennap   6

Zennor   Halestown   Praze-an-
Beeble   Perranarworthal   Trelissick
Garden   Feock

Gurnard's Head   247   Hayle (Λ)   Stithians   Mylor
Bridge

Pendeen Watch   252   St. Erth   11   Leedstown(Λ)   252   **Penryn**

Penwith   Madron   Ludgvan   Carleen (Λ)   Lamanva   St. Just

Cape Cornwall   Trengwainton   Marazion   Wendron   205   5   St. Ma

(Λ) St. Just   Sancreed   Relubbus   Constantine   Mawnan
Smith

Rosudgeon   Sithney   **Falmouth**

9 **Penzance**   St Michael's
Mount   Breage   **Helston**   Glendurgan   *Falmouth Bay*

Cross-
an-Wra   Newlyn   *Cudden Point*   14   Culdrose   Mawgan   Gweek   Mawnan

Whitesand Bay   Mousehole   Praa
Sands   23   Porthleven   *Helford*   *Nare Point*

Sennen   St. Buryan   (Λ)   Helford   Gillan

Longships   Lamorna   Gunwalloe   Trelowarren   Manaccan

Land's End   Treen   11   *Lizard*   Porthallow

Porthcurno   *Poldhu Point*   113   St. Keverne

Gwennap Head   Porthgwarra   (Λ) Mullion   *Manacle Point*

Mount's Bay   *Mullion Cove*   *Peninsula*   (Λ) Coverack

Black Head

Kynance Cove   Ruan Minor

Wolf Rock   Lizard

Lizard Pt.

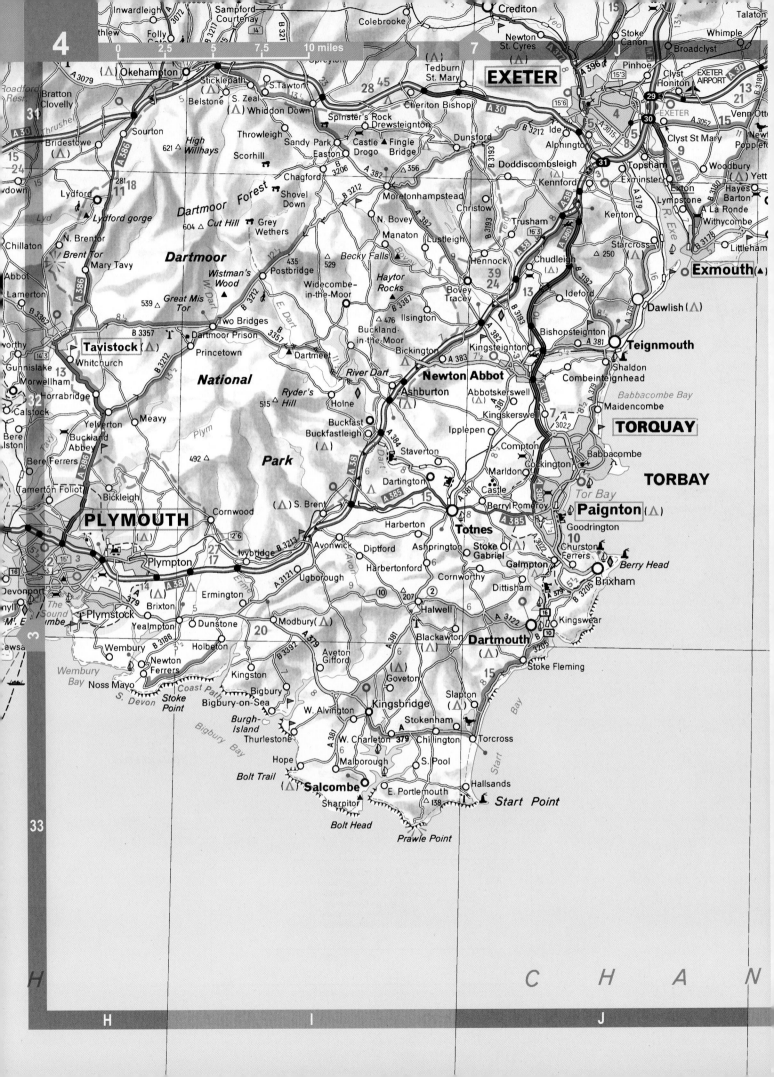

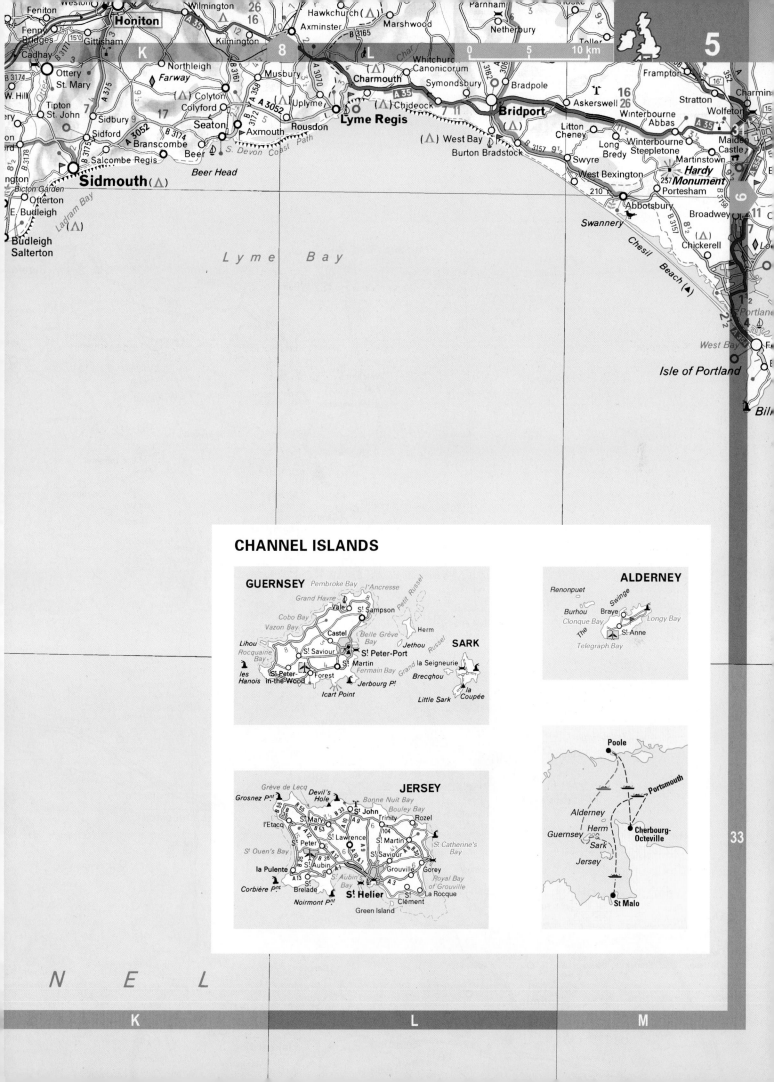

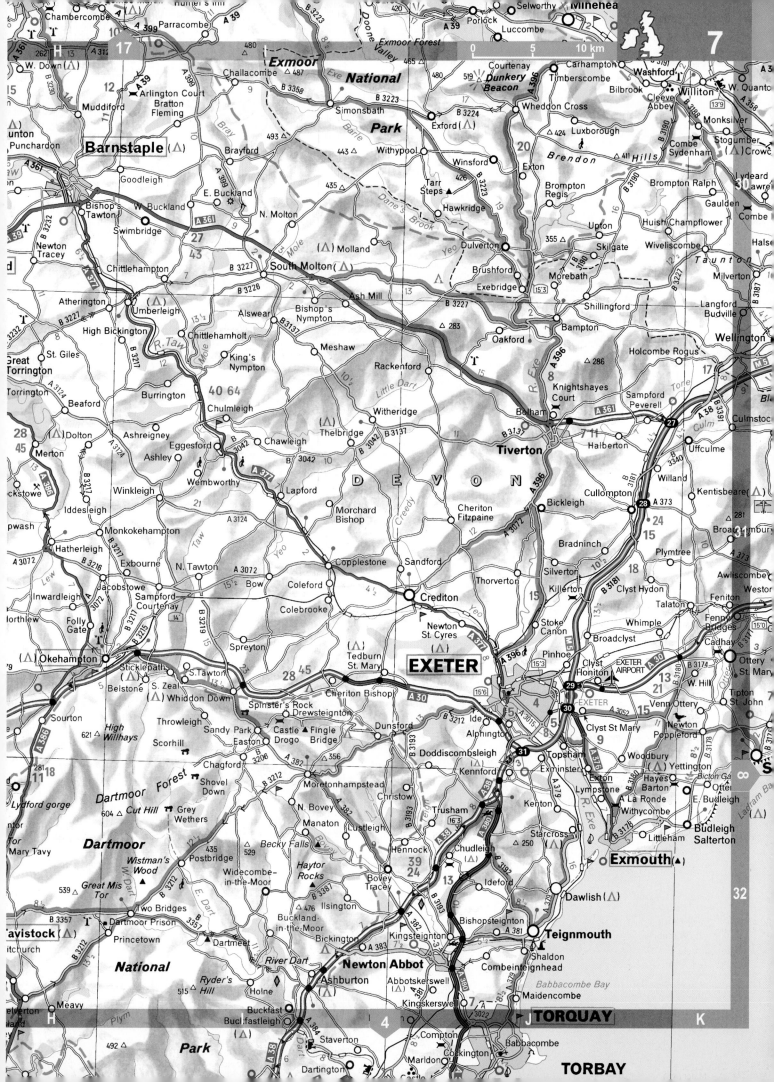

0   2.5   5   7.5   10 miles

E H
C
E
O
R
G
E'S

Rosslare

Pembrokeshire Coast

Trwyn
Dinas
Head   Newp

Strumble
Head
(▲)

Fishguard
Bay

213   Goodwick
3½

Bryn-
Henllan

A 487

Dinas

St. Nicholas

Fishguard /Ab
Pen

Llanychaer

Ynysdeullyn   Abercastle

Trecwn

334

Penclegyr   Mathry

Trevine

Porthgain

17   B 4331   Letterston

Puncheston

347

Abereiddy   Croes-goch

Welsh Hook

St. David's Head (▲)

181   Carn Llidi
Whitesand
Bay   2½   Bishop's
Palace

Wolf's Castle

164

B 4330

Solva

P E M B R O K E S
Llandeloy

Hayscastle

6

A 487   14   15
24

Spittal   Wa

Bishops and Clerks

Ramsey
Island

Ramsey Sound

St. David's
Tyddewi (▲)

A 487

Solva

100

Newgale

Scolton Mar

Camrose

Rudbaxton

Cla
Roa

Wiston

St. Bride's Bay

16

Nolton

5

B 4329

B 4327

A 487

Haverfordwest

A 40

14'9   **Hwlffordd**

Picto
Park

Broad Haven
(▲)

B 4341

Lit. Haven   13   A 4076

National Park

The Smalls

Skomer Island
(▲)

Martin's
Haven

St. Brides

B 4327

Johnston

Steynton

10

Llangwm

Lawrenny

Grassholme I.

Broad Sound

Marloes

5½
St.
Ishmael's   Herbrandston

Rosemarket

Skokholm Island (▲)

Dale

6   71

Milford Haven
Aberdaugleddau

Neyland

Milford Haven

Thorn I.   Angle

Pembroke Dock
Doc Penfro

16   Ca
10

Rhoscrowther   **Pembroke** /
Penfro

4½   27

15   A

Bist
P

Rosslare

St. Ann's Head (▲)

Freshwater
West

Hundleton

Lamphey

14'6

A 4
J

National Park   Castlemartin   12

B 4319

Freshwater
East

Linney
Head

Bosherston   Stackpole

Stack   Rocks   **St. Govan's
Head** (▲)

Stackpole

P e m b r o k e s h i r e

D   E   F

0   2.5   5   7.5   10 miles

Carmarthen
Caerfyrddin

Nantgaredig
Abergwili
Llangunnor
A 40
B 4298
Meidrim
Cwmfelin
Boeth
Whitland
Bancyfelin
St. Clears
Sanclêr
Llanddarog
A 48
A 40
B 4299
151
A 4300
H

Clarbeston Road
Rudbaxton
51
Llandissilio
Llanfallteg
B 4313
A 40
B 4314
Robeston Wathen
18
11
Haverfordwest
Hwlffordd
National Park
Narberth
Arberth
Templeton
Llangynog
Langain
Llan-y-bri
Llansteffan
Llanddowror
Red Roses
Tavernspite
Laugharne
Castle
Castle
Castle
Ferryside
Llandyfaelog
Llangyndeyrn
Llangain
Pontyberem
B 4306
B 4309
Pontyates
A 484
262
B 4317
18

Johnston
Steynton
Rosemarket
Llangwm
Martletwy
Cresswell
Jeffreyston
Kilgetty
Marros
Amroth
Pendine
Kidwelly
Cydweli
Trimsaran
Milford Haven
Aberdaugleddau
Neyland
Pembroke Dock
Doc Penfro
Lawrenny
Carew
Saundersfoot
Monkstone Point
Pendine Sands
Burry Port
Porth Tywyn
Pembrey

Pembroke
Penfro
Hundleton
Lamphey
Jameston
Bishop's Palace
St. Florence
Tenby
Dinbych-y-pysgod
Carmarthen Bay
Llanelli
Whitford Point

Castlemartin
Freshwater East
Manorbier
Lydstep
Penally
Caldey Sound
Caldey Island
Penrhyn Gŵyr
Burry Holms
Llanmadoc
Weobley
Arthur's Stone
G
O
Reynoldston
Rhossili Bay
Oxwich

National Park
Bosherston
Stackpole
Stackpole Head
Stack Rocks
St. Govan's Head
Worms Head
Rhossili
Port-Eynon
Horton

Pembrokeshire Coast
Port-Eynon-Point

29

B R I S T O L

30

Lundy
Ilfracom
Morte Point
Lee
Mortehoe
Woolacombe
Baggy Point
Putsborough
Croyde
Morte Bay
Georgeha

F   6   G   H

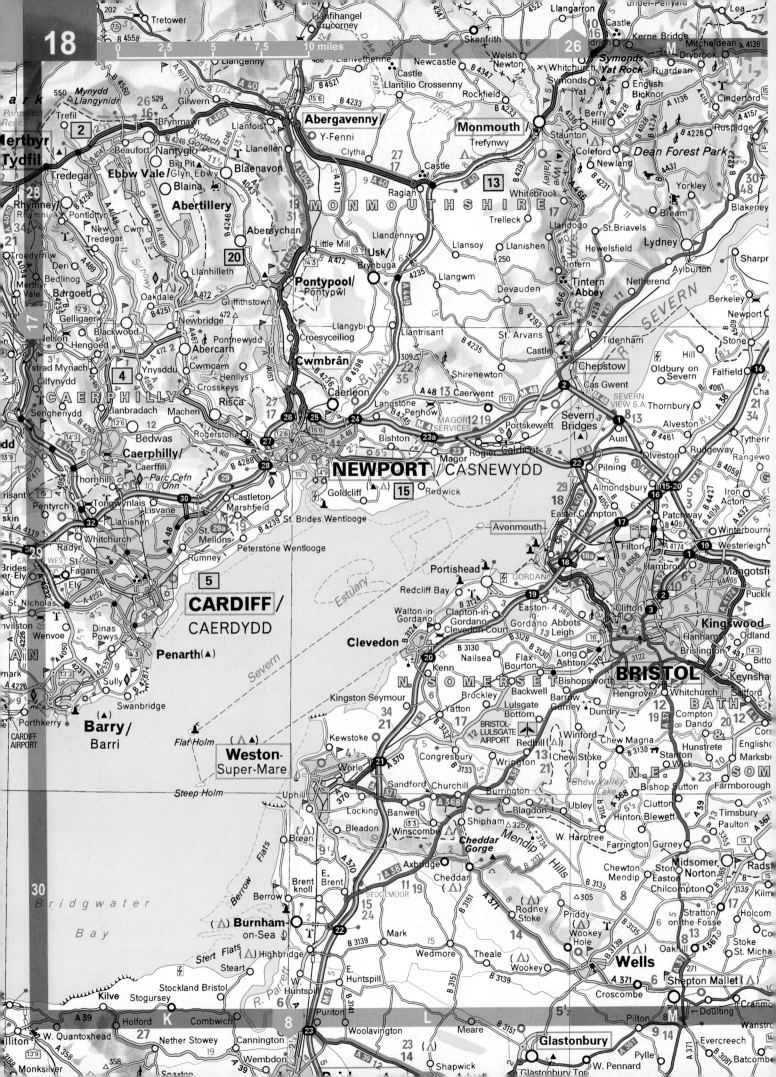

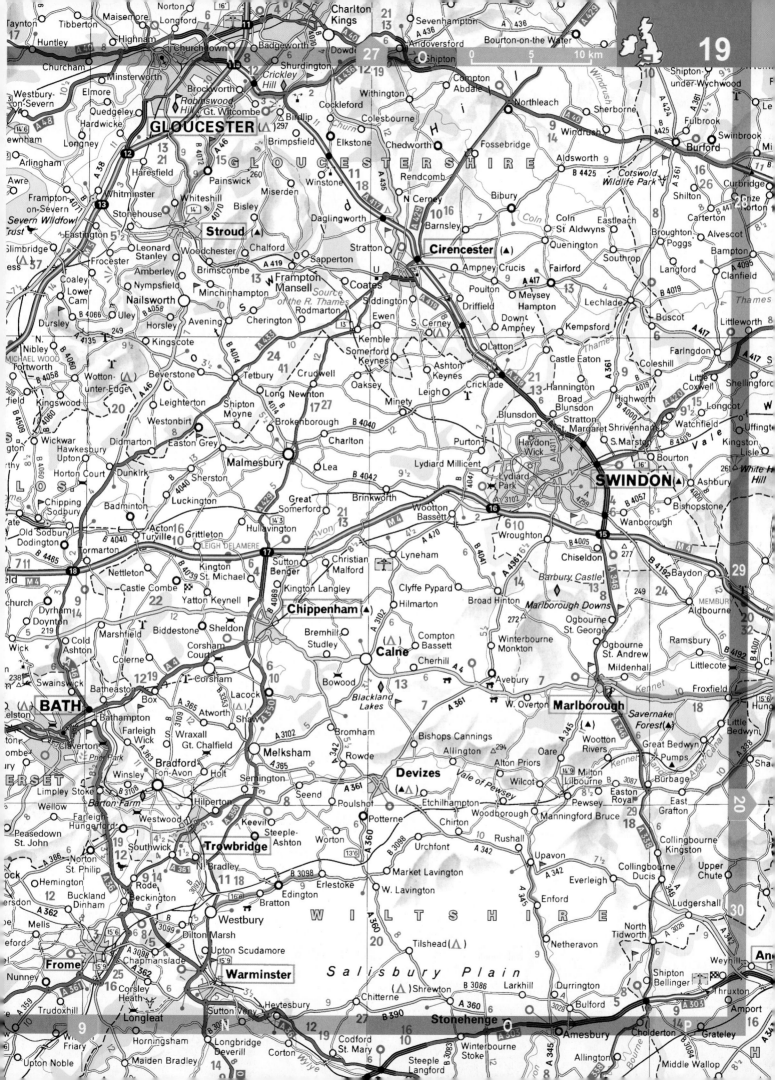

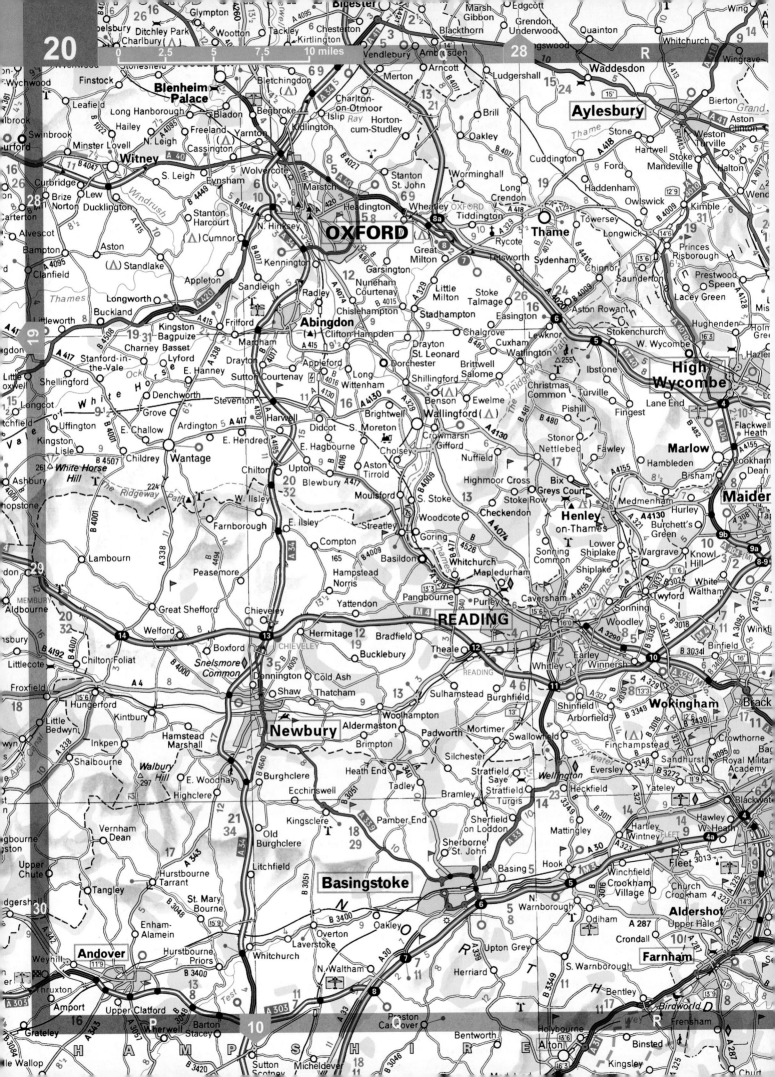

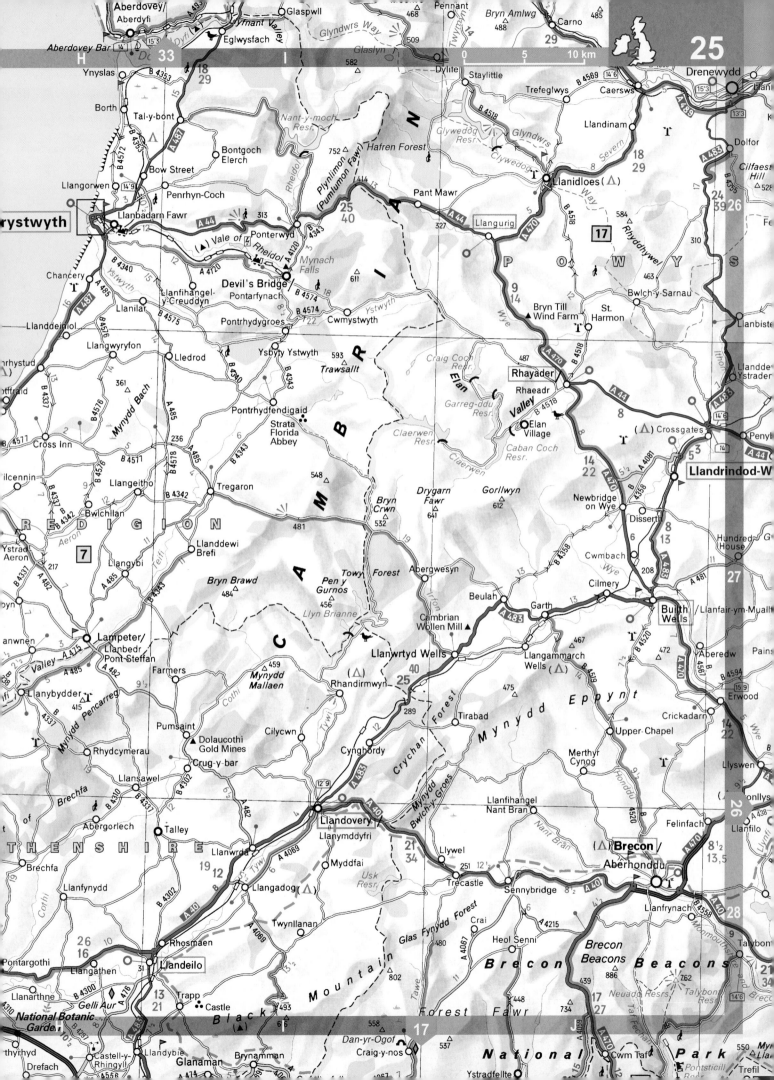

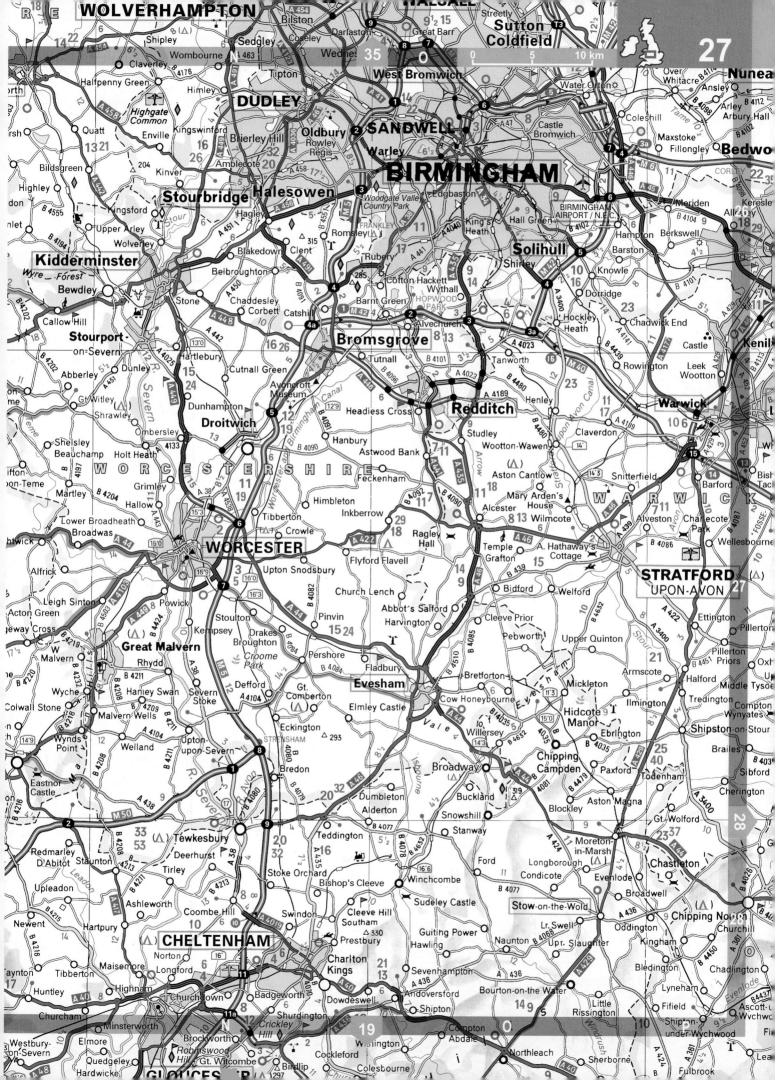

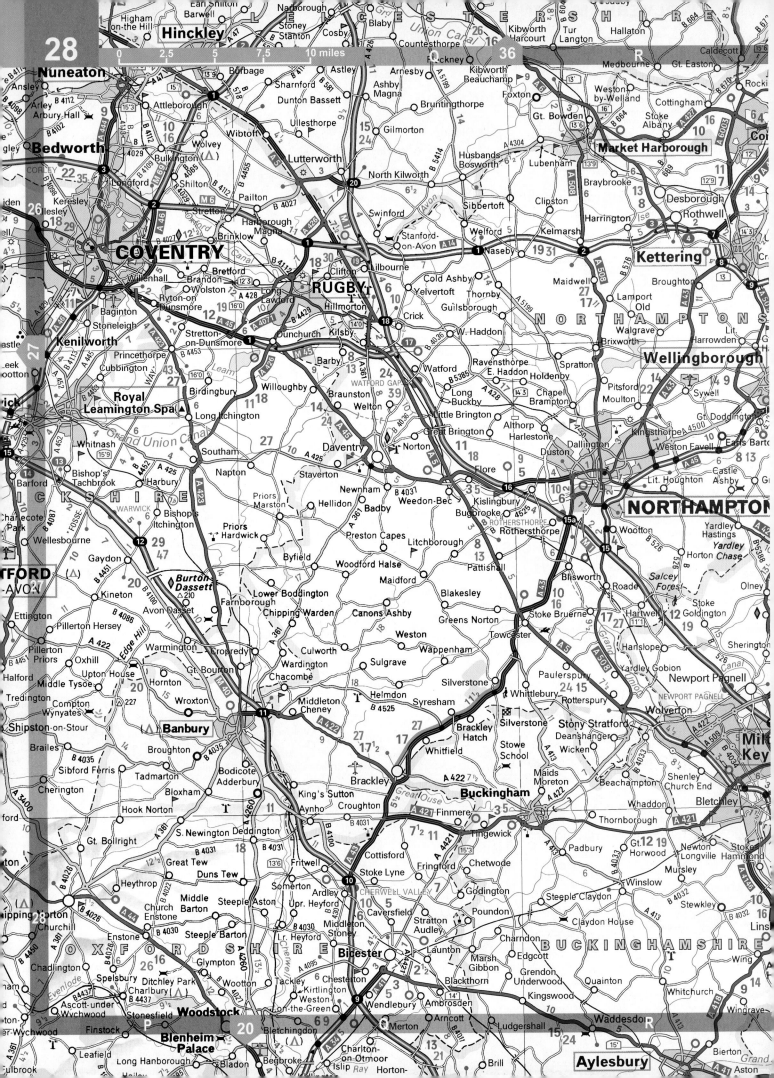

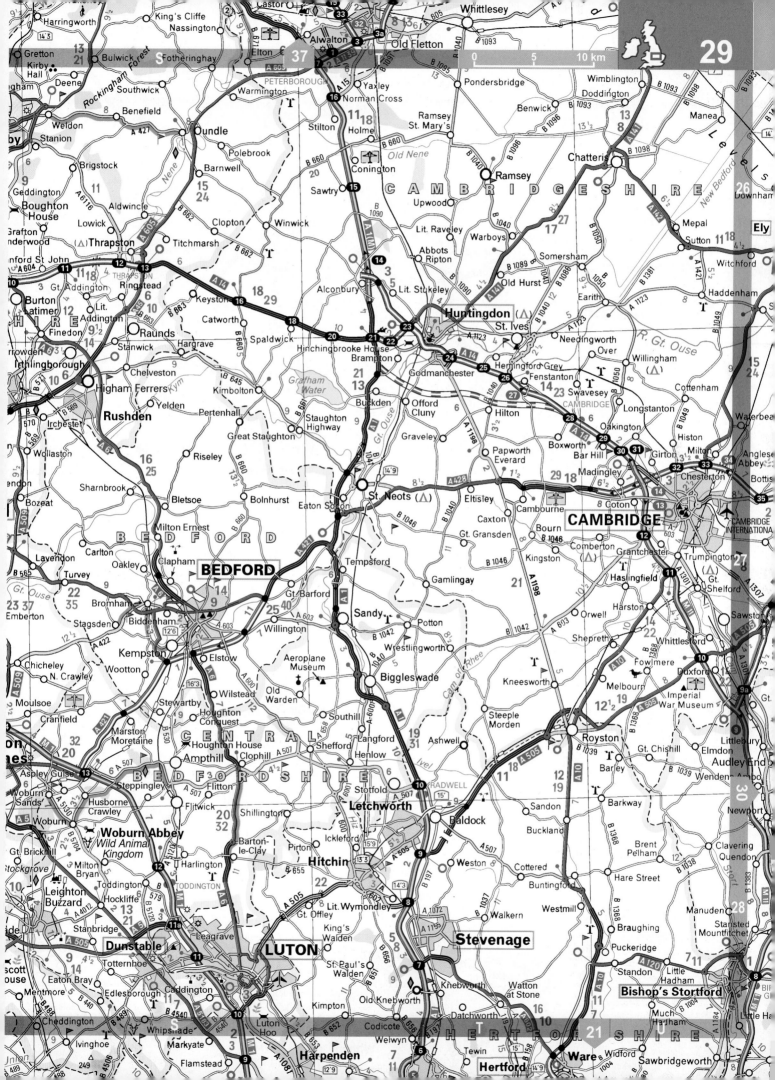

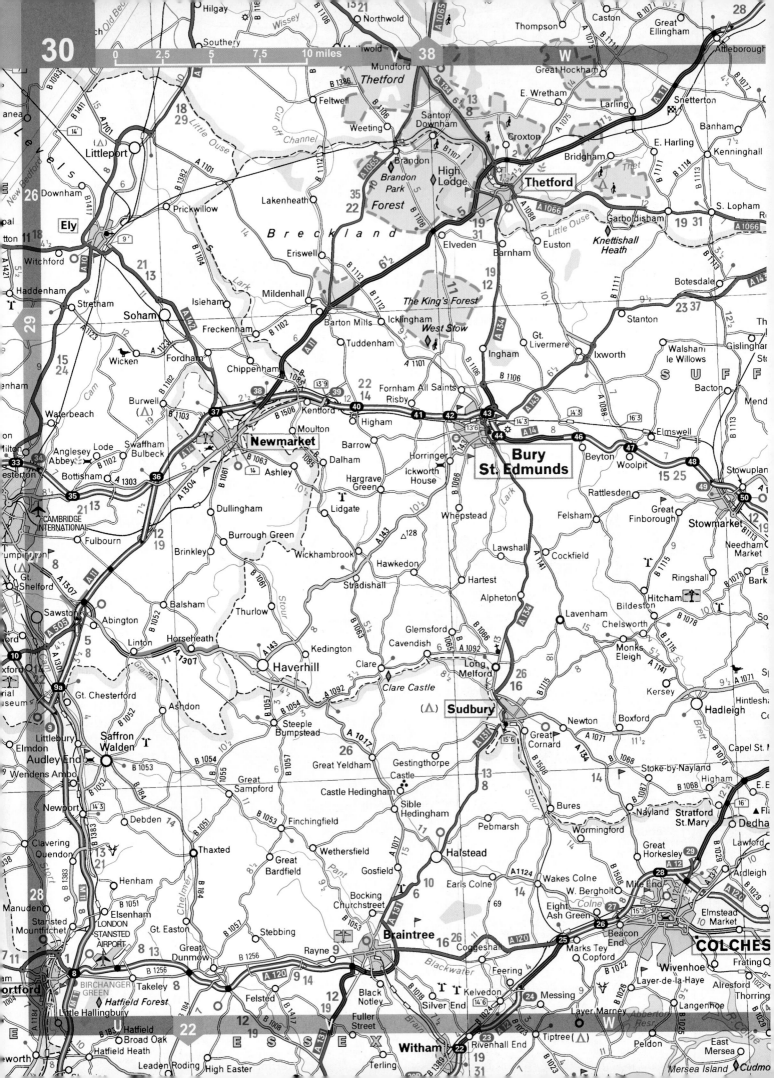

0   2.5   5   7.5   10 miles

F ANGLESEY
40

Rhosneigr Llanfaelog 32 5
(Δ) Pentre Berw
A 4080 B 4422 Llanfair-Pw
Bryn-Celli-
ddu
Aberffraw B 4421 Plas New
10½ Brynsiencyn A 4080
Bordogan A 4080 B 4419 Mer
Newborough B 4419
Malltraeth Bay Mermaid Inn
(Δ)
Llanddwyn- Caernarfon
Island
Bontnewydd
53
Caernarfon Llanwn
Bay Dinas Dinlle (Δ)
Llandwrog A 499 14
(Δ) Pen-y-g
Pontlyfni 13½ Llanllyfni
(Δ)
Clynnog- 22
Fawr 35
21
Trevor A 499 Δ
Trwyn y Gorlech Yr Eifl 522
564 Δ Llanaelhaearn
Llithfaen B 4417 7½
Carreg Ddu 6 Peninsula A 4411
Morfa Nefyn Nefyn Y Ffor (Δ) Llanystumdwy
Porth Ysgaden B A 497 B 4354 (Δ) Chwilog 14
10 B 4354 7 Lleyn A 499 A 497 Cricciet
Tudweiliog Efailnewydd 9½ (Δ)
B 4417 312 Δ Pwllheli
Llangwnnadl (Δ) Tremado
Penrhyn Mawr Sarn Meyllteyrn B 4413 Bay
103 Botwnnog 13 Llanbedrog
305 8½ A 499
Aberdaron St. Tudwal's
Mynydd Mawr Llanengan Road
Braich y Pwll Δ 160 Y Rhiw Abersoch
Bwlchtocyn
Bardsey Sound Porth Neigwl St. Tudwal's Islands
or Hell's Mouth
Trwyn Cilan
Bardsey Island (▲)

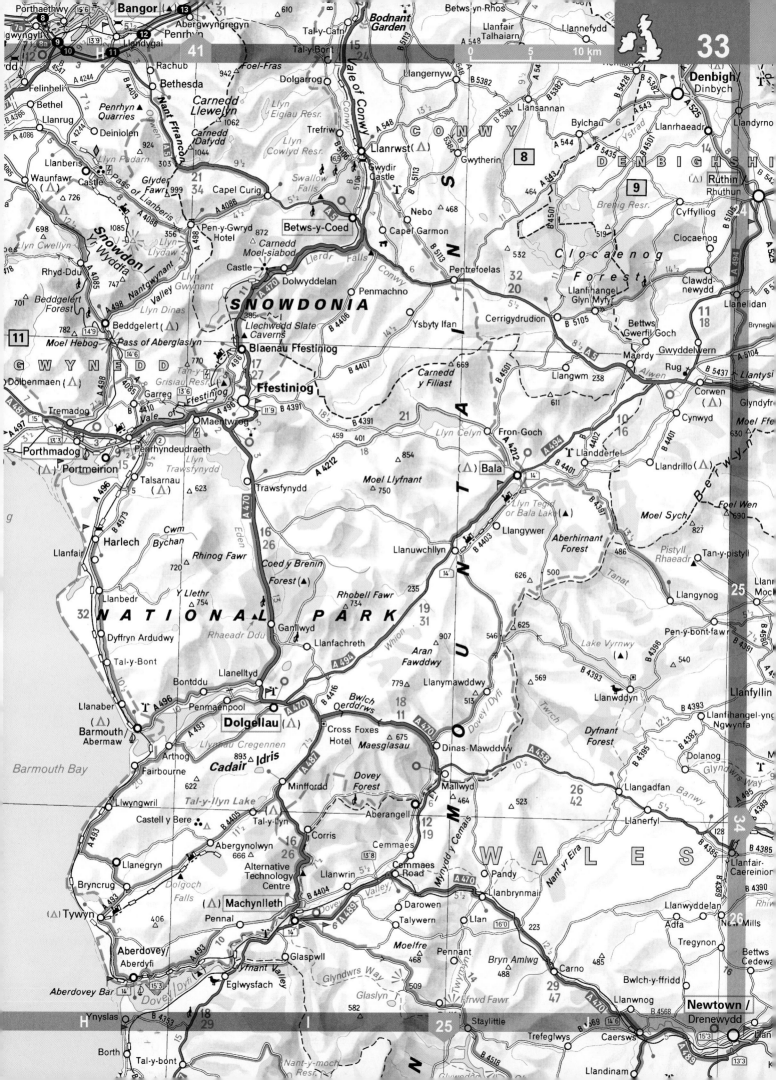

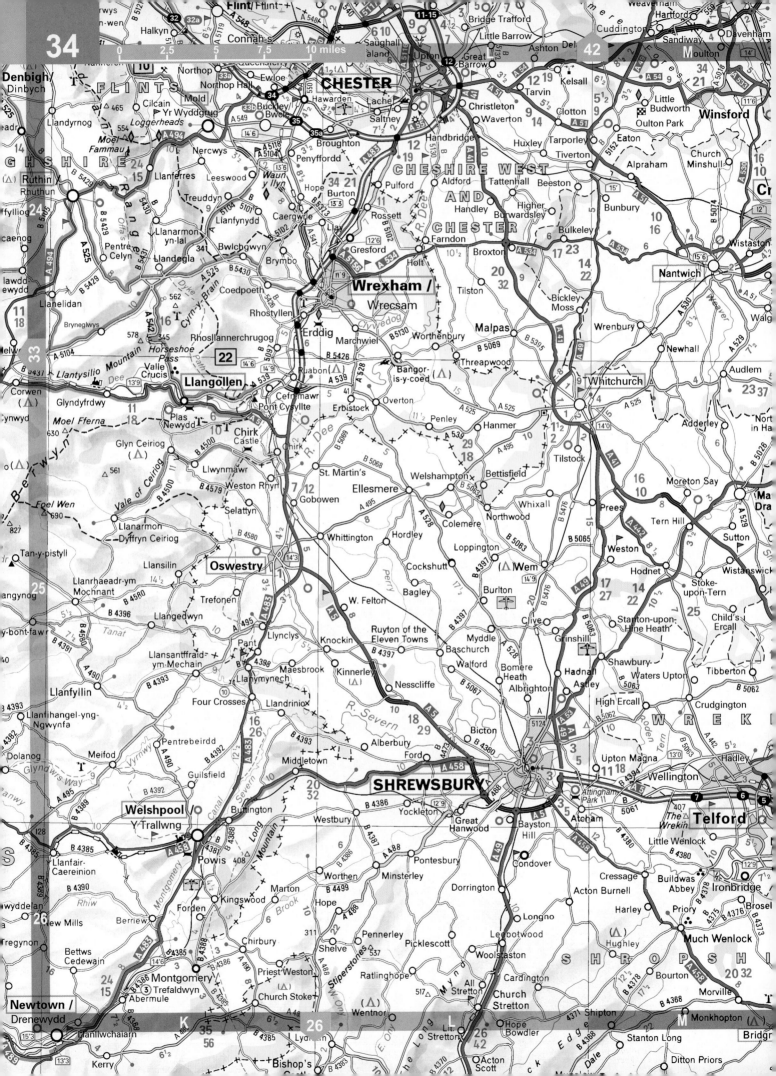

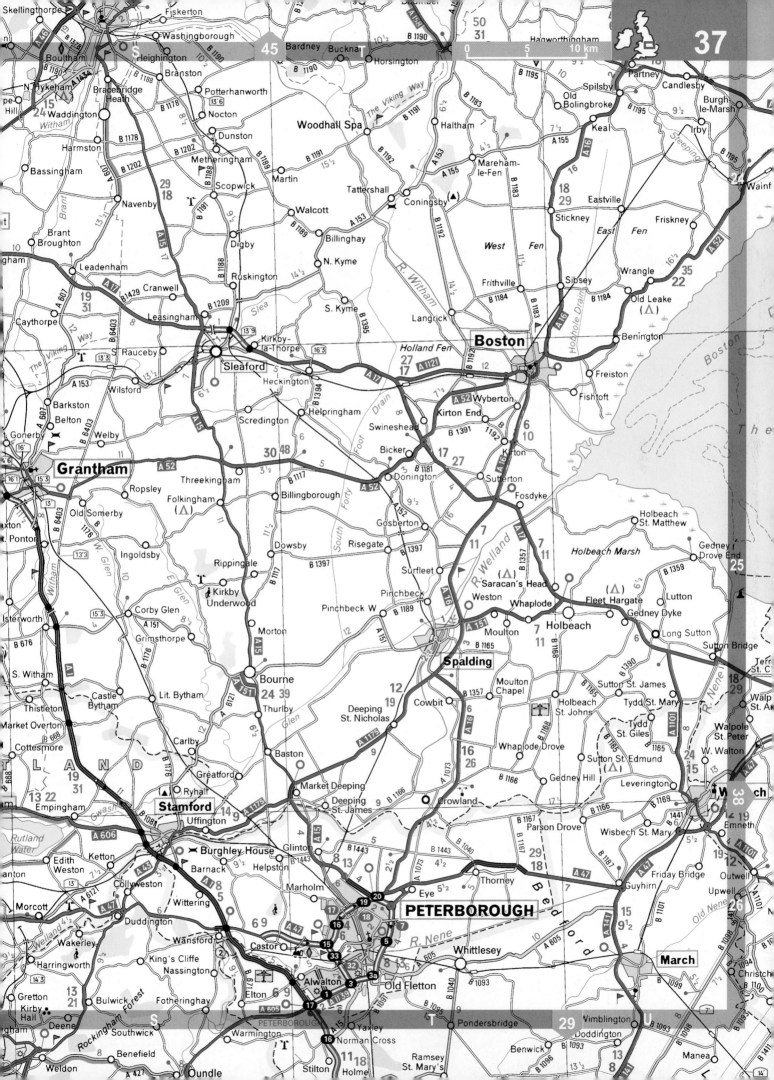

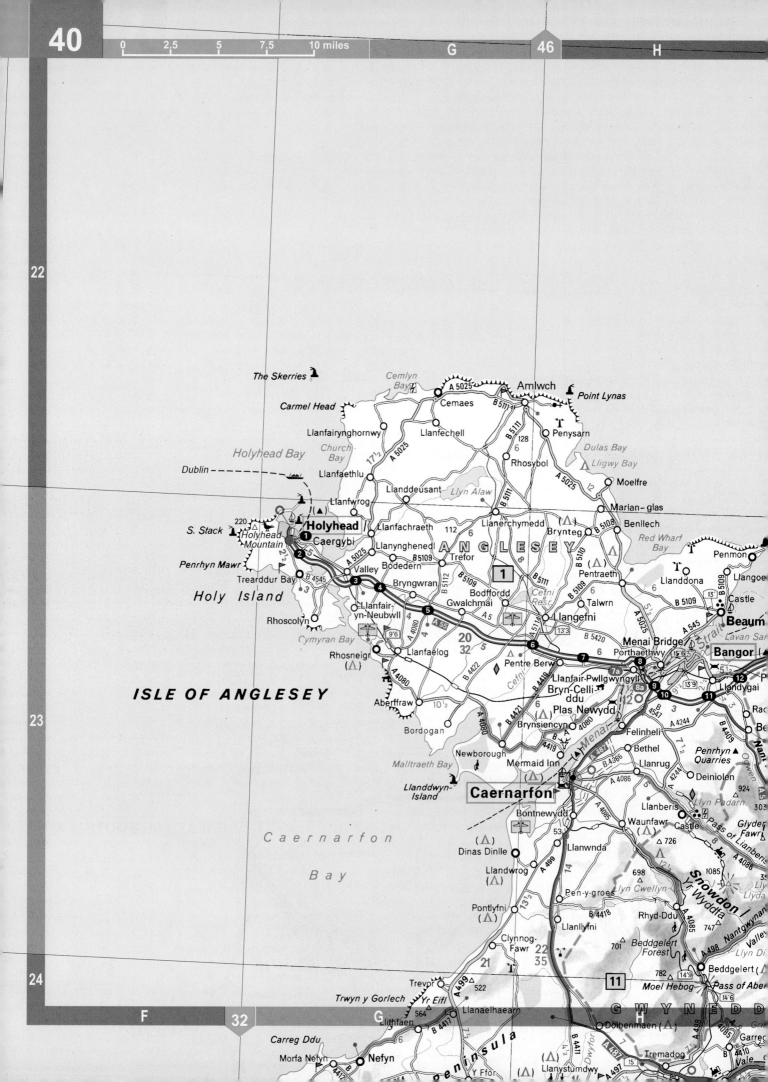

0 2.5 5 7.5 10 miles

The Skerries

Cemlyn Bay

Amlwch

Point Lynas

Carmel Head

Cemaes

A 5025

B 5111

Llanfairynghornwy

Llanfechell

Penysarn

Holyhead Bay

Church Bay

128

Rhosybol

6

Dulas Bay

Lligwy Bay

Llanfaethlu

A 5025

17½

Llanddeusant

Llyn Alaw

A 5025

12

Moelfre

Dublin

Llanfwrog

Marian-glas

220

Holyhead

S. Stack

Holyhead Mountain

Caergybi

Llanfachraeth

Llanerchymedd

Brynteg

B 5108

Benllech

ANGLESEY

112

6

Red Wharf Bay

Penmon

Penrhyn Mawr

Llanynghened

B 5109

Trefor

8

B 5110

Pentraeth

Llanddona

Llangoe

2½

Valley

Bodedern

B 5112

B 5109

B 5111

B 5109

13

Castle

Trearddur Bay

B 4545

Bryngwran

Bodffordd

Talwrn

A 5025

Beaum

Holy Island

3

Gwalchmai

A 5

Cefni Resr.

Llangefni

A 545

Rhoscolyn

Llanfair-yn-Neubwll

A 55

13·3

B 5420

Menai Bridge

Bangor

Cymyran Bay

9·6

A 4080

20 32

5

Porthaethwy

15·6

Lavan San

Rhosneigr (△)

Llanfaelog

Pentre Berw

Llanfair-Pwllgwyngyll

Llandygai

ISLE OF ANGLESEY

A 4080

A 4422

A 5114

Bryn-Celli-ddu

8a

10

11

Rad

Aberffraw

10½

A 4080

Plas Newydd

12

A 4547

Be

Bordogan

A 4080

Brynsiencyn

A 4080

Menai

Felinheli

7½

Penrhyn Quarries

B 4403

Nant Ogwen

Newborough

Mermaid Inn

B 4419

A 4087

Bethel

Llanrug

Deiniolen

924

Ogwen

Malltraeth Bay

A 4366

A 4086

Penrhyn

303

Llanddwyn Island

Caernarfon

Llanberis

Llyn Padarn

Caernarfon Bay

Bontnewydd

A 4086

Waunfawr

Castle

Pass of Llanberis

A 4086

Dinas Dinlle (△)

Llanwnda

53

726

698

1085

Glyder Fawr

Glyder Fach

Llandwrog (△)

A 499

14

Llyn Cwellyn

Snowdon

Yr Wyddfa

Llyd

Pen-y-groes

3

747

Pontlyfni (△)

13½

B 4418

Rhyd-Ddu

A 4085

Nantgwynan

Valle

Llanllyfni

Llyn Di

Clynnog-Fawr

22 35

701

Beddgelert Forest

A 498

21

782

14·9

Beddgelert

11

Moel Hebog

Pass of Aber

Trevor

A 499

522

14·6

GWYNEDD

Trwyn y Gorlech

Yr Eifl

Llithfaen

564

Llanaelhaearn

B 4417

Dolbenmaen (△)

A 498

4085

Gar

Carreg Ddu

6

eninsula

B 4417

Y Ffor

A 487

15

Tremadog

Vale

Morfa Nefyn

Nefyn

B 4417

Llanystumdwy

A 497

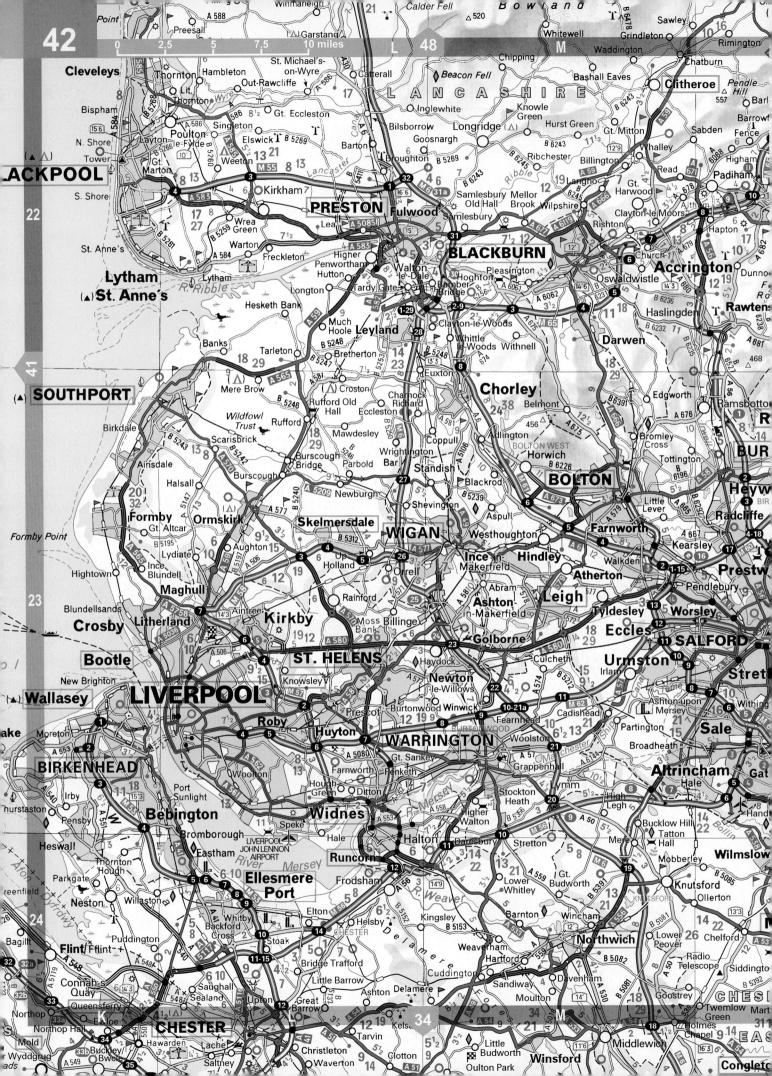

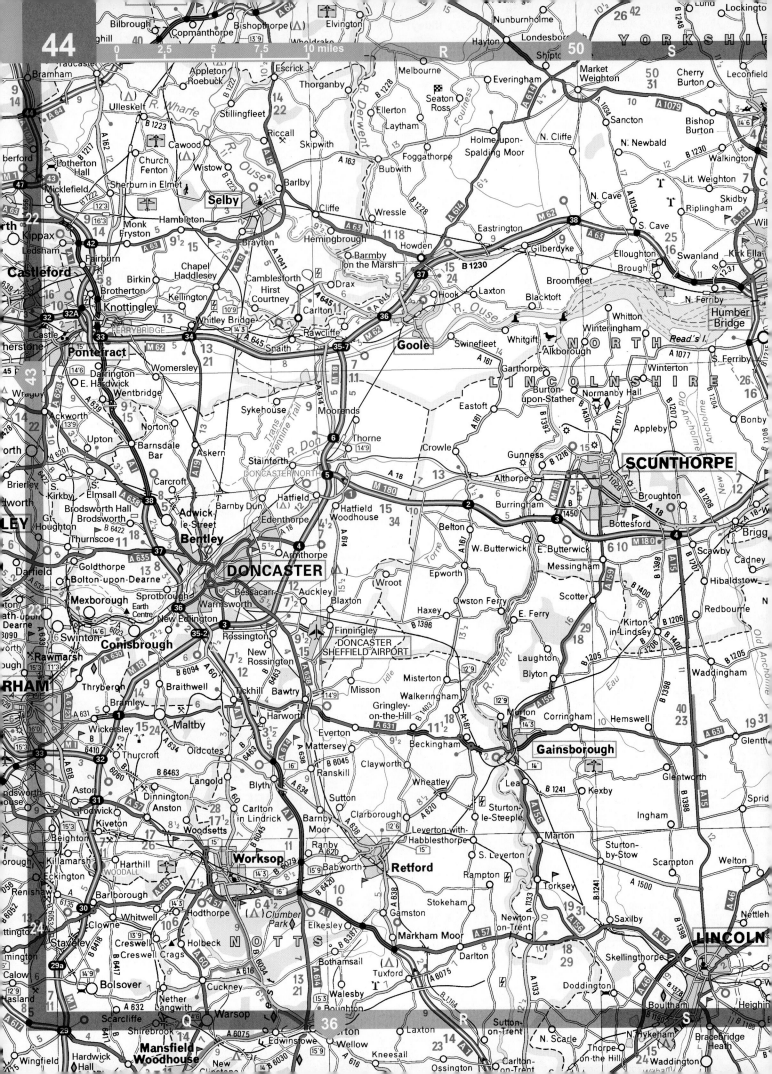

KINGSTON-UPON-HULL

GRIMSBY

Cleethorpes

Beverley

Hornsea

Brandesburton

Leven

Sigglesthorne

Mappleton

Routh

Arram

Withernwick

Skirlaugh

Aldbrough

Burton Constable Hall

Humbleton

Sproatley

Tunstall

Sutton-on-Hull

Bilton

Burton Pidsea

Roos

Preston

Hedon

Burstwick

Withernsea

Paull

Keyingham

Winestead

Hollym

Ottringham

Patrington

Holmpton

New Holland

Goxhill

Sunk Island

Easington

Thornton E. Halton

Abbey

Kilnsea

Thornton Curtis

S. Killingholme

Immingham Dock

Ulceby

Immingham

Barton-upon-Humber

Spurn Head

Mouth of the Humber

Elsham

Kirmington

Stallingborough

Keelby

Healing

Gt. Coates

Humberside Airport

Laceby

Humberston

Barnetby-le-Wold

Gt. Limber

Waltham

New Waltham

Holton-le-Clay

Rotterdam
Zeebrugge

Grasby

Swallow

Tetney

Marshchapel

Caistor

N. Thoresby

Fulstow

Grainthorpe

N. Somercotes

Kelsey

Nettleton

Wold Newton

Ludborough

Conisholme

Saltfleet

Moortown

S. Kelsey

Thoresway

Binbrook

Fotherby

Theddlethorpe St. Helen

Osgodby

Stainton-le-Vale

Alvingham

Tealby

Market Rasen

Ludford

Welton-le-Wold

Louth

Grimoldby

Mablethorpe

Middle Rasen

Willingham Forest

Legbourne

Trusthorpe

Linwood

Hainton

Donington-on-Bain

Tathwell

Withern

Maltby-le-Marsh

Sutton-on-Sea

Faldingworth

East Barkwith

Cadwell Park

Burwell

S. Thoresby

Thurlby

Huttoft

Wickenby

Holton

Scamblesby

Alford

Mumby

Wragby

Belchford

Tetford

Ulceby

Hogsthorpe

Chapel St. Leonards

Reepham

Minting

Baumber

Hagworthingham

Willoughby

Ingoldmells

Bardney

Bucknall

Horsington

Horncastle

Partney

Candlesby

Potterhanworth

Spilsby

Burgh-le-Marsh

Nocton

Woodhall Spa

Haltham

Old Bolingbroke

Keal

Irby

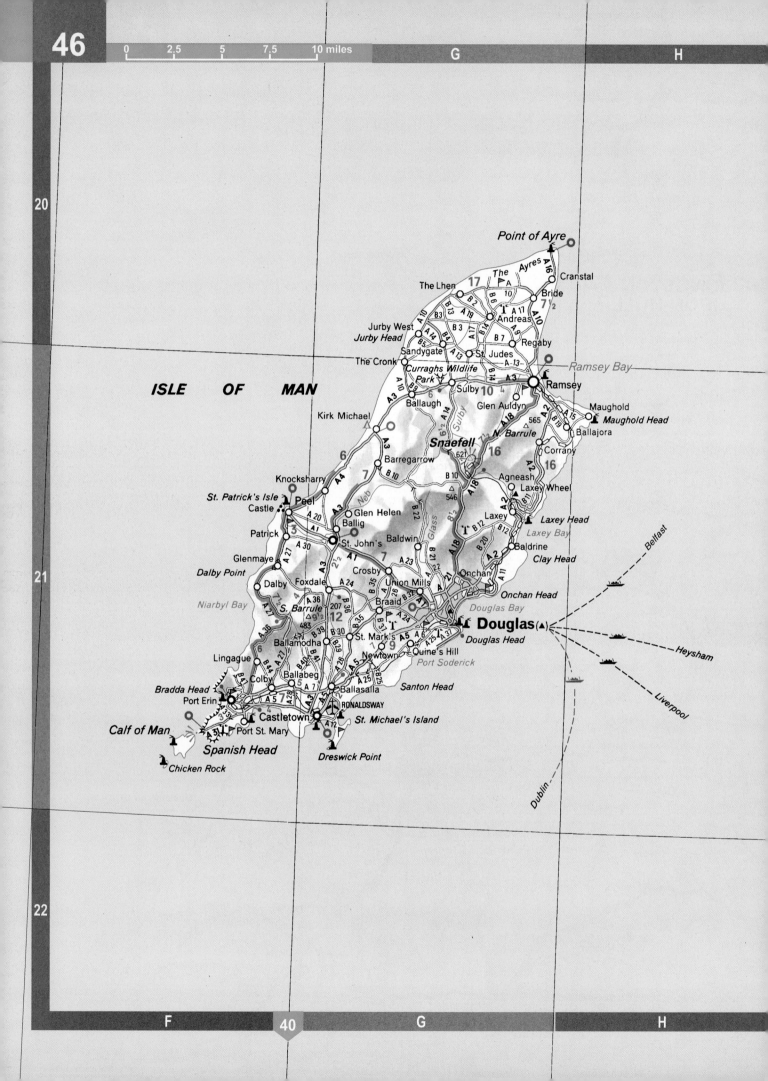

I

Distington Ullock

Lowca

△ 247 16 (△)

Partn Mor

Whitehaven

B 5294 A 5086 Frizington

Ennerdale Bridge

Buttermere Grange

Buttermere (▲) △ 754 Rosthw

B 5295 Ennerdale Water B 5289 △ 358 14 5

6 Cleator Moor Honister Pass

A 595 10 Seathwaite

St. Bees Head Great Gable

B 5345 △ 899 Wasdale Head

(△) St. Bees Egremont Copeland Forest △ 692

B 5345 Scafell Pikes △ 977

CUMBRIAN

Beckermet Calder Bridge 20

Nether △ 902 (△) Lang

Wasdale Wast (▲)

Gosforth Water Lit.

7 10'9 △ 390 Pa

Santon Hard Knott

Bridge Eskdale Green Boot Pass 393 Furness

Seascale Irt Eskdale 17

B 5344 The Old Man △ 80

Holmrook Esk △ Cor

Drigg B 5344c

Ravenglass Seathwaite

(△) Muncaster Ulpha (△) Torver

Whitfell A 593 18

572 △ A 506

Selker Bay A 595 9

43 Broughton Mills

69

Bootle Broughton- Blawit

in-Furness

Black Combe △ 600 22 A 595 Lowick Bridg

A 5092 Low

A 5093 7½ Grizebeck Gr

Silecroft Sand Side

(△) Millom (△) Ulverston

A 595

Haverigg Ireleth Gt.

A 590 21 Lit.

Askam Urswick

in Furness 12 19

Dalton-in-Furness

Duddon Sands Gt.

Sands

(△) **Barrow** -in-Furness Furness Gleaston

Abbey

14 3 A 5087

Isle of Walney Biggar Rampside

Hilpsford Point

Douglas (I.

Fleet

Rossa

I J K **Clev**

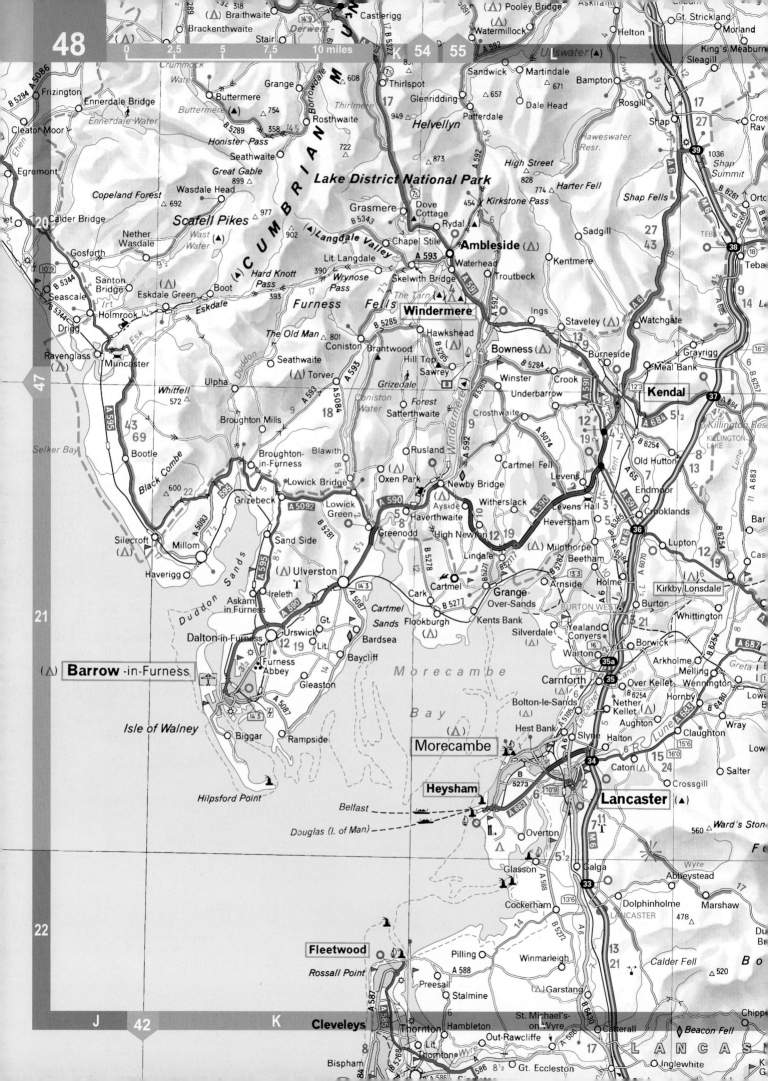

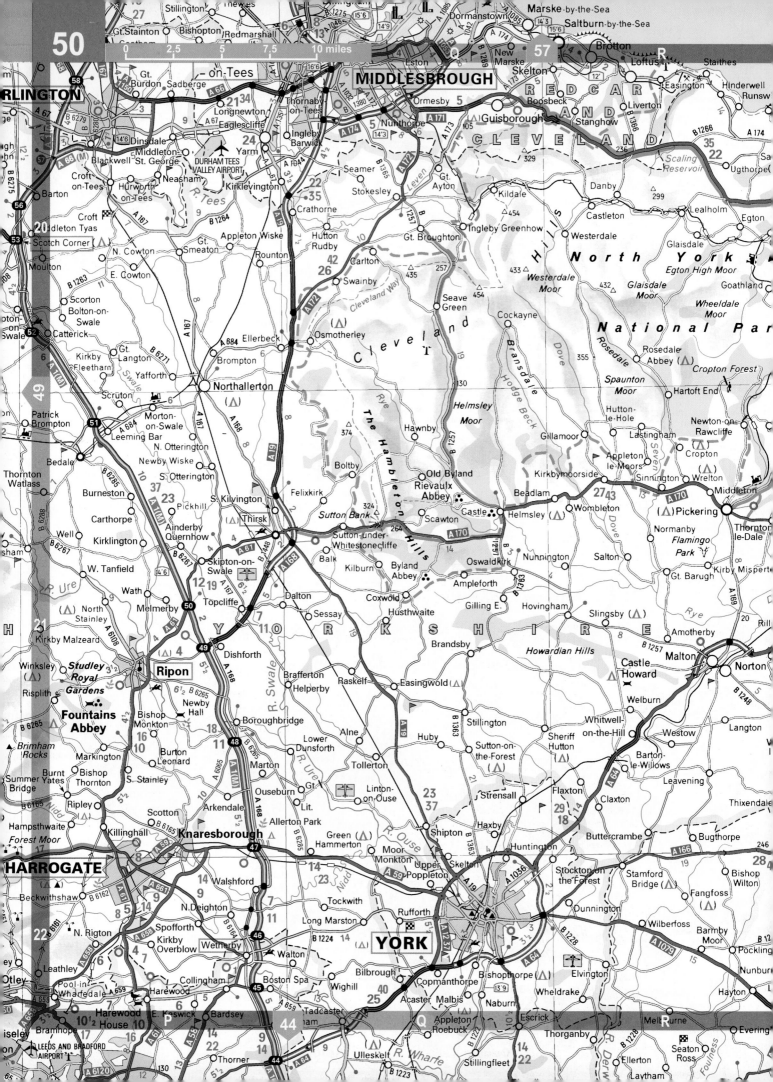

20

Bay
ttleness
-ythe
Whitby (Λ)
send
Abbey
Ruswarp
eights
Esk
Hawsker
smont
(Λ)
B 1447
Robin Hood's Bay
oors
206
B 1416
34
21
288
Ravenscar
Cleveland
299
Fylingdales Moor Λ
Way
A 171
201
Staintondale
k
280
Harwood Dale
Langdale Forest
Cloughton
evisham
Burniston
Derwent
A 165
Dalby
Langdale
Scalby
Forest
End
Hackness
Wykeham Forest
Ayton
B 1261
SCARBOROUGH (Λ Λ)
Ebberston (Λ)
Wykeham (Λ)
Seamer
7½
Eastfield
Allerston
Snainton
17 27
Cayton
(Λ)
B 1415
B 1258
A 170
Brompton
by Sawdon
A 64
Lebberston
A 1039
Yedingham
The
Gristhorpe
Filey (Λ)
Carrs
Hertford
6 Muston
Filey Bay
B 1258
A 1039
Sherburn
Staxton
Hunmanby
A 165
A 64
Ganton
(Λ)
W. Heslerton
22
Reighton
ton
16
35
B 1249
Speeton
19 11
Wintringham
Foxholes
Wold Newton
B 1229
Bempton
-cagglethorpe
Burton Fleming
15 9
13½ B
Flamborough
199
Weaverthorpe
B 1255
Head
Grimston
W. Lutton
12
B 1253
6
B 1255 B 1259
arram
175
Duggleby
Langtoft
Rudston
Carnaby
Bridlington (Λ)
Street
12
(Λ)
B 1253
B 1251
Sledmere
A 614
5½
A 165
Monument
B 1252
B 1249
Kilham
Bridlington
B 1248
Garton-on-
13 21
Burton Agnes
Bay
B 1251
Wetwang
the-Wolds
7½
Nafferton
10
Barmston
Fridaythorpe
A 166
Gt. Driffield
Lissett
6
1
Kelk Beck
Huggate
Kirkburn
4½
Wansford
B 1249
Skipsea (Λ)
8½
Old Howe
B 1242
N. Dalton
Bainton
Foston-on-
B 1246
the-Wolds
Hutton
A 164
N. Frodingham
Beeford
Watton
12
Cranswick
Middleton-
Atwick
on-the-Wolds
Lund
Burshill
Bewholme
B 1242
Hornsea
olme
26 42
Lockington
(Λ)
Brandesburton
ndesborough
B 1248
B 1244
7
YORKSHIRE
Leven
Sigglesthorne
35
Shiptonthorpe
Mappleton

Market
50
Cherry
Arram
22
Weighton
31
Burton
Leconfield
A 1035
Routh
Withernwick
A 1079
10
A 1035
Sancton
Bishop
Beverley
Yorkshire
EAST RIDING OF
21
22

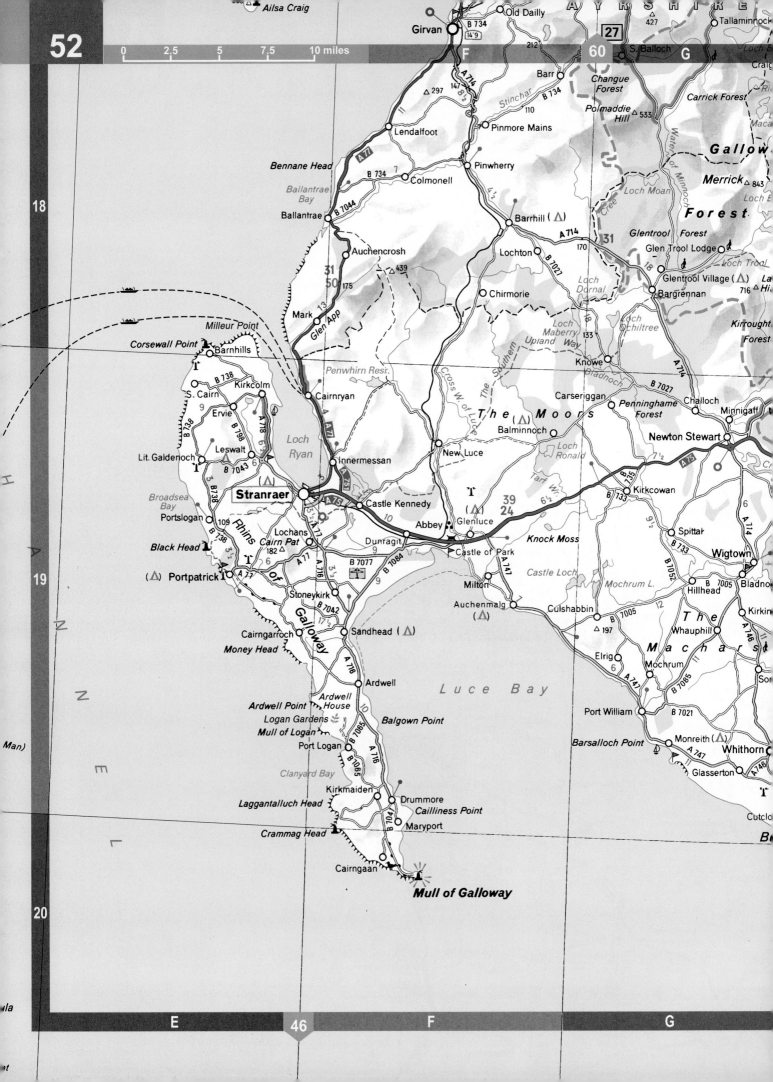

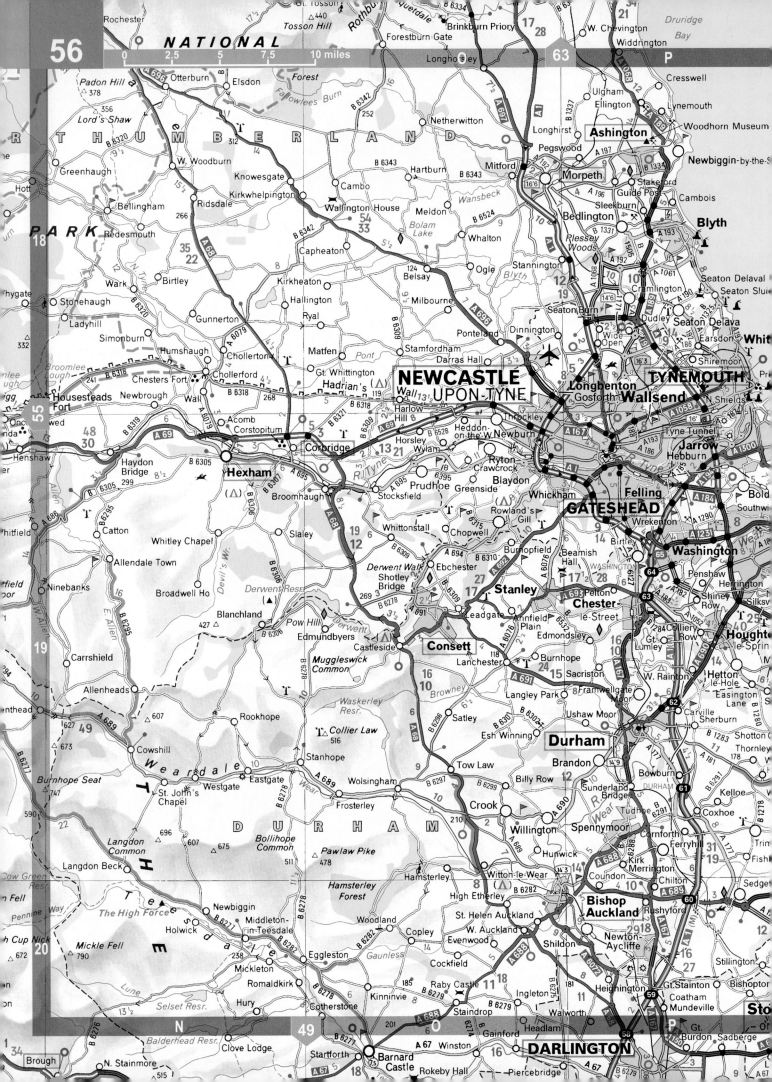

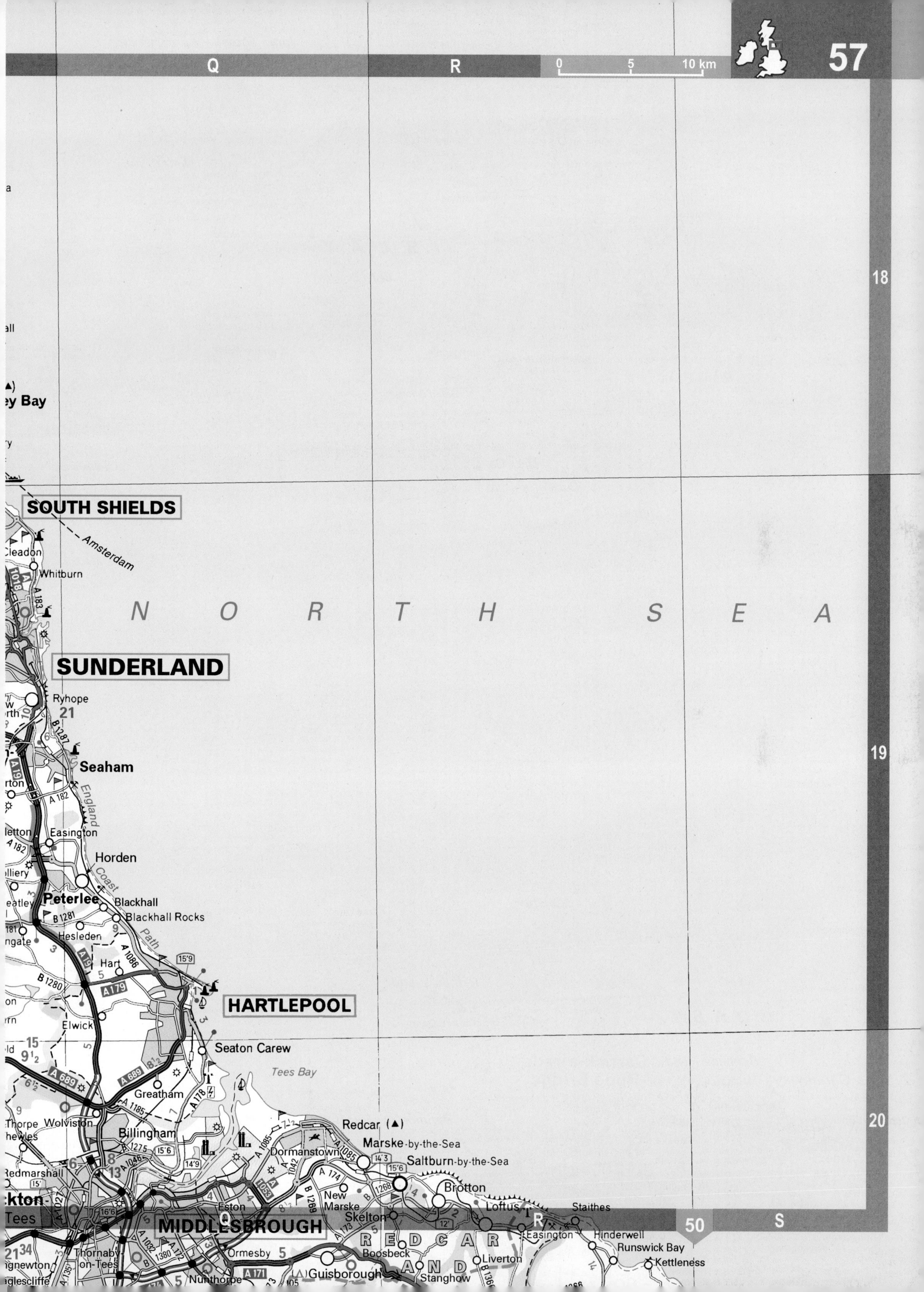

18

SOUTH SHIELDS

Amsterdam

Cleadon

Whitburn

N O R T H S E A

SUNDERLAND

Ryhope

21

Seaham

Easington

Horden

Peterlee Blackhall

Blackhall Rocks

Hesleden

Hart

15'9

HARTLEPOOL

Elwick

15
9'2

Seaton Carew

Tees Bay

Greatham

19

20

Thorpe Wolviston

Billingham

Redcar (▲)

Marske-by-the-Sea

Dormanstown

Saltburn-by-the-Sea

Brotton

MIDDLESBROUGH

New Marske

Skelton

Loftus

Staithes

Easington Hinderwell

50 S

R E D C A R

Ormesby 5

Boosbeck

Liverton

Runswick Bay

Kettleness

Nunthorpe

Guisborough

Stanghow

A N D

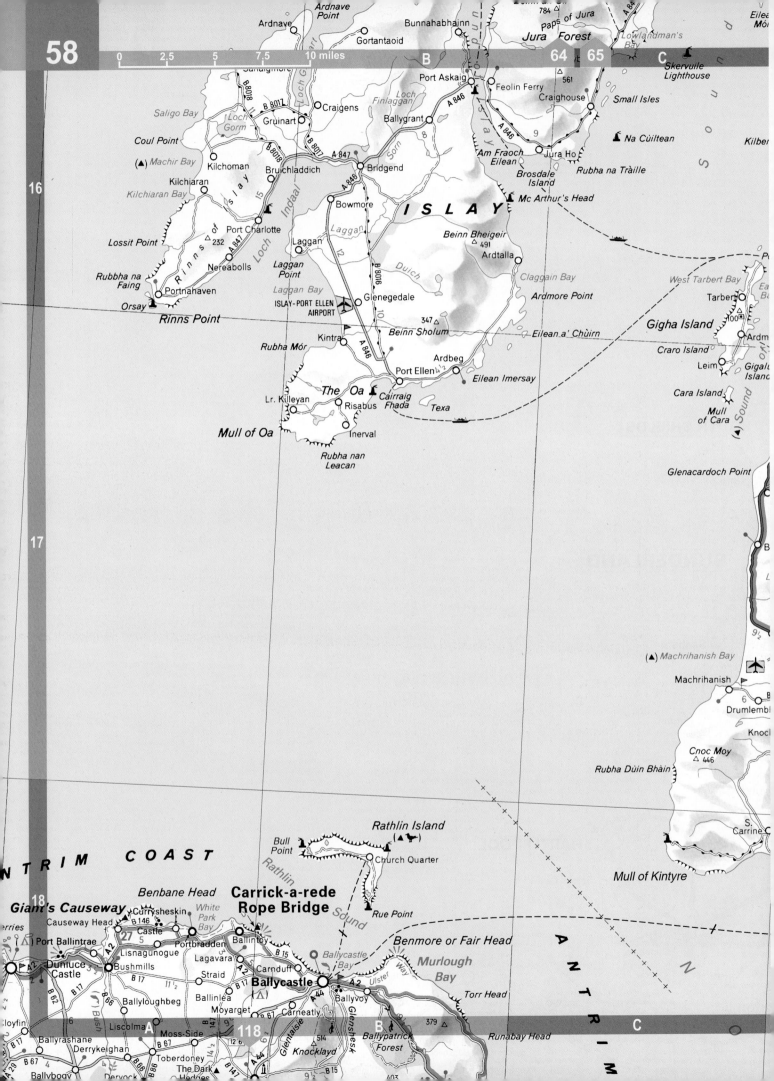

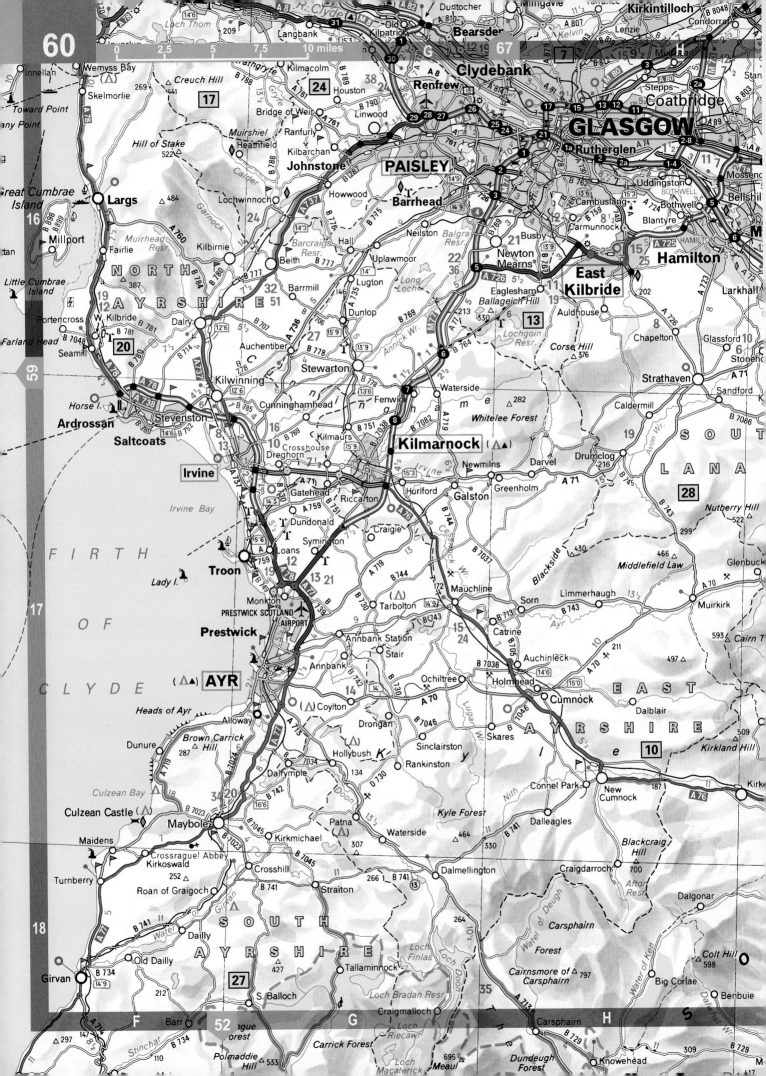

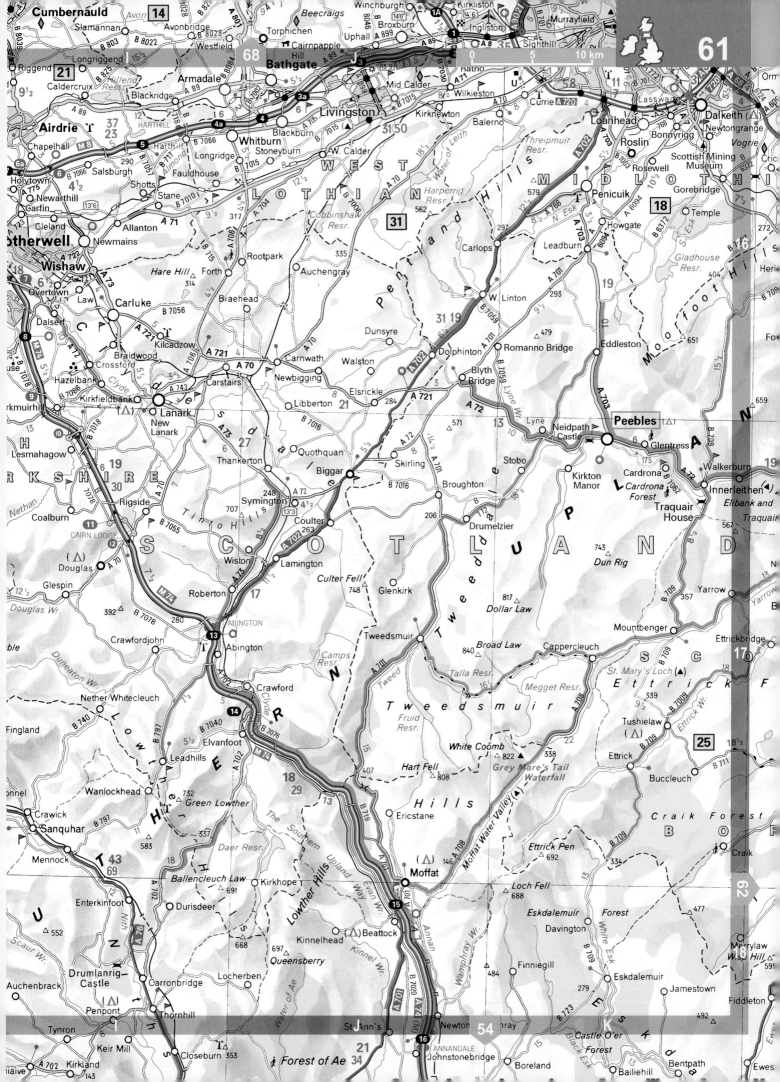

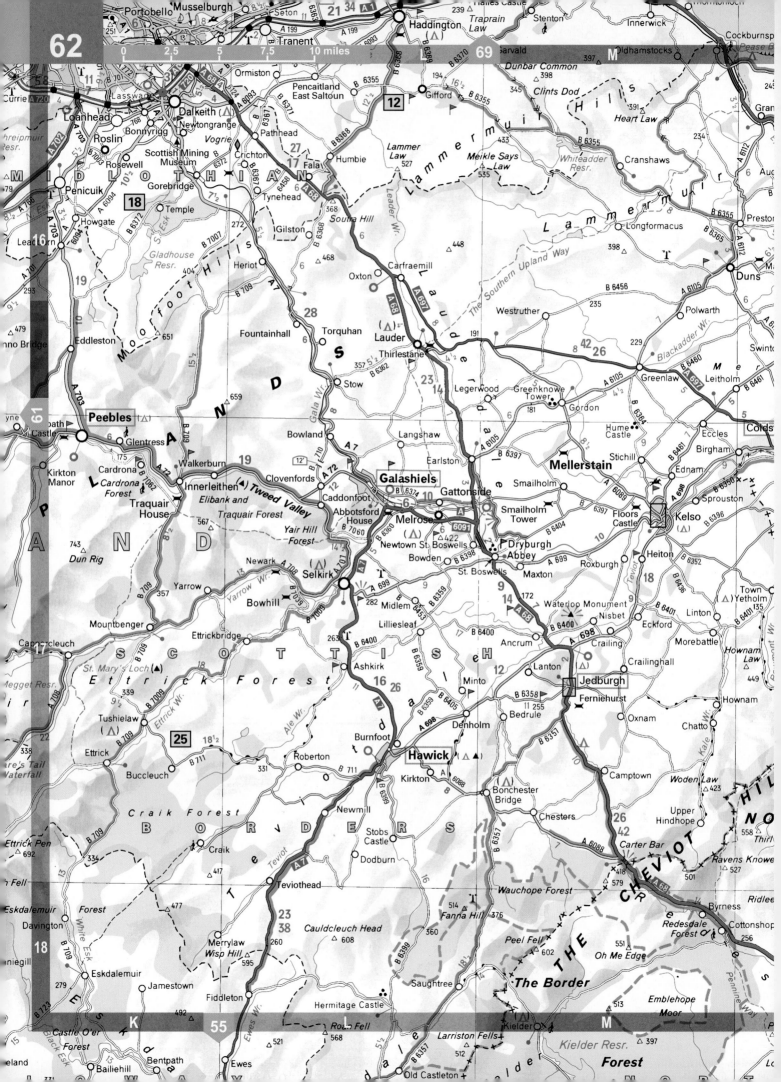

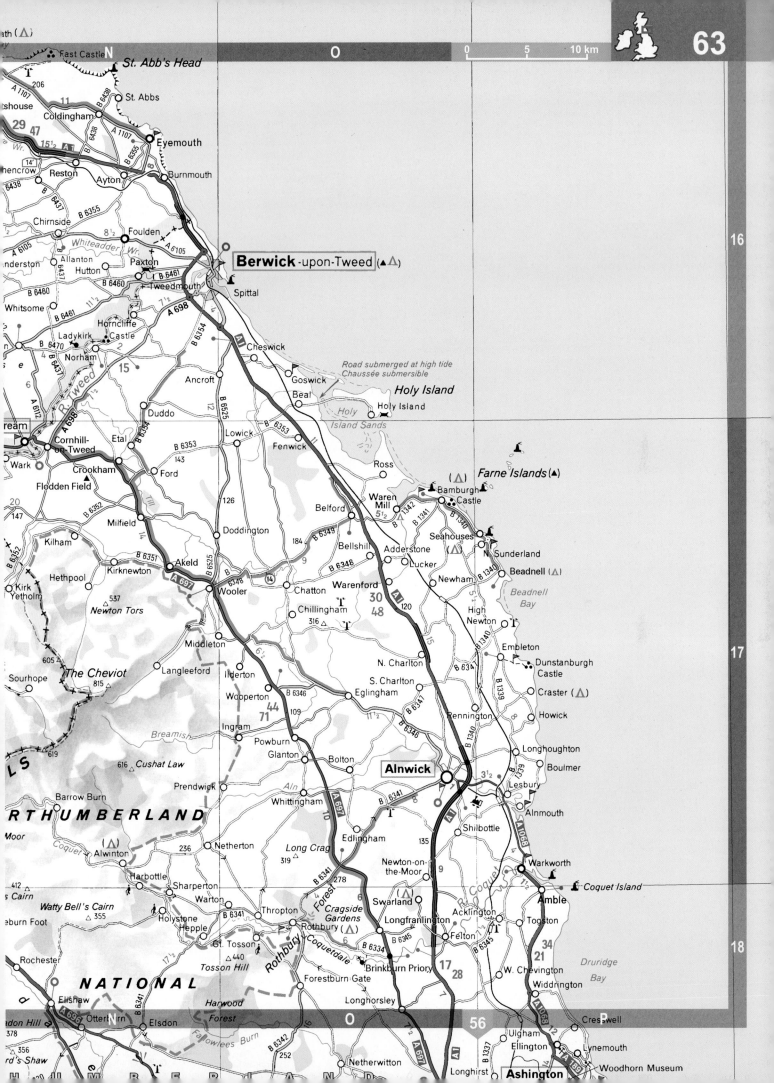

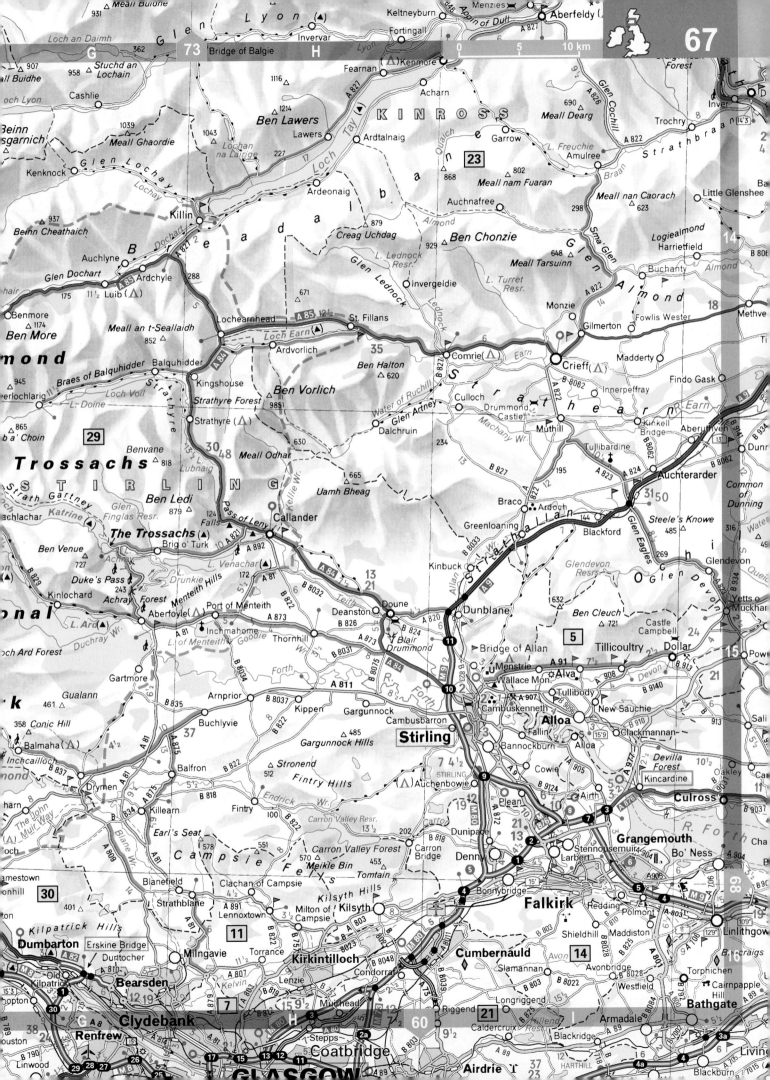

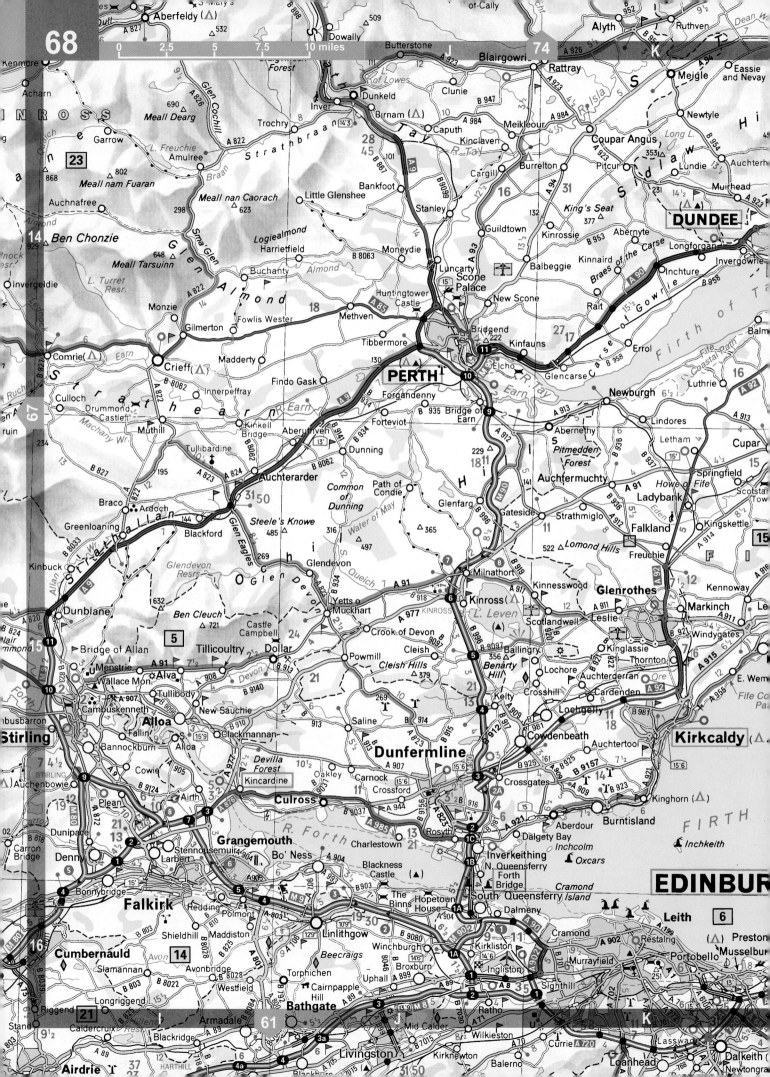

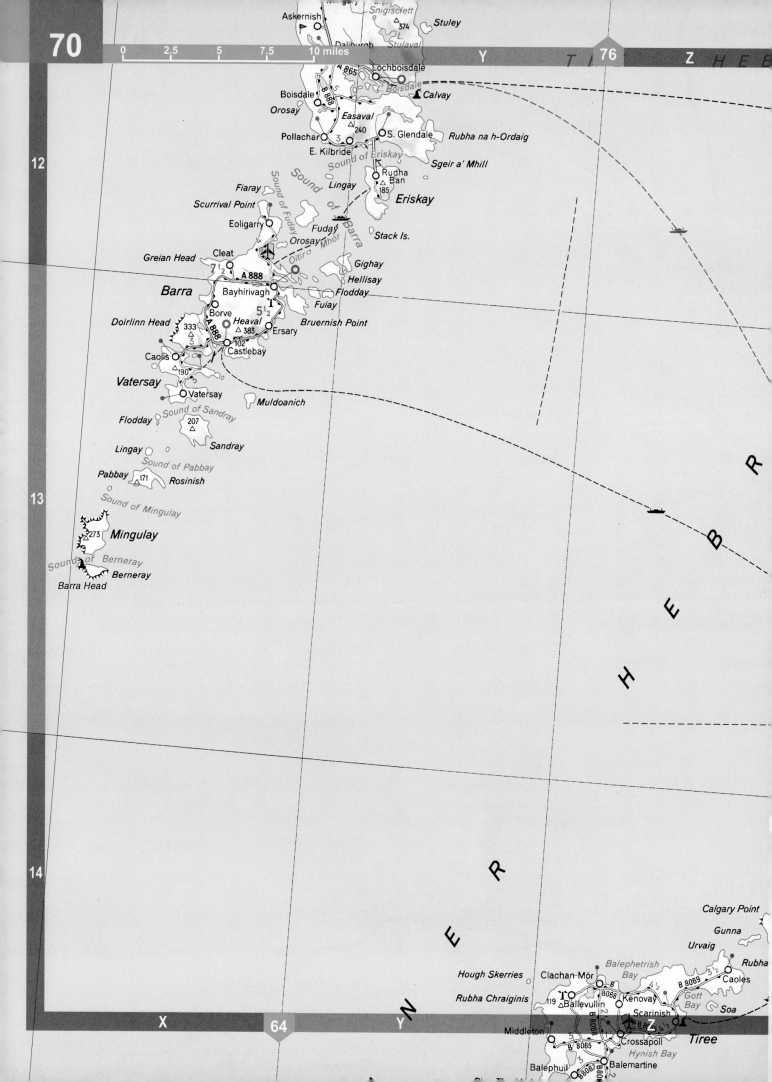

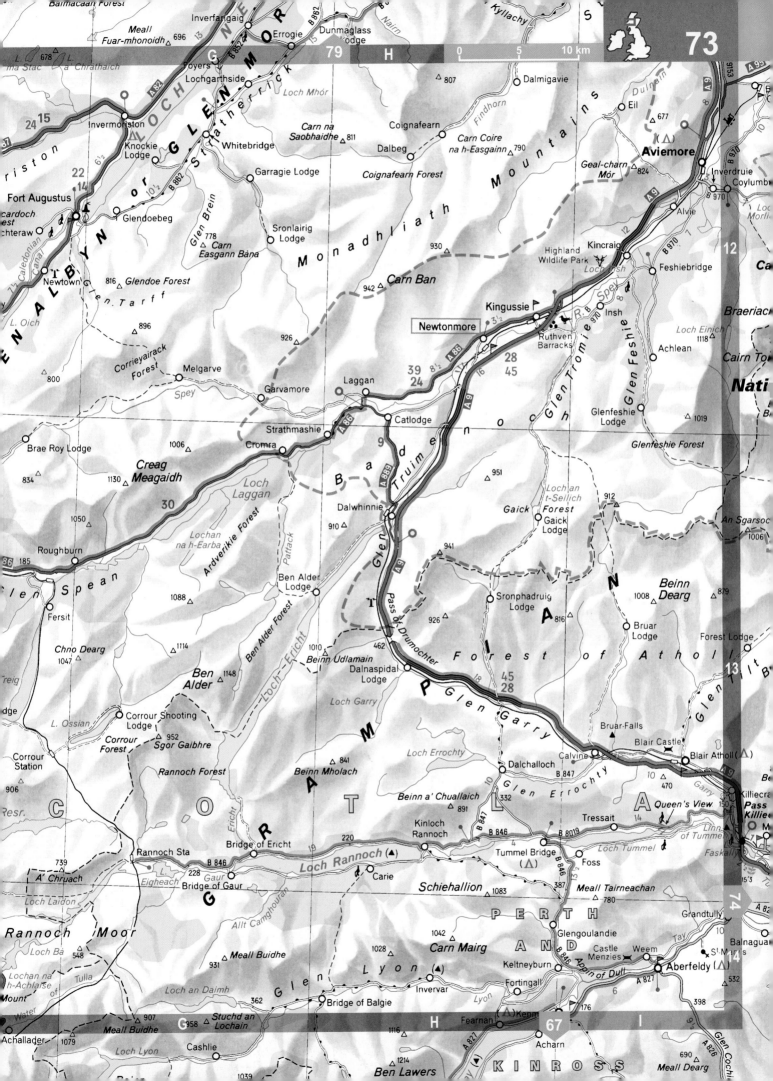

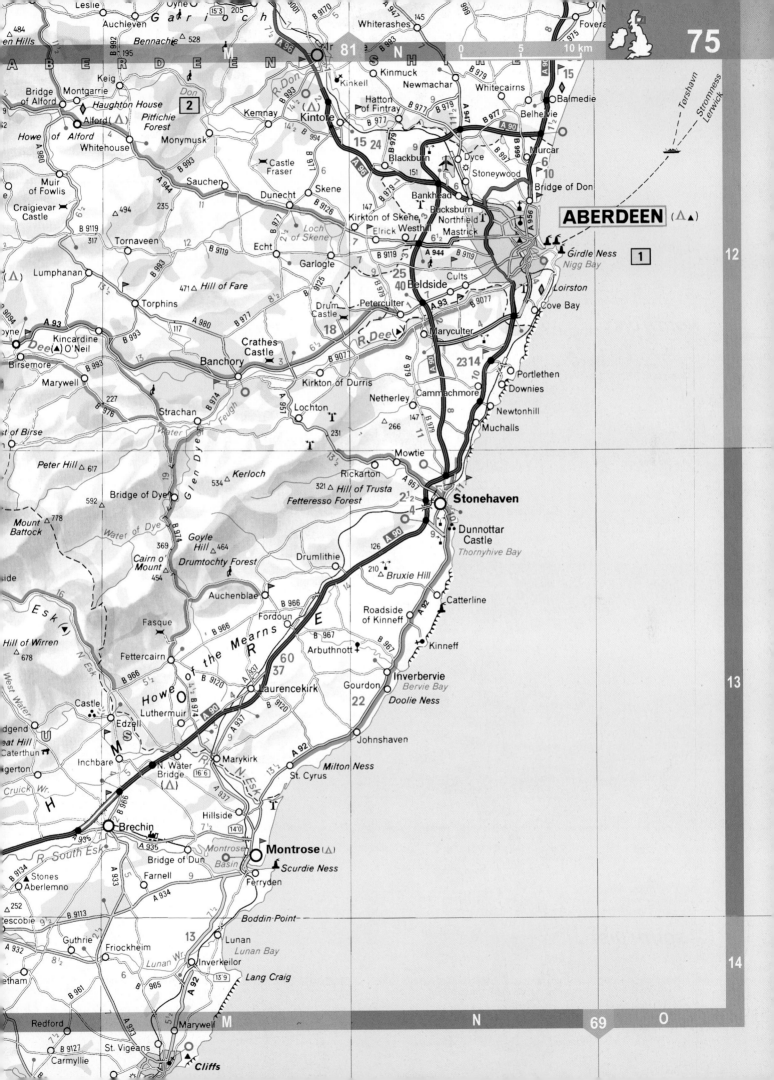

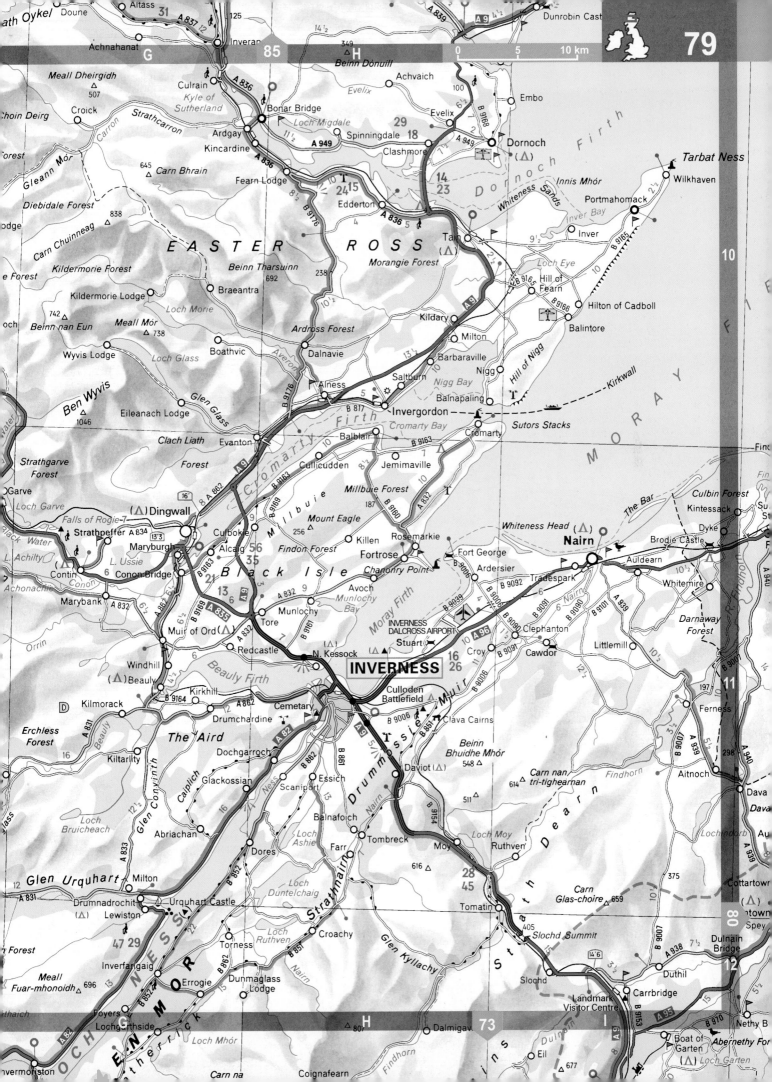

0 2.5 5 7.5 10 miles

Z   A

8

9

10

B R I D E S

E

HARRIS

ISLE OF LEWIS
AND HARRIS

LEWIS

Galson

Borve

Shader

15

Barvas

Arnol

Bragar

50 Shawbost

12

Garenin

Carloway

Dun Carloway Broch

Tolsta Chaolais

Breasclete

Eilean
Kearstay

Callanish

Garynahine

Standing Stones

Achmore

112

Newmarket

Stornoway

L. Urrahag

28

A 857

110

12

Tong

Beinn Mholach

△ 292

L. Laxavat Ard

Loch Breivat

261

A 858

B 8059

B 8011

13

8½

13½

7

A 858

A 859

B 897

9

Leurbost

Crossbost

5

Ranish

Barkin Isles

Eilean Chaluim Chil

Cromore

Eilean T

Marvig

L. Orasay

L. nam
Falcag

L. Trealaval

Loch Airigh
na h-Airde

281
△

Laxay

Keose

Balallan

Kershader

B 8060

L. Erisort

Arivruaich

L. Sgibacleit

Seaforth
Head

36

A 859

492
△

Park
or
Pairc

Glenside

Gravir

Lemreway

Eishken

L. Odhairn

Keb

B 8060

Eilean Iubhard

Gallan Head

West Loch Roag

Tobson

Little Bernera

Pabay Mór

Breaclete

Great
Bernera

Vuia Mór

Cruivig

Aird Uig

Valtos

Miavaig

Floday

205

Timsgarry

Uig

Camas Uig

Mangersta

Islivig

Aird Brenish

Brenish

574
△

L.
Grunavat

Suainaval

L. Tamanavay

Bràigh Mór

Loch Roag

Little Loch Roag

East Loch Roag

Enaclete

B 8011

20

Morsgail Forest

Loch Langavat

Loch Resort

Ulladale

303

△

Mealasta I.

Kearstay

Scarp

308
△

Gasker

Hushinish

Hushinish Point

B 887

Forest of Harris

Amhuinnsuidhe

13

Meavaig

Clisham

△ 799

North Harris

Tirga Mór

△ 679

Stúlaval
△

579

Ardvourlie

17½

217

Seaforth
Island

Beinn Mhór

572
△

Crionaig

△
467

371
△

Taransay Glorigs

Soay Mór

HARRIS

Taransay

Maaruig

Rhenigidale

Lo ch
Trollamarig

Eilean Mór
a'Bhàigh

Sound of Shiant

Eilea

Isay

Ardhasaig

West Loch Tarbert

267
△

Sound of Taransay

506
△

Luskentyre

South Harris
Forest

Scotasay

Tarbert

3

4

Kyles
Scalpay

334
△

Scalpay

104

Shiant Islands

Toe Head

Coppay

Shillay

Borv

Scarista

365
△

398
△

76

Z

Drinnishadder

South Harris

A 859

East Loch
Tarbert

Scalpay

Grosebay

A

GLES)

N A N

E

Loch Seaforth

Loch Shell or Loch Sealg

0   5   10 km

B

C

8

Butt of Lewis

Eoropie
Port of Ness
Habost
B 8015
Skigersta
Cross
Dell
Ness

Loch Langavat

Cellar Head

248
△
Muirneag
Tolsta
Tolsta Head

B 895

Gress

Back

12 ½

Portnaguran
Tiumpan Head

Broad Bay
(▲)

A 866

Melbost   12
Garraboste
Eye Peninsula
Knock
Bayble

Chicken Head

THE MINCH

Edrachillis
Bay

Point of Stoer

Culkein
Eilean
Chrona
Clashnessie
Stoer
Clachtoll
B 869
L. Croca
Achmelvich
9
Baddidarach
Soyea Island
A' Chleit
Kirkaig
Point
Inve

Rubha Còigeach
Eilean Mór

Enard Bay
Rubha Mór
Reiff
Brae of Achnahaird
6
Eilean
Mullagrach
Altandhu
Osgaig
Badnagyle
Isle Ristol
Polbain
Sta
Glas-leac Mór
L. Bad a' Ghaill
Achiltibuie
Tanera
Mór
Badenscallie
Tanera Beg
Summer Is.
84
Horse I.
Culnacraig
Eilean Dubh
Achduart
Priest Island
Bottle I.
C

Càrn nan Sgeir
10
Martin

òraidh

ck Head

Mhuire

B

77

C

Gob a' Ghe

Eilean Furadh Mór

Rubha Réidh

Greenstone Point
Cailleach Head
Annat Bay

Opinan
Rubha Beag
Scoraig
Stattic Point

Mellon Udrigle
Gruinard
Island
Badluarach
Beinn Ghobhla
△ 635

D

Achgarve
Mellon
Charles
Laide
Mungasdale
Allt na h-A
Badrallach

Cove
Gruinard
Bay
932
Badcaul

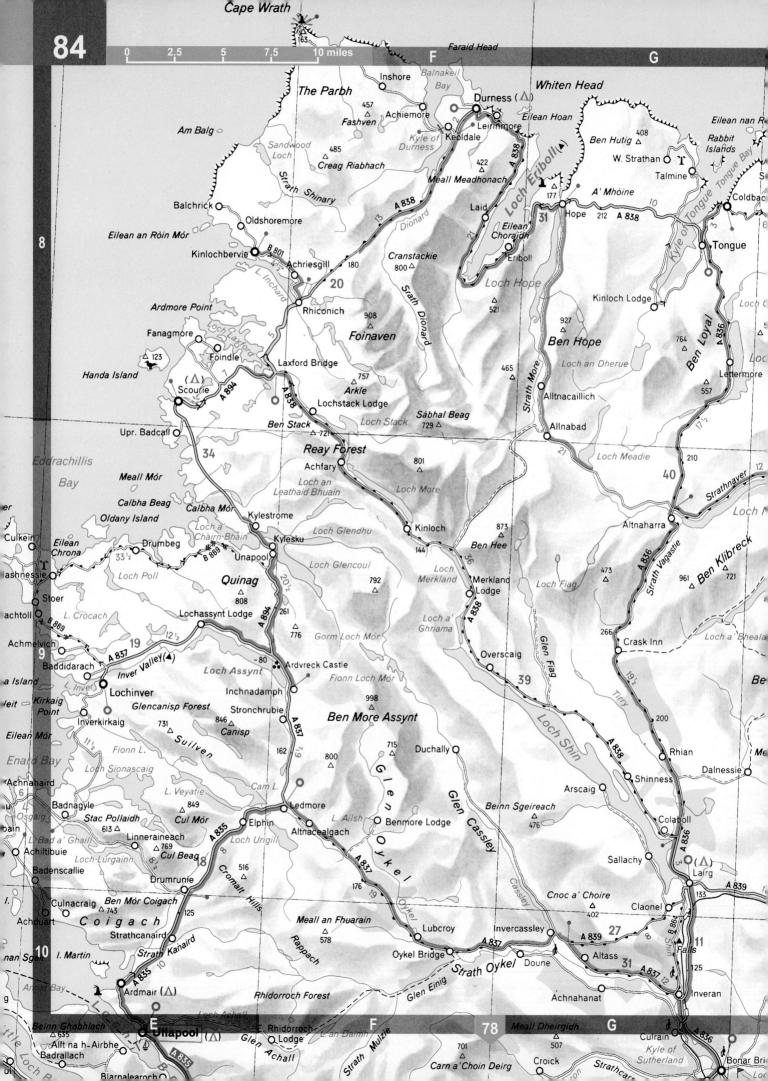

ORKNEY ISLANDS

0 2.5 5 7.5 10 miles

Flotta
Fara
Lyness
Water Sound
Burray
Causeway
St. Margaret's Hope
Grim Ness
B 9044
Herston
B 9042
Langhorpe
Bow
Switha
B 9041
Swona
South Ronaldsay
Burwick
Cleat
Old Head
Brough Ness
South Walls
Cantick Head
Tor Ness
Waterinhouse
Hurliness
B 9041
118

Pentland Firth

Langaton Point
Island of Stroma
Nethertown
Pentland Skerries
Uppertown
51
St. John's Point
Duncansby Head

Dunnet Head
B 855
Scarfskerry
Brough
Gills
John o' Groats
St. John's Loch
Mey
A 836
Canisbay
124
Dunnet
Barrock
Skirza
Brims Ness
Holborn Head
Skirza Head
Crosskirk
Scrabster
Dunnet Bay
Castletown
Freswick
Freswick Bay
Achreamie
A 882
A 836
Thurso
Loch Heilen
Slickly
Auckengill
Westfield
141
Bower
Lyth
Sortat
Keiss
Calder Mains
Roadside
B 874
B 876
Myrelandhorn
17
Shurrery
Halkirk
Lt Scarmclate
B 870
Sinclair's Bay
Noss Head
Olgrinmore
Banniskirk
Loch Watten
Reiss
Girnigoe and Sinclair Castles
Spittal
Watten
A 882
B 874
A 99
Staxigoe
Loch Shurrery
Mybster
B 870
21
Haster
North Head
Westerdale
Wick
South Head
Badlipster
44
71
Tannach
Loch More
13
Grey Cairns of Camster
Thrumster
211
212
Sarclet
348
Loch Ruard
Ulbster
60 37
287
Hill o' Many Stanes
Houstry
Lybster
Latheron
Forse
W. Clyth
Janetstown
706
Braemore
626 Scaraben
Dunbeath
20
Borgue
Langwell Forest
Berriedale
200
A 897
Helmsdale

Inset (Orkney)

J K

Sule Skerry
Bow He
Noup Head
Westray
Stack Skerry
169
Midbea

Rousay
Wasb
(▲) Brough of Birsay
Brough Head
250
B 9064
Kitchener Memorial
Birsay
Georth
Gurness Broch
A 967
Twatt
B 9057
Skara Brae
Dounby
221
Yesnaby
Maes Howe
Finstown
Mainland
Ring of Brodgar
Stenness
268
Wideford Hill Cairn
Stromness
A 965
Orphir
Graemsay
St. Mary
Moaness
479
Cava
Old Man of Hoy
Scapa Flow
Rora Head
Rackwick
Fara
Lyness
Flotta
Hoy
Tor Ness
South Walls
Pentland Firth
Dunnet Head
Scarfskerry
Stroma
Scrabster
Dunnet
Gills
A 836
Thurso
Castletown

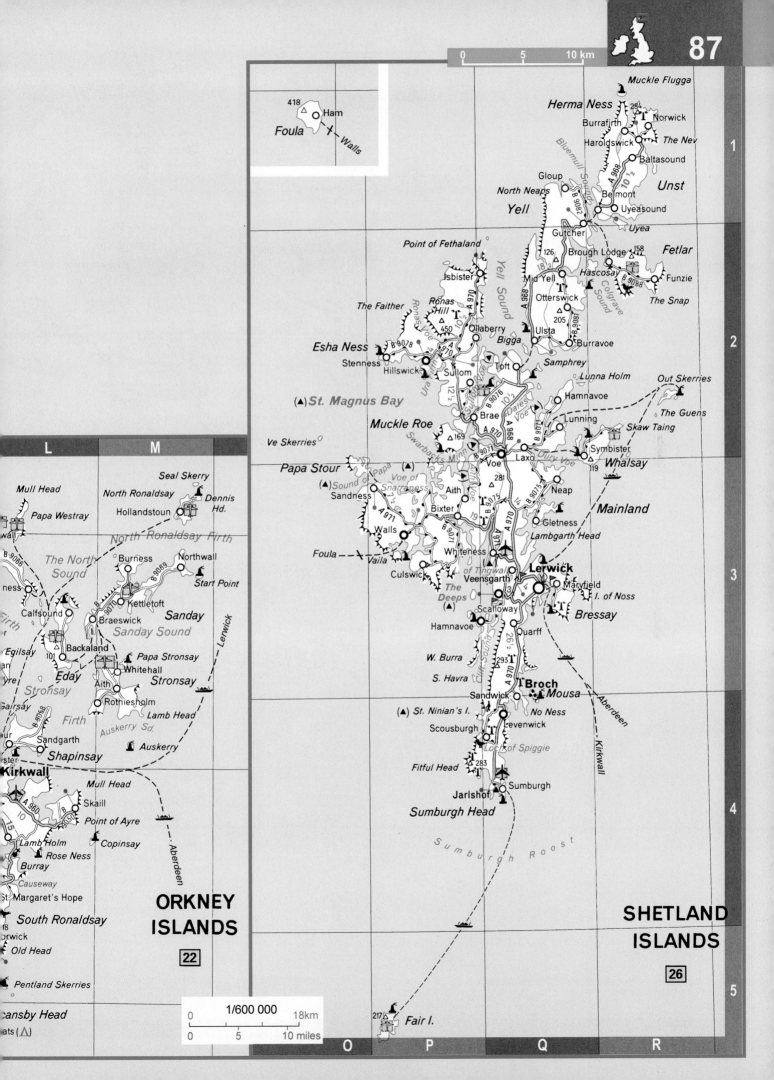

0   5   10 km

Foula
418 △ — Ham
Walls

SHETLAND ISLANDS

Muckle Flugga
Herma Ness 284
Burrafirth ⌖ Norwick
Haroldswick *The Nev*
Baltasound
Unst
A 968 10½

Gloup
North Neaps
Belmont
Yell B 9082 Uyeasound
Uyea

Gutcher
126 Brough Lodge 158 **Fetlar**
Point of Fethaland 18½ △ Hascosay Funzie
Isbister B 9088 *The Snap*
Rônas Hill Mid Yell
450 △ 10½ Otterswick
The Faither A 970 Ulsta 205 B 9087
Esha Ness B 9078 Ollaberry *Lunna Holm* *Out Skerries*
Stenness A 970 Bigga Hamnavoe *The Guens*
Hillswick Sullom *Samphrey* *Skaw Taing*
(▲)St. Magnus Bay 12½ Toft Lunning Symbister
Brae B 9076 10½ *Dales Voe* 119 **Whalsay**
Ve Skerries ° **Muckle Roe** A 970 A 968 B 9071
A 169 △ Voe **Mainland**
Papa Stour A 907 Laxo *Dury Voe*
(▲)Sound of Papa 281 Neap
Sandness *Voe of Snarraness* Aith △ Gletness
Bixter 19 *Lambgarth Head*
Walls A 971 A 971
Foula B 9071 Whiteness A 970 A 971
Vaila *L. of Tingwall* **Lerwick**
Culswick *The Deeps* Veensgarth Maryfield
(▲) Scalloway *I. of Noss*
Hamnavoe 3 **Bressay**
Quarff
W. Burra 26½
S. Havra 293 A 970 **⊤Broch**
Sandwick *Mousa*
St. Ninian's I. (▲) No Ness
Scousburgh Levenwick
Loch of Spiggie
Fitful Head △ 283
217 △ Sumburgh
Jarlshof
Sumburgh Head
Sumburgh Roost

Fair I. 217 △

**SHETLAND
ISLANDS**
26

ORKNEY ISLANDS

L | M
Mull Head
Papa Westray *Seal Skerry*
North Ronaldsay *Dennis Hd.*
Hollandstoun
North Ronaldsay Firth
The North Sound Burness Northwall
B 9069 *Start Point*
Calfsound Kettletoft **Sanday**
Braeswick *Sanday Sound*
Backaland Whitehall
Eday Aith *Papa Stronsay*
Egilsay 101 △ Rothiesholm **Stronsay**
Stronsay *Lamb Head*
Firth *Auskerry Sd.*
Sandgarth ▲ *Auskerry*
Shapinsay
Kirkwall *Mull Head*
A 960 Skaill
B 9050 *Point of Ayre*
10 *Lamb Holm* *Copinsay*
Rose Ness
Burray
Causeway
St. Margaret's Hope
South Ronaldsay
Old Head
Pentland Skerries
ansby Head
ats (△)

**ORKNEY
ISLANDS**
22

1/600 000
0 — 18km
0 5 10 miles

O | P | Q | R

1 2 3 4 5

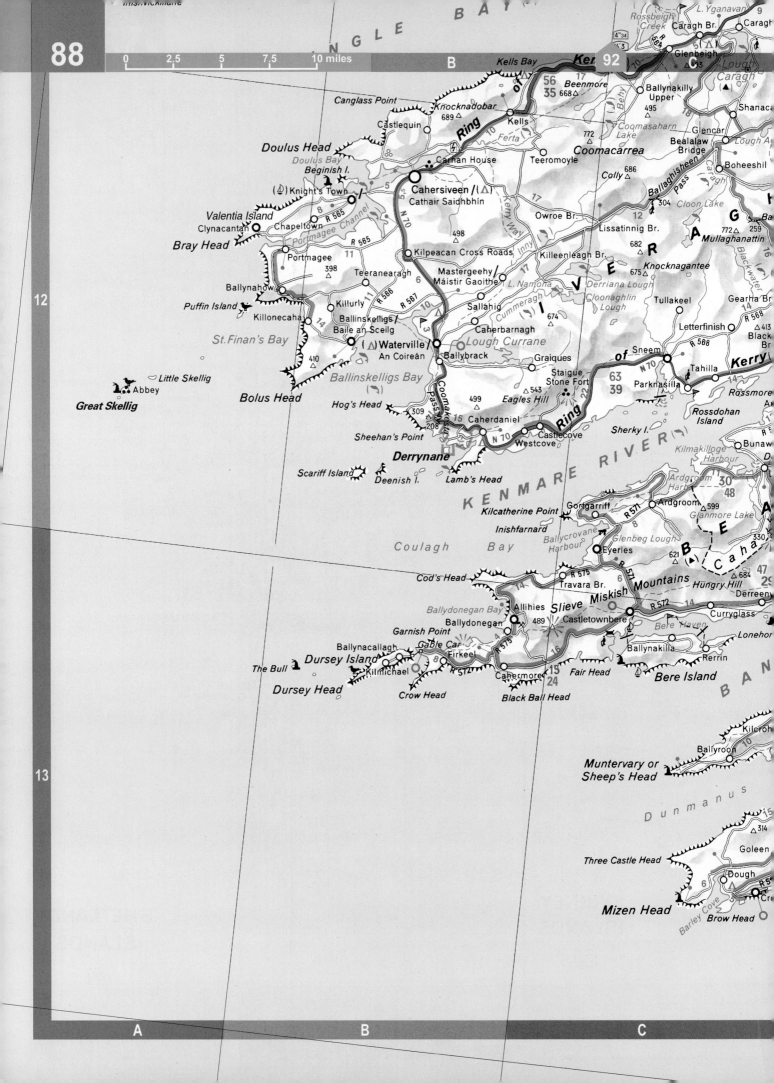

INGLE BAY

0   2.5   5   7.5   10 miles

L. Yganavan

Rossbeigh
Creek
Caragh Br.   Caragh

4"34
R 3   R
564

Glenbeigh

Kells Bay

Kerry

70

Caragh

Lough

Canglass Point

Knocknadobar
689 △

Kells

Ring
of

56
35

Beenmore
668 △

495

Ballynakilly
Upper

18

Shanaca

Castlequin

Doulus Head

Doulus Bay

Beginish I.

Carhan House

Teeromoyle

772

Coomacarrea

Coomasaharn
Lake

Glencar

Bealalaw
Bridge

Lough A

Shanaca

Boheeshil

Knight's Town

N70

Cahersiveen /(△)
Cathair Saidhbhín

Colly

686
△

304

Ballaghisheen
Pass

Cloon Lake

Bray Head

Valentia Island
Clynacantan

Chapeltown

R 565

R 565

Portmagee Channel

498

Owroe Br.

Kerry Way

Lissatinnig Br.

12

Mullaghanattin

772 △   259

Black

Portmagee

11

398
△

Teeranearagh

Kilpeacan Cross Roads

Inny

Mastergeehy
Máistir Gaoithe

17

Killeenleagh Br.

682
△

675 △

Knocknagantee

Derriana Lough

Gearha Br

14

R 568

Ballynahow

Puffin Island

Killurly

R 566

R 567

6

10

Sallahig

L. Namona

Cloonaghlin
Lough

Tullakeel

Letterfinish

△ 413
Black
Br

Killonecaha

St. Finan's Bay

Ballinskelligs /
Baile an Sceilg

(△) Waterville /
An Coireán

△
3

Caherbarnagh

674
△

Lough Currane

Ballybrack

Graiques

Sneem

Tahilla

R 568

KERRY

Little Skellig

Abbey

Great Skellig

Bolus Head

Ballinskelligs Bay

Hog's Head

Staigue
Stone Fort

Eagles Hill

△ 543

499
△

63
39

Ring

Parknasilla

Rossmore

Rossdohan
Island

Sheehan's Point

309

208
△

Coomakesta
Pass

15

Caherdaniel

N 70

Westcove

Castlecove

Sherky I.

of

Bunaw

Derrynane

Scariff Island

Deenish I.

Lamb's Head

KENMARE RIVER

Kilmakilloge
Harbour

Kilcatherine Point

Ardgroom
Harb.

11
30
48

Inishfarnard

Coulagh   Bay

Ballycrovane
Harbour

Gortgarriff

Ardgroom

R 571

599
△

Glanmore Lake

330

BEA

Eyeries

621
△

B

Caha

47

△ 684

Cod's Head

14

Travara Br.

R 575

Slieve Miskish Mountains

Hungry Hill

29

Derreen

Ballydonegan Bay

Ballydonegan

489

R 571

R 572

14

Curryglass

Lonehor

Garnish Point

Cable Car

Firkeel

4

R 575

Castletownbere

16

Bere Haven

Ballynakilla

Rerrin

Ballynacallagh

R 512

8

Cahermore

15
24

Fair Head

Bere Island

Dursey Island

Kilmichael

The Bull

Dursey Head

Crow Head

Black Ball Head

BAN

Kilcroh

Ballyroon

10

Muntervary or
Sheep's Head

Dunmanus

△ 314

Three Castle Head

Goleen

6

Dough

R5

Mizen Head

Barley Cove

Cre

Brow Head

12

13

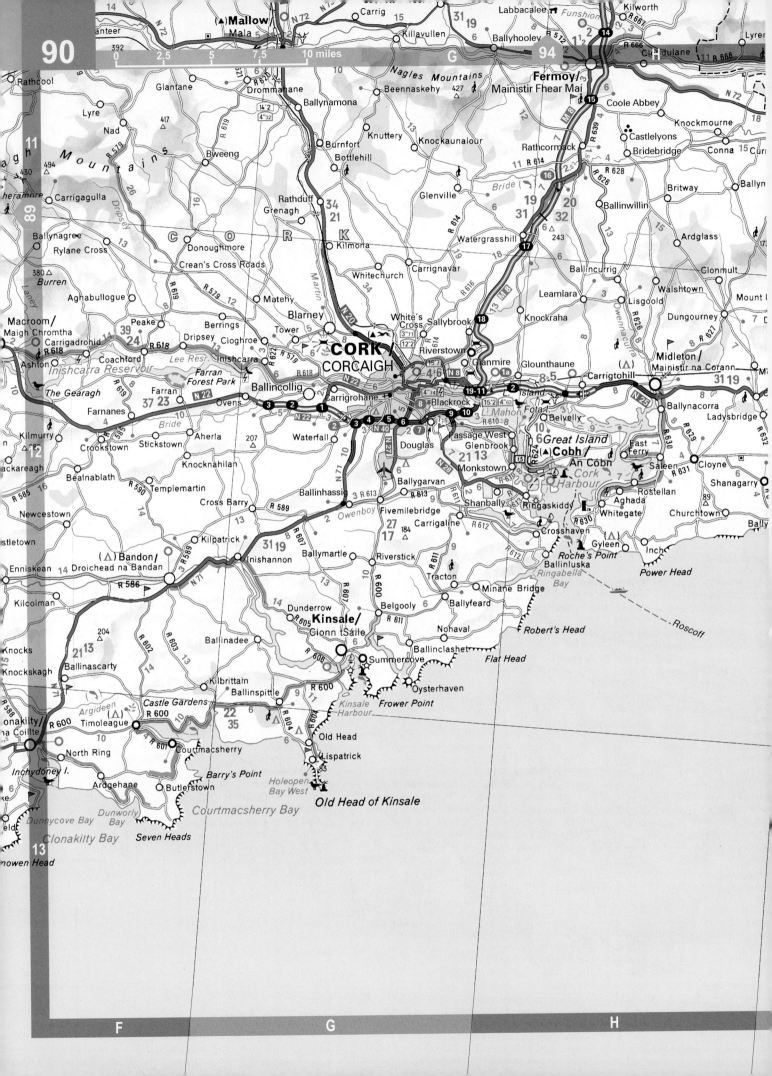

0   2.5   5   7.5   10 miles

B

10

MO

THE

Loop Head (71)

Kerry Head

Dreenagh

218

Glenderry

(△) Bally

Ballyheige B

The Seven Hogs or
Magharee Islands

Illauntannig

Rough Point

Fahamore

Kilshannig

Brandon Point

Brandon Bay

Tralee Bay

Brandon /
Cé Bhréanainn

Ballyquin

Lough Gill

Castlegregory (△)

Strand Killmey

Brandon Head

Dingle Way

Brandon Creek

Brandon
Mountain

△ 951

Cloghane

Owenmore

Stradbally

Aughacasla

Derrymore

Ballydavid Head

Tiduff

Kilcummin

Feohanagh

Kilcummin

Ballyduff

Beenoskee

△ 825

11

Smerwick
Harbour

Feohanagh

Camp

I 68

Smerwick

Ballydavid

Ballinloghig

D I N G L E

(△) L. Slat

Sybil Head

Murreagh

Kilmalkedar

△ 623

456 △ 616

Owenascaul

825

Caherconree

Ballyferriter /
Baile an Fheirtéaraigh

Gallarus Oratory

(△)

Connor Pass

594

△

50
31

Lougher

N 86

Slie

Clogher Head

Ballineanig

Ballynana

R 559

13

17

Aughils

R 561

Inishtooskert

18

R 559

Dingle /
Daingean Uí Chúis

Anascaul

7

Inch

Blasket Islands /(\△)

Na Blascaodaí

Ventry

Milltown

Dingle
Harb.

N 86

Inch

Castlema
Harbou

Great Blasket
Island

Dunquin /
Dún Chaoin

516 △ Mount Eagle

Beehive
Huts

R 559

17

Ventry
Harbour

Lispole /
Lios Póil

18

Doonmanagh

Cromane

Knockaunnag

Tearaght I.

Blasket Sound

Parkmore Pt.

Bull's Head

Castle

Minard Head

Illaunstookagh

Tullig

Inishnabro

Slea Head

Dunmore Head

L. Yganavar

Inishvickillane

(\△)

Rossbeigh
Creek

Caragh Br.

Caragh

D I N G L E   B A Y

4ᴬ34

R

14'3

R 564

5

Glenbeigh

N 70

△ 493

Lough
Caragh

Kells Bay

Kerry (\△)

Ballynakilly
Upper

Canglass Point

56
35

Beenmore

668 △

495

Shanaca

Knocknadobar

689 △

Kells

17

Coomasaharn
Lake

Glencar

Castlequin

Ring

Ferta

10

772 △

Bealalaw
Bridge

Lough Ac

12

Doulus Head

Coomacarrea

Colly

686 △

Boheeshil

Doulus Bay

Carhan House

Teeromoyle

Caragh

Beginish I.

N 70

Ballaghisheen
Pass

304

Cloon Lake

(⚓) Knight's Town

Cahersiveen /(\△)

Cathair Saidhbhín

Ballaghbeama

Valentia Island

R 565

Owroe Br.

12

Lissatinnig Br.

682 △

772△ 259

Clynacartan

Cha

5'5

N 70

Kerry Way

C

Mullaghanattin

A

88

B

498

Inny

△

V   E   R

Bray Head

R 565

11

Kilpeacan Cross Roads

Killeenleagh Br.

675 △

Knocknagantee

Blackwat

Portmagee

398 △

Teeranearagh △

Mastergeehy /
Máistir Gaoithe

17

L. Namona

Derriana Lough

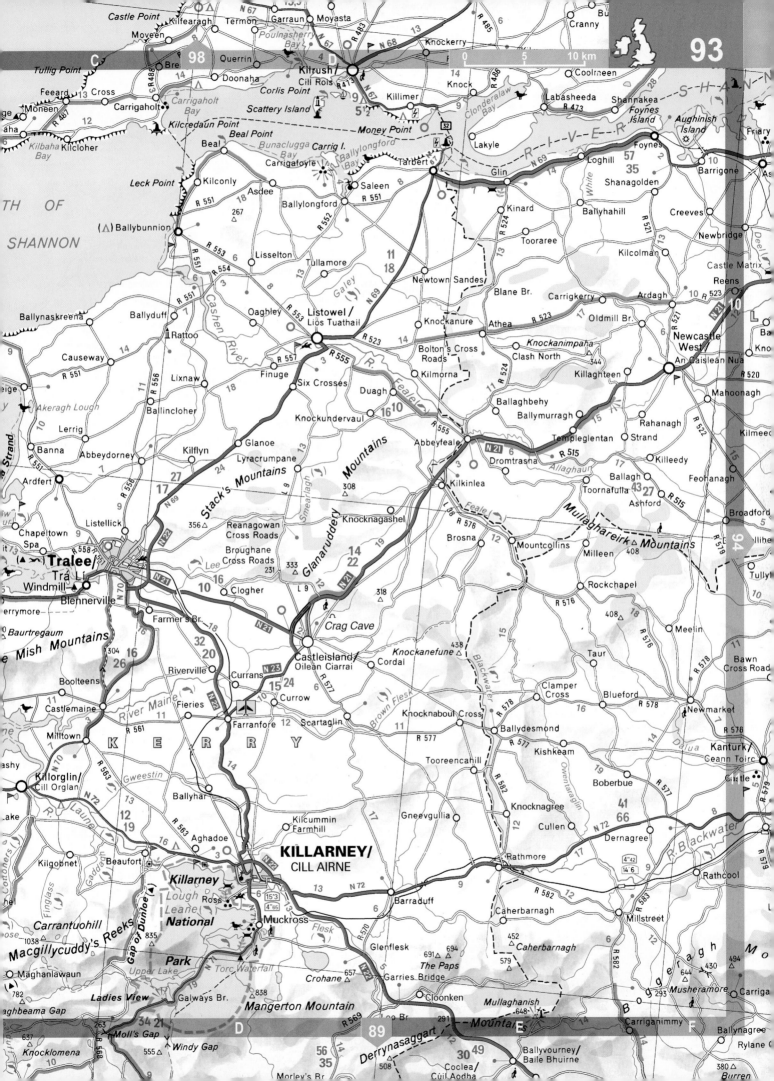

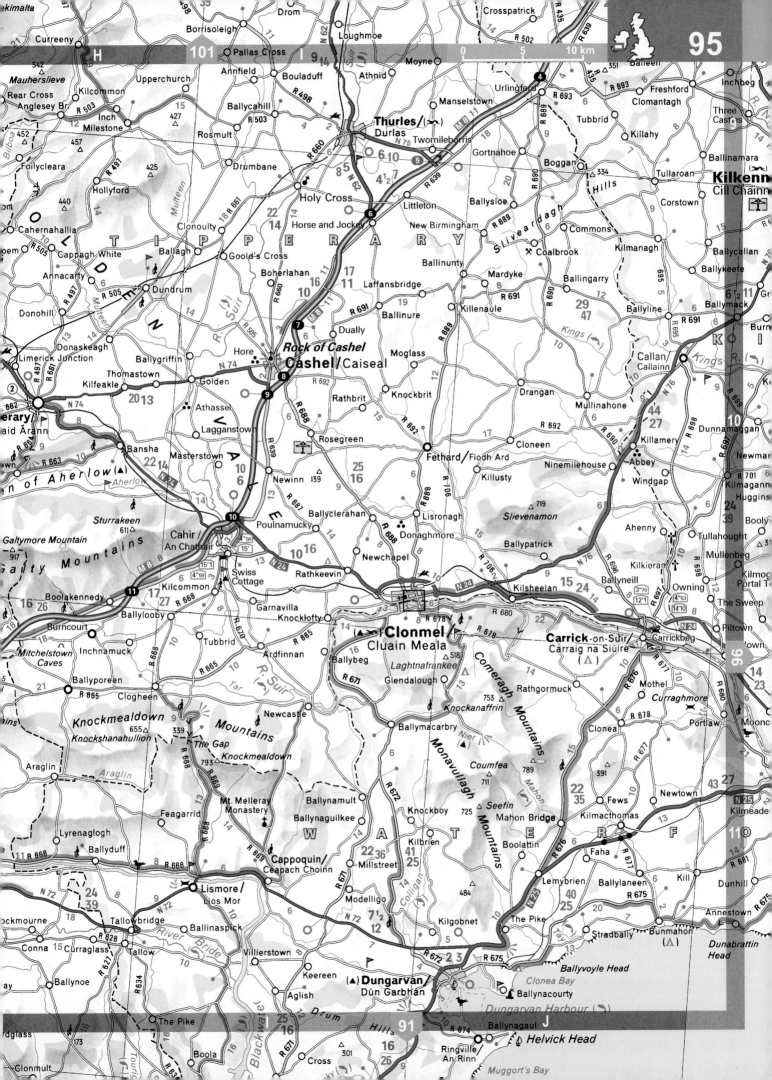

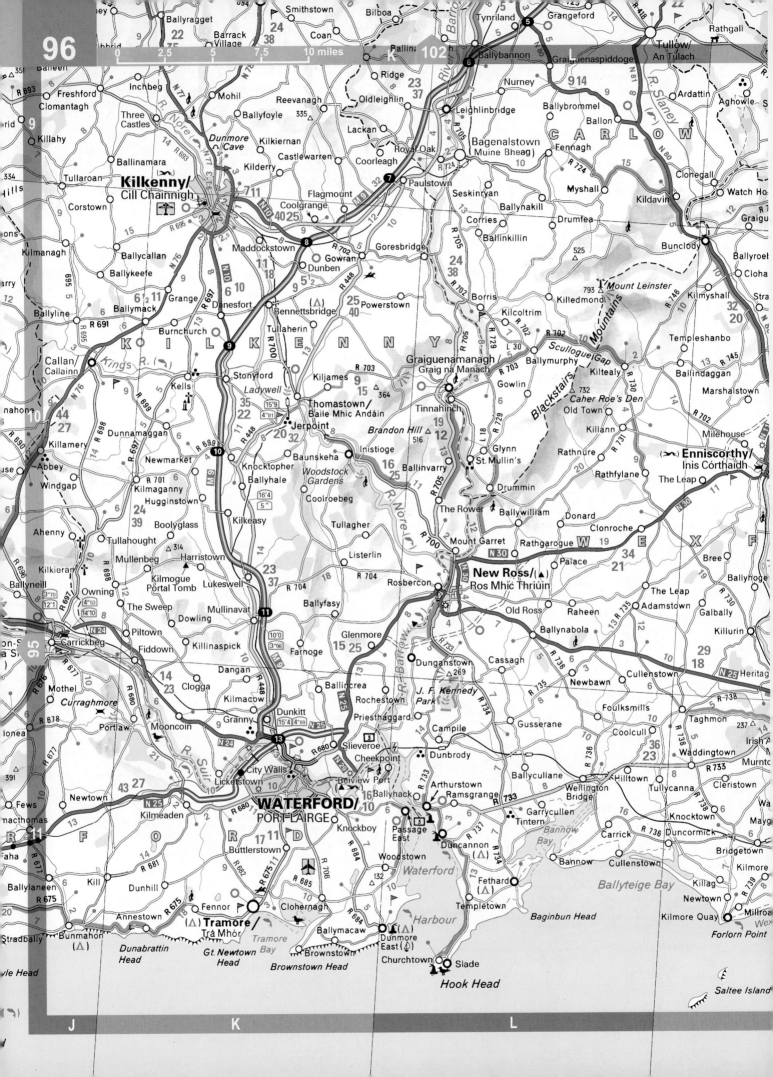

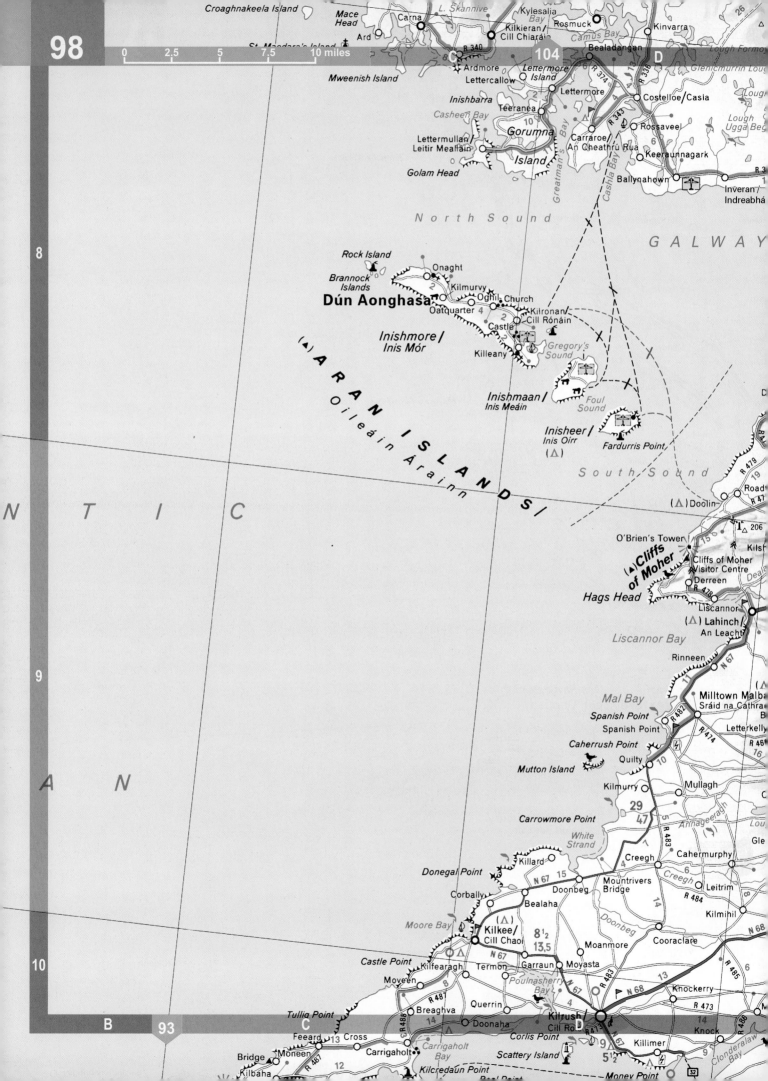

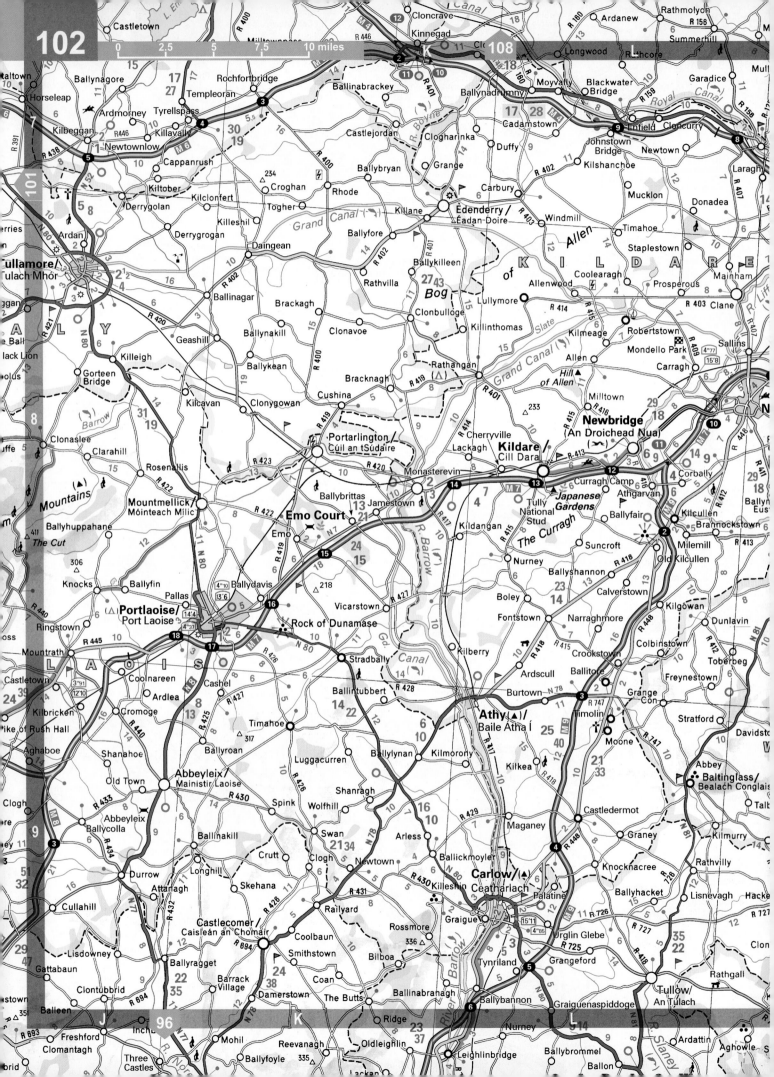

FINGAL

Portrane
Donab
Newbridge
Lambay Island

Ratoath
Donaghmore
Corduff

Kilbride
Fairyhouse
Swords
Sord
Kinsaley
Malahide/Mullach Íde
Portmarnock
Baldoyle
Ireland's Eye

Batterstown
Kils
Ward
St. Margaret's
Santry
Artane
Nose of Howth

Ballynare
Dunboyne
Clonee
Mulhuddart
Clonsilla
Finglas
Clontarf
Howth /
Binn Éadair
Douglas (I. of Man)

Maynooth /
Maigh Nuad
Leixlip
Blanchardstown
Phoenix
Park
Dublin
Bay
Holyhead

Castletown House
Celbridge
Lucan
Liverpool

Milltown
DUBLIN / BAILE ÁTHA CLIATH

Straffan
Newcastle
Clondalkin
Rathmines
Blackrock
Dún Laoghaire

Grand Canal
Rathcoole
Saggart
Tallaght
Dundrum
Stillorgan
Dalkey
Killiney

Kill
Johnstown
Furness
Kilteel
Brittas
Killakee
Sandyford
Stepaside
Ballybrack
Loughlinstown
Killiney Bay

as/An Nás
Kilbride
Three Rock Mt.
Kilternan
Shankill
Little
Bray
Bray/Bré

Kilbride
Glencullen
Enniskerry
Bray Head

Blessington
Glencree
Powerscourt Demesne
Killrúddery

Russborough House
Lackan
Kippure
WICKLOW
Killough
Kilmacanoge

Valleymount
Sally Gap
Waterfall
Great Sugar Loaf
Greystones/
Na Clocha Liatha

Hollywood
Mullaghcleevaun
Lough Tay
The Downs
Carriggower
Delgany

Glenbridge Lodge
MOUNTAINS
Kilpedder
Kilcoole

Granabeg
Waterfall
Glenmacnass
Sraghmore
Newtown
Mt. Kennedy

Donard
Wicklow Gap
Roundwood
Vartry Reservoir
Leamore Strand

Table Mountain
NATIONAL PARK
Newcastle

Ballinclea
Glendalough
Upper Lake
Laragh
Annamoe
The Devil's Glen
Killiskey

Lower Lake
Ballycullen
Ashford
Mount Usher

WICKLOW
Clara
Ballinalea
Rathnew

Lugnaquilla Mountain
Drumgoft
Ballinderry
Glenealy
Wicklow/Cill Mhantáin

Rathdangan
Rathdrum/
Ráth Droma
Greenan
Kilmacurragh
Wicklow Head

Kiltegan
Aghavannagh
Kilbride
Kilpoole

Knockananna
Sheeanamore
Ballinaclash
Avondale Forest Park
Kilmacco
Ballinacor
Ardmore Point

Askanagap
Motte Stone
Redcross

Moyne
Craffield
Aughrim
Avoca
Ardanairy
Mizen Head

Bridgeland
Tinahely
Woodenbridge
Johnstown
Brittas Bay

Croghan Mountain
Ferrybank
Arklow/An tInbhear Mór

Coolboy
Ballyfad
Johnstown
Coolgreany
Clogga

Crosspatrick
Coolattin
Scarnagh

0   2.5   5   7.5   10 miles

B

A T L A N T

4

5

6

Benwee He

Erris Head   Kid Island

Eagle Island   *Broad Haven*

Aghadoon   Rinroe Point

138   266

Corclogh   6   Knocknalina

Annagh Head

10

Inver

Inishglora   Belmullet /
                              Beal an Mhuirthead

R 313

Corraun Point   R 313   11

An Geata Mór   7   R 314   Barna
                                   Barr na

Mullet Peninsula   Drumreagh   *Trawmore*   Bunnahowen /
                                    Bay   Bun na hAbhna
                                                                      240
                                 Elly Bay   **12**
Inishkea North   **19**

                        Doolough Point   Srahmor

Inishkea South   Tristia

                        Aghleam   Dooyork

                        105
                        10   **Blacksod**   10   6   Geesala /
                        Fallmore Point   Gaoth Saile

Black Rock   Duvillaun More   Duvillaun Beg   *Blacksod*   *Tullaghan*
                                                  Bay   *Bay*   Shranama

                                        Doohooma

                                                                               N 59
                                        Ridge Point   *Fahy Lough*   Doona

Saddle Head   Slievemore   Ballycroy

                     671   Valley
                     Doogort   Bellag
Achill Head Croaghaun   4   Inishbiggle Castlehill
                 667   Dooagh   Keel   River   2   63
                 R 319   2   5   2   Bunacurry Annagh   39
Moyteoge Head   Keem Strand   Island   Claggan

                        Cathedral Rocks
(▲) ACHILL ISLAND   Cashel   Sala
Dooega Head   464
Dooega /Dumha Éige   Knockmore   340   Achill

C D

0 5 10 km

A T L A N T I C   O C E A N

4

Rathli

112

Stags of Broad Haven

Downpatrick Head (▲)

Portacloy
232 △
Carrowteige /
athrú Thaidhg
Porturlin
Port Durlainne
305 △ Glinsk
Belderg
Harbour
Creevagh Head
14

Ross Port
14
Muingnabo
340 △
16
Belderrig /
Béal Deirg
Ceide
Fields
R 314
Gortmore
Rathlackan
Lackan
Bay
Lenadoon Point
Easky (△)

Pollatomish
8
Annie Brady
Bridge
Glenamoy /
Gleann na Múaidhe
11
R 314
31
50
Maumakeogh
379 △
Benmore
△ 351
Ballycastle
Way
R 315
9
Killogeary
Carrowmore
5
Kilcummin
Killala Bay
Rathlee
R 297
7

ocknalower
Bellanaboy Bridge
5
Glenamoy
Way
Western
7
R 314
17
27
Rathfran
6
Kilglass
12
N 59
Dromore
53
33

arrowmore Lake
331 △
Sheskin
Slieve Fyagh
Creevagh
Kilcon
Killala
2
Inishcrone
R 297
Drinaghan
14
Owenbeg
5

Gortmore
11
Attavally
Bangor
R 315
Corvoley
7
Rathoma
16
Moyne
R 297
Culleens
7
5

Largan
14
Owenmore
Bangor
367 △
Doobehy
Belville
R 315
Rosserk
R 297
N 59
Corbally
Ox Mountains
19

Bellacorick
N 59
42 26
Eskeragh
Muing
Lough Dahybaun
R 315
10
Knockanillaun
R 314
Castleconor
Crockets Town
Bunnyconnellan
R 294
416 △
Easky Lou
329 △

Slieve Car
720 △
Deel Bridge
18
Crossmolina /
Crois Mhaoilíona
R 315
N 59
Ballina /
Béal an Átha
R 294
16
Slieve Gamph of the
Largan
6
32
20
Masshill

Nephin
Trail
Rake Street
15
Garrycloonagh
R 310
Lough Talt
Bellanagraugh Br.

Nephin Beg
628 △
Keenagh
387 △
Castlehill
9
R 315
Errew
Newtown
Cloghans
Corroy
Mount Falcon
333 △
Attymass
Mullany's Cross
Kilmacteige
Arinagh

Srahduggaun
628 △
Lahardaun
Cuilkillew
804 △
Brackwanshagh
15
Moy
River
16
Corlee
Aclare
Bahada

Glennamong
712 △
581 △
Srahmore
Birreencorragh
698 △
Derreen
Ballynagoraher
Bofeenaun
Nephin
Glen Nephin
CONN
105
Knockmore
25
40
Church Village
Cullin
13
Carrowmore
Curraghbonaun

D E F

5

0   2.5   5   7.5   10 miles

G

2

West Town
East Town

Tory

Bloody Foreland Head

R 257
316   Meenaclady
Brinlack
Bun na Leaca

13   Gweedore
Gort

Gola Island /
Gabhla   Derrybeg   Tievea
△ 431

Owey Island /
Llaighe   Middletown
Bunbeg   R 258   Gweedore /
An Bun Beag   Gaoth Dobha

Cruit
Island   Inishfree
Bay   DONEGAL
AIRPORT   Dore   Clady   3
L.
Torneady Point   Rosses   Kincasslagh   R 259   Crolly /   Nac
Bay   Annagary   Croithlí
Aran or
Aranmore Island /
Árainn Mhór   228   Leabgarrow   The   Loughanure
Rosses   Burtonport /
Ballintra   Ailt an Chorráin   519
The   Anure
Rutland   Rosses   Meencorwick
Island   (▲)   N 56   Owenator
Inishfree Upper   R 259   384
Crohy Head   Dungloe /   (△)   Lough   396
Maghery   An Clochán Liath   Croangar   Com
Meenatotan
Derrydruel   R 252   R 254
Meenacross   Doocharry   Owen
N 56   An Dúchoraidh   Gweebarra
Roaninish   Gweebarra   Trawenagh   17   R 252
Dooey Point   Bay   27   9
Gweebarra   Derrylough   Ballynacarrick   Baile
Bay   Lettermacaward /   Aghla M
Dunmore Head   Leitir Mhic an Bhaird   596
(△) Portnoo   Clooney   14
Dawros Head   Narin   Gweebarra   335
Rossbeg   Maas   Bridge   D   Graff
Kilclooney   R 250
Loughros More   N 56   Glenties   14
Bay   R 261   Stracashel   Tanga
Loughros Point   L.   R 253
Glendorragha   Machugh   Kilrean   60
Slievetooey   Grannogeboy   Owenea   9
443   Maghera   N 56
Laconnell   Ardara   Owentocker   Carnaween
Glen Head   Glencolmcille   374   50   521
Folk Village   502 △ 31   Neck of the Ballagh   H
F   Glen Bay   112   Stravally   Lough   G
Rossan Point   Nalughraman   Glengesh
Malin More   Glencolumbkille   Crove   Pass   Meenybtaddan
Malin Beg   Gleann Cholm Cille   Meenaneary /   Meentullynagarn   Tullynaha
Málainn Bhig   Mín na Aoire   R 263
Malin   Meenavean
Bay   6   9   3   R 262

0   2.5   5   7.5   10 miles

L   M

1

Inishtrahull

Inishtrahull Sound

117

△ 284

lyhillin

Ballygorman

Irbalreagh   14   *Glengad Head*

Lag   Portaleen

Malin   R 243   *Dunmore Head*

R 242   11   Culdaff   *Culdaff Bay*

R 238   R 238   Clonca   6   Ballymagaraghy

donagh/   R 244   10   *Kinnagoe Bay*

Domhnach   Carrowmore   Gleneely

R 238   *Crocknasmug*   *Inishowen Head*

327 △   Leckemy

12   Glentogher   326 △   Stroove   *Dunagree Pt.*

S H O W E N   32   Greencastle   8

(△)   51   R 241   *Magilligan Pt.*

2   341 △   Castle Cary   *Magilligan Pt.*   *Magilligan Strand*

Moville   *Downhill*

398 △   Redcastle   Bun an Phobail   B 202   *Mussenden Temple*

R 240   10   White Castle   Magilligan   △ (△)   Castlerock

Quigley's Point   Bellarena   Articlave

R 238   4   *Binevenagh*   5½

Muff   Crindle   385 △   Stradreagh   Macosquin

Culmore   B 69   4½   Bolea   13   21   *Springwell Forest*

Coolkeeragh   A 2   5   Limavady   Keady Mountain   B 186   Ballybogy

Campsey   Carrickhugh   337 △   B 66   9

LONDONDERRY/   A 2   Ballykelly   B 69   *Roe Valley*   Ringsend

DERRY   17   Glenhead   3   B 68   *Cam Forest*   Boleran

27   Eglinton   Greysteel   Drumsurn   399 △

Drumahoe   *Loughermore*   396 △   9½   Aghadowey

A6   Ervey Cross Roads   7   9   B 192   B 190   Garvagh

Ness Wood   Bovevagh   B 64   6

Killaloo   19   31   Burnfoot   B 64   Moneydig

Claudy   Ballymoney   B 74   Dungiven   Mac Laughlins Corner

Millbrook   Priory   Boviel   7½   21   34   Kilrea

3   Feeny   Banagher   2½   13   21   Swatragh

Ballyneaner   Park   B 44   *Banagher Forest*

D STRABANE   Carnanreagh   Dreon   481 △   *Mullaghmore*   555 △

Craig   4½   Mullaghash   10   B 40   Lisnamuck

678 △   *Sperrin Mountains*   Moneyneany

△ 635   *Sawel Mountain*

Mullaghcloga   K   *Glenelly Valley*   114

Cranagh 10   Mount Hamilton   562 △   Draperstown

Glenelly   or Sperrin   *Carnanelly*

ANTRIM COAST

Benbane Head   Carr

Giant's Causeway   Currysheskin   Ro

The Skerries   Causeway Head   B 146   Castle   *White Park Bay*   Ballin

Ramore Head   Port Ballintrae   27   5   Portbradden

(△) Portrush   A 2   Dunluce Castle   Bushmills   Lagavara   Straid

Portstewart   B 62   Lisnagunogue   B 17   11½

B 185   Cloyfin   B 66   Ballyloughbeg   Moyarget

13 6   A 2   B 17   Ballyrashane   Liscolman   Moss-Side   B 147   Ballinlea

14 6   Coleraine   B 67   Derrykeighan   B 67   Toberdoney   The Dark Hedges

B 201   Castleroe   Ballybogy   Dervock   CAUSEWAY COA

Damhead   B 147   Kirkhills   Stranocum   The Drones   AND GLENS

A 54   Crossgare   (△)   Ballymoney   Dunaghy   Kilraghts

Ballylintagh   Balnamore   Milltown   43   27

Mullan   Agivey   B 66   Bendooragh   B 16   Garryduff   Killagan Corner   A 44

A 29   Ardreagh   B 62   Clou

Vow   Finvoy   Dunloy   A 26

Moneydig   Kilrea   3½   Rasharkin   B 64   Glenvale   Glarryford   Mac

Lislea   B 96   Aughnacleagh   B 93   Graigs

Upperlands   Clady   Cullybackey   12

Culnady   Portglenone   Galgorm   16

Maghera   Ahoghill   A 42   Gracehill

Gulladuff   A 54   B 52   B 18

A 29   Tobermore   M   Knockcloghrim   Newferry

Curran   Bellaghy   Chesney's   Whitesides

Castledawson   *Lough Beg*   Corner   Corner   Caddy

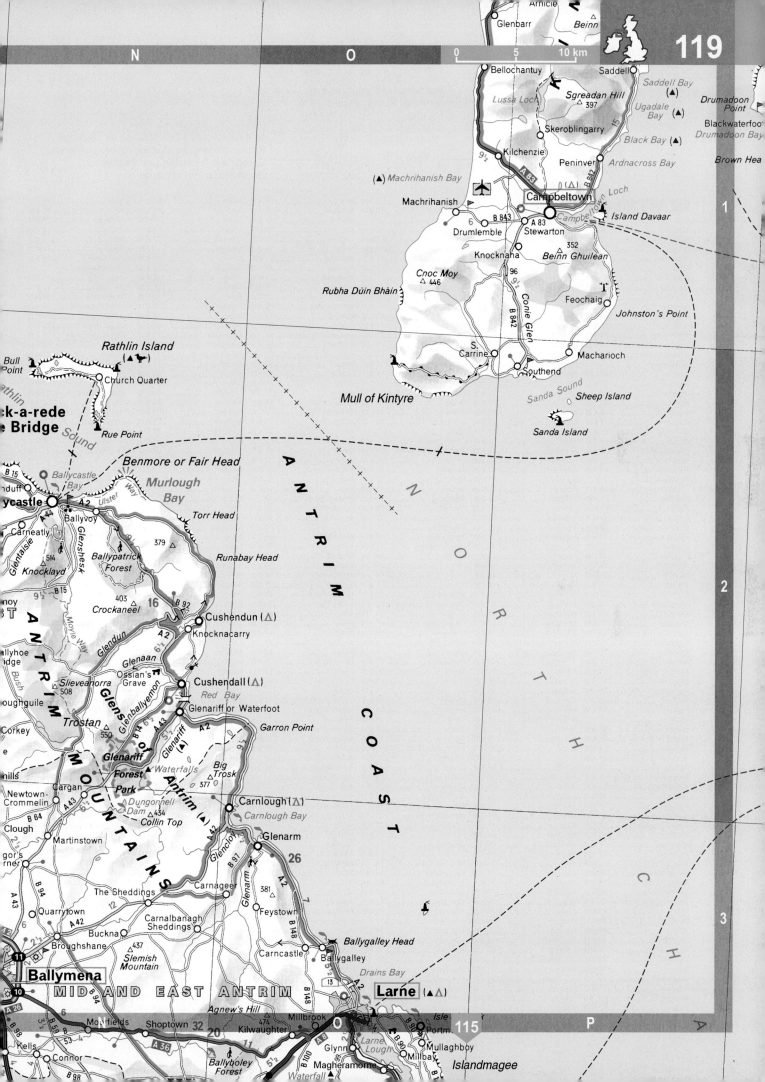

0   5   10 km

Arnicle

Glenbarr   Beinn

Bellochantuy   Saddell

Saddell Bay (▲)

Lussa Loch   Sgreadan Hill
△ 397   Ugadale
Bay (▲)   Drumadoon
Point

Skeroblingarry   Black Bay (▲)   Blackwaterfoo
Drumadoon Bay

Kilchenzie   9½   Peninver   Ardnacross Bay   Brown Hea

(▲) Machrihanish Bay

Machrihanish   Campbeltown   Island Davaar

6   B 843   A 83   Campbeltown Loch
Drumlemble   Stewarton

Knocknaha   352   Beinn Ghuilean
96
Cnoc Moy
△ 446   Feochaig
Rubha Dùin Bhàin   Johnston's Point

S. Carrine   Macharioch
Southend   Sanda Sound   Sheep Island
Mull of Kintyre   Sanda Island

Bull   Rathlin Island
Point   (▲)   Church Quarter

k-a-rede   Rue Point
Bridge   Sound

Benmore or Fair Head   A   N
B 15   Ballycastle
duff   Bay   Murlough   T
ycastle   A 2   Bay
A 44   Ballyvoy   Torr Head   R
Carneatly   Glenshesk   379 △   I
514   Ballypatrick   Runabay Head   M
Knocklayd   Forest
9½   B 15
403 △   16   B 92   Cushendun (△)
noy   Crockaneel   Knocknacarry
403
Glenaan   C
Slieveanorra   Ossian's   Cushendall (△)   O
508   Grave
oughguile   Glenariff or Waterfoot   A
Trostan   Glenballyemon   Red Bay   S
Corkey   550   Garron Point   T
ills   Glenariff (△)
Glenariff   Waterfalls   Big
Forest   Trosk
Newtown-   Park   377
Crommelin   Cargan   A 43   Dungonnell   Carnlough (△)
B 64   Dam   434   Carnlough Bay
Clough   Collin Top
Martinstown   Glenarm
Carnageer   26
Quarrytown   12   381   Glencloy   B 97
A 42   Feystown
Buckna   Carnalbanagh   B 148
Sheddings   Carncastle   Ballygalley Head
The Sheddings   437   Ballygalley
Broughshane   Slemish   13   Drains Bay
11   Mountain   Larne (▲ △)

Ballymena   MID AND EAST ANTRIM

10   Agnew's Hill
A 26   Monfields   Shoptown 32   474   Millbrook   O   115
6   Kilwaughter   Portm   P
Kells   Connor   Glynn   Mullaghboy
Ballyboley   Larne   Millbay   A
Forest   Lough
Magheramorne   Islandmagee
Waterfall

A B C D E F G H I J K L M N O P Q R S T U V W X Y Z

Page number / Numéro de page / Seitenzahl
Paginanummer / Numero di pagina / Número de Página

Place / Localité / Ort
Plaatsen / Località / Localidad

Achmelvich ....84 E 9

Grid coordinates / Coordonnées de carroyage
Koordinatenangabe / Verwijstekens ruitsysteem
Coordinate riferite alla quadrettatura
Coordenadas en los mapas

A

A Chill 71 A 12
A La Ronde 4 J 32
Abbas Combe 9 M 30
Abberley 27 M 27
Abbey 23 X 30
Abbey Dore 26 L 28
Abbey Town 54 K 19
Abbeydale 43 P 23
Abbeystead 48 L 22
Abbots Bromley 35 O 25
Abbots Langley 21 S 28
Abbots Leigh 18 M 29
Abbots Ripton 29 T 26
Abbotsbury 5 M 32
Abbotsford House 62 L 17
Abbotskerswell 4 J 32
Aber Banc 15 G 27
Aberaeron 24 H 27
Aberaman 17 J 28
Aberangell 33 I 25
Abercarn 18 K 29
Abercastle 14 E 28
Aberchirder 81 M 11
Abercynon 17 J 29
Aberdâr / Aberdare 17 J 28
Aberdare / Aberdâr 17 J 28
Aberdaron 32 F 25
Aberdaugleddau / Milford Haven 14 E 28
Aberdeen 75 N 12
Aberdour 68 K 15
Aberdour Bay 81 N 10
Aberdovey / Aberdyfi 33 H 26
Aberdyfi / Aberdovey 33 H 26
Aberedw 25 J 27
Abereiddy 14 E 28
Aberfeldy 73 I 14
Aberffraw 32 G 24
Aberford 43 P 22
Aberfoyle 67 G 15
Abergavenny / Y-Fenni 18 K 28
Abergele 41 J 23
Abergolech 15 H 28
Abergwaun / Fishguard 24 F 28
Abergwesyn 25 I 27
Abergwili 15 H 28
Abergwynfi 17 J 29
Abergwyngregyn 41 H 23
Abergynolwyn 33 I 26
Aberhonddu / Brecon 25 J 28
Aberkenfig 17 J 29
Aberlady 69 L 15
Aberlemno 75 L 13
Aberlour 80 K 11
Abermaw / Barmouth 33 H 25
Abermule 34 K 26
Abernethy 68 K 15
Abernyte 68 K 14
Aberpennar / Mountain Ash 17 J 28
Aberporth 15 G 27
Abersoch 32 G 25
Abersychan 18 K 28
Abertawe / Swansea 17 I 29
Aberteifi / Cardigan 15 G 27
Abertillery 18 K 28
Aberuthven 67 J 15
Aberystwyth 25 H 26
Abingdon 20 Q 28
Abinger Common 21 S 30
Abinger Hammer 21 S 30
Abington *Cambs.* 30 U 27
Abington *South Lanarkshire* 61 I 17
Aboyne 75 L 12
Abriachan 79 G 11
Abridge 21 U 29
Accrington 42 M 22
Achahoish 65 D 16
Achallader 66 F 14
Achanalt 78 F 11
Achaphubuil 72 E 13
Acharacle 71 C 13
Achargary 85 H 8
Acharn 67 H 14
Achduart 83 E 10
Achgarve 78 D 10
Achiemore 84 F 8
Achiltibuie 83 D 9
Achintee 78 D 11
Achintraid 78 D 11
Achlean 73 I 12
Achleck 64 B 14
Achmelvich 84 E 9
Achmore 78 D 11
Achnahanat 84 G 10
Achnamara 65 D 15
Achnanellan 72 E 13
Achnasheen 78 E 11
Achnashellach Forest 78 E 11
Achosnich 71 B 13
Achranich 71 C 14
Achray (Loch) 67 G 15
Achreamie 85 I 8
Achriesgill 84 F 8
Achtalean 77 B 11
Achvaich 79 H 10
Acklington 63 P 18
Ackworth 44 P 23
Acle 39 Y 26
Acomb 55 N 19
Acrise Place 13 X 30
Acton Burnell 34 L 26
Acton Scott 26 L 26
Acton Turville 19 N 29
Adbaston 35 M 25
Adderbury 28 Q 27
Adderley 34 M 25
Adderstone 63 O 17
Addingham 49 O 22
Addlestone 21 S 29
Adfa 33 J 26
Adlington 42 M 23
Adlington Hall 43 N 24
Advie 80 J 11
Adwick-le-Street 44 Q 23
Ae (Forest of) 53 J 18
Ae Village 53 J 18
Afan Argoed 17 J 29
Affric (Glen) 78 F 12
Affric Lodge 78 E 12
Afon Dyfrdwy / Dee (River) 34 K 24
Afon Dyfrdwy (River) / Dee *Wales* 41 K 23
Afon-wen 41 K 23
Agneash 46 G 21
Aikton 54 K 19
Ailort (Loch) 72 C 13
Ailsa Craig 59 E 18
Ainderby Quernhow 50 P 21
Ainort (Loch) 77 B 12
Ainsdale 42 K 23
Air Uig 82 Y 9
Aird 65 D 15
Aird (The) 79 G 11
Aird of Sleat 71 C 12
Airdrie 61 I 16
Airigh na h-Airde (Loch) 82 Z 9
Airor 72 C 12
Airth 67 I 15
Airton 49 N 21
Aith *Orkney Is.* 87 M 6
Aith *Shetland Is.* 87 P 3
Aitnoch 80 I 11
Akeld 63 N 17
Albourne 11 T 31
Albrighton 35 N 26
Albyn or Mor (Glen) 73 F 12
Alcaig 79 G 11
Alcester 27 O 27
Alconbury 29 T 26
Aldborough 39 X 25
Aldbourne 19 P 29
Aldbrough 45 T 22
Aldbrough St. John 49 O 20
Aldbury 21 S 28
Alde (River) 31 Y 27
Aldeburgh 31 Y 27
Aldenham 21 S 28
Alderbury 9 O 30
Alderholt 9 O 31
Alderley Edge 43 N 24
Alderney *Channel I.* 5
Aldershot 20 R 30
Alderton 27 N 28
Aldford 34 L 24
Aldingbourne 11 R 31
Aldridge 35 O 26
Aldringham 31 Y 27
Aldsworth 19 O 28
Aldunie 80 K 12
Aldwick 11 R 31
Alexandria 66 G 16
Alfold Crossways 11 S 30
Alford *Aberdeenshire* 75 L 12
Alford *Lincs.* 45 U 24
Alfreton 36 P 24
Alfrick 27 M 27
Alfriston 12 U 31
Aline (Loch) 65 C 14
Alkborough 44 S 22
Alkham 13 X 30
All Stretton 34 L 26
Allanaquoich 74 J 12
Allanton *North Lanarkshire* 61 I 16
Allanton *Scottish Borders* 63 N 16
Allendale Town 55 N 19
Allenheads 55 N 19
Allensmore 26 L 27
Allerford 17 J 30
Allerston 51 S 21
Allestree 36 P 25
Allhallows 22 V 29
Alligin Shuas 78 D 11
Allington *Kennet* 19 O 29
Allington *Salisbury* 9 O 30
Allnabad 84 G 8
Alloa 67 I 15
Allonby 54 J 19
Alloway 60 G 17
Allt na h-Airbhe 78 E 10
Alltan Fhèarna (Loch an) 85 H 9
Alltnacaillich 84 G 8
Almond (Glen) 67 I 14
Almondbank 68 J 14
Almondsbury 18 M 29
Alness 79 H 10
Alnmouth 63 P 17
Alnwick 63 O 17
Alpheton 30 W 27
Alphington 4 J 31
Alpraham 34 M 24
Alresford 30 X 28
Alrewas 35 O 25
Alsager 35 N 24
Alsh (Loch) 78 D 12
Alston 55 M 19
Alstonefield 35 O 24
Alswear 7 I 31
Altadnduin 85 H 9
Altandhu 83 D 9
Altarnun 3 G 32
Altass 84 G 10
Alternative Technology Centre 33 I 26
Altham 42 M 22
Althorne 22 W 29
Althorpe 44 R 23
Altnabreac Station 85 I 8
Altnacealgach 84 F 9
Altnaharra 84 G 9
Alton *Hants.* 10 R 30
Alton *Staffs.* 35 O 25
Alton Pancras 9 M 31
Alton Priors 19 O 29
Alton Towers 35 O 25
Altrincham 42 M 23
Alum Bay 10 P 31
Alva 67 I 15
Alvaston 36 P 25
Alvechurch 27 O 26
Alvediston 9 N 30
Alves 80 J 11
Alvescot 19 P 28
Alvie 73 I 12
Alvingham 45 U 23
Alwinton 63 N 17
Alyth 74 K 14
Amberley 11 S 31
Amble 63 P 18
Amblecote 27 N 26
Ambleside 48 L 20
Ambrosden 28 Q 28
Amersham 21 S 29
Amesbury 9 O 30
Amhuinnsuidhe 82 Y 10
Amisfield 53 J 18
Amlwch 40 G 22
Ammanford / Rhydaman 15 I 28
Amotherby 50 R 21
Ampleforth 50 Q 21
Amport 20 P 30
Ampthill 29 S 27
Amroth 15 G 28
Amulree 67 I 14
An Riabhachan 78 E 11
An Socach 74 J 13
An Teallach 78 E 10
Anchor 26 K 26
Ancroft 63 O 16
Ancrum 62 M 17
Andover 20 P 30
Andoversford 27 O 28
Andreas 46 G 20
Angle 14 E 28
Anglesey (Isle of) 40
Anglesey Abbey 30 U 27
Angmering 11 S 31
Annan 54 K 19
Annan (River) 61 J 18
Annat 78 D 11
Annat Bay 83 E 10
Annbank 60 G 17
Annbank Station 60 G 17
Anne Hathaway's Cottage 27 O 27
Annesley-Woodhouse 36 Q 24
Annfield Plain 56 O 19
Ansley 28 P 26
Anstey 36 Q 25
Anston 44 Q 23
Anstruther 69 L 15
Anthorn 54 K 19
Antony House 3 H 32
Appin 72 E 14
Appleby *Eden* 55 M 20
Appleby *North Lincolnshire* 44 S 23
Appleby Magna 36 P 25
Applecross 77 C 11
Appledore *Devon* 6 H 30
Appledore *Kent* 12 W 30
Appleford 20 Q 29
Appleton 20 P 28
Appleton Roebuck 44 Q 22
Appleton Wiske 50 P 20
Appletreewick 49 O 21
Aran Fawddwy 33 I 25
Arberth / Narberth 15 F 28
Arbigland 53 J 19
Arbirlot 69 M 14
Arbor Low 35 O 24
Arborfield 20 R 29
Arbroath 69 M 14
Arbury Hall 28 P 26
Arbuthnott 75 N 13
Archiestown 80 K 11
Ard (Loch) 67 G 15
Ardanaiseig 66 E 14
Ardarroch 78 D 11
Ardcharnich 78 E 10
Ardchiavaig 64 B 15
Ardchuilk 78 F 11
Ardchyle 67 G 14
Ardechive 72 E 13
Arden 66 G 15
Ardentallen 65 D 14
Ardeonaig 67 H 14
Ardersier 79 H 11
Ardery 72 C 13
Ardfern 65 D 15
Ardgartan 66 F 15
Ardgay 79 G 10
Ardgour 72 D 13
Ardhasaig 82 Z 10
Ardingly 11 T 30
Ardington 20 P 29
Ardivachar 76 X 11
Ardleigh 30 W 28
Ardley 28 Q 28
Ardlui 66 F 15
Ardlussa 65 C 15
Ardmair 84 E 10
Ardminish 58 C 16
Ardmore Point *Isle of Skye* 77 A 11
Ardnacross 71 C 14
Ardnamurchan 71 B 13
Ardnastang 72 D 13
Ardnave 64 A 16
Ardnave Point 64 B 16
Ardpatrick 59 D 16
Ardrishaig 65 D 15
Ardrossan 59 F 17
Ardshealach 71 C 13
Ardslignish 71 C 13
Ardtalla 58 B 16
Ardtalnaig 67 H 14
Ardtoe 71 C 13
Ardvasar 71 C 12
Ardverikie Forest 73 G 13
Ardvorlich 67 H 14
Ardwell 52 F 19
Argyll 65 D 15
Argyll Forest Park 66 F 15
Arichastlich 66 F 14
Arienas (Loch) 71 C 14
Arileod 71 A 14
Arinacrinachd 77 C 11
Arinagour 71 A 14
Arisaig 71 C 13
Arivruaich 82 Z 9
Arkaig (Loch) 72 E 13
Arkendale 50 P 21
Arkengarthdale 49 O 20
Arkholme 48 M 21
Arklet (Loch) 66 G 15
Arley 27 P 26
Arlingham 19 M 28
Arlington Court 7 I 30
Armadale *Highland* 85 H 8
Armadale *West Lothian* 61 I 16
Armadale Bay 71 C 12
Armitage 35 O 25
Armthorpe 44 Q 23
Arnabost 71 A 14
Arncliffe 49 N 21
Arncott 20 Q 28
Arncroach 69 L 15
Arne 9 N 31
Arnesby 28 Q 26
Arnicle 59 D 17
Arnisdale 72 D 12
Arnish 77 B 11
Arnol 82 A 8
Arnold 36 Q 25
Arnprior 67 H 15
Arnside 48 L 21
Aros 65 B 14
Arram 45 S 22
Arran (Isle of) 59 E 17
Arreton 10 Q 31
Arrochar 66 F 15
Arscaig 84 G 9
Arundel 11 S 31
Ascog 59 E 16
Ascot 21 R 29
Ascott House 29 R 28
Ascott-under-Wychwood 28 P 28
Ascrib Islands 77 A 11
Asfordby 36 R 25
Ash *Kent* 23 X 30
Ash *Surrey* 20 R 30
Ash Mill 7 I 31
Ashbourne 35 O 24
Ashburton 4 I 32
Ashbury 19 P 29
Ashby de la Zouch 36 P 25
Ashby Magna 28 Q 26
Ashcott 8 L 30
Ashdon 30 U 27
Ashford *Kent* 12 W 30
Ashford *Surrey* 21 S 29
Ashford-in-the-Water *Derbs.* 43 O 24
Ashie (Loch) 79 H 11
Ashill *Breckland* 38 W 26
Ashill *South Somerset* 8 L 31
Ashingdon 22 W 29
Ashington *Northumb* 56 P 18
Ashington *West Sussex* 11 S 31
Ashkirk 62 L 17
Ashleworth 27 N 28
Ashley *East Cambridgeshire* 30 V 27
Ashley *Newcastle-under-Lyme* 35 M 25
Ashley *Torridge* 7 I 31
Ashley Green 21 S 28
Ashmore 9 N 31
Ashover 36 P 24
Ashperton 26 M 27
Ashreigney 7 I 31
Ashtead 21 T 30
Ashton 34 L 24
Ashton-in-Makerfield 42 M 23
Ashton Keynes 19 O 29
Ashton-under-Lyne 43 N 23
Ashton-upon-Mersey 42 M 23
Ashurst 10 P 31
Ashwell *North Hertfordshire* 29 T 27
Ashwell *Rutland* 36 R 25
Ashwellthorpe 39 X 26
Askam in Furness 47 K 21
Askern 44 Q 23
Askernish 76 X 12
Askerswell 5 L 31
Askham 55 L 20
Askrigg 49 N 21
Askwith 49 O 22
Aslacton 31 X 26
Aslockton 36 R 25
Aspatria 54 K 19
Aspley Guise 29 S 27
Assynt (Loch) 84 E 9
Astley 34 L 25
Aston *Vale Royal* 44 Q 23
Aston *West Oxfordshire* 20 P 28
Aston Clinton 20 R 28
Aston Magna 27 O 27
Aston Rowant 20 R 28
Aston Tirrold 20 Q 29
Astwood Bank 27 O 27
Atcham 34 L 25
Athelhampton Hall 9 N 31
Athelney 8 L 30
Athelstaneford 69 L 16
Atherington 7 H 31
Athersley 43 P 23
Atherstone 36 P 26
Atherton 42 M 23
Atholl (Forest of) 73 H 13
Attadale 78 D 11
Attleborough *Breckland* 38 X 26
Attleborough *Nuneaton and Bedworth* 28 P 26
Attlebridge 39 X 25
Atwick 51 T 22
Atworth 19 N 29
Aucharnie 81 M 11
Auchavan 74 K 13
Auchenblae 75 M 13
Auchenbowie 67 I 15
Auchenbrack 61 I 18
Auchenbreck 65 E 16
Auchencairn 53 I 19
Auchencrosh 52 F 18
Auchencrow 63 N 16
Auchengray 61 J 16
Auchenmalg 52 F 19
Auchentiber 60 G 16

Auchindrean ...78 E 10
Auchinleck ...60 H 17
Auchleven ...81 M 12
Auchlyne ...67 G 14
Auchnafree ...67 I 14
Auchnagallin ...80 J 11
Auchnagatt ...81 N 11
Aucholzie ...74 K 12
Auchronie ...74 L 13
Auchterarder ...67 I 15
Auchteraw ...73 F 12
Auchterderran ...68 K 15
Auchterhouse ...68 K 14
Auchtermuchty ...68 K 15
Auchtertyre ...78 D 12
Auckengill ...86 K 8
Auckley ...44 Q 23
Audenshaw ...43 N 23
Audlem ...34 M 25
Audley ...35 N 24
Audley End ...30 U 27
Aughton near Lancaster ...48 L 21
Aughton near Ormskirk ...42 L 23
Auldearn ...79 I 11
Auldgirth ...53 I 18
Auldhouse ...60 H 16
Ault a' Chruinn ...72 D 12
Aultbea ...78 D 10
Aust ...18 M 29
Austrey ...35 P 26
Austwick ...49 N 21
Avebury ...19 O 29
Aveley ...22 U 29
Avening ...19 N 28
Aveton Gifford ...4 I 33
Aviemore ...73 I 12
Avoch ...79 H 11
Avon (Glen) ...74 J 12
Avon (River) R. Severn ...28 O 26
Avon (River) Wilts. ...9 O 31
Avonbridge ...67 I 16
Avonmouth ...18 L 29
Avonwick ...4 I 32
Awe (Loch) ...65 E 15
Awliscombe ...8 K 31
Awre ...19 M 28
Axbridge ...18 L 30
Axminster ...8 L 31
Axmouth ...5 K 31
Aylburton ...18 M 28
Aylesbury ...20 R 28
Aylesford ...22 V 30
Aylesham ...23 X 30
Aylsham ...39 X 25
Aylton ...26 M 27
Aymestrey ...26 L 27
Aynho ...28 Q 28
Ayr ...60 G 17
Aysgarth ...49 O 21
Ayside ...48 L 21
Ayton Scarborough ...51 S 21
Ayton Scottish Borders ...63 N 16

B

Bà (Loch) ...65 C 14
Babbacombe Bay ...4 J 32
Babcary ...8 M 30
Babell ...41 K 23
Babworth ...44 R 24
Back ...83 B 9
Backaland ...87 L 6
Backmuir of New Gilston ...69 L 15
Backwater Reservoir ...74 K 13
Backwell West Town ...18 L 29
Baconsthorpe ...39 X 25
Bacton Mid Suffolk ...30 X 27
Bacton North Norfolk ...39 Y 25
Bacup ...43 N 22
Bad a' Ghaill (Loch) ...84 E 9
Bad an Sgalaig (Loch) ...78 D 10
Badachro ...77 C 10
Badanloch (Loch) ...85 H 9
Badanloch Lodge ...85 H 9
Badcaul ...78 D 10
Baddesley Ensor ...35 P 26
Baddidarach ...84 E 9
Badenoch ...73 H 13
Badenscallie ...83 E 9
Badenyon ...74 K 12
Badlipster ...86 K 8
Badluarach ...78 D 10
Badminton ...19 N 29
Badrallach ...78 E 10
Bae Colwyn / Colwyn Bay ...41 I 23
Bagh nam Faoileann ...76 Y 11
Bagillt ...41 K 23
Bagley ...34 L 25

Bagshot ...21 R 29
Bagworth ...36 P 25
Bagwyllydiart ...26 L 28
Baile Mòr ...64 A 15
Bailiehill ...54 K 18
Bainbridge ...49 N 21
Bainton ...51 S 22
Bakewell ...35 O 24
Bala ...33 J 25
Balallan ...82 A 9
Balbeggie ...68 J 14
Balblair ...79 H 10
Balcary Point ...53 I 19
Balchrick ...84 E 8
Balcombe ...11 T 30
Balderton ...36 R 24
Baldock ...29 T 28
Baldrine ...46 G 21
Baldwin ...46 G 21
Balemartine ...64 Z 14
Balephetrish Bay ...70 Z 14
Balephuil ...64 Z 14
Balephuil Bay ...64 Z 14
Balerno ...61 J 16
Baleshare ...76 X 11
Balevulin ...65 B 14
Balfour ...87 L 6
Balfron ...67 H 15
Balgray ...69 L 14
Balgy ...78 D 11
Balintore Angus ...74 K 13
Balintore Highland ...79 I 10
Balivanich ...76 X 11
Balk ...50 Q 21
Ballabeg ...46 F 21
Ballachulish ...72 E 13
Ballajora ...46 G 21
Ballamodha ...46 G 21
Ballantrae ...52 E 18
Ballasalla ...46 G 21
Ballater ...74 K 12
Ballaugh ...46 G 21
Ballevullin ...70 Z 14
Balliemore near Dunoon ...65 E 15
Balliemore near Oban ...65 D 14
Ballig ...46 G 21
Ballingry ...68 K 15
Ballinluig ...74 J 14
Ballochan ...75 L 12
Ballochroy ...59 D 16
Ballyhaugh ...71 A 14
Balmacellan ...53 H 18
Balmaha ...67 G 15
Balmedie ...75 N 12
Balminnoch ...52 F 19
Balmoral Castle ...74 K 12
Balmullo ...69 L 14
Balnacra ...78 D 11
Balnafoich ...79 H 11
Balnaguard ...74 I 14
Balnahard ...64 B 14
Balnakeil Bay ...84 F 8
Balnaknock ...77 B 11
Balnapaling ...79 H 10
Baltonsborough ...8 M 30
Balvicar ...65 D 15
Balvraid ...72 D 12
Bamburgh Castle ...63 O 17
Bamford ...43 O 23
Bampton Cumbria ...48 L 20
Bampton Devon ...7 J 31
Bampton Oxon. ...20 P 28
Banavie ...72 E 13
Banbury ...28 P 27
Banchory ...75 M 12
Bancyfelin ...15 G 28
Bandenscoth ...81 M 11
Banff ...81 M 10
Bangor ...40 H 23
Bankend ...53 J 18
Bankfoot ...68 J 14
Bankhead ...75 N 12
Banks ...42 L 22
Bankshill ...54 K 18
Banniskirk ...85 J 8
Bannockburn ...67 I 15
Banstead ...21 T 30
Banwell ...18 L 30
Bapchild ...22 W 30
Bar Hill ...29 U 27
Barbaraville ...79 H 10
Barbon ...48 M 21
Barcaldine ...65 E 14
Barcombe Cross ...11 U 31
Bardney ...45 T 24
Bardsea ...48 K 21
Bardsey ...43 P 22
Bardsey Island ...32 F 25

Barford ...39 X 26
Barford-St. Martin ...9 O 30
Barfreston ...23 X 30
Bargoed ...18 K 28
Bargrennan ...52 G 18
Barham ...23 X 30
Barking ...30 X 27
Barking and Dagenham
   London Borough ...21 U 29
Barkston ...37 S 25
Barkway ...29 U 28
Barlaston ...35 N 25
Barlborough ...44 Q 24
Barlestone ...36 P 26
Barley North Hertfordshire ...29 U 27
Barley Pendle ...42 N 22
Barmby on the Marsh ...44 R 22
Barming ...22 V 30
Barmouth / Abermaw ...33 H 25
Barmouth Bay ...33 H 25
Barmston ...51 T 21
Barnack ...37 S 26
Barnard Castle ...49 O 20
Barnby Dun ...44 Q 23
Barnby Moor
   East Riding of Yorks. ...50 R 22
Barnby Moor Notts. ...44 Q 23
Barney ...38 W 25
Barnham ...30 W 26
Barnham Broom ...38 X 26
Barnhill ...80 J 11
Barnhills ...52 E 18
Barningham ...49 O 20
Barnoldswick ...49 N 22
Barnsley ...43 P 23
Barnstaple ...7 H 30
Barnton ...42 M 24
Barnwell ...29 S 26
Barr ...52 F 18
Barra ...70 X 13
Barra (Sound of) ...70 X 12
Barra Head ...70 X 13
Barregarrow ...46 G 21
Barrhead ...60 G 16
Barrhill ...52 F 18
Barri / Barry ...18 K 29
Barrington ...8 L 31
Barrisdale ...72 D 12
Barrisdale Bay ...72 D 12
Barrmill ...60 G 16
Barrock ...86 K 8
Barrow ...52 F 18
Barrow Burn ...63 N 17
Barrow Gurney ...18 L 29
Barrow-in-Furness ...47 K 21
Barrow-upon-Humber ...45 S 22
Barrow-upon-Soar ...36 Q 25
Barrowby ...36 R 25
Barrowford ...43 N 22
Barry Angus ...69 L 14
Barry / Barri
   Vale of Glamorgan ...18 K 29
Barsham ...31 Y 26
Barston ...27 O 26
Bartestree ...26 M 27
Barton Eden ...49 P 20
Barton Lancs. ...42 L 22
Barton-le-Clay ...29 S 28
Barton le Willows ...50 R 21
Barton Mills ...30 V 26
Barton-on-Sea ...9 P 31
Barton-under-Needwood ...35 O 25
Barton-upon-Humber ...44 S 22
Barvas ...82 A 8
Barwell ...36 P 26
Barwick-in-Elmet ...43 P 22
Baschurch ...34 L 25
Bashall Eaves ...42 M 22
Basildon Berks. ...20 Q 29
Basildon Essex ...22 V 29
Basing ...20 Q 30
Basingstoke ...20 Q 30
Baslow ...43 P 24
Bass Rock ...69 M 15
Bassenthwaite ...54 K 19
Bassingham ...37 S 24
Baston ...37 T 25
Bastwick ...39 Y 25
Batcombe ...8 M 31
Bath ...19 N 29
Bathampton ...19 N 29
Batheaston ...19 N 29
Bathgate ...61 J 16
Batley ...43 P 22

Battle ...12 V 31
Baumber ...45 T 24
Bawburgh ...39 X 26
Bawdeswell ...38 X 25
Bawdsey ...31 Y 27
Bawtry ...44 Q 23
Bayble ...83 B 9
Baycliff ...48 K 21
Baydon ...19 P 29
Bayhead ...76 X 11
Bayston Hill ...34 L 25
Beachampton ...28 R 27
Beachy Head ...12 U 31
Beacon (The) ...2 E 33
Beacon End ...30 W 28
Beaconsfield ...21 S 29
Beadlam ...50 R 21
Beadnell Bay ...63 P 17
Beaford ...7 H 31
Beal ...63 O 16
Beaminster ...8 L 31
Beamish Hall ...56 P 19
Beamsley ...49 O 22
Bearsden ...67 G 16
Bearsted ...22 V 30
Beattock ...61 J 18
Beauchief ...43 P 24
Beaufort ...18 K 28
Beaulieu ...10 P 31
Beauly ...79 G 11
Beauly Firth ...79 G 11
Beaumaris ...40 H 23
Beaumont ...54 K 19
Beaupré Castle ...17 J 29
Bebington ...42 L 23
Beccles ...31 Y 26
Beckfoot ...54 J 19
Beckingham ...44 R 23
Beckington ...19 N 30
Beckley ...12 V 31
Beckton ...21 U 29
Bedale ...50 P 21
Beddau ...17 J 29
Beddgelert ...33 H 24
Beddingham ...11 U 31
Bedford ...29 S 27
Bedgebury Pinetum ...12 V 30
Bedlington ...56 P 18
Bedlinog ...17 K 28
Bedrule ...62 M 17
Bedwas ...18 K 29
Bedworth ...28 P 26
Bee (Loch) ...76 X 11
Beer ...5 K 31
Beeston ...36 Q 25
Beeswing ...53 I 18
Begbroke ...20 Q 28
Beguildy ...26 K 26
Beighton ...44 P 23
Beinn a' Ghlò ...74 I 13
Beinn a' Mheadhoin (Loch) ...78 F 12
Beinn Dearg Highland ...78 F 10
Beinn Dearg
   Perthshire and Kinross ...73 I 13
Beinn Heasgarnich ...67 G 14
Beinn Ime ...66 F 15
Beith ...60 G 16
Belbroughton ...27 N 26
Belchford ...45 T 24
Belford ...63 O 17
Belhelvie ...75 N 12
Bellabeg ...74 K 12
Bellanoch ...65 D 15
Bellingham ...55 N 18
Bellshill
   Berwick-upon-Tweed ...63 O 17
Bellshill North Lanarkshire ...60 H 16
Belmont ...87 R 1
Belnacraig ...74 K 12
Belnahua ...65 C 15
Belper ...36 P 24
Belsay ...56 O 18
Belstead ...31 X 27
Belstone ...4 I 31
Belton Lincs. ...37 S 25
Belton Norfolk ...39 Y 26
Belton North Lincs. ...44 R 23
Belton Rutland ...36 R 25
Belvoir ...36 R 25
Bembridge ...10 Q 31
Bempton ...51 T 21
Ben Alder ...73 G 13
Ben Alder Lodge ...73 G 13
Ben Armine Forest ...85 H 9
Ben Armine Lodge ...85 H 9
Ben Chonzie ...67 I 14
Ben Cruachan ...65 E 14
Ben-damph Forest ...78 D 11

Ben Hope ...84 G 8
Ben Klibreck ...84 G 9
Ben Lawers ...67 H 14
Ben Ledi ...67 H 15
Ben Lomond ...66 G 15
Ben Loyal ...84 G 8
Ben Macdui ...74 I 12
Ben More Argyll and Bute ...65 B 14
Ben More Stirling ...67 G 14
Ben More Assynt ...84 F 9
Ben Nevis ...72 E 13
Ben Starav ...66 E 14
Ben Vorlich ...67 H 14
Ben Wyvis ...79 G 10
Benbecula ...76 X 11
Benbuie ...60 H 18
Benderloch Argyll and Bute ...65 D 14
Benderloch Mountain ...65 E 14
Bendronaig Lodge ...78 E 11
Benenden ...12 V 30
Benfleet ...22 V 29
Benington ...37 U 25
Benllech ...40 H 23
Benmore ...67 G 14
Benmore Lodge ...84 F 9
Benson ...20 Q 29
Bentley Doncaster ...44 Q 23
Bentley East Hampshire ...20 R 30
Bentpath ...54 K 18
Bentworth ...10 Q 30
Benwick ...29 T 26
Beoraid (Loch) ...72 D 13
Bere Alston ...3 H 32
Bere Ferrers ...3 H 32
Bere Regis ...9 N 31
Berkeley ...18 M 28
Berkhamsted ...21 S 28
Berneray near Barra ...70 X 13
Berneray near North Uist ...76 Y 10
Bernice ...66 E 15
Bernisdale ...77 B 11
Berriew ...34 K 26
Berrington Hall ...26 L 27
Berrow ...18 K 30
Berry Hill ...18 M 28
Berry Pomeroy ...4 J 32
Berrynarbor ...17 H 30
Bervie Bay ...75 N 13
Berwick-St. John ...9 N 31
Berwick-upon-Tweed ...63 O 16
Berwyn ...33 J 25
Bessacarr ...44 Q 23
Bethel ...33 H 24
Bethersden ...12 W 30
Bethesda ...33 H 24
Betley ...35 M 24
Bettisfield ...34 L 25
Bettws Cedewain ...34 K 26
Bettws Evan ...15 G 27
Bettws Gwerfil Goch ...33 J 24
Bettyhill ...85 H 8
Betws-y-Coed ...33 I 24
Betws yn Rhos ...41 J 23
Beulah near Cardigan ...15 G 27
Beulah
   near Llandrindod-Wells ...25 J 27
Beverley ...45 S 22
Beverstone ...19 N 29
Bewaldeth ...54 K 19
Bewcastle ...55 L 18
Bewdley ...27 N 26
Bewholme ...51 T 22
Bexhill ...12 V 31
Bexley London Borough ...21 U 29
Beyton ...30 W 27
Bhaid-Luachraich (Loch) ...78 D 10
Bhealaich (Loch a') ...84 G 9
Bhraoin (Loch a') ...78 E 10
Bhrollum (Loch) ...82 A 10
Bibury ...19 O 28
Bicester ...28 Q 28
Bicker ...37 T 25
Bickington ...4 I 32
Bickleigh Mid Devon ...7 J 31
Bickleigh South Hams ...4 H 32
Bicton ...34 L 25
Bicton gardens ...5 K 31
Bidborough ...12 V 30
Biddenden ...12 V 30
Biddenham ...29 S 27
Biddestone ...19 N 29
Biddulph ...35 N 24
Bidean nam Bian ...72 E 13
Bideford ...6 H 30
Bidford ...27 O 27
Bieldside ...75 N 12
Bierton ...20 R 28

Big Corlae ...60 H 18
Bigbury ...4 I 33
Bigbury-on-Sea ...4 I 33
Biggar Barrow-in-Furness ...47 K 21
Biggar South Lanarkshire ...61 J 17
Biggin Hill ...21 U 30
Biggleswade ...29 T 27
Bignor ...11 S 31
Bildeston ...30 W 27
Bildsgreen ...27 M 26
Bill of Portland ...8 M 32
Billericay ...22 V 29
Billesdon ...36 R 26
Billingborough ...37 S 25
Billinge ...42 L 23
Billingham ...57 Q 20
Billinghay ...37 T 24
Billingshurst ...11 S 30
Billingsley ...27 M 26
Billockby ...39 Y 26
Billy Row ...56 O 19
Bilsborrow ...42 L 22
Bilsington ...12 W 30
Bilston ...35 N 26
Bilton ...45 T 22
Binbrook ...45 T 23
Binfield ...20 R 29
Bingham ...36 R 25
Bingley ...43 O 22
Binham ...38 W 25
Binns (The) ...68 J 16
Binsted ...10 R 30
Birchington ...23 X 29
Birdham ...10 R 31
Birdingbury ...28 P 27
Birdwell ...43 P 23
Birdworld ...10 R 30
Birgham ...62 N 17
Birkdale ...42 K 23
Birkenhead ...42 K 23
Birkin ...44 Q 22
Birling Gap ...12 U 31
Birmingham ...27 O 26
Birnam ...68 J 14
Birsay ...86 K 6
Birsemore ...75 L 12
Birstall ...36 Q 25
Birtley Gateshead ...56 P 19
Birtley Tynedale ...55 N 18
Birtsmorton Court ...27 N 27
Bisham ...20 R 29
Bishop Auckland ...56 P 20
Bishop Burton ...44 S 22
Bishop Monkton ...50 P 21
Bishop Sutton ...18 M 29
Bishop Thornton ...50 P 21
Bishop Wilton ...50 R 22
Bishops Cannings ...19 O 29
Bishop's Castle ...26 L 26
Bishop's Caundle ...9 M 31
Bishop's Cleeve ...27 N 28
Bishop's Itchington ...28 P 27
Bishops Lydeard ...8 K 30
Bishop's Nympton ...7 I 31
Bishop's Palace
   near St. David's ...14 E 28
Bishop's Palace near Tenby ...16 F 28
Bishop's Stortford ...30 U 28
Bishop's Tachbrook ...28 P 27
Bishop's Tawton ...7 H 30
Bishop's Waltham ...10 Q 31
Bishopsteignton ...4 J 32
Bishopstocke ...10 Q 31
Bishopston ...15 H 29
Bishopstone Salisbury ...9 O 30
Bishopstone Swindon ...19 O 29
Bishopthorpe ...50 Q 22
Bishopton Darlington ...56 P 20
Bishopton Renfrewshire ...67 G 16
Bishton ...18 L 29
Bisley ...19 N 28
Bispham ...42 K 22
Bix ...20 R 29
Bixter ...87 P 3
Blaby ...36 Q 26
Black Bay ...59 D 17
Black Isle ...79 G 11
Black Corries ...72 F 13
Black Down Hills ...8 K 31
Black Mount ...66 F 14
Black Mountain ...25 I 28
Black Mountains ...26 K 28
Black Notley ...30 V 28
Black Torrington ...6 H 31
Black Water Valley ...78 F 11
Blackawton ...4 I 32

A B C D E F G H I J K L M N O P Q R S T U V W X Y Z

Blackburn *Aberdeenshire* ...75 N 12
Blackburn *Lancs.* .....42 M 22
Blackburn *West Lothian* ......61 J 16
Blackfield ......10 P 31
Blackford *Cumbria* ......54 L 19
Blackford
  Perthshire and Kinross .....67 I 15
Blackhall ......57 Q 19
Blackhall Rocks ......57 Q 19
Blackhill *Aberdeenshire* ......81 O 11
Blackhill *Highland* ......77 A 11
Blacklunans ......74 J 13
Blackmoor Gate ......17 I 30
Blackmore ......22 U 28
Blackness Castle ......68 J 15
Blacko ......43 N 22
Blackpool ......42 K 22
Blackridge ......61 I 16
Blackthorn ......28 Q 28
Blacktoft ......44 R 22
Blackwater *Hart* ......20 R 30
Blackwater *Isle of Wight* ...10 Q 31
Blackwater *(River)* ......22 W 28
Blackwater Reservoir ......72 F 13
Blackwaterfoot ......59 D 17
Blackwell ......50 P 20
Blackwood ......18 K 29
Bladnoch ......52 G 19
Bladon ......20 P 28
Blaenannherch ......15 G 27
Blaenau Ffestiniog ......33 I 25
Blaenavon ......18 K 28
Blaengarw ......17 J 29
Blaengrwrach ......17 J 28
Blagdon ......18 L 30
Blaich ......72 E 13
Blaina ......18 K 28
Blair Atholl ......73 I 13
Blair Castle ......73 I 13
Blairgowrie ......68 J 14
Blairmore ......66 F 16
Blakeney *Glos.* ......18 M 28
Blakeney *Norfolk* ......38 X 25
Blakesley ......28 Q 27
Blamerino ......68 K 14
Blandford Forum ......9 N 31
Blanefield ......67 H 16
Blàr a Chaorainn ......72 E 13
Blarmachfoldach ......72 E 13
Blarnalearoch ......78 E 10
Blawith ......48 K 21
Blaxton ......44 R 23
Blaydon ......56 O 19
Bleadon ......18 L 30
Bleaklow Hill ......43 O 23
Blean ......23 X 30
Bleasby ......36 R 24
Blenheim Palace ......20 P 28
Bletchingdon ......20 Q 28
Bletchley ......28 R 27
Bletsoe ......29 S 27
Blewbury ......20 Q 29
Blickling ......39 X 25
Blickling Hall ......39 X 25
Blidworth ......36 Q 24
Blindley Heath ......21 T 30
Blisland ......3 F 32
Blisworth ......28 R 27
Blithe ......35 O 25
Blithfield Hall ......35 O 25
Blithfield Reservoir ......35 O 25
Blockley ......27 O 27
Blofield ......39 Y 26
Bloxham ......28 P 27
Blubberhouses ......49 O 22
Blue John Cavern ......43 O 23
Bluemull Sound ......87 Q 1
Blundellsands ......42 K 23
Blundeston ......39 Z 26
Blyth *Northumb.* ......56 P 18
Blyth *Notts.* ......44 Q 23
Blythburgh ......31 Y 27
Blythe Bridge ......35 N 25
Blyton ......44 R 23
Bo' Ness ......68 J 15
Boarhills ......69 L 15
Boat of Garten ......74 I 12
Boathvic ......79 G 10
Bocking Churchstreet ......30 V 28
Boddam ......81 O 11
Bodedern ......40 G 23
Bodelwyddan ......41 J 23
Bodenham ......26 L 27
Bodfari ......41 J 23
Bodffordd ......40 G 23
Bodham Street ......39 X 25
Bodiam Castle ......12 V 30

Bodicote ......28 Q 27
Bodmin ......3 F 32
Bodmin Moor ......3 G 32
Bodnant Garden ......41 I 23
Bognor Regis ......11 R 31
Bogue ......53 H 18
Boisdale ......70 X 12
Boisdale *(Loch)* ......70 Y 12
Boldon ......56 P 19
Bolham ......7 J 31
Bollin *(River)* ......42 N 23
Bollington ......43 N 24
Bolney ......11 T 31
Bolnhurst ......29 S 27
Bolsover ......44 Q 24
Boltby ......50 Q 21
Bolton *Alnwick* ......63 O 17
Bolton *Bolton* ......42 M 23
Bolton Abbey ......49 O 22
Bolton-by-Bowland ......49 N 22
Bolton-le-Sands ......48 L 21
Bolton on Swale ......50 P 20
Bolton-upon-Dearne ......44 Q 23
Bomere Heath ......34 L 25
Bonar Bridge ......79 G 10
Bonawe Quarries ......65 E 14
Bonby ......44 S 23
Boncath ......15 G 27
Bonchester Bridge ......62 M 17
Bonhill ......66 G 16
Bonnybridge ......67 I 16
Bonnyrigg ......61 K 16
Bont-faen / Cowbridge ......17 J 29
Bontgoch Elerch ......25 I 26
Bontnewydd ......32 H 24
Boosbeck ......50 R 20
Boot ......47 K 20
Bootle *Cumbria* ......47 J 21
Bootle *Merseyside* ......42 K 23
Border Forest Park (The) ...55 M 18
Bordogan ......32 G 24
Boreham ......22 V 28
Boreham Street ......12 V 31
Borehamwood ......21 T 29
Boreland ......54 K 18
Borgue
  Dumfries and Galloway ...53 H 19
Borgue *Highland* ......85 J 9
Borness ......53 H 19
Borough Green ......22 U 30
Boroughbridge ......50 P 21
Borreraig ......77 Z 11
Borrobol Forest ......85 H 9
Borrowash ......36 P 25
Borth ......25 H 26
Borve *Barra Isle* ......70 X 13
Borve *Eilean Siar* ......70 X 13
Borve *Isle of Lewis* ......82 A 8
Borve *South Harris* ......76 Y 10
Borwick ......48 L 21
Bosbury ......27 M 27
Boscastle ......6 F 31
Boscombe ......9 O 31
Bosham ......10 R 31
Bosherston ......16 F 29
Bosley ......35 N 24
Boston ......37 T 25
Boston Spa ......50 P 22
Boswinger ......3 F 33
Botesdale ......30 W 26
Bothamsall ......44 R 24
Bothel ......54 K 19
Bothwell ......60 H 16
Botley ......10 Q 31
Botolph Melton ......36 R 25
Bottesford
  North Lincolnshire ......44 S 23
Bottisham ......30 U 27
Botwnnog ......32 G 25
Boughton ......36 Q 24
Boughton House ......29 R 26
Boughton Street ......22 W 30
Boulmer ......63 P 17
Boultham ......44 S 24
Bourn ......29 T 27
Bourne ......37 S 25
Bournemouth ......9 O 31
Bourton *North Dorset* ......9 N 30
Bourton
  Vale of White Horse ...19 P 29
Bourton-on-the-Water ......27 O 28
Bovey Tracey ......4 I 32
Bovingdon ......21 S 28
Bow ......7 I 31
Bow Street ......25 H 26
Bowden ......62 L 17
Bower *Highland* ......85 K 8

Bower *Tynedale* ......55 M 18
Bowerchalke ......9 O 30
Bowes ......49 N 20
Bowhill ......62 L 17
Bowland ......62 L 17
Bowland (Forest of) ......49 M 22
Bowmore ......58 B 16
Bowness ......48 L 20
Bowness-on-Solway ......54 K 19
Bowood House ......19 N 29
Box ......19 N 29
Box Hill ......21 T 30
Boxford *Babergh* ......30 W 27
Boxford *West Berkshire* ...20 P 29
Boxley ......22 V 30
Boxworth ......29 T 27
Boyton ......6 G 31
Bozeat ......29 R 27
Braaid ......46 G 21
Brabourne Lees ......12 W 30
Bracadale *(Loch)* ......77 A 12
Bracebridge Heath ......37 S 24
Brackley ......28 Q 27
Brackley Hatch ......28 Q 27
Bracknell ......20 R 29
Braco ......67 I 15
Bracora ......72 C 13
Bradan Resr *(Loch)* ......60 G 18
Bradfield *Sheffield* ......43 P 23
Bradfield *West Berkshire* ...20 Q 29
Bradford *Bradford* ......43 O 22
Bradford *Taunton Deane* ...8 K 31
Bradford Abbas ......8 M 31
Bradford-on-Avon ......19 N 29
Brading ......10 Q 31
Bradninch ......7 J 31
Bradpole ......5 L 31
Bradwell ......43 O 24
Bradwell-on-Sea ......22 W 28
Bradworthy ......6 G 31
Brae ......87 P 2
Brae of Achnahaird ......83 D 9
Brae Roy Lodge ......73 F 13
Braeantra ......79 G 10
Braedownie ......74 K 13
Braehead ......61 J 16
Braemar ......74 J 12
Braemore ......85 J 9
Braeriach ......74 I 12
Braeswick ......87 L 6
Brafferton Helperby ......50 Q 21
Bragar ......82 A 8
Braglenbeg ......65 D 15
Braich y Pwll ......32 F 25
Braidwood ......61 I 16
Bràigh Mòr ......82 Y 9
Brailes ......28 P 27
Brailsford ......35 P 25
Braintree ......30 V 28
Braishfield ......10 P 30
Braithwell ......44 Q 23
Bramcote ......36 Q 25
Bramfield ......31 Y 27
Bramford ......31 X 27
Bramhall ......43 N 23
Bramham ......43 P 22
Bramhope ......43 P 22
Bramley
  Basingstoke and Deane ...20 Q 30
Bramley
  South Yorks. ......44 Q 23
Bramley *Surrey* ......21 S 30
Brampton *Cambs.* ......29 T 27
Brampton *Cumbria* ......55 L 19
Brampton *Eden* ......55 M 20
Brampton *Rotherham.* ......43 P 23
Brampton *Suffolk* ......31 Y 26
Brampton Bryan ......26 L 26
Brancaster ......38 V 25
Branderburgh ......80 K 10
Brandesburton ......51 T 22
Brandon *Durham* ......56 P 19
Brandon *Suffolk* ......30 V 26
Brandsby ......50 Q 21
Branscombe ......5 K 31
Bransgore ......9 O 31
Branston ......37 S 24
Brant Broughton ......37 S 24
Brassington ......35 P 24
Bratton ......19 N 30
Bratton Clovelly ......6 H 31
Bratton Fleming ......7 I 30
Braughing ......29 U 28
Braunston *Daventry* ......28 Q 27
Braunston *Rutland* ......36 R 26
Braunton ......6 H 30
Bray-on-Thames ......21 R 29

Bray Shop ......3 G 32
Braybrooke ......28 R 26
Brayford ......7 I 30
Brayton ......44 Q 22
Breaclete ......82 Z 9
Breadalbane ......67 G 14
Breage ......2 D 33
Bream ......18 M 28
Breamore House ......9 O 31
Brean ......18 K 30
Breasclete ......82 Z 9
Breaston ......36 Q 25
Brechin ......75 M 13
Breckland ......30 V 26
Brecon / Aberhonddu ......25 J 28
Brecon Beacons
  National Park ......25 J 28
Bredbury ......43 N 23
Brede ......12 V 31
Bredenbury ......26 M 27
Bredgar ......22 W 30
Bredon ......27 N 27
Bredwardine ......26 L 27
Bremhill ......19 N 29
Brenchley ......12 V 30
Brendon Hills ......7 J 30
Brendon ......18 K 30
Brenig Reservoir ......33 J 24
Brenish ......82 Y 9
Brent *London Borough* ......21 T 29
Brent Knoll ......18 L 30
Brent Pelham ......29 U 28
Brentwood ......22 U 29
Brenzett ......12 W 30
Brereton ......35 O 25
Bressay ......87 Q 3
Bretford ......28 P 26
Bretherton ......42 L 22
Brewham ......9 M 30
Brewlands Bridge ......74 K 13
Brewood ......35 N 25
Bride ......46 G 20
Bridestowe ......4 H 31
Bridge ......23 X 30
Bridge of Alford ......75 L 12
Bridge of Allan ......67 I 15
Bridge of Avon ......80 J 11
Bridge of Balgie ......73 H 14
Bridge of Brown ......74 J 12
Bridge of Buchat ......74 L 12
Bridge of Craigisla ......74 K 13
Bridge of Dee ......53 I 19
Bridge of Don ......75 N 12
Bridge of Dun ......75 M 13
Bridge of Dye ......75 M 13
Bridge of Earn ......68 J 14
Bridge of Ericht ......73 G 13
Bridge of Gairn ......74 K 12
Bridge of Gaur ......73 G 13
Bridge of Orchy ......66 F 14
Bridge of Weir ......60 G 16
Bridge Trafford ......42 L 24
Bridgemary ......10 Q 31
Bridgend *Aberdeenshire* ...80 L 11
Bridgend *Angus* ......75 L 13
Bridgend *Argyll and Bute* ...65 D 15
Bridgend *Islay* ......58 B 16
Bridgend
  Perthshire and Kinross ...68 J 14
Bridgend / Pen-y-bont ......17 J 29
Bridgend of Lintrathen ......74 K 13
Bridgerule ......6 G 31
Bridgham ......30 W 26
Bridgnorth ......27 M 26
Bridgwater ......8 L 30
Bridlington ......51 T 21
Bridport ......5 L 31
Brierfield ......43 N 22
Brierley ......43 P 23
Brierley Hill ......27 N 26
Brigham ......54 J 20
Brighouse ......43 O 22
Brighstone ......10 P 32
Brighstone Forest ......10 P 32
Brightling ......12 V 31
Brightlingsea ......23 X 28
Brighton ......11 T 31
Brightwell ......20 Q 29
Brigstock ......29 S 26
Brill ......20 Q 28
Brimfield ......26 L 27
Brimham Rocks ......49 O 21
Brimington ......43 P 24
Brimpsfield ......19 N 28
Brimpton ......20 Q 29
Brinkburn Priory ......63 O 18
Brinkley ......30 V 27

Brinklow ......28 P 26
Brinkworth ......19 O 29
Brinyan ......86 L 6
Brisley ......38 W 25
Brislington ......18 M 29
Bristol ......18 M 29
Briston ......38 X 25
Briton Ferry ......17 I 29
Brittle *(Loch)* ......71 B 12
Brittwell Salome ......20 Q 29
Brixham ......4 J 32
Brixton ......4 H 32
Brixworth ......28 R 27
Brize Norton ......20 P 28
Broad Bay ......83 B 9
Broad Blunsdon ......19 O 29
Broad Chalke ......9 O 30
Broad Haven ......14 E 28
Broad Hinton ......19 O 29
Broad Law ......61 J 17
Broad Oak ......12 V 31
Broadbrige Heath ......11 S 30
Broadclyst ......7 J 31
Broadford ......77 C 12
Broadlands ......10 P 31
Broadmayne ......9 M 31
Broadstairs ......23 Y 29
Broadstone ......9 O 31
Broadwas ......27 M 27
Broadway ......27 O 27
Broadwell Ho ......55 N 19
Broadwey ......8 M 32
Broadwindsor ......8 L 31
Broadwoodwidger ......6 H 31
Brochel ......77 B 11
Brockdish ......31 X 26
Brockenhurst ......10 P 31
Brockley ......18 L 29
Brockworth ......19 N 28
Brodick ......59 E 17
Brodick Bay ......59 E 17
Brodick Castle ......59 E 17
Brodie Castle ......79 I 11
Brodsworth ......44 Q 23
Brodsworth Hall ......44 Q 23
Brokenborough ......19 N 29
Brolass ......65 B 14
Bromborough ......42 L 24
Brome ......31 X 26
Bromfield ......26 L 26
Bromham *Bedford* ......29 S 27
Bromham *Kennet* ......19 N 29
Bromley *London Borough* ...21 U 29
Brompton *Kent* ......22 V 29
Brompton *near Northallerton* 50 P 20
Brompton-by-Sawdon ......51 S 21
Brompton on Swale ......49 O 20
Brompton Ralph ......7 K 30
Brompton Regis ......7 J 30
Bromsgrove ......27 N 26
Bromyard ......26 M 27
Bronllys ......26 K 27
Brook ......22 W 30
Brooke ......39 Y 26
Brookmans Park ......21 T 28
Broom *(Loch)* ......78 E 10
Broomfield *Chelmsford* ......22 V 28
Broomfield *Sedgemoor* ...8 K 30
Broomfleet ......44 S 22
Broomhaugh ......56 O 19
Brora ......85 I 9
Broseley ......34 M 26
Brotherton ......44 Q 22
Brotton ......57 R 20
Brough
  East Riding of Yorkshire ...44 S 22
Brough *Eden* ......49 N 20
Brough *Highland* ......86 J 8
Brough Head ......86 J 6
Brough Lodge ......87 R 2
Brough of Birsay ......86 J 6
Broughton *Cumbria* ......54 J 19
Broughton
  Flintshire / Sir y Fflint ...34 L 24
Broughton *Hants.* ......10 P 30
Broughton *Lancs.* ......42 L 22
Broughton *North Lincs.* ...44 S 23
Broughton *Northants.* ......28 R 26
Broughton *Oxon.* ......28 P 27
Broughton *Scottish Borders* .61 J 17
Broughton-in-Furness ......47 K 21
Broughton Mills ......47 K 21
Broughton Moor ......54 J 19
Broughton Poggs ......19 P 28
Broughty Ferry ......69 L 14
Brownhills ......35 O 26
Brownsea Island ......9 O 31

Broxbourne ......21 T 28
Broxburn ......68 J 16
Bruar Lodge ......73 I 13
Bruichladdich ......58 A 16
Brundall ......39 Y 26
Brushford ......7 J 30
Bruton ......8 M 30
Brydekirk ......54 K 18
Brymbo ......34 K 24
Bryn-Henllan ......24 F 27
Brynamman ......17 I 28
Brynberian ......17 J 29
Bryngwran ......40 G 23
Bryngwyn ......26 K 27
Brynhoffnant ......15 G 27
Brynmawr ......18 K 28
Brynsiencyn ......32 H 24
Brynteg ......40 H 23
Bualintur ......71 B 12
Bubwith ......44 R 22
Buccleuch ......61 K 17
Buchanty ......67 I 14
Buchlyvie ......67 H 15
Buckden *Cambs.* ......29 T 27
Buckden *North Yorks.* ......49 N 21
Buckfast ......4 I 32
Buckfast Abbey ......4 I 32
Buckfastleigh ......4 I 32
Buckhaven ......68 K 15
Buckhorn Weston ......9 M 30
Buckie ......80 L 10
Buckingham ......28 R 27
Buckland *Herts.* ......29 T 28
Buckland *Oxon.* ......20 P 28
Buckland Abbey ......4 H 32
Buckland Brewer ......6 H 31
Buckland Dinham ......19 M 30
Buckland in-the-Moor ......4 I 32
Buckland Newton ......8 M 31
Buckland St. Mary ......8 K 31
Bucklebury ......20 Q 29
Bucklers Hard ......10 P 31
Buckley / Bwcle ......34 K 24
Buckminster ......36 R 25
Bucknall ......37 T 24
Bucknell ......26 L 26
Bucks green ......11 S 30
Bucksburn ......75 N 12
Bude ......6 G 31
Budleigh Salterton ......5 K 32
Bugbrooke ......28 Q 27
Bugle ......3 F 32
Bugthorpe ......50 R 21
Buildwas Abbey ......34 M 26
Builth Wells /
  Llanfair-ym-Muallt ......25 J 27
Bulford ......19 O 30
Bulkéley ......34 L 24
Bulkington ......28 P 26
Bulwell ......36 Q 24
Bulwick ......37 S 26
Bunarkaig ......72 F 13
Bunessan ......64 B 15
Bungay ......31 Y 26
Bunnahabhainn ......64 B 16
Bunny ......36 Q 25
Buntingford ......29 T 28
Burbage *Leics.* ......28 P 26
Burbage *Wilts.* ......19 O 29
Burchett's Green ......20 R 29
Bures ......30 W 28
Burford ......19 P 28
Burgess Hill ......11 T 31
Burgh-by-Sands ......54 K 19
Burgh Castle ......39 Y 26
Burgh-le-Marsh ......38 U 24
Burgh-St. Peter ......39 Y 26
Burghead ......80 J 10
Burghfield ......20 Q 29
Burghill ......26 L 27
Burghley House ......37 S 26
Burham ......22 V 30
Burley ......9 O 31
Burley-in-Wharfedale ......49 O 22
Burlton ......34 L 25
Burneside ......48 L 20
Burneston ......50 P 21
Burnfoot ......62 L 17
Burnham ......21 S 29
Burnham Market ......38 W 25
Burnham-on-Crouch ......22 W 28
Burnham-on-Sea ......18 L 30
Burnhaven ......81 O 11
Burnhope ......56 O 19
Burniston ......51 S 21

Burnley	43	N 22
Burntisland	68	K 15
Burrafirth	87	R 1
Burravoe	87	Q 2
Burray	87	L 7
Burrelton	68	K 14
Burringham	44	R 23
Burrington *North Devon*	7	I 31
Burrington *North Somerset*	18	L 30
Burrough Green	30	V 27
Burrow Head	53	G 19
Burry Port /Porth Tywyn	15	H 28
Burscough	42	L 23
Burscough Bridge	42	L 23
Burshill	51	S 22
Bursledon	10	Q 31
Burslem	35	N 24
Burstwick	45	T 22
Burton *Christchurch*	9	O 31
Burton *Ellesmere* Port and Neston	48	L 21
Burton *South Lakeland*	48	L 21
Burton *Wrecsam / Wrexham*	34	L 24
Burton Agnes	51	T 21
Burton Bradstock	5	L 31
Burton Constable Hall	45	T 22
Burton Fleming	51	S 21
Burton in Lonsdale	49	M 21
Burton Joyce	36	Q 25
Burton Latimer	29	R 26
Burton Leonard	50	P 21
Burton Pidsea	45	T 22
Burton-upon-Stather	44	R 23
Burton-upon-Trent	35	O 25
Burwarton	26	M 26
Burwash	12	V 31
Burwell *Cambs.*	30	U 27
Burwell *Lincs.*	45	U 24
Bury *Bury*	42	N 23
Bury *Chichester*	11	S 31
Bury St. Edmunds	30	W 27
Busby	60	H 16
Buscot	19	P 28
Bushey	21	S 29
Bute (Island of)	59	E 16
Bute (Kyles of)	59	E 16
Bute (Sound of)	59	E 16
Butleigh	8	L 30
Butley	31	Y 27
Butt of Lewis	83	B 8
Buttercrambe	50	R 21
Buttermere	47	K 20
Butterstone	68	J 14
Buttington	34	K 25
Buxted	12	U 31
Buxton *Derbs.*	43	O 24
Buxton *Norfolk*	39	X 25
Bwcle / Buckley	34	K 24
Bwlch	26	K 28
Bwlch Oerddrws	33	I 25
Bwlch y Ffridd	33	J 26
Bwlch-y-Groes	25	I 28
Bwlch-y-Sarnau	25	J 26
Bwlchgwyn	34	K 24
Bwlchllan	25	H 27
Byfield	28	Q 27
Byfleet	21	S 30
Byland Abbey	50	Q 21
Byrness	62	M 18

C		
Cabrach	80	K 12
Cadair Idris	33	I 25
Caddington	29	S 28
Caddonfoot	62	L 17
Cadhay	5	K 31
Cadishead	42	M 23
Cadnam	10	P 31
Cadney	44	S 23
Cadwell Park	45	T 24
Caerau	17	J 29
Caerdydd / Cardiff	18	K 29
Caerffili / Caerphilly	18	K 29
Caerfyrddin / Carmarthen	15	H 28
Caergwrle	34	K 24
Caergybi / Holyhead	40	G 23
Caerlaverock Castle	53	J 19
Caerleon	18	L 29
Caernarfon	32	H 24
Caernarfon Bay	32	G 24
Caerphilly / Caerffili	18	K 29
Caersws	25	J 26
Caerwent	18	L 29
Caerwys	41	K 23
Cailliness Point	52	F 19
Cairn Edward Forest	53	H 18
Cairn Gorm	74	J 12

Cairn Table	60	H 17
Cairn Toul	74	I 12
Cairnborrow	80	L 11
Cairndow	66	F 15
Cairngaan	52	F 20
Cairngarroch	52	E 19
Cairnie	80	L 11
Cairnpapple Hill	67	J 16
Cairnryan	52	E 19
Cairnsmore of Carsphairn	60	H 18
Cairnsmore of Fleet	53	G 19
Cairraig Fhada	58	B 17
Caister-on-Sea	39	Z 26
Caistor	45	T 23
Calbourne	10	P 31
Caldbeck	54	K 19
Caldecott	36	R 26
Calder (Loch)	85	J 8
Calder Bridge	47	J 20
Calder Mains	85	J 8
Caldercruix	61	I 16
Calderdale	43	N 22
Caldermill	60	H 17
Caldey Island	15	F 29
Caldicot	18	L 29
Caldwell	49	O 20
Calf of Man	46	F 21
Calfsound	87	L 6
Calgary	71	B 14
Calgary Bay	71	B 14
Caliach Point	71	B 14
Calke Abbey	36	P 25
Callander	67	H 15
Callater (Glen)	74	J 13
Callington	3	H 32
Calne	19	N 29
Calow	43	P 24
Calstock	3	H 32
Calthwaite	55	L 19
Calvay	70	Y 12
Calver	43	P 24
Calverton	36	Q 24
Calvine	73	I 13
Cam	29	U 27
Cam Loch	84	E 9
Camas Chil Mhalieu	72	D 14
Camas-luinie	78	D 12
Camasnacroise	72	D 14
Camastianavaig	77	B 11
Camber	12	W 31
Camberley	20	R 30
Camblesforth	44	Q 22
Cambo	56	O 18
Cambois	56	P 18
Camborne	2	E 33
Cambrian Mountains	25	I 27
Cambridge	29	U 27
Cambusbarron	67	I 15
Cambuskenneth	67	I 15
Camden *London Borough*	21	T 29
Camelford	6	F 32
Cammachmore	75	N 12
Campbeltown	59	D 17
Campsie Fells	67	H 15
Camptown	62	M 17
Campville	35	P 25
Camrose	24	E 28
Camusnagaul	78	E 10
Candlesby	37	U 24
Canewdon	22	W 29
Canisbay	86	K 8
Canna	71	A 12
Cannich	78	F 11
Cannich (Glen)	78	F 11
Cannington	8	K 30
Cannock	35	N 25
Canonbie	54	L 18
Canons Ashby	28	Q 27
Canterbury	23	X 30
Cantley	39	Y 26
Canvey Island	22	V 29
Caol	72	E 13
Caolas a' Mhòrain	76	Y 10
Caoles	70	Z 14
Caolis	70	X 13
Caolisport (Loch)	65	D 16
Cape Cornwall	2	C 33
Cape Wrath	84	E 8
Capel	11	T 30
Capel Curig	33	I 24
Capel Garmon	33	I 24
Capel Le Ferne	13	X 30
Capel St. Mary	31	X 27
Capel-y-Ffin	26	K 28
Capesthorne Hall	43	N 24
Capheaton	56	O 18
Cappercleuch	61	K 17

Caputh	68	J 14
Cara Island	58	C 17
Carbis Bay	2	D 33
Carbost *Minginish*	77	A 12
Carbost *Trotternish*	77	B 11
Cardenden	68	K 15
Cardiff / Caerdydd	18	K 29
Cardigan / Aberteifi	15	G 27
Cardigan Bay	24	G 26
Cardington	34	L 26
Cardinham	3	G 32
Cardrona	61	K 17
Cardross	66	G 16
Cardurnock	54	K 19
Carew	15	F 28
Carfraemill	62	L 16
Cargill	68	J 14
Carhampton	7	J 30
Carie	73	H 13
Carinish	76	Y 11
Carisbrooke	10	Q 31
Cark	48	L 21
Carlbt	37	S 25
Carleen	2	D 33
Carleton	49	N 22
Carlisle	55	L 19
Carlops	61	J 16
Carloway	82	Z 9
Carlton *Bedford*	29	S 27
Carlton *Hambleton*	50	Q 20
Carlton *Hinckley and Bosworth*	36	P 26
Carlton *North Yorks.*	44	Q 22
Carlton *Notts.*	36	Q 25
Carlton Colville	31	Z 26
Carlton in Lindrick	44	Q 23
Carlton-on-Trent	36	R 24
Carluke	61	I 16
Carmarthen / Caerfyrddin	15	H 28
Carmel Head	40	G 22
Carmunnock	60	H 16
Carmyllie	69	L 14
Carn Ban	73	H 12
Carn Coire na h-Easgainn	73	H 12
Carn Eige	78	E 12
Carn Glas-choire	79	I 11
Carn Mairg	73	H 14
Carnaby	51	T 21
Carnach	78	E 12
Carnassarie Castle	65	D 15
Carnedd Llewelyn	33	I 24
Carnforth	48	L 21
Carno	33	J 26
Carnock	68	J 15
Carnoustie	69	L 14
Carnwath	61	J 16
Carradale	59	D 17
Carradale Bay	59	D 17
Carrbridge	79	I 12
Carrick	66	F 15
Carrick Roads	2	E 33
Carron	80	K 11
Carron (Loch)	77	C 11
Carron Bridge	67	H 15
Carrshield	55	N 19
Carrutherstown	54	J 18
Carsaig	65	C 15
Carse of Gowrie	68	K 14
Carseriggan	52	G 19
Carsethorn	53	J 19
Carsluith	53	G 19
Carsphairn	53	H 18
Carstairs	61	I 16
Carterton	19	P 28
Carterway Heads	56	O 19
Carthew	3	F 32
Carthorpe	50	P 21
Cartmel	48	L 21
Carville	56	P 19
Cas-Gwent / Chepstow	18	M 29
Cashlie	67	G 14
Casnewydd / Newport	18	L 29
Cassington	20	P 28
Cassley (Glen)	84	F 9
Castell-Nedd / Neath	17	I 29
Castell Newydd Emlyn / Newcastle Emlyn	15	G 27
Castell-y-Rhingyll	15	H 28
Castle Acre	38	W 25
Castle Ashby	28	R 27
Castle Bolton	49	O 21
Castle Bytham	37	S 25
Castle Campbell	67	I 15
Castle Cary	8	M 30
Castle Combe	19	N 29
Castle Donington	36	P 25
Castle Douglas	53	I 19

Castle Drogo	4	I 31
Castle Eaton	19	O 29
Castle Fraser	75	M 12
Castle frome	26	M 27
Castle Hedingham	30	V 28
Castle Howard	50	R 21
Castle Kennedy	52	F 19
Castle Lachlan	65	E 15
Castle Loch	52	F 19
Castle Rising	38	V 25
Castlebay	70	X 13
Castleford	43	P 22
Castlemartin	16	E 29
Castlerigg	54	K 20
Castleton *Casnewydd / Newport*	18	K 29
Castleton *Derbs.*	43	O 23
Castleton *North Yorks.*	50	R 20
Castletown *Highland*	85	J 8
Castletown *Isle of Man*	46	G 21
Caston	38	W 26
Catacol	59	E 16
Catacol Bay	59	D 16
Caterham	21	T 30
Catfield	39	Y 25
Catlodge	73	H 12
Caton	48	L 21
Catrine	60	H 17
Catterall	42	L 22
Catterick	50	P 20
Catterick Garrison	49	O 20
Catterline	75	N 13
Cattistock	8	M 31
Catton *Broadland*	39	X 26
Catton *Tynedale*	55	N 19
Catworth	29	S 26
Cauldcleuch Head	62	L 18
Cauldon	35	O 24
Caulkerbush	53	I 19
Cautley	49	M 20
Cava	86	K 7
Cavendish	30	V 27
Caversfield	28	Q 28
Caversham	20	R 29
Cawdor	79	I 11
Cawood	44	Q 22
Cawsand	3	H 32
Cawston	39	X 25
Caxton	29	T 27
Caynham	26	M 26
Caythorpe	37	S 24
Cayton	51	S 21
Ceall (Loch nan)	71	C 13
Cefn Bryn	15	H 29
Cefn-Coed-y-cymmer	17	J 28
Cefn-mawr	34	K 25
Cefn-y-Pant	15	G 28
Ceinewydd / New Quay	24	G 27
Ceiriog (Vale of)	34	K 25
Cemaes	40	G 22
Cemaes Head	15	F 27
Cemmaes	33	I 26
Cemmaes road	33	I 26
Cenarth	15	G 27
Ceres	69	L 15
Cerne Abbas	8	M 31
Cerrigydrudion	33	J 24
Chacewater	2	E 33
Chacombe	28	Q 27
Chadderton	43	N 23
Chaddesden	36	P 25
Chadlington	28	P 28
Chadwell St. Mary	22	V 29
Chagford	4	I 31
Chailey	11	T 31
Chàirn Bhain (Loch a')	84	E 9
Chalfont St. Giles	21	S 29
Chalfont St. Peter	21	S 29
Chalford	19	N 28
Chalgrove	20	Q 29
Challacombe	7	I 30
Challoch	52	G 19
Challock	22	W 30
Chambercombe Manor	17	H 30
Chandler's Ford	10	P 31
Channel Islands	5	
Chapel Brampton	28	R 27
Chapel-en-le-Frith	43	O 24
Chapel Haddlesey	44	Q 22
Chapel le Dale	49	M 21
Chapel St. Leonards	45	V 24
Chapel Stile	48	K 20
Chapelhall	61	I 16
Chapelknowe	54	K 18
Chapelton	60	H 16
Chapeltown *Moray*	74	K 12
Chapeltown *Sheffield*	43	P 23
Chapmanslade	19	N 30
Chard	8	L 31

Chardstock	8	L 31
Charfield	19	M 29
Charing	22	W 30
Charlbury	28	P 28
Charlecote *Park*	27	P 27
Charleston *Manor*	12	U 31
Charlestown *Restormel*	3	F 33
Charlton	19	N 29
Charlton Horethorne	8	M 30
Charlton Kings	27	N 28
Charlton Marshall	9	N 31
Charlton Musgrove	9	M 30
Charlton on Otmoor	20	Q 28
Charlwood	11	T 30
Charminster	8	M 31
Charmouth	5	L 31
Charney Basset	20	P 29
Charsfield	31	X 27
Chartham	23	X 30
Chartridge	21	S 28
Chartwell	21	U 30
Chastleton	27	P 28
Chatburn	42	M 22
Chatham	22	V 29
Chatsworth House	43	P 24
Chatteris	29	U 26
Chatto	62	M 17
Chatton	63	O 17
Chawleigh	7	I 31
Cheadle *Gtr. Mches.*	43	N 23
Cheadle *Staffs.*	35	O 25
Checkendon	20	Q 29
Cheddar	18	L 30
Cheddar Gorge	18	L 30
Cheddington	21	S 28
Cheddleton	35	N 24
Chedington	8	L 31
Chedworth	19	O 28
Cheese Bay	76	Y 11
Chelford	42	N 24
Chellaston	36	P 25
Chelmarsh	27	M 26
Chelmsford	22	V 28
Cheltenham	27	N 28
Chelveston	29	S 27
Chelwood Gate	11	U 30
Chepstow / Cas-Gwent	18	L 29
Cherhill	19	O 29
Cherington *Cotswold*	19	N 28
Cherington *Stratford-on-Avon*	27	P 27
Cheriton	10	Q 30
Cheriton Bishop	4	I 31
Cheriton Fitzpaine	7	J 31
Cherry Burton	44	S 22
Chertsey	21	S 29
Cherwell (River)	28	Q 28
Cheselbourne	9	M 31
Chesham	21	S 28
Chesham Bois	21	S 28
Cheshunt	21	T 28
Chesil Beach	8	M 32
Cheslyn Hay	35	N 26
Chester	34	L 24
Chester-le-Street	56	P 19
Chesterfield	43	P 24
Chesters	62	M 17
Chesters Fort	55	N 18
Chesterton *Cambridge*	29	U 27
Chesterton *Cherwell*	28	Q 28
Cheswardine	35	M 25
Cheswick	63	O 16
Cheviot (The)	63	N 17
Cheviot Hills (The)	62	M 17
Chew Magna	18	M 29
Chew Stoke	18	M 29
Chewton Mendip	18	M 30
Chicheley	29	R 27
Chichester	10	R 31
Chickerell	5	M 32
Chicklade	9	N 30
Chiddingfold	11	S 30
Chiddingly	12	U 31
Chiddingstone	22	U 30
Chideock	5	L 31
Chieveley	20	Q 29
Chigwell	21	U 29
Chilcompton	18	M 30
Child Okeford	9	N 31
Childrey	20	P 29
Child's Ercall	34	M 25
Chilham	22	W 30
Chillingham	63	O 17
Chilmark	9	N 30
Chiltern Hills	20	R 29
Chilton *Sedgefield*	56	P 20

Chilton *Vale of White Horse*	20	Q 29
Chilton Folia	20	P 29
Chippenham *East Cambridgeshire*	30	V 27
Chippenham *North Wiltshire*	19	N 29
Chipping	42	M 22
Chipping Campden	27	O 27
Chipping Norton	28	P 28
Chipping Ongar	22	U 28
Chipping Sodbury	19	M 29
Chipping Warden	28	Q 27
Chirbury	34	K 26
Chirk	34	K 25
Chirk Castle	34	K 25
Chirmorie	52	F 18
Chirnside	63	N 16
Chirton	19	O 30
Chiseldon	19	O 29
Chislet	23	X 30
Chiswell Green	21	S 28
Chitterne	19	N 30
Chittlehamholt	7	I 31
Chittlehampton	7	I 30
Chobham	21	S 29
Choire (Loch)	84	H 9
Cholderton	9	O 30
Cholesbury	21	S 28
Chollerton	55	N 18
Cholsey	20	Q 29
Chon (Loch)	67	G 15
Chopwell	56	O 19
Chorley	42	M 23
Chorleywood	21	S 29
Christchurch *Christchurch*	9	O 31
Christchurch *Fenland*	38	U 26
Christian Malford	19	N 29
Christleton	34	L 24
Christmas Common	20	R 29
Christow	4	J 32
Chroisg (Loch a')	78	E 11
Chudleigh	4	J 32
Chulmleigh	7	I 31
Church	42	M 22
Church Crookham	20	R 30
Church Eaton	35	N 25
Church Enstone	28	P 28
Church Fenton	44	Q 22
Church Knowle	9	N 32
Church Leigh	35	O 25
Church Lench	27	O 27
Church Minshull	34	M 24
Church Stoke	34	K 26
Church Stretton	34	L 26
Churcham	19	M 28
Churchdown	27	N 28
Churchill *North Somerset*	18	L 29
Churchill *Oxon.*	27	P 28
Churchingford	8	K 31
Churnet	35	N 24
Churnsike Lodge	55	M 18
Churston Ferrers	4	J 32
Churt	10	R 30
Chwilog	32	H 25
Cifynydd	17	K 29
Cilcain	34	K 24
Cilcennin	25	H 27
Cilgerran	15	G 27
Cilmery	25	J 27
Cilrhedyn	15	G 28
Cilybebyll	17	I 28
Cilycwn	25	I 27
Cinderford	18	M 28
Cirencester	19	O 28
City of London *London Borough*	21	T 29
Clachaig	66	E 16
Clachan *Argyl*	66	F 15
Clachan *Kintyre*	59	D 16
Clachan Mòr	70	Z 14
Clachan of Campsie	67	H 16
Clachan of Glendaruel	65	E 15
Clachtoll	83	E 9
Clackavoid	74	J 13
Clackmannan	67	I 15
Clacton-on-Sea	23	X 28
Claggain Bay	58	B 16
Claggan	71	C 14
Claidh (Loch)	82	A 10
Claigan	77	A 11
Claines	27	N 27
Clandon Park	21	S 30
Clanfield	10	Q 31
Claonel	84	G 9
Clapham *Beds.*	29	S 27
Clapham *North Yorks.*	49	M 21
Clapton-in-Gordano	18	L 29

A B C D E F G H I J K L M N O P Q R S T U V W X Y Z

A B C D E F G H I J K L M N O P Q R S T U V W X Y Z

Clàr (Loch nan) .... 85 H 9
Clarbeston Road .... 24 F 28
Clare .... 30 V 27
Clashindarroch .... 80 L 11
Clashmore .... 79 H 10
Clashnessie .... 84 E 9
Clatt .... 80 L 12
Clatteringshaws (Loch) .... 53 H 18
Clauchlands Point .... 59 E 17
Clavering .... 29 U 28
Claverley .... 27 N 26
Claverton Manor .... 19 N 29
Clawdd-newydd .... 33 J 24
Clawton .... 6 G 31
Claxton Ryedale .... 50 R 21
Claxton South Norfolk .... 39 Y 26
Clay Cross .... 36 P 24
Claydon .... 31 X 27
Claydon House .... 28 R 28
Claypole .... 36 R 24
Clayton .... 11 T 31
Clayton-le-Moors .... 42 M 22
Clayton West .... 43 P 23
Cleadale .... 71 B 13
Cleadon .... 57 P 19
Cleat .... 70 X 12
Cleator Moor .... 47 J 20
Cleckheaton .... 43 O 22
Cleedownton .... 26 M 26
Cleehill .... 26 M 26
Cleethorpes .... 45 T 23
Cleeve Abbey .... 7 J 30
Cleeve Prior .... 27 O 27
Clehonger .... 26 L 27
Cleigh .... 65 D 14
Clenchwarton .... 38 V 25
Clent .... 27 N 26
Cleobury Mortimer .... 26 M 26
Cleobury North .... 26 M 26
Clephanton .... 79 I 11
Clevedon .... 18 L 29
Clevedon-Court .... 18 L 29
Cleveland Hills .... 50 Q 20
Cleveleys .... 42 K 22
Cley Next the Sea .... 38 X 25
Cliburn .... 55 M 20
Cliffe Edway .... 22 V 29
Cliffe Selby .... 44 R 22
Clifton
    City of Nottingham .... 36 Q 25
Clifton Eden .... 55 L 20
Clifton
    Rugby .... 28 Q 26
Clifton Hampden .... 20 Q 29
Clifton-upon-Teme .... 27 M 27
Clipston .... 28 R 26
Clisham .... 82 Z 10
Clitheroe .... 42 M 22
Clive .... 34 L 25
Cliveden House .... 21 R 29
Clocaenog .... 33 J 24
Clocaenog Forest .... 33 J 24
Clola .... 81 O 11
Clophill .... 29 S 27
Clopton .... 29 S 26
Closeburn .... 53 I 18
Clotton .... 34 L 24
Clouds Hill .... 9 N 31
Cloughton .... 51 S 20
Clova .... 74 K 13
Clova (Glen) .... 74 K 13
Clove Lodge .... 49 N 20
Clovelly .... 6 G 31
Clovenfords .... 62 L 17
Clovulin .... 72 E 13
Clowne .... 44 Q 24
Cluanie Loch .... 72 E 12
Cluanie Lodge .... 72 E 12
Clumber Park .... 44 Q 24
Clun .... 26 K 26
Clunbury .... 26 L 26
Clunes Forest .... 72 F 13
Clungunford .... 26 L 26
Clunie .... 68 J 14
Clutton .... 18 M 30
Clwydian Range .... 34 K 24
Clydach .... 17 I 28
Clyde (Firth of) .... 59 F 17
Clyde (River) .... 61 J 17
Clydebank .... 60 G 16
Clydesdale .... 61 I 16
Clyffe Pypard .... 19 O 29
Clynnog-Fawr .... 32 G 24
Clyro .... 26 K 27
Clyst Honiton .... 4 J 31
Clyst Hydon .... 7 J 31
Clytha .... 18 L 28
Clywedog Resr. .... 25 J 26

Coalburn .... 61 I 17
Coaley .... 19 N 28
Coalville .... 36 P 25
Coast .... 78 D 10
Coatbridge .... 60 H 16
Coates .... 19 N 28
Cobham .... 21 S 30
Cock Bridge .... 74 K 12
Cockayne .... 50 Q 20
Cockburnspath .... 69 M 16
Cockenzie and Port Seton .. 69 L 16
Cockerham .... 48 L 22
Cockermouth .... 54 J 20
Cockfield Babergh .... 30 W 27
Cockfield Teesdale .... 56 O 20
Cocking .... 10 R 31
Cockleford .... 19 N 28
Cockshutt .... 34 L 25
Coddington .... 36 R 24
Codford St. Mary .... 9 N 30
Codicote .... 21 T 28
Codnor .... 36 P 24
Codsall .... 35 N 26
Coe (Glen) .... 72 F 14
Coed y Brenin Forest ...... 33 I 25
Coedpoeth .... 34 K 24
Coggeshall .... 30 W 28
Coigach .... 84 E 10
Coignafearn .... 73 H 12
Coignafearn Forest .... 73 H 12
Coille Mhorgil .... 72 E 12
Colaboll .... 84 G 9
Colbost .... 77 A 11
Colby Eden .... 55 M 20
Colby Isle of Man .... 46 F 21
Colchester .... 30 W 28
Cold Ash .... 20 Q 29
Cold Ashby .... 28 Q 26
Cold Ashton .... 19 M 29
Cold Fell .... 55 M 19
Cold Norton .... 22 W 28
Coldbackie .... 84 G 8
Colden Common .... 10 Q 31
Coldingham .... 63 N 16
Coldstream .... 63 N 17
Colebrooke .... 7 I 31
Coleford Glos. .... 18 M 28
Coleford Somerset .... 18 M 30
Colemere .... 34 L 25
Coleorton .... 36 P 25
Coleshill
    North Warwickshire .... 27 O 26
Coleshill
    Vale of White Horse .. 19 P 29
Colgrave Sound .... 87 R 2
Colkirk .... 38 W 25
Coll Argyll and Bute ...... 71 A 14
Coll Eilean Siar .... 83 B 9
Colliery Row .... 56 P 19
Collieston .... 81 O 11
Collin .... 53 J 18
Collingbourne Ducis .... 19 P 30
Collingbourne Kingston .... 19 P 30
Collingham Notts. .... 36 R 24
Collingham West Yorks. .... 50 P 22
Collington .... 26 M 27
Collyweston .... 37 S 26
Colmonell .... 52 F 18
Coln (River) .... 19 O 28
Colnabaichin .... 74 K 12
Colne .... 43 N 22
Colne (River) .... 22 X 28
Colonsay .... 64 B 15
Colpy .... 81 M 11
Colsterworth .... 37 S 25
Coltishall .... 39 Y 25
Colwall Stone .... 27 M 27
Colwinston .... 17 J 29
Colwyn Bay / Bae Colwyn .. 41 I 23
Colyton .... 5 K 31
Combe Florey .... 8 K 30
Combe Martin .... 17 H 30
Combe-St. Nicholas .... 8 L 31
Combeinteignhead .... 4 J 32
Comberton .... 29 U 27
Combwich .... 8 K 30
Come-to-Good .... 2 E 33
Compton Berks. .... 20 Q 29
Compton Guildford .... 21 S 30
Compton West Sussex ...... 10 R 31
Compton Abdale .... 19 O 28
Compton Basset .... 19 O 29
Compton Castle .... 4 J 32
Compton Dando .... 18 M 29
Compton Wynyates .... 28 P 27
Comrie .... 67 I 14
Cona Glen .... 72 D 13

Conchra .... 65 E 15
Condicote .... 27 O 28
Condover .... 34 L 26
Congleton .... 35 N 24
Congresbury .... 18 L 29
Coningsby .... 37 T 24
Conington .... 29 T 26
Conisbrough .... 44 Q 23
Coniston .... 48 K 20
Connah's Quay .... 42 K 24
Connel .... 65 D 14
Connel Park .... 60 H 17
Conon Bridge .... 79 G 11
Consett .... 56 O 19
Constantine Bay .... 2 E 32
Contin .... 79 G 11
Convinth (Glen) .... 79 G 11
Conway Falls .... 33 I 24
Conwy .... 41 I 23
Conwy (River) .... 33 I 24
Conwy (Vale of) .... 33 I 24
Cooden Beach .... 12 V 31
Cookham .... 21 R 29
Copthorne .... 11 T 30
Coquet (River) .... 63 N 17
Corbridge .... 55 N 19
Corby .... 28 R 26
Corby Glen .... 37 S 25
Corfe Castle .... 9 N 32
Corfe Mullen .... 9 N 31
Corgarff Castle .... 74 K 12
Corhampton .... 10 Q 31
Cornforth .... 56 P 19
Cornhill .... 81 L 11
Cornhill-on-Tweed .... 63 N 17
Cornwood .... 4 I 32
Cornworthy .... 4 J 32
Corpach .... 72 E 13
Corpusty .... 39 X 25
Corran .... 72 E 13
Corrany .... 46 G 21
Corrie .... 59 E 17
Corrie Common .... 54 K 18
Corrimony .... 78 F 11
Corringham Thurrock ...... 22 V 29
Corringham West Lindsey .. 44 R 23
Corris .... 33 I 26
Corry .... 77 C 12
Corryvreckan (Gulf of) .... 65 C 15
Corscombe .... 8 L 31
Corsham .... 19 N 29
Corsham Court .... 19 N 29
Corsley Heath .... 19 N 30
Corsock .... 53 I 18
Corstopitum .... 55 N 19
Corton .... 9 N 30
Corwen .... 33 J 25
Cosby .... 36 Q 26
Cosham .... 10 Q 31
Costessey .... 39 X 26
Cot-town .... 81 N 11
Cotehill .... 55 L 19
Cotgrave .... 36 R 24
Cotham .... 36 R 24
Cotherstone .... 49 O 20
Cothi River .... 25 H 28
Coton .... 29 U 27
Cotswold Wildlife Park .... 19 O 28
Cottenham .... 29 U 27
Cottered .... 29 T 28
Cottesmore .... 37 S 25
Cottingham
    East Riding of Yorks. .. 45 S 22
Cottingham Northants. .... 28 R 26
Cottisford .... 28 Q 27
Cottonshopeburn Foot ...... 62 M 18
Coulags .... 78 D 11
Coulport .... 66 F 15
Coulter .... 61 J 17
Coundon .... 56 P 20
Countesthorpe .... 36 Q 26
Coupar Angus .... 68 K 14
Coustonn .... 66 E 16
Cove Argyll and Bute ...... 66 F 15
Cove Highland .... 78 C 10
Cove Bay .... 75 N 12
Coverack .... 2 E 33
Cow Honeybourne .... 27 O 27

Cowal .... 65 E 15
Cowan Bridge .... 48 M 21
Cowbit .... 37 T 25
Cowbridge / Bont-faen .... 17 J 29
Cowdenbeath .... 68 J 15
Cowdray House .... 10 R 31
Cowes Isle of Wight ...... 10 Q 31
Cowfold .... 11 T 31
Cowie .... 67 I 15
Cowling .... 43 N 22
Cowplain .... 10 Q 31
Coxheath .... 22 V 30
Coxwold .... 50 Q 21
Coylton .... 60 G 17
Coylumbridge .... 74 I 12
Crackington Haven .... 6 G 31
Crafthole .... 3 H 32
Cragside Gardens .... 63 O 18
Crai .... 25 J 28
Craig .... 78 E 11
Craig Lodge .... 65 E 16
Craig-y-nos .... 17 I 28
Craigdarroch .... 60 H 18
Craigellachie .... 80 K 11
Craigencallie .... 53 G 18
Craigendoran .... 66 F 16
Craigens .... 58 B 16
Craighead .... 69 M 15
Craighouse .... 58 C 16
Craigie .... 60 G 17
Craigievar Castle .... 75 L 12
Craigmalloch .... 53 G 18
Craignish (Loch) .... 65 D 15
Craignure .... 65 C 14
Craigrothie .... 69 L 15
Craigton .... 74 K 14
Craik .... 62 K 17
Crail .... 69 M 15
Crailing .... 62 M 17
Crailinghall .... 62 M 17
Crakaig .... 85 I 9
Cramlington .... 56 P 18
Cramond .... 68 K 16
Cranborne .... 9 O 31
Cranbrook .... 12 V 30
Crane Moor .... 43 P 23
Cranford St. John .... 29 S 26
Cranleigh .... 11 S 30
Cranmore .... 18 M 30
Cranshaws .... 62 M 16
Cranstal .... 46 G 20
Cranwell .... 37 S 24
Cranworth .... 38 W 26
Crask Inn .... 84 G 9
Craster .... 63 P 17
Crathes Castle .... 75 M 12
Crathie .... 74 K 12
Crathorne .... 50 Q 20
Craven Arms .... 26 L 26
Crawcrook .... 56 O 19
Crawford .... 61 J 17
Crawfordjohn .... 61 I 17
Crawick .... 61 I 17
Crawley Hants. .... 10 P 30
Crawley West Sussex ...... 11 T 30
Crawley Down .... 11 T 30
Creag Meagaidh .... 73 G 13
Creagan .... 65 E 14
Creagorry .... 76 Y 11
Creake South .... 38 W 25
Credenhill .... 26 L 27
Crediton .... 7 J 31
Creech St. Michael .... 8 K 30
Creetown .... 53 G 19
Creggans .... 66 E 15
Creran (Loch) .... 65 D 14
Cressage .... 34 M 26
Cresswell Castle Morpeth .. 56 P 18
Cresswell Pembrokeshire /
    Sir Benfro .... 15 F 28
Creswell .... 44 Q 24
Cruden Bay .... 81 O 11
Crewe .... 35 M 24
Crewkerne .... 8 L 31
Crianlarich .... 66 G 14
Cribyn .... 15 H 27
Criccieth .... 33 H 25
Crich .... 36 P 24
Crichton .... 62 L 16
Crick .... 28 Q 26
Crickadarn .... 25 K 27
Cricket St. Thomas .... 8 L 31
Crickhowell .... 26 K 28
Crickley Hill .... 19 N 28
Cricklade .... 19 O 29
Crieff .... 67 I 14

Crimond .... 81 O 11
Crimplesham .... 38 V 26
Crinan .... 65 D 15
Crinan (Loch) .... 65 D 15
Cringleford .... 39 X 26
Croachy .... 79 H 12
Crocketford .... 53 I 18
Crockham Hill .... 21 U 30
Croes-goch .... 14 E 28
Croesyceiliog .... 18 L 29
Croft Herefordshire ...... 26 L 27
Croft Richmondshire ...... 50 P 20
Croft-on-Tees .... 50 P 20
Crofty .... 15 H 29
Croggan .... 65 C 14
Croglin .... 55 M 19
Croick .... 79 G 10
Croig .... 71 B 14
Cromalt Hills .... 84 E 9
Cromar .... 74 L 12
Cromarty .... 79 H 10
Cromarty Bay .... 79 H 10
Cromarty Firth .... 79 H 11
Cromdale .... 80 J 11
Cromdale (Hills of) .... 80 J 12
Cromer .... 39 X 25
Cromford .... 35 P 24
Cromore .... 82 A 9
Cromra .... 73 G 13
Crondall .... 20 R 30
Cronk (The) .... 46 G 21
Crook South Lakeland .... 48 L 20
Crook Wear Valley .... 56 O 19
Crook of Devon .... 68 J 15
Crookham .... 63 N 17
Crookham Village .... 20 R 30
Crooklands .... 48 L 21
Cropredy .... 28 Q 27
Cropston .... 36 Q 25
Cropwell Bishop .... 36 R 25
Crosby Allerdale .... 54 J 19
Crosby Isle of Man .... 46 G 21
Crosby Sefton .... 42 K 23
Crosby Ravensworth ...... 48 M 20
Croscombe .... 18 M 30
Cross .... 83 B 8
Cross Fell .... 55 M 19
Cross Hands .... 15 H 28
Cross Inn .... 25 H 27
Crossaig .... 59 D 16
Crossapol .... 64 Z 14
Crossbost .... 82 A 9
Crossford .... 61 I 16
Crossgates .... 68 J 15
Crossgill .... 48 L 21
Crosshill Fife .... 68 K 15
Crosshill South Ayrshire .. 60 G 18
Crosshouse .... 60 G 17
Crosskeys .... 18 K 29
Crosskirk .... 85 J 8
Crossmichael .... 53 I 19
Crossraguel Abbey .... 60 F 18
Crossways .... 9 N 31
Croston .... 42 L 23
Crouch (River) .... 22 W 29
Croughton .... 28 Q 28
Crow Hill .... 26 M 28
Crowborough .... 12 U 30
Crowcombe .... 8 K 30
Crowhurst .... 12 V 31
Crowland .... 37 T 25
Crowle Doncaster .... 44 R 23
Crowle Wychavon .... 27 N 27
Crowlin Island .... 77 C 11
Crowmarsh Gifford .... 20 Q 29
Crowthorne .... 20 R 29
Croxley Green .... 21 S 29
Croxton .... 30 W 26
Croxton Kerrial .... 36 R 25
Croy .... 79 H 11
Croyde .... 6 H 30
Croydon London Borough .. 21 T 29
Cruden Bay .... 81 O 11
Crudgington .... 34 M 25
Crudwell .... 19 N 29
Crug-y-bar .... 25 I 27
Crulivig .... 82 Z 9
Crymmych .... 15 G 28
Crynant .... 17 I 28
Cuaig .... 77 C 11
Cubbington .... 28 P 27
Cubert .... 2 E 32
Cuckfield .... 11 T 30
Cucklington .... 9 M 30
Cuckney .... 44 Q 24
Cuddington Aylesbury .... 20 R 28
Cuddington Vale Royal .. 42 M 24

Cudworth .... 43 P 23
Cuffley .... 21 T 28
Cuhxham .... 20 Q 29
Cuilicudden .... 79 H 11
Cuillin Sound .... 71 B 12
Cuillin (The) .... 77 B 12
Culbokie .... 79 G 11
Culdrose .... 2 E 33
Culgaith .... 55 M 20
Culkein .... 83 D 9
Cullen .... 80 L 10
Cullen Bay .... 80 L 10
Cullingworth .... 43 O 22
Cullipool .... 65 D 15
Culloch .... 67 I 14
Cullompton .... 7 J 31
Culmington .... 26 L 26
Culmstock .... 8 K 31
Culnacraig .... 84 E 10
Culrain .... 79 G 10
Culross .... 68 J 15
Culshabbin .... 52 G 19
Culswic .... 87 P 3
Culter Fell .... 61 J 17
Cults .... 75 N 12
Culzean Castle .... 59 F 17
Cumbernauld .... 67 I 16
Cumbrian Moutains .... 48 K 20
Cuminestown .... 81 N 11
Cummersdale .... 54 L 19
Cummertrees .... 54 J 19
Cumnock .... 60 H 17
Cumnor .... 20 P 28
Cumwhitton .... 55 L 19
Cunninghamhead .... 60 G 17
Cupar .... 69 K 15
Curbridge .... 20 P 28
Curdridge .... 10 Q 31
Currie .... 61 K 16
Curry Rivel .... 8 L 30
Cutcloy .... 53 G 19
Cutnall green .... 27 N 27
Cuxton .... 22 V 29
Cwm .... 18 K 28
Cwm Bychan .... 33 H 25
Cwm Taf .... 17 J 28
Cwmafan .... 17 I 29
Cwmaman .... 17 J 28
Cwmbach Carmarthenshire /
    Sir Gaerfyrddin ...... 15 G 28
Cwmbach Powys / Powys .. 25 J 27
Cwmbach Rhondda, Cynon, Taf /
    Rhondda, Cynon, Taff 17 J 28
Cwmbrân .... 18 L 29
Cwmcarn .... 18 K 29
Cwmcoy .... 15 G 27
Cwmllynfell .... 17 I 28
Cwmystwyth .... 25 I 26
Cwnduad .... 15 G 28
Cwnfelin Boeth .... 15 G 28
Cwrt-Newydd .... 15 H 27
Cydweli / Kidwelly .... 15 H 28
Cyffylliog .... 33 J 24
Cymmer .... 17 J 29
Cymyran Bay .... 40 G 23
Cynwyl Elfed .... 15 G 28

D

Dacre Eden .... 55 L 20
Dacre Harrogate .... 49 O 21
Daglingworth .... 19 N 28
Daily .... 60 F 18
Daimh (Loch an) .... 73 G 14
Dairsie or Osnaburgh .... 69 L 14
Dalavich .... 65 E 15
Dalbeattie .... 53 I 19
Dalbeg .... 73 H 12
Dalby .... 46 F 21
Dalblair .... 60 H 17
Dalchalloch .... 73 H 13
Dalchruin .... 67 H 15
Dale .... 14 E 28
Dale Head .... 48 L 20
Dalgonar .... 60 H 18
Dalham .... 30 V 27
Dalhavaig .... 85 I 8
Daliburgh .... 76 X 12
Dalkeith .... 61 K 16
Dallas .... 80 J 11
Dalleagles .... 60 H 17
Dallington Northampton .. 28 R 27
Dallington Rother .... 12 V 31
Dalmally .... 66 F 14
Dalmellington .... 60 G 18
Dalmeny .... 68 J 16
Dalmigavie .... 73 H 12
Dalnabreck .... 71 C 13

Dalnaspidal Lodge ....73 H 13
Dalnavaid ....74 J 13
Dalnavie ....79 H 10
Dalness ....72 F 14
Dalry
  Dumfries and Galloway ....53 H 18
Dalry North Ayrshire ....60 F 16
Dalrymple ....60 G 17
Dalston ....54 L 19
Dalswinton ....53 I 18
Dalton
  Dumfries and Galloway ....54 J 18
Dalton North Yorks. ....50 P 21
Dalton in Furness ....47 K 21
Damerham ....9 O 31
Damh (Loch) ....78 D 11
Dan-yr-Ogof ....17 I 28
Danbury ....22 V 28
Danby ....50 R 20
Dane ....35 N 24
Danehill ....11 U 30
Darenth ....22 U 29
Darfield ....43 P 23
Darlington ....50 P 20
Darowen ....33 I 26
Darras Hall ....56 O 18
Darrington ....44 Q 22
Darsham ....31 Y 27
Dartford ....22 U 29
Dartford Tunnel ....22 U 29
Dartington ....4 I 32
Dartmeet ....4 I 32
Dartmoor National Park ....4 I 32
Dartmouth ....4 J 32
Darton ....43 P 23
Darvel ....60 H 17
Darwen ....42 M 22
Datchet ....21 S 29
Datchworth ....29 T 28
Dava ....80 J 11
Daventry ....28 Q 27
Davidstow ....6 G 32
Davington ....61 K 18
Daviot ....79 H 11
Dawley ....34 M 26
Dawlish ....4 J 32
Deal ....23 Y 30
Dean ....54 J 20
Dean Forest Park ....18 M 28
Deanich Lodge ....78 F 10
Deanston ....67 H 15
Dearham ....54 J 19
Debden ....30 U 28
Deben (River) ....31 X 27
Debenham ....31 X 27
Deddington ....28 Q 28
Dedham ....30 W 28
Dee / Afon Dyfrdwy (River)
  Wales ....41 K 23
Dee (River) Scotland ....75 N 12
Dee (River) / Afon Dyfrdwy ..34 K 24
Deene ....29 S 26
Deepcut ....21 R 30
Deepdale ....49 M 21
Deeping-St. James ....37 T 25
Deeping St. Nicholas ....37 T 25
Deeps (The) ....87 P 3
Defford ....27 N 27
Deiniolen ....33 H 24
Delabole ....6 F 32
Delamere ....34 M 24
Delamere Forest ....42 L 24
Dell ....83 B 8
Dellifure ....80 J 11
Delnadamph Lodge ....74 K 12
Delph ....43 N 23
Denbigh / Dinbych ....33 J 24
Denby Dale ....43 P 23
Denchworth ....20 P 29
Denham ....21 S 29
Denholm ....62 L 17
Denmead ....10 Q 31
Dennington ....31 Y 27
Denny ....67 I 15
Dent ....49 M 21
Denton South Kesteven ......36 R 25
Denton Stockport ....43 N 23
Denver ....38 V 26
Derby ....36 P 25
Deri ....18 K 28
Dersingham ....38 V 25
Dervaig ....71 B 14
Derwent (River) R. Ouse .....44 R 22
Derwent (River) R. Trent .....36 P 24
Derwent (River) R. Tyne ......56 O 19
Derwent Dale ....43 O 23
Derwent Reservoir Derbs. ..43 O 23

Derwent Reservoir
  Northumb. ....56 N 19
Derwent Water ....54 K 20
Desborough ....28 R 26
Desford ....36 Q 26
Detling ....22 V 30
Devauden ....18 L 28
Deveron (River) ....81 M 11
Devil's Beef Tub ....61 J 17
Devil's Bridge / Pontarfynach 25 I 26
Devil's Elbow ....74 J 13
Devil's Punch Bowl ....10 R 30
Devizes ....19 O 29
Devonport ....3 H 32
Dewsbury ....43 P 22
Dherue (Loch an) ....84 G 8
Dial Post ....11 S 31
Dickleburgh ....31 X 26
Didcot ....20 Q 29
Diddlebury ....26 L 26
Digby ....37 S 24
Dilhorne ....35 N 25
Dilton Marsh ....19 N 30
Dilwyn ....26 L 27
Dinas ....24 F 27
Dinas Dinlle ....32 G 24
Dinas Head ....24 F 27
Dinas-Mawddwy ....33 I 25
Dinas Powys ....18 K 29
Dinbych / Denbigh ....33 J 24
Dinbych-y-pysgod / Tenby ..15 F 28
Dingwall ....79 G 11
Dinnet ....74 L 12
Dinnington
  Newcastle upon Tyne ....56 O 18
Dinnington Rotherham ....44 Q 23
Dinsdale ....50 P 20
Dinton ....9 O 30
Diptford ....4 I 32
Dirleton ....69 L 15
Dishforth ....50 P 21
Diss ....31 X 26
Disserth ....25 J 27
Distington ....53 J 20
Ditcheat ....8 M 30
Ditchingham ....31 Y 26
Ditchley Park ....28 P 28
Ditchling ....11 T 31
Ditton Priors ....26 M 26
Doc Penfro /
  Pembroke Dock ....16 F 28
Docherty (Glen) ....78 E 11
Dochgarroch ....79 H 11
Docking ....38 V 25
Dockray ....54 L 20
Dodburn ....62 L 17
Doddington Cambs. ....29 U 26
Doddington Kent ....22 W 30
Doddington Lincs. ....44 S 24
Doddington Northumb. ....63 O 17
Dodington ....19 M 29
Dodman Point ....3 F 33
Dodworth ....43 P 23
Doirlinn ....71 C 13
Dolanog ....33 J 25
Dolbenmaen ....33 H 25
Dolfor ....26 K 26
Dolgarrog ....33 I 24
Dolgellau ....33 I 25
Dolgoch Falls ....33 I 26
Dollar ....67 I 15
Dolphinholme ....48 L 22
Dolton ....7 H 31
Don (River) R. Ouse ....44 R 22
Don (River) R. Spey ....74 K 12
Doncaster ....44 Q 23
Donhead-St. Andrew ....9 N 30
Donhead-St. Mary ....9 N 30
Donington ....37 T 25
Donington-on-Bain ....45 T 24
Donington Park Circuit ....36 P 25
Donisthorpe ....36 P 25
Donnington Berks. ....20 Q 29
Donnington Salop ....35 M 25
Donyatt ....8 L 31
Doon (Loch) ....60 G 18
Dorback Lodge ....74 J 12
Dorchester Dorset ....8 M 31
Dorchester Oxon. ....20 Q 29
Dordon ....35 P 26
Dore ....43 P 24
Dores ....79 H 11
Dorking ....21 T 30
Dormansland ....11 U 30
Dormanstown ....57 Q 20
Dornie ....78 D 12
Dornoch ....79 H 10

Dornoch Firth ....79 H 10
Dornock ....54 K 19
Dorrington ....34 L 26
Dorstone ....26 K 27
Dorusduain ....78 D 12
Douchary (Glen) ....78 F 10
Dougarie ....59 D 17
Douglas Isle of Man ....46 G 21
Douglas
  South Lanarkshire ....61 I 17
Douglastown ....74 L 14
Dounby ....86 K 6
Doune Highland ....84 G 10
Doune Stirling ....67 H 15
Dove (River) ....35 O 24
Dove Cottage ....48 K 20
Dove Holes ....43 O 24
Dovedale ....35 O 24
Dover ....13 X 30
Dovercourt ....31 X 28
Doveridge ....35 O 25
Dovey / Dyfi (River) ....33 I 26
Dowally ....74 J 14
Dowdeswell ....27 N 28
Dowlish Wake ....8 L 31
Down Ampney ....19 O 28
Downderry ....3 G 32
Downham ....30 U 26
Downham Market ....38 V 26
Downies ....75 N 12
Downton ....9 O 31
Dowsby ....37 S 25
Doynton ....19 M 29
Drakes Broughton ....27 N 27
Draughton ....49 O 22
Drax ....44 R 22
Draycott ....36 P 25
Draycott-in-the-Clay ....35 O 25
Draycott-in-the-Moors ....35 N 25
Drayton Norfolk ....39 X 25
Drayton Oxon. ....20 Q 29
Drayton-St. Leonard ....20 Q 29
Drefach near Carmarthen ...15 H 28
Drefach
  near Newcastle-Emlyn .....15 G 27
Dreghorn ....60 G 17
Drem ....69 L 15
Drenewydd / Newtown ....26 K 26
Dreswick Point ....46 G 21
Driffield ....19 O 28
Drigg ....47 J 20
Drighlington ....43 P 22
Drimnin ....71 C 14
Drinnishadder ....76 Z 10
Drissaig ....65 E 15
Droitwich ....27 N 27
Dronfield ....43 P 24
Drongan ....60 G 17
Droxford ....10 Q 31
Druidibeg (Loch) ....76 Y 12
Druim a' Chliabhain (Loch) ..85 H 8
Druimindarroch ....71 C 13
Drum Castle ....75 M 12
Drumbeg ....84 E 9
Drumblade ....81 L 11
Drumburgh ....54 K 19
Drumchardine ....79 G 11
Drumclog ....60 H 17
Drumelzier ....61 J 17
Drumfearn ....71 C 12
Drumlanrig Castle ....61 I 18
Drumlemble ....58 C 17
Drumlithie ....75 M 13
Drummond Castle ....67 I 14
Drummore ....52 F 19
Drummossie Muir ....79 H 11
Drumnadrochit ....79 G 11
Drumrunie ....84 E 9
Drumsallie ....72 D 13
Drumtochty Forest ....75 M 13
Druridge Bay ....63 P 18
Drybrook ....18 M 28
Dryburgh Abbey ....62 M 17
Drygarn Fawr ....25 J 27
Drymen ....67 G 15
Drynoch ....77 B 12
Duchally ....84 F 9
Ducklington ....20 P 28
Duddington ....37 S 26
Duddo ....63 N 16
Dudley Dudley ....27 N 26
Dudley North Tyneside ....56 P 18
Duff House ....81 M 11
Dufftown ....80 K 11
Duffus ....80 J 10
Dufton ....55 M 20

Duggleby ....51 S 21
Duich (Loch) ....78 D 12
Duirinish ....77 C 12
Duke's Pass ....67 G 15
Dukinfield ....43 N 23
Dullingham ....30 V 27
Dulnain Bridge ....80 J 12
Duloe ....3 G 32
Dulverton ....7 J 30
Dumbarton ....67 G 16
Dumbleton ....27 O 27
Dumfries ....53 J 18
Dun Carloway Broch ....82 Z 9
Dunan ....66 F 16
Dunbar ....69 M 15
Dunbeath ....85 J 9
Dunblane ....67 I 15
Duncansby Head ....86 K 8
Dunchurch ....28 Q 26
Duncow ....53 J 18
Duncton ....11 S 31
Dundee ....69 K 14
Dundonald ....60 G 17
Dundrennan ....53 I 19
Dundry ....18 M 29
Dunecht ....75 M 12
Dunfermline ....68 J 15
Dungeness ....13 W 31
Dunholme ....44 S 24
Dunino ....69 L 15
Dunipace ....67 I 15
Dunkeld ....68 J 14
Dunkery Beacon ....7 J 30
Dunkeswell ....8 K 31
Dunkirk ....19 N 29
Dunley ....27 N 27
Dunlop ....60 G 16
Dunmaglass Lodge ....79 H 12
Dunnet ....85 J 8
Dunnet Bay ....85 J 8
Dunnet Head ....86 J 7
Dunning ....68 J 15
Dunnington ....50 R 22
Dunnockshaw ....42 N 22
Dunnottar Castle ....75 N 13
Dunoon ....66 F 16
Dunragit ....52 F 19
Dunrobin Castle ....85 I 10
Dunstable ....29 S 28
Dunstaffnage Castel ....65 D 14
Dunstanburgh Castle ....63 P 17
Dunster ....17 J 30
Dunston ....37 S 24
Dunsyre ....61 J 16
Duntelchaig (Loch) ....79 H 11
Dunton bassett ....28 Q 26
Dunure ....59 F 17
Dunvegan ....77 A 11
Dunvegan (Loch) ....77 A 11
Dunvegan Castle ....77 A 11
Dunvegan Head ....76 Z 11
Dunwich ....31 Y 27
Durdle Door ....9 N 32
Durham ....56 P 19
Durisdeer ....61 I 18
Durlston Head ....9 O 32
Durness ....84 F 8
Durrington ....19 O 30
Dursley ....19 M 28
Dury Voe ....87 Q 2
Duston ....28 R 27
Duthil ....79 I 12
Duxford ....29 U 27
Dyce ....75 N 12
Dyfi / Dovey (River) ....33 I 26
Dymchurch ....13 W 30
Dymock ....27 M 28
Dyrham ....19 M 29
Dyserth ....41 J 23

E

Eaglescliffe ....50 P 20
Eaglesfield ....54 K 18
Eaglesham ....60 H 16
Eakring ....36 R 24
Ealing London Borough ....21 T 29
Earba (Lochan na h-) ....73 G 13

Earby ....49 N 22
Eardisley ....26 K 27
Earl Shilton ....36 Q 26
Earl Soham ....31 X 27
Earl Stonham ....31 X 27
Earley Winnersh ....20 R 29
Earlish ....77 A 11
Earls Barton ....28 R 27
Earls Colne ....30 W 28
Earlsferry ....69 L 15
Earlston ....62 L 17
Earn (Loch) ....67 H 14
Earn (River) ....67 J 14
Earsdon ....56 P 18
Earsham ....31 Y 26
Eartham ....11 S 31
Easdale ....65 D 15
Easebourne ....10 R 31
Easington Easington ....57 P 19
Easington
  East Riding of Yorkshire ...45 U 23
Easington
  Redcar and Cleveland .....50 R 20
Easington
  South Oxfordshire ....20 Q 28
Easington Lane ....56 P 19
Easingwold ....50 Q 21
Eassie and Nevay ....68 K 14
East Aberthaw ....17 J 29
East Barkwith ....45 T 24
East Bergholt ....30 X 28
East Brent ....18 L 30
East Budleigh ....5 K 32
East Butterwick ....44 R 23
East-Challow ....20 P 29
East Chinnock ....8 L 31
East-Coker ....8 M 31
East Cowes ....10 Q 31
East Cowton ....50 P 20
East Dereham ....38 W 25
East Ferry ....44 R 23
East Glen (River) ....37 S 25
East Grafton ....19 P 29
East Grinstead ....11 T 30
East Hagbourne ....20 Q 29
East-Halton ....45 T 23
East Hanney ....20 P 29
East Hardwick ....44 Q 23
East Harling ....30 W 26
East Haven ....69 L 14
East Hendred ....20 P 29
East Hoathly ....12 U 31
East Horsley ....21 S 30
East Huntspill ....18 L 30
East Ilsley ....20 Q 29
East Keswick ....50 P 22
East Kilbride Eilean Siar .....70 X 12
East Kilbride
  South Lanarkshire ....60 H 16
East-Knoyle ....9 N 30
East Knoyle ....9 N 30
East Lambrook ....8 L 31
East Leake ....36 Q 25
East Linton ....69 M 16
East Loch Roag ....82 Z 9
East Loch Tarbet ....77 Z 10
East Looe ....3 G 32
East Lulworth ....9 N 32
East-Malling ....22 V 30
East Markham ....44 R 24
East Meon ....10 Q 31
East Mersea ....22 W 28
East Midlands Airport ....36 Q 25
East Moor ....35 P 24
East Norton ....36 R 26
East-Poringland ....39 Y 26
East Portlemouth ....4 I 33
East Rhidorroch Lodge ....78 F 10
East-Rudham ....38 W 25
East-Saltoun ....62 L 16
East Tisted ....10 R 30
East Wemyss ....68 K 15
East-Winch ....38 V 25
East Wittering ....10 R 31
East Witton ....49 O 21
East-Woodhay ....20 P 29
East-Wretham ....30 W 26
Eastbourne ....12 U 31
Eastchurch ....22 W 29
Eastdean ....12 U 31
Easter-Compton ....18 M 29
Easter Ross ....79 G 10
Eastergate ....11 S 31
Eastfield ....51 S 21
Eastgate ....55 N 19
Eastham ....42 L 24
Eastington ....19 N 28

Eastleach ....19 O 28
Eastleigh ....10 P 31
Eastoft ....44 R 23
Easton Carlisle ....55 L 18
Easton Dorset ....8 M 32
Easton Norfolk ....39 X 26
Easton-Grey ....19 N 29
Easton-in-Gordano ....18 L 29
Easton-Royal ....19 O 29
Eastriggs ....54 K 19
Eastrington ....44 R 22
Eastry ....23 X 30
Eastville ....37 U 24
Eastwood ....36 Q 24
Eaton ....34 M 24
Eaton Bray ....29 S 28
Eaton Socon ....29 T 27
Ebbw Vale / Glyn Ebwy ......18 K 28
Ebchester ....56 O 19
Ebrington ....27 O 27
Eccels ....62 M 17
Ecchinswell ....20 Q 29
Ecclefechan ....54 K 18
Eccles ....42 M 23
Eccleshall ....35 N 25
Echt ....75 M 12
Eckford ....62 M 17
Eckington Derbs. ....43 P 24
Eckington Worc. ....27 N 27
Edale ....43 O 23
Eday ....87 L 6
Eddelston ....61 K 16
Edderton ....79 H 10
Eddrachillis Bay ....84 E 9
Eden (River) ....55 M 19
Eden Project ....3 F 32
Edenbridge ....21 U 30
Edentaggart ....66 F 15
Edenthorpe ....44 Q 23
Edgefield ....39 X 25
Edgmond ....35 M 25
Edgton ....26 L 26
Edinbane ....77 A 11
Edinburgh ....68 K 16
Edington ....19 N 30
Edith Weston ....37 S 26
Edlesborough ....29 S 28
Edlingham ....63 O 17
Edmondsley ....56 P 19
Edmundbyers ....56 O 19
Ednalton ....36 Q 25
Edwalton ....36 Q 25
Edwinstowe ....36 Q 24
Edzell ....75 M 13
Efailnewydd ....32 G 25
Egerton ....22 W 30
Eggerness Point ....53 G 19
Eggleston ....56 N 20
Egham ....21 S 29
Egilsay ....87 L 6
Eglingham ....63 O 17
Egloskerry ....6 G 32
Eglwys Brewis ....17 J 29
Eglwysfach ....33 I 26
Eglwyswrw ....15 F 27
Egremont ....47 J 20
Egton ....50 R 20
Eha ....71 B 13
Eigheach (Loch) ....73 G 13
Eight Ash Green ....30 W 28
Eil ....73 I 12
Eil (Loch) ....72 E 13
Eilde Mór (Loch) ....72 F 13
Eilean a' Chalmain ....64 A 15
Eilean Beag ....77 C 11
Eilean Chathastail ....71 B 13
Eilean Donan Castle ....78 D 12
Eilean Flodigarry ....77 B 10
Eilean Mhuire ....82 A 10
Eilean Mòr ....77 C 11
Eilean na Bà ....77 C 11
Eilean nan Each ....71 B 13
Eilean Trodday ....77 B 10
Eileanach Lodge ....79 G 10
Eilt (Loch) ....72 D 13
Eishken ....82 A 9
Eishort (Loch) ....71 C 12
Elan Valley ....25 J 27
Elan Village ....25 J 27
Elcho ....68 J 14
Elgin ....80 K 11
Elgol ....71 B 12
Elie ....69 L 15
Eling ....10 P 31
Elkesley ....44 R 24
Elkstone ....19 N 28

A B C D E F G H I J K L M N O P Q R S T U V W X Y Z

Elland ....43 O 22
Ellastone ....35 O 25
Ellen's Green ....11 S 30
Ellerbeck ....50 P 20
Ellerton ....44 R 22
Ellesmere ....34 L 25
Ellesmere Port ....42 L 24
Ellingham ....31 Y 26
Ellington ....56 P 18
Ellon ....81 N 11
Elloughton ....44 S 22
Elmdon ....29 U 27
Elmley Castle ....27 N 27
Elmore ....19 N 28
Elmstead Market ....30 W 28
Elmswell ....30 W 27
Elphin ....84 E 9
Elrick ....75 N 12
Elrig ....52 G 19
Elsdon ....55 N 18
Elsenham ....30 U 28
Elsham ....45 S 23
Elsrickle ....61 J 16
Elstead ....21 R 30
Elstree ....21 T 29
Elswick ....42 L 22
Eltisley ....29 T 27
Elton ....37 S 26
Elveden ....30 W 26
Elvington ....50 R 22
Elwick ....57 Q 19
Elworth ....35 M 24
Ely ....30 U 26
Emberton ....28 R 27
Embleton *Allerdale* ....54 K 20
Embleton *Alnwick* ....63 P 17
Embo ....79 I 10
Embsay ....49 O 22
Emneth ....37 U 26
Empingham ....37 S 25
Emsworth ....10 R 31
Enaclete ....82 Z 9
Enard Bay ....83 D 9
Enderby ....36 Q 26
Endmoor ....48 L 21
Endon ....35 N 24
Enfield *London Borough* ....21 T 29
Enford ....19 O 30
Englefield Green ....21 S 29
English Bicknor ....18 M 28
Englishcombe ....19 M 29
Enham Alamein ....20 P 30
Enmore ....8 K 30
Ensay ....71 B 14
Enstone ....28 P 28
Enterkinfoot ....61 I 18
Enville ....27 N 26
Eochar ....76 X 11
Eoligarry ....70 X 12
Eoropie ....83 B 8
Eorsa ....65 B 14
Eport (Loch) ....76 Y 11
Epping ....21 U 28
Epping Forest ....21 U 29
Epsom ....21 T 30
Epworth ....44 R 23
Erddig ....34 K 24
Eredine ....65 E 15
Eredine Forest ....65 D 15
Eriboll ....84 F 8
Eriboll (Loch) ....84 F 8
Ericht (Loch) ....73 G 13
Ericstane ....61 J 17
Eridge Green ....12 U 30
Eriska ....65 D 14
Eriskay ....70 Y 12
Erisort (Loch) ....82 A 9
Eriswell ....30 V 26
Erlestoke ....19 N 30
Ermington ....4 I 32
Erpingham ....39 X 25
Erraid ....64 A 15
Errochty (Loch) ....73 H 13
Errogie ....79 G 12
Errol ....68 K 14
Ersary ....70 X 13
Erskine Bridge ....67 G 16
Ervie ....52 E 19
Erwood ....25 K 27
Esh Winning ....56 O 19
Esha Ness ....87 P 2
Esher ....21 S 29
Esk (Glen) ....75 L 13
Esk (River) ....54 K 19
Eskdale ....54 K 18
Eskdalemuir ....61 K 18
Essendon ....21 T 28

Essich ....79 H 11
Eston ....57 Q 20
Etal ....63 N 17
Etchilhampton ....19 O 29
Etchingham ....12 V 30
Etherow (River) ....43 N 23
Etherow Park ....43 N 23
Etive (Glen) ....72 F 14
Etive (Loch) ....65 E 14
Eton ....21 S 29
Ettington ....27 P 27
Ettrick ....61 K 17
Ettrick Forest ....62 K 17
Ettrick Pen ....61 K 17
Etwall ....35 P 25
Euston ....30 W 26
Euxton ....42 L 22
Evanton ....79 G 11
Evelix ....79 H 10
Evenlode ....27 O 28
Evenwood ....56 O 20
Evercreech ....8 M 30
Everingham ....44 R 22
Everleigh ....19 O 30
Evershot ....8 M 31
Eversley ....20 R 29
Everton ....44 R 23
Evesham ....27 O 27
Evesham (Vale of) ....27 O 27
Ewe (Isle of) ....78 D 10
Ewell ....21 T 29
Ewelme ....20 Q 29
Ewenny ....17 J 29
Ewes ....54 L 18
Ewhurst ....11 S 30
Exbourne ....7 I 31
Exe (River) ....7 J 31
Exebridge ....7 J 30
Exeter ....4 J 31
Exford ....7 J 30
Exminster ....4 J 31
Exmoor National Park ....7 I 30
Exmouth ....4 J 32
Exton ....7 J 30
Eyam ....43 O 24
Eye *Cambs.* ....37 T 26
Eye *Suffolk* ....31 X 27
Eye Peninsula ....83 B 9
Eyemouth ....63 N 16
Eynort (Loch) *Highland* ....77 A 12
Eynort (Loch) *Western Isles* ....76 Y 12
Eynsford ....22 U 29
Eynsham ....20 P 28
Eyre Point ....77 B 12
Eythorne ....23 X 30

F

Fada (Loch) ....76 Y 11
Failsworth ....43 N 23
Fair Isle ....87 P 5
Fair Oak ....10 Q 31
Fairbourne ....33 H 25
Fairburn ....44 Q 22
Fairford ....19 O 28
Fairlie ....59 F 16
Fairlight ....12 V 31
Fakenham ....38 W 25
Fala ....62 L 16
Faldingworth ....45 S 23
Falfield ....18 M 29
Falkirk ....67 I 16
Falkland ....68 K 15
Fallford ....54 K 18
Fallin ....67 I 15
Falmer ....11 T 31
Falmouth ....2 E 33
Falstone ....55 M 18
Fanagmore ....84 E 8
Fanmore ....65 B 14
Fannich (Loch) ....78 E 11
Fannich Lodge ....78 F 11
Fara ....86 K 7
Fareham ....10 Q 31
Faringdon ....19 P 29
Farlam ....55 L 19
Farleigh-Hungerford ....19 N 30
Farley ....9 O 30
Farley Mount ....10 P 30
Farlow ....26 M 26
Farmborough ....18 M 29
Farmers ....25 I 27
Farmtown ....80 L 11
Farnborough *Hants.* ....20 R 30
Farnborough *Warw.* ....28 P 27
Farnborough
  West Berkshire ....20 P 29

Farndon *Chester* ....34 L 24
Farndon
  Newark and Sherwood ....36 R 24
Farne Islands ....63 P 17
Farnell ....75 M 13
Farnham *Dorset* ....9 N 31
Farnham *Surrey* ....20 R 30
Farnham Royal ....21 S 29
Farningham ....22 U 29
Farnley ....49 O 22
Farnsfield ....36 Q 24
Farnworth ....42 M 23
Farr ....85 H 8
Farrington Gurney ....18 M 30
Farway ....5 K 31
Fasnakyle ....78 F 12
Fasnakyle Forest ....78 F 11
Fasque ....75 M 13
Fassfern ....72 E 13
Fauldhouse ....61 I 16
Faversham ....22 W 30
Fawley ....10 P 31
Fazeley ....35 O 26
Fearby ....49 O 21
Fearn Lodge ....79 H 10
Fearnan ....67 H 14
Fearnmore ....77 C 11
Featherstone *Staffs.* ....35 N 26
Featherstone *West Yorks.* ....43 P 22
Feelindre ....15 F 27
Feering ....30 W 28
Feetham ....49 N 20
Felbridge ....11 T 30
Felindre *Carmarthenshire /
  Sir Gaerfyrddin* ....25 I 28
Felindre *Powys* ....26 K 26
Felinfach ....25 K 28
Felinheli ....33 H 24
Felixkirk ....50 Q 21
Felixstowe ....31 Y 28
Felling ....56 P 19
Felmingham ....39 Y 25
Felpham ....11 S 31
Felsham ....30 W 27
Felsted ....30 V 28
Feltham ....21 S 29
Felthorpe ....39 X 25
Felton ....63 O 18
Feltwell ....30 V 26
Fence ....42 N 22
Feniton ....8 K 31
Fenny Bentley ....35 O 24
Fenstanton ....29 T 27
Fenton *Stoke-on-Trent* ....35 N 25
Fenton *West Lindsey* ....44 R 24
Fenwick
  Berwick-upon-Tweed ....63 O 17
Fenwick *East Ayrshire* ....60 G 17
Feochaig ....59 D 17
Feochan (Loch) ....65 D 14
Feock ....2 E 33
Feolin Ferry ....58 B 16
Fern ....74 L 13
Ferndown ....9 O 31
Ferness ....79 I 11
Fernhurst ....11 R 30
Fernie ....75 M 13
Ferryhill ....56 P 19
Ferryside ....15 G 28
Fersit ....73 F 13
Feshie (Glen) ....73 I 12
Feshiebridge ....73 I 12
Fetcham ....21 S 30
Fetlar ....87 R 2
Fetterangus ....81 N 11
Fettercairn ....75 M 13
Fewston ....49 O 22
Ffestiniog ....33 I 25
Ffestiniog (Vale of) ....33 H 25
Fflint / Flint ....42 K 24
Fforest Fawr ....17 J 28
Ffostrasol ....15 G 27
Fiaray ....70 X 12
Fiddleton ....62 L 18
Fifield ....27 P 28
Filey ....51 T 21
Fillongley ....27 P 26
Filton ....18 M 29
Finchampstead ....20 R 29
Finchingfield ....30 V 28
Findhorn ....80 J 11
Findhorn (River) ....73 H 12
Findhorn Bay ....80 J 11
Findo Gask ....68 J 14
Findochty ....80 L 10
Findon ....11 S 31

Finedon ....29 S 26
Fingest ....20 R 29
Fingland ....60 I 17
Finiskaig ....72 D 13
Finmere ....28 Q 28
Finniegill ....61 K 18
Finningley ....44 R 23
Finsbay ....76 Z 10
Finstock ....20 P 28
Finstown ....86 K 6
Fintry *Aberdeenshire* ....81 M 11
Fintry *Stirling* ....67 H 15
Fionn Loch ....78 D 10
Fionn Loch Mór ....84 F 9
Fionnphort ....64 A 15
Fishbourne *Chichester* ....10 R 31
Fishbourne *Isle of Wight* ....10 Q 31
Fishburn ....56 P 19
Fisherfield Forest ....78 D 10
Fisherford ....81 M 11
Fishguard / Abergwaun ....24 F 28
Fishnish Bay ....65 B 14
Fiskavaig ....77 A 12
Fiskerton ....44 S 24
Fittleworth ....11 S 31
Fiunary ....71 C 14
Fivehead ....8 L 30
Flackwell Heath ....21 R 29
Fladbury ....27 N 27
Fladda-Chùain ....77 A 10
Flagg ....35 O 24
Flamborough ....51 T 21
Flamborough Head ....51 T 21
Flamingo Park ....50 R 21
Flamstead ....21 S 28
Flash ....35 O 24
Flashader ....77 A 11
Flatford Mill ....30 X 28
Flax Bourton ....18 L 29
Flaxton ....50 R 21
Fleckney ....36 Q 26
Fleet ....20 R 30
Fleet (Islands of) ....53 H 19
Fleet (Loch) ....79 H 10
Fleet Hargate ....37 U 25
Fleetwood ....48 K 22
Flimby ....53 J 19
Flint / Fflint ....42 K 24
Flintham ....36 R 24
Flitton ....29 S 27
Flitwick ....29 S 27
Flixton ....31 Y 26
Flodday *near Hellisay* ....70 X 13
Flodday *near Sandray* ....70 X 13
Flodden Field ....63 N 17
Flodigarry ....77 B 11
Flookburgh ....48 L 21
Floors Castle ....62 M 17
Flotta ....86 K 7
Flowerdale Forest ....78 D 11
Flyford Flavell ....27 N 27
Fochabers ....80 K 11
Fockerby ....44 R 22
Foindle ....84 E 8
Folkestone ....13 X 30
Folkingham ....37 S 25
Folly Gate ....7 H 31
Fontmell Magna ....9 N 31
Ford *Argyll and Bute* ....65 D 15
Ford *Arun* ....11 S 31
Ford
  Berwick-upon-Tweed ....63 N 17
Ford
  Buckinghamshire ....20 R 28
Ford *Cotswold* ....27 O 28
Ford
  Shrewsbury and Atcham ..34 L 25
Forde Abbey ....8 L 31
Forden ....34 K 26
Fordham ....30 V 27
Fordingbridge ....9 O 31
Fordoun ....75 M 13
Fordwich ....23 X 30
Fordyce ....80 L 11
Foreland ....10 Q 31
Foreland Point ....17 I 30
Foremark Reservoir ....36 P 25
Forest Lodge ....74 I 13
Forest Row ....11 U 30
Forestburn Gate ....63 O 18
Forfar ....74 L 14
Forgandenny ....68 J 14
Formby ....42 K 23
Formby Point ....42 K 23
Fornham All Saints ....30 W 27

Forres ....80 J 11
Forrest Lodge ....53 H 18
Forse ....85 K 9
Forsinard ....85 I 8
Fort Augustus ....73 F 12
Fort George ....79 H 11
Fort Victoria ....10 P 31
Fort William ....72 E 13
Forter ....74 K 13
Forteviot ....68 J 14
Forth ....61 I 16
Forth (Firth of) ....68 K 15
Forth (River) ....67 G 15
Forth Bridges ....68 J 15
Fortingall ....73 H 14
Forton ....35 M 25
Fortrose ....79 H 11
Fortuneswell ....8 M 32
Fosdyke ....37 T 25
Foss ....73 I 13
Foston ....36 R 25
Foston on the Wolds ....51 T 22
Fotherby ....45 T 23
Fotheringhay ....29 S 26
Foulden ....63 N 16
Foulness Point ....22 W 29
Foulridge ....43 N 22
Foulsham ....38 X 25
Fountainhall ....62 L 16
Fountains Abbey ....50 P 21
Four Crosses ....34 K 25
Four Elms ....21 U 30
Four Marks ....10 Q 30
Fovant ....9 O 30
Foveran ....81 N 12
Fowey ....3 G 32
Fowlmere ....29 U 27
Fownhope ....26 M 27
Foxdale ....46 G 21
Foxholes ....51 S 21
Foxton ....28 R 26
Foxup ....49 N 21
Foyers ....73 G 12
Fraddon ....3 F 32
Framfield ....12 U 31
Framlingham ....31 Y 27
Frampton-on-Severn ....19 M 28
Framwellgate Moor ....56 P 19
Frant ....12 U 30
Fraserburgh ....81 O 10
Fraserburgh Bay ....81 O 10
Freckenham ....30 V 27
Freckleton ....42 L 22
Freeland ....20 P 28
Freethorpe ....39 Y 26
Freevater Forest ....79 F 10
Freiston ....37 U 25
Fremington ....7 H 30
Frensham ....10 R 30
Freshwater ....10 P 31
Freshwater Bay ....10 P 31
Freshwater East ....16 F 29
Freshwater West ....14 E 29
Fressingfield ....31 X 26
Freswick ....86 K 8
Freuchie ....68 K 15
Freuchie (Loch) ....67 I 14
Friday Bridge ....37 U 26
Fridaythorpe ....51 S 21
Frimley ....21 R 30
Fringford ....28 Q 28
Frinton-on-Sea ....31 X 28
Friockheim ....75 M 14
Frisa (Loch) ....71 B 14
Friskney ....37 U 24
Frithville ....37 T 24
Frittenden ....12 V 30
Fritton ....28 Q 28
Frizington ....47 J 20
Frocester ....19 N 28
Frodsham ....42 L 24
Froggatt ....43 P 24
Frome ....19 N 30
Frosterley ....56 O 19
Froxfield ....20 P 29
Fuday ....70 X 12
Fuiay ....70 X 13
Fulbourn ....30 U 27
Fulking ....11 T 31
Fuller Street ....22 V 28
Fulwood ....42 M 22
Funtington ....10 R 31
Funzie ....87 R 2
Furness Abbey ....47 K 21
Furness Fells ....48 K 20
Fyfield ....22 U 28
Fyvie ....81 M 11

G

Gaddesby ....36 R 25
Gaick Lodge ....73 H 13
Gainford ....49 O 20
Gainsborough ....44 R 23
Gairloch ....78 C 10
Gairlochy ....72 E 13
Gairsay ....87 L 6
Gaitsgill ....54 L 19
Galashiels ....62 L 17
Galgate ....48 L 22
Gallan Head ....82 Y 9
Gallanach ....65 D 14
Galloway Forest Park ....52 G 18
Galltair ....72 D 12
Galmisdale ....71 B 13
Galmpton ....4 J 32
Galson ....82 A 8
Galston ....60 G 17
Galtrigill ....76 Z 11
Gamblesby ....55 M 19
Gamlingay ....29 T 27
Gamston ....44 R 24
Ganavan ....65 D 14
Ganton ....51 S 21
Garboldisham ....30 W 26
Gardenstown ....81 N 10
Garelochhead ....66 F 15
Garenin ....82 Z 9
Garforth ....43 P 22
Gargrave ....49 N 22
Gargunnock ....67 H 15
Garioch ....81 M 12
Garlieston ....53 G 19
Garlogie ....75 M 12
Garmony ....65 C 14
Garmouth ....80 K 11
Garrabost ....83 B 9
Garragie Lodge ....73 G 12
Garraron ....65 D 15
Garreg ....33 H 25
Garrigill ....55 M 19
Garrisdale Point ....71 A 12
Garros ....77 B 11
Garrow ....67 I 14
Garry (Glen) *Highland* ....72 E 12
Garry (Glen)
  Perthshire and Kinross ....73 H 13
Garry (Loch) ....72 F 12
Garsington ....20 Q 28
Garten (Loch) ....74 I 12
Garth ....25 J 27
Garthorpe ....44 R 23
Gartmore ....67 G 15
Gartocharn ....67 G 15
Garton-on-The-Wolds ....51 S 21
Garvald ....69 M 16
Garvamore ....73 G 12
Garve ....79 F 11
Garvellachs ....65 C 15
Garvestone ....38 W 26
Garvock ....66 F 16
Garway ....26 L 28
Garynahine ....82 Z 9
Gatehouse of Fleet ....53 H 19
Gateshead ....56 P 19
Gateside ....68 K 15
Gatley ....42 N 23
Gatwick Airport ....11 T 30
Gaulden Manor ....8 K 30
Gavard ....64 B 15
Gaydon ....28 P 27
Gayton *King's Lynn
  and West Norfolk* ....38 V 25
Gayton *Stafford* ....35 N 25
Gaywood ....38 V 25
Geary ....77 A 11
Geddington ....29 R 26
Gedney Drove End ....37 U 25
Gedney Hill ....37 T 25
Gelligaer ....18 K 29
Gelston ....53 I 19
Georgeham ....6 H 30
Georth ....86 K 6
Gerrards Cross ....21 S 29
Gestingthorpe ....30 V 27
Gifford ....62 L 16
Gigha (Sound of) ....58 C 17
Gigha Island ....58 C 16
Gighay ....70 Y 12
Gilberdyke ....44 R 22
Gildersome ....43 P 22
Gilfach Goch ....17 J 29
Gillamour ....50 R 21
Gilling East ....50 Q 21

Great Britain 127

Gilling West 49 O 20
Gillingham *Dorset* 9 N 30
Gillingham *Kent* 22 V 29
Gillingham *South Norfolk* 31 Y 26
Gills 86 K 8
Gilmerton 67 I 14
Gilmorton 28 Q 26
Gilston 62 L 16
Gilwern 18 K 28
Girthon 53 H 19
Girton 29 U 27
Girvan 59 F 18
Gisburn 49 N 22
Gisland 55 M 19
Gittisham 8 K 31
Gladestry 26 K 27
Glaisdale 50 R 20
Glamis 74 K 14
Glamis Castle 74 L 14
Glanaman 17 I 28
Glandwr 15 G 28
Glanton 63 O 17
Glas-allt-Shiel 74 K 13
Glas-leac Mór 83 D 9
Glas Maol 74 J 13
Glasbury 26 K 27
Glascarnoch (Loch) 78 F 10
Glascwm 26 K 27
Glasdrum 72 E 14
Glasgow 60 H 16
Glasphein 76 Z 11
Glaspwll 33 I 26
Glass (Loch) 79 G 10
Glassburn 78 F 11
Glasserton 52 G 19
Glassford 60 H 16
Glasshouses 49 O 21
Glasson 48 L 22
Glassonby 55 M 19
Glastonbury 8 L 30
Gleadless 43 P 23
Gleann Beag 78 F 10
Gleann Mór 79 G 10
Gleaston 48 K 21
Glecknabae 59 E 16
Glemsford 30 V 27
Glen auldyn 46 G 21
Glen Brittle Forest 77 B 12
Glen Finglas Reservoir 67 G 15
Glen More Forest Park 74 I 12
Glen Shee 74 J 13
Glen Trool Lodge 52 G 18
Glenbarr 59 C 17
Glenborrodale 71 C 13
Glenbranter 66 E 15
Glenbrittle House 77 B 12
Glenbuchat Castle 74 K 12
Glenbuck 60 I 17
Glencaple 53 J 18
Glencarse 68 K 14
Glencoe 72 E 13
Glencoul (Loch) 84 F 9
Glendoebeg 73 G 12
Glendurgan Garden 2 E 33
Glenegedale 58 B 16
Glenelg 72 D 12
Glenelg Bay 72 D 12
Glenfarg 68 J 15
Glenfeshie Lodge 73 I 12
Glenfiddich Lodge 80 K 11
Glenfield 36 Q 26
Glenfinnan 72 D 13
Glenforsa Airport 65 C 14
Glenfyne Lodge 66 F 15
Glengorm 71 B 14
Glengoulandie 73 H 14
Glengrasco 77 B 11
Glenkens (The) 53 H 18
Glenkin die 74 L 12
Glenkirk 61 J 17
Glenlivet 80 J 11
Glenluce 52 F 19
Glenmassan 66 E 15
Glenmaye 46 F 21
Glenmore 71 C 13
Glenprosen Village 74 K 13
Glenridding 48 L 20
Glenrothes 68 K 15
Glenside 82 A 9
Glenstriven 66 E 16
Glentham 44 S 23
Glentress 61 K 17
Glentrool Village 52 G 18
Glentworth 44 S 23
Glenuachdarach 77 B 11
Glenuig 71 C 13
Glespin 61 I 17
Gletness 87 Q 3
Glinton 37 T 26
Glossop 43 O 23
Gloucester 27 N 28
Gloup 87 Q 1
Glusburn 49 O 22
Glutt Lodge 85 I 9
Glympton 28 P 28
Glyn Ceiriog 34 K 25
Glyn-Ebwy / Ebbw Vale 18 K 28
Glyn-neath 17 J 28
Glyncorrwg 17 J 28
Glynde 11 U 31
Glyndebourne 11 U 31
Glyndyfrdwy 34 K 25
Gnosall 35 N 25
Goadby 36 R 26
Goat Fell 59 E 17
Goathland 50 R 20
Gobowen 34 K 25
Godalming 21 S 30
Godmanchester 29 T 27
Godmanstone 8 M 31
Godshill 10 Q 32
Godstone 21 T 30
Goil (Loch) 66 F 15
Golborne 42 M 23
Goldcliff 18 L 29
Goldhanger 22 W 28
Goldthorpe 44 Q 23
Golspie 85 I 10
Gomersal 43 O 22
Gometra 64 B 14
Gomshall 21 S 30
Gooderstone 38 V 26
Goodleigh 7 I 30
Goodrich 26 M 28
Goodrington 4 J 32
Goodwick 24 F 27
Goodwood House 10 R 31
Goole 44 R 22
Goonhavern 2 E 32
Goostrey 42 M 24
Gordon 62 M 16
Gordonbush 85 I 9
Gordonstown 80 L 11
Gorebridge 61 K 16
Goring 20 Q 29
Gorm Loch Mór 84 F 9
Gorran Haven 3 F 33
Gorseinon 15 H 29
Gorsleston-on-Sea 39 Z 26
Gortantaoid 64 B 16
Gosberton 37 T 25
Gosfield 30 V 28
Gosforth *Cumbria* 47 J 20
Gosforth
Newcastle upon Tyne 56 P 18
Gosport 10 Q 31
Goswick 63 O 16
Gotham 36 Q 25
Gott Bay 70 Z 14
Goudhurst 12 V 30
Gourdon 75 N 13
Gourock 66 F 16
Gowerton 15 H 29
Goxhill 45 T 22
Graemsay 86 K 7
Grafton Underwood 29 S 26
Grain 22 W 29
Grainthorpe 45 U 23
Granby 36 R 25
Grandtully 74 I 14
Grange-over-Sands 48 L 21
Grangemouth 67 I 15
Grantchester 29 U 27
Grantham 37 S 25
Grantown-on-Spey 80 J 12
Grantshouse 62 N 16
Grasby 45 S 23
Grasmere 48 K 20
Grassington 49 O 21
Grateley 9 P 30
Graveley 29 T 27
Gravesend 22 V 29
Gravir 82 A 9
Grayrigg 48 M 20
Grays Thurrock 22 V 29
Grayshott 10 R 30
Grayswood 11 R 30
Greasbrough 43 P 23
Great Addington 29 S 26
Great Altcar 42 K 23
Great Amwell 21 T 28
Great Asby 49 M 20
Great Ayton 50 Q 20
Great Baddow 22 V 28
Great Bardfield 30 V 28
Great Barford 29 S 27
Great Barr 35 O 26
Great Barrow 34 L 24
Great Barugh 50 R 21
Great Bedwyn 19 P 29
Great Bentley 31 X 28
Great Bernera 82 Z 9
Great Bircham 38 V 25
Great-Bollright 28 P 28
Great Bookham 21 S 30
Great Bourton 28 Q 27
Great Bowden 28 R 26
Great Brickhill 29 R 28
Great Bridgeford 35 N 25
Great Bromley 30 X 28
Great Broughton 50 Q 20
Great-Budworth 42 M 24
Great Burdon 50 P 20
Great Chalfield 19 N 29
Great Chesterford 30 U 27
Great Chishill 29 U 27
Great Clifton 53 J 20
Great Coates 45 T 23
Great-Comberton 27 N 27
Great Cornard 30 W 27
Great Cubley 35 O 25
Great Cumbrae Island 59 F 16
Great-Dalby 36 R 25
Great Doddington 28 R 27
Great Driffield 51 S 21
Great-Dunham 38 W 25
Great Dunmow 30 V 28
Great Easton *Essex* 30 U 28
Great Easton *Leics.* 28 R 26
Great Eccleston 42 L 22
Great Ellingham 38 W 26
Great Finborough 30 W 27
Great Glen 36 Q 26
Great Gonerby 37 S 25
Great Gransden 29 T 27
Great Harrowden 28 R 27
Great Harwood 42 M 22
Great Hockham 30 W 26
Great Horkesley 30 W 28
Great Horwood 28 R 28
Great Houghton 43 P 23
Great Langton 50 P 20
Great-Limber 45 T 23
Great Livermere 30 W 27
Great Lumley 56 P 19
Great Malvern 27 N 27
Great Marton 42 K 22
Great Massingham 38 W 25
Great Milton 20 Q 28
Great Missenden 21 R 28
Great Mitton 42 M 22
Great Musgrave 49 M 20
Great Oakley 31 X 28
Great Ormes Head 41 I 22
Great Orton 54 K 19
Great Ouse (River) 38 V 25
Great Ouseburn 50 Q 21
Great Ponton 37 S 25
Great Ryburgh 38 W 25
Great Salkeld 55 L 19
Great Sampford 30 V 28
Great Shefford 20 P 29
Great Shelford 29 U 27
Great Smeaton 50 P 20
Great Somerford 19 N 29
Great Stainton 56 P 20
Great Strickland 55 L 20
Great Torrington 6 H 31
Great Tosson 63 O 18
Great Totham 22 W 28
Great Urswick 48 K 21
Great Wakering 22 W 29
Great Waltham 22 V 28
Great Whernside 49 O 21
Great Whittington 56 O 18
Great Witley 27 M 27
Great Wolford 27 P 27
Great Wyrley 35 N 26
Great Yarmouth 39 Z 26
Great Yeldham 30 V 27
Greatford 37 S 25
Greatham *Cleveland* 57 Q 20
Greatham *Hants.* 10 R 30
Greatstone-on-Sea 12 W 31
Green Hammerton 50 Q 21
Greenfield
Flintshire / Sir y Fflint 41 K 23
Greenfield *Highland* 72 F 12
Greenhaugh 55 N 18
Greenhead 55 M 19
Greenholm 60 H 17
Greenhow Hill 49 O 21
Greenlaw 62 M 16
Greenloaning 67 I 15
Greenock 66 F 16
Greenodd 48 K 21
Greens Norton 28 Q 27
Greenside 56 O 19
Greenwich
London Borough 21 U 29
Grendon 28 R 27
Grendon Underwood 28 Q 28
Gresford 34 L 24
Greshornish 77 A 11
Greshornish (Loch) 77 A 11
Gress 83 B 9
Gretna 54 K 19
Gretton 37 R 26
Greys Court 20 R 29
Greysouthen 54 J 20
Greystoke 55 L 19
Griffithstown 18 K 28
Griminish 76 X 11
Grimley 27 N 27
Grimoldby 45 U 23
Grimsay 76 Y 11
Grimsby 45 T 23
Gringley on the Hill 44 R 23
Grinshill 34 L 25
Grinton 49 O 20
Gristhorpe 51 T 21
Grittleton 19 N 29
Groby 36 Q 26
Grogport 59 D 17
Groombridge 12 U 30
Grosebay 76 Z 10
Grosmont *Monmouthshire /*
Sir Fynwy 26 L 28
Grosmont *Scarborough* 50 R 20
Grove 20 P 29
Gruinard Bay 78 D 10
Gruinard Island 78 D 10
Gruinart 58 B 16
Gruinart (Loch) 64 B 16
Grunavat (Loch) 82 Z 9
Grundisburgh 31 X 27
Gualachulain 66 E 14
Guardbridge 69 L 14
Guernsey *Channel I.* 5
Guesting 12 V 31
Guildford 21 S 30
Guildtown 68 J 14
Guilsborough 28 Q 26
Guisborough 50 Q 20
Guiseley 43 O 22
Guist 38 W 25
Gullane 69 L 15
Gunna 70 Z 14
Gunnerside 49 N 20
Gunnerton 55 N 18
Gunness 44 R 23
Gunnislake 3 H 32
Gunthorpe 36 R 25
Gurnard 10 Q 31
Gurness Broch 86 K 6
Gurnos 17 I 28
Gussage All Saints 9 O 31
Gutcher 87 Q 1
Guthrie 75 L 14
Guyhirn 37 U 26
Gwalchmai 40 G 23
Gwaun-Cae-Gurwen 17 I 28
Gwbert-on-Sea 15 F 27
Gweek 2 E 33
Gwennap 2 E 33
Gwithian 2 D 33
Gwyddelwern 33 J 24
Gwyddgrug 15 H 28
Gwydir Castle 33 I 24
Gwytherin 33 I 24

H

Habost 83 B 8
Hackney *London Borough* 21 T 29
Haddenham *Bucks.* 20 R 28
Haddenham *Cambs.* 29 U 26
Haddington 69 L 16
Haddiscoe 39 Y 26
Haddo House 81 N 11
Haddon Hall 35 P 24
Hadfield 43 O 23
Hadleigh *Essex* 22 V 29
Hadleigh *Suffolk* 30 W 27
Hadley 34 M 25
Hadlow 22 V 30
Hadnall 34 L 25
Hadrian's Wall 55 M 18
Haggbeck 55 L 18
Hagley 27 N 26
Hagworthingham 45 U 24
Hailsham 12 U 31
Hainford 39 X 25
Hainton 45 T 23
Halam 36 R 24
Halberton 7 J 31
Hale 42 M 23
Hales 39 Y 26
Halesowen 27 N 26
Halesworth 31 Y 26
Halford 27 P 27
Halifax 43 O 22
Halistra 77 A 11
Halkirk 85 J 8
Hall 60 G 16
Halland 12 U 31
Hallaton 36 R 26
Halling 22 V 29
Hallington 55 N 18
Halloughton 36 R 24
Hallow 27 N 27
Hallsands 4 J 33
Halsall 42 L 23
Halse 8 K 30
Halsetown 2 D 33
Halstead 30 V 28
Halstock 8 M 31
Haltham 37 T 24
Halton *Aylesbury Vale* 20 R 28
Halton *Lancaster* 48 L 21
Halton Gill 49 N 21
Haltwhistle 55 M 19
Halwell 4 I 32
Halwill Junction 6 H 31
Hamble 10 Q 31
Hambleden 20 R 29
Hambledon *Hants.* 10 Q 31
Hambledon *Surrey* 11 S 30
Hambleton *Lancs.* 42 L 22
Hambleton *North Yorks.* 44 Q 22
Hambleton Hills (The) 50 Q 21
Hambridge 8 L 31
Hamilton 60 H 16
Hammersmith and Fulham
London Borough 21 T 29
Hamnavoe *near Brae* 87 Q 2
Hamnavoe *near Scallway* 87 P 3
Hampreston 9 O 31
Hampstead Norris 20 Q 29
Hampsthwaite 50 P 21
Hampton Court 21 S 29
Hampton in Arden 27 O 26
Hamstead Marshall 20 P 29
Hamsterley 56 O 19
Hamstreet 12 W 30
Hamworthy 9 N 31
Handa Island 84 E 8
Handbridge 34 L 24
Handbury 27 N 27
Handcross 11 T 30
Handforth 43 N 23
Handley 34 L 24
Handsworth 43 P 23
Hanham 18 M 29
Hanley 35 N 24
Hanley Swan 27 N 27
Hanningfield 22 V 28
Hannington 19 O 29
Hanslope 28 R 27
Happisburgh 39 Y 25
Hapton 42 N 22
Harberton 4 I 32
Harbertonford 4 I 32
Harbledown 23 X 30
Harborough Magna 28 Q 26
Harbottle 63 N 17
Harbury 28 P 27
Harby 36 R 25
Hardham 11 S 31
Hardwick 44 Q 24
Hardwick Hall 36 Q 24
Hardwicke 19 N 28
Hardy Monument 5 M 31
Hardy's Cottage 9 M 31
Hare Street 29 U 28
Haresfield 19 N 28
Harewood House 50 P 22
Hargrave 29 S 27
Hargrave Green 30 V 27
Haringey *London Borough* 21 T 29
Harlaxton 36 R 25
Harlech 33 H 25
Harleston 31 X 26
Harlestone 28 R 27
Harley 34 M 26
Harlington 29 S 28
Harlosh 77 A 11
Harlow 21 U 28
Harlow Hill 56 O 18
Harmston 37 S 24
Haroldswick 87 R 1
Harpenden 21 S 28
Harpley 38 V 25
Harport (Loch) 77 A 12
Harray (Loch of) 86 K 6
Harrietfield 67 J 14
Harrington *Allerdale* 53 J 20
Harrington *Kettering* 28 R 26
Harringworth 37 S 26
Harris *Highland* 71 A 13
Harris *Western Isles* 82 Y 10
Harris (Sound of) 76 Y 10
Harrogate 50 P 22
Harrow *London Borough* 21 S 29
Harston 29 U 27
Hartburn 56 O 18
Hartest 30 W 27
Hartfield 11 U 30
Harthill *North Lanarkshire* 61 I 16
Harthill *Rotherham* 44 Q 24
Harting 10 R 31
Hartington 35 O 24
Hartland 6 G 31
Hartland Quay 6 G 31
Hartlebury 27 N 26
Hartlepool 57 Q 19
Hartley 22 U 29
Hartley Wintney 20 R 30
Hartpury 27 N 28
Hartshill 36 P 26
Hartwell 20 R 28
Hartwell 28 R 27
Harvington 27 O 27
Harwell 20 Q 29
Harwich 31 X 28
Harwood Dale 51 S 20
Harworth 44 Q 23
Hascosay 87 R 2
Haselbury Plucknett 8 L 31
Hasland 43 P 24
Haslemere 11 R 30
Haslingden 42 N 22
Haslingfield 29 U 27
Haslington 35 M 24
Hassocks 11 T 31
Haster 86 K 8
Hastings 12 V 31
Hatch Court 8 L 31
Hatfield
County of Herefordshire 26 M 27
Hatfield *Herts.* 21 T 28
Hatfield *South Yorks.* 44 Q 23
Hatfield Broad Oak 22 U 28
Hatfield Heath 22 U 28
Hatfield Peverel 22 V 28
Hatfield Woodhouse 44 R 23
Hatherleigh 7 H 31
Hathern 36 Q 25
Hathersage 43 P 24
Hatton *Aberdeenshire* 81 O 11
Hatton *Derbs.* 35 O 25
Hatton of Fintray 75 N 12
Haugh of Urr 53 I 19
Haughton 35 N 25
Haunn 71 B 14
Havant 10 R 31
Havenstreet 10 Q 31
Haverfordwest / Hwlffordd 16 F 28
Haverhill 30 V 27
Haverigg 47 K 21
Havering *London Borough* 22 U 29
Haverthwaite 48 K 21
Hawarden 34 K 24
Hawes 49 N 21
Hawick 62 L 17
Hawkchurch 8 L 31
Hawkedon 30 V 27
Hawkesbury Upton 19 M 29
Hawkhurst 12 V 30
Hawkridge 7 J 30
Hawkshead 48 L 20
Hawkwell 22 V 29
Hawley 20 R 30
Hawling 27 O 28
Haworth 43 O 22
Hawsker 51 S 20
Haxby 50 Q 21
Haxey 44 R 23
Hay-on-Wye 26 K 27
Haydock 42 M 23
Haydon Bridge 55 N 19
Haydon Wick 19 O 29
Hayfield 43 O 23

A B C D E F G H I J K L M N O P Q R S T U V W X Y Z

A B C D E F G H I J K L M N O P Q R S T U V W X Y Z

Hayle .... 2 D 33
Hayling Island .... 10 R 31
Hayscastle .... 14 E 28
Hayton .... 50 R 22
Haywards Heath .... 11 T 31
Hazel Grove .... 43 N 23
Hazelbank .... 61 I 16
Hazelbury Bryan .... 9 M 31
Hazlemere .... 21 R 29
Heacham .... 38 V 25
Headcorn .... 22 V 30
Headington .... 20 Q 28
Headless Cross .... 27 O 27
Headley .... 10 R 30
Heads of Ayr .... 60 F 17
Healey .... 49 O 21
Healing .... 45 T 23
Heanor .... 36 P 24
Heast .... 71 C 12
Heath End .... 20 Q 29
Heath Hayes .... 35 O 25
Heather .... 36 P 25
Heathfield *Renfrewshire* .... 60 F 16
Heathfield *Wealden* .... 12 U 31
Heathrow Airport .... 21 S 29
Hebburn .... 56 P 19
Hebden Bridge .... 43 N 22
Hebrides (Sea of the) .... 76 Z 12
Heckfield .... 20 R 29
Heckington .... 37 T 25
Heddon on the Wall .... 56 O 19
Hedge End .... 10 Q 31
Hednesford .... 35 O 25
Hedon .... 45 T 22
Heighington *Durham* .... 56 P 20
Heighington *Lincs.* .... 44 S 24
Heights of Kinlochewe .... 78 E 11
Helensburgh .... 66 F 15
Helford .... 2 E 33
Hellifield .... 49 N 22
Hellingly .... 12 U 31
Hellisay .... 70 X 12
Hell's Mouth
   or Porth Neigwl .... 32 G 25
Helmdon .... 28 Q 27
Helmsdale .... 85 J 9
Helmsley .... 50 Q 21
Helpringham .... 37 T 25
Helpston .... 37 S 26
Helsby .... 42 L 24
Helston .... 2 E 33
Helton .... 55 L 20
Helvellyn .... 48 K 20
Hemel Hempstead .... 21 S 28
Hemingbrough .... 44 R 22
Hemingford Grey .... 29 T 27
Hemington .... 19 M 30
Hempnall .... 39 X 26
Hempton .... 38 W 25
Hemsby .... 39 Z 25
Hemswell .... 44 S 23
Hemsworth .... 43 P 23
Hemyock .... 8 K 31
Hendy .... 15 H 28
Henfield .... 11 T 31
Hengoed .... 18 K 29
Henham .... 30 U 28
Henley .... 27 O 27
Henley-on-Thames .... 20 R 29
Henllan .... 33 J 24
Henllys .... 18 K 29
Henlow .... 29 T 27
Hennock .... 4 J 32
Henshaw .... 55 M 19
Henstead .... 31 Y 26
Henstridge .... 9 M 31
Heol Senni .... 25 J 28
Hepple .... 63 N 18
Heptonstall .... 43 N 22
Herbrandston .... 14 E 28
Hereford .... 26 L 27
Heriot .... 62 L 16
Herm *Channel I.* 5
Herma Ness .... 87 R 1
Hermitage .... 20 Q 29
Hermitage Castle .... 62 L 18
Herne Bay .... 23 X 29
Herriard .... 20 Q 30
Herrington .... 56 P 19
Herstmonceux .... 12 U 31
Hertford .... 21 T 28
Hesket Newmarket .... 54 K 19
Hesketh Bank .... 42 L 22
Hesleden .... 57 Q 19
Hessenford .... 3 G 32
Hessle .... 45 S 22
Hest Bank .... 48 L 21

Heswall .... 42 K 24
Hethersgill .... 55 L 19
Hethpool .... 63 N 17
Hetton-le-Hole .... 56 P 19
Heveningham .... 31 Y 27
Hever .... 21 U 30
Heversham .... 48 L 21
Hevingham .... 39 X 25
Hewelsfield .... 18 M 28
Hexham .... 55 N 19
Heybridge .... 22 W 28
Heysham .... 48 L 21
Heyshott .... 11 R 31
Heytesbury .... 9 N 30
Heythrop .... 28 P 28
Heywood .... 43 N 23
Hibaldstow .... 44 S 23
Hickling .... 36 R 25
Hickling Green .... 39 Y 25
Hidcote Manor Garden .... 27 O 27
High Bentham .... 49 M 21
High Bickington .... 7 I 31
High Birkwith .... 49 N 21
High Easter .... 22 V 28
High Ercall .... 34 M 25
High Etherley .... 56 O 20
High Force (The) .... 55 N 20
High Halden .... 12 W 30
High Halstow .... 22 V 29
High Ham .... 8 L 30
High Hesket .... 55 L 19
High Newton *Alnwick* .... 63 P 17
High Newton
   South Lakeland .... 48 L 21
High Offley .... 35 N 25
High Ongar .... 22 U 28
High Peak .... 43 O 23
High Willhays .... 4 I 31
High Wycombe .... 20 R 29
Higham *Kent* .... 22 V 29
Higham *Lancs.* .... 42 N 22
Higham
   North East Derbyshire .... 36 P 24
Higham *Suffolk* .... 30 V 27
Higham Ferrers .... 29 S 27
Higham on the Hill .... 36 P 26
Highbridge .... 18 L 30
Highclere .... 20 P 29
Highcliffe .... 9 O 31
Higher Penwortham .... 42 L 22
Highland Wildlife Park .... 73 I 12
Highley .... 27 M 26
Highmoor Cross .... 20 R 29
Hightae .... 54 J 18
Hightown *Congleton* .... 35 N 24
Hightown *Sefton* .... 42 K 23
Highworth .... 19 O 29
Hilborough .... 38 W 26
Hildenborough .... 22 U 30
Hilderstone .... 35 N 25
Hilgay .... 38 V 26
Hill .... 18 M 29
Hill of Fearn .... 79 I 10
Hill of Tarvit .... 69 L 15
Hillhead .... 52 G 19
Hillingdon
   London Borough .... 21 S 29
Hillington .... 38 V 25
Hillside .... 75 M 13
Hillswick .... 87 P 2
Hilmarton .... 19 O 29
Hilperton .... 19 N 30
Hilpsford Point .... 47 K 21
Hilton *Aberdeenshire* .... 81 N 11
Hilton *Eden* .... 55 M 20
Hilton *Huntingdonshire* .... 29 T 27
Hilton *North Dorset* .... 9 N 31
Hilton *South Derbyshire* .... 35 P 25
Hilton of Cadboll .... 79 I 10
Himbleton .... 27 N 27
Hinchingbrooke House .... 29 T 27
Hinckley .... 36 P 26
Hinderwell .... 50 R 20
Hindhead .... 10 R 30
Hindley .... 42 M 23
Hindolveston .... 38 X 25
Hindon .... 9 N 30
Hingham .... 38 W 26
Hinstock .... 34 M 25
Hintlesham .... 31 X 27
Hinton-Blewett .... 18 M 30
Hirst Courtney .... 44 Q 22
Hirwaun .... 17 J 28
Histon .... 29 U 27
Hitcham .... 30 W 27
Hitchin .... 29 T 28

Hockering .... 38 X 25
Hockerton .... 36 R 24
Hockley .... 22 V 29
Hockley Heath .... 27 O 26
Hockliffe .... 29 S 28
Hoddesdon .... 21 T 28
Hodnet .... 34 M 25
Hodthorpe .... 44 Q 24
Hogsthorpe .... 45 U 24
Holbeach .... 37 U 25
Holbeach-St. Johns .... 37 T 25
Holbeach-St. Matthew .... 37 U 25
Holbeck .... 44 Q 24
Holbrook .... 31 X 28
Holbury .... 10 P 31
Holcombe .... 18 M 30
Holcombe Rogus .... 7 J 31
Holdenby .... 28 R 27
Holford .... 8 K 30
Holkam Hall .... 38 W 25
Hollandstoun .... 87 M 5
Hollesley .... 31 Y 27
Hollesley Bay .... 31 Y 27
Hollingbourne .... 22 V 30
Hollingworth .... 43 O 23
Hollybush .... 60 G 17
Hollym .... 45 U 22
Holmbridge .... 43 O 23
Holme *Huntingdonshire* .... 29 T 26
Holme *South Lakeland* .... 48 L 21
Holme-next-the-Sea .... 38 V 25
Holme
   upon Spalding-Moor .... 44 R 22
Holmer Green .... 21 R 29
Holmes Chapel .... 35 M 24
Holmesfield .... 43 P 24
Holmfirth .... 43 O 23
Holmhead .... 60 H 17
Holmpton .... 45 U 22
Holnest .... 8 M 31
Holsworthy .... 6 G 31
Holt *Dorset* .... 9 O 31
Holt *Norfolk* .... 38 X 25
Holt *Wilts.* .... 19 N 29
Holt *Wrexham* .... 34 L 24
Holt Heath .... 27 N 27
Holton *Lincs.* .... 45 T 24
Holton *Norfolk* .... 31 Y 26
Holton *South Somerset* .... 8 M 30
Holton Heath .... 9 N 31
Holton-le-Clay .... 45 T 23
Holwick .... 55 N 20
Holy Island *Anglesey* .... 40 F 23
Holy Island *North Ayrshire* .... 59 E 17
Holy Island *Northumb.* .... 63 O 16
Holybourne .... 10 R 30
Holyhead / Caergybi .... 40 G 23
Holystone .... 63 N 18
Holywell .... 2 E 32
Holywell / Treffynnon .... 41 K 23
Holywell Bay .... 2 E 32
Holywood .... 53 J 18
Honing .... 39 Y 25
Honiton .... 8 K 31
Hoo St. Werburgh .... 22 V 29
Hook
   Basingstoke and Deane .... 20 R 30
Hook
   East Riding of Yorkshire .... 44 R 22
Hook Norton .... 28 P 28
Hooke .... 8 M 31
Hope *Derbs.* .... 43 O 23
Hope *Flintshire* .... 34 K 24
Hope *Highland* .... 84 G 8
Hope *South Shropshire* .... 34 L 26
Hope (Loch) .... 84 G 8
Hope Bowdler .... 26 L 26
Hope under Dinmore .... 26 L 27
Hopeman .... 80 J 10
Hopetoun House .... 68 J 16
Hopton .... 39 Z 26
Horam .... 12 U 31
Horbury .... 43 P 23
Horden .... 57 Q 19
Hordley .... 34 L 25
Horeb .... 15 G 27
Horley .... 21 T 30
Hornby .... 48 M 21
Horncastle .... 45 T 24
Hornchurch .... 22 U 29
Horncliffe .... 63 N 16
Horning .... 39 Y 25
Horninglow .... 35 P 25
Horn's Cross .... 6 H 31
Hornsea .... 51 T 22
Hornton .... 28 P 27
Horrabridge .... 4 H 32

Horseheath .... 30 V 27
Horsehouse .... 49 O 21
Horsell .... 21 S 30
Horsford .... 39 X 25
Horsforth .... 43 P 22
Horsham .... 11 T 30
Horsham St. Faith .... 39 X 25
Horsington *East Lindsey* .... 37 T 24
Horsington
   South Somerset .... 9 M 30
Horsley *Stroud* .... 19 N 28
Horsley *Tynedale* .... 56 O 19
Horsmonden .... 12 V 30
Horstead .... 39 Y 25
Horsted Keynes .... 11 T 30
Horton *Abertawe /
   Swansea* .... 15 H 29
Horton *East Dorset* .... 9 O 31
Horton *South Somerset* .... 8 L 31
Horton Court .... 19 M 29
Horton-in-Ribblesdale .... 49 N 21
Horwich .... 42 M 23
Hoton .... 36 Q 25
Hott .... 55 M 18
Houghton .... 10 P 30
Houghton Hall .... 38 V 25
Houghton House .... 29 S 27
Houghton-le-Spring .... 56 P 19
Houghton-on-the-Hill .... 36 R 26
Hougton .... 55 L 19
Hounslow
   London Borough .... 21 S 29
Hourn (Loch) .... 72 D 12
Housesteads Fort .... 55 N 18
Houston .... 60 G 16
Houstry .... 85 J 9
Hove .... 11 T 31
Hoveton .... 39 Y 25
Hovingham .... 50 R 21
How Caple .... 26 M 28
Howden .... 44 R 22
Howe of the Mearns .... 75 M 13
Howick .... 63 P 17
Howmore .... 76 X 12
Hownam .... 62 M 17
Howwood .... 60 G 16
Hoxa (Sound of) .... 86 K 7
Hoxne .... 31 X 26
Hoy .... 86 J 7
Hoylake .... 41 K 22
Hoyland Nether .... 43 P 23
Huby .... 50 Q 21
Hucknall .... 36 Q 24
Huddersfield .... 43 O 23
Huggate .... 51 S 22
Hugh Town *I. of Scilly* 2
Hughenden .... 20 R 29
Hughley .... 34 M 26
Huish Champflower .... 7 J 30
Huish Episcopi .... 8 L 30
Hull (River) .... 45 S 22
Hulland .... 35 P 24
Hullavington .... 19 N 29
Hullbridge .... 22 V 29
Humber (River) .... 45 T 23
Humber Bridge .... 44 S 22
Humberston .... 45 T 23
Humbleton .... 45 T 22
Hume Castle .... 62 M 17
Humshaugh .... 55 N 18
Hundleton .... 16 F 28
Hundred House .... 26 K 27
Hungerford .... 20 P 29
Hunmanby .... 51 T 21
Hunstanton .... 38 V 25
Hunter's Inn .... 17 I 30
Hunter's Quay .... 66 F 16
Huntingdon .... 29 T 26
Huntington .... 50 Q 22
Huntingtower Castle .... 68 J 14
Huntly .... 80 L 11
Hunton .... 49 O 21
Huntspill .... 18 L 30
Hunwick .... 56 O 19
Hurlford .... 60 G 17
Hurn .... 9 O 31
Hursley .... 10 P 30
Hurst Green .... 12 V 30
Hurstbourne Priors .... 20 P 30
Hurstbourne Tarrant .... 20 P 30
Hurstpierpoint .... 11 T 31
Hurworth-on-Tees .... 50 P 20
Hury .... 55 N 20
Husbands Bosworth .... 28 Q 26
Huthwaite .... 36 Q 24
Huttoft .... 45 U 24
Hutton *Scottish Borders* .... 63 N 16

Hutton *South Ribble* .... 42 L 22
Hutton Cranswick .... 51 S 22
Hutton Rudby .... 50 Q 20
Huxley .... 34 L 24
Huyton .... 42 L 23
Hyde .... 43 N 23
Hynish .... 64 Z 14
Hynish Bay .... 64 Z 14
Hythe *Hants.* .... 10 P 31
Hythe *Kent* .... 13 X 30

I

Ibsley .... 9 O 31
Ibstock .... 36 P 25
Ickleford .... 29 T 28
Icklingham .... 30 V 27
Ickworth House .... 30 V 27
Iddesleigh .... 7 H 31
Ideford .... 4 J 32
Iden .... 12 W 31
Iden Green .... 12 V 30
Idmiston .... 9 O 30
Idrigill Point .... 77 A 12
Ightham .... 22 U 30
Ightham Mote .... 22 U 30
Ilchester .... 8 L 30
Ilderton .... 63 O 17
Ilfracombe .... 17 H 30
Ilkeston .... 36 Q 25
Ilkley .... 49 O 22
Illogan .... 2 E 33
Ilmington .... 27 O 27
Ilminster .... 8 L 31
Ilsington .... 4 I 32
Ilton .... 8 L 31
Immingham .... 45 T 23
Immingham Dock .... 45 T 23
Ince Blundell .... 42 K 23
Ince-in-Makerfield .... 42 M 23
Inch Kenneth .... 64 B 14
Inchard (Loch) .... 84 E 8
Inchbare .... 75 M 13
Inchgrundle .... 74 L 13
Inchkeith .... 68 K 15
Inchlaggan .... 72 E 12
Inchmarnock .... 59 E 16
Inchnadamph .... 84 F 9
Inchture .... 68 K 14
Indaal (Loch) .... 58 A 16
Inerval .... 58 B 17
Ingatestone .... 22 V 28
Ingbirchworth .... 43 P 23
Ingham .... 30 W 27
Ingleby Barwick .... 50 Q 20
Ingleton *Durham* .... 56 O 20
Ingleton *North Yorks.* .... 49 M 21
Inglewhite .... 42 L 22
Inglewood Forest .... 55 L 19
Ingliston .... 68 J 16
Ingoldmells .... 38 V 24
Ingoldsby .... 37 S 25
Ingram .... 63 O 17
Ings .... 48 L 20
Inkpen .... 20 P 29
Innellan .... 59 F 16
Inner Hebrides .... 70 Y 14
Inner Sound .... 77 C 11
Innerleithen .... 61 K 17
Innerpeffray .... 67 I 14
Innerwick .... 69 M 16
Insch .... 81 M 11
Insh .... 73 I 12
Inshore .... 84 F 8
Inver *Highland* .... 79 I 10
Inver *Perth and Kinross* .... 68 J 14
Inver (Loch) .... 84 E 9
Inver Bay .... 79 I 10
Inver Mallie .... 72 E 13
Inver Valley .... 84 E 9
Inveralligin .... 78 D 11
Inverallochy .... 81 O 10
Inveran .... 84 G 10
Inveraray .... 66 E 15
Inverarity .... 69 L 14
Inverarnan .... 66 F 15
Inverbeg .... 66 G 15
Inverbervie .... 75 N 13
Invercassley .... 84 G 10
Invercauld House .... 74 J 12
Inverchapel .... 66 F 15
Invercreran .... 72 E 14
Inverdruie .... 73 I 12
Inverewe Gardens .... 78 C 10
Inverey .... 74 J 13
Inverfarigaig .... 79 G 12

Invergarry .... 72 F 12
Invergeldie .... 67 H 14
Invergordon .... 79 H 10
Invergowrie .... 68 K 14
Inverie .... 72 C 12
Inverinan .... 65 E 15
Inverinate .... 78 D 12
Inverkeithing .... 68 J 15
Inverkeithny .... 81 M 11
Inverkip .... 66 F 16
Inverkirkaig .... 84 E 9
Inverliever Forest .... 65 D 15
Inverlochlarig .... 67 G 15
Invermoriston .... 73 G 12
Inverness .... 79 H 11
Inversanda .... 72 D 13
Inversnaid Hotel .... 66 F 15
Inveruglas .... 66 F 15
Inverurie .... 81 M 12
Invervar .... 73 H 14
Inwardleigh .... 7 H 31
Iona .... 64 A 15
Ipplepen .... 4 J 32
Ipstones .... 35 O 24
Ipswich .... 31 X 27
Irby *East Lindsey* .... 37 U 24
Irby *Wirral* .... 42 K 23
Irchester .... 29 S 27
Ireby .... 54 K 19
Ireleth .... 47 K 21
Irlam .... 42 M 23
Iron Acton .... 18 M 29
Ironbridge .... 34 M 26
Irthington .... 55 L 19
Irthlingborough .... 29 S 27
Irvine .... 60 F 17
Irwell (River) .... 42 N 23
Isbyty Ystwyth .... 25 I 27
Isla (Glen) .... 74 K 13
Islay (Sound of) .... 64 B 16
Isle of Whithorn .... 53 G 19
Isleham .... 30 V 26
Isleornsay .... 71 C 12
Isleworth .... 21 S 29
Islington *London Borough* .... 21 T 29
Islip .... 20 Q 28
Islivig .... 82 Y 9
Itchingfield .... 11 S 30
Ithon (River) .... 25 K 27
Itteringham .... 39 X 25
Iver .... 21 S 29
Iver Heath .... 21 S 29
Ivinghoe .... 21 S 28
Ivybridge .... 4 I 32
Ivychurch .... 12 W 30
Iwade .... 22 W 29
Iwerne Minster .... 9 N 31
Ixworth .... 30 W 27

J

Jacobstow .... 6 G 31
Jacobstowe .... 7 H 31
Jameston .... 15 F 29
Jamestown
   Dumfries and Galloway .... 61 K 18
Jamestown
   West Dunbartonshire .... 66 G 16
Janetstown .... 85 J 9
Jarrow .... 56 P 19
Jaywick .... 23 X 28
Jedburgh .... 62 M 17
Jedburgh Abbey .... 62 M 17
Jeffreyston .... 15 F 28
Jemimaville .... 79 H 11
Jersey *Channel I.* 5
Jevington .... 12 U 31
John Muir .... 69 M 15
John o' Groats .... 86 K 8
Johnshaven .... 75 N 13
Johnston .... 16 F 28
Johnstone .... 60 G 16
Johnstonebridge .... 54 J 18
Jura (Isle of) .... 58 B 16
Jura (Sound of) .... 65 C 16
Jura Forest .... 65 B 16
Jura Ho .... 58 B 16
Jurby West .... 46 G 20

K

Kainakill .... 77 C 11
Kames .... 65 E 16
Katrine (Loch) .... 67 G 15
Kea .... 2 E 33
Keal .... 37 U 24
Keal (Loch na) .... 65 B 14
Kearsley .... 42 M 23
Keasden .... 49 M 21

Kebock Head ... 82 A 9
Kedington ... 30 V 27
Kedleston Hall ... 36 P 25
Keelby ... 45 T 23
Keevil ... 19 N 30
Kegworth ... 36 Q 25
Keig ... 75 M 12
Keighley ... 43 O 22
Keillmore ... 65 C 16
Keinton Mandeville ... 8 M 30
Keir Mill ... 53 I 18
Keiss ... 86 K 8
Keith ... 80 L 11
Keld ... 49 N 20
Kellas *Angus* ... 69 L 14
Kellas *Moray* ... 80 J 11
Kelleth ... 49 M 20
Kellie Castle ... 69 L 15
Kellington ... 44 Q 22
Kelloe ... 56 P 19
Kelly Bray ... 3 H 32
Kelmarsh ... 28 R 26
Kelsall ... 34 L 24
Kelso ... 62 M 17
Kelston ... 19 M 29
Keltneyburn ... 73 H 14
Kelty ... 68 J 15
Kelvedon ... 30 W 28
Kelvedon Hatch ... 22 U 29
Kemble ... 19 N 28
Kemnay ... 75 M 12
Kempley ... 26 M 28
Kempsey ... 27 N 27
Kempsford ... 19 O 28
Kempston ... 29 S 27
Kemsing ... 22 U 30
Kendal ... 48 L 21
Kenfig ... 17 I 29
Kenilworth ... 27 P 26
Kenknock ... 67 G 14
Kenmore *Highland* ... 77 C 11
Kenmore *Perthshire and Kinross* ... 67 I 14
Kenn ... 18 L 29
Kennet (River) ... 19 O 29
Kennethmont ... 80 L 11
Kenninghall ... 30 X 26
Kennington *Kent* ... 22 W 30
Kennington *Oxon.* ... 20 Q 28
Kennoway ... 68 K 15
Kenovay ... 70 Z 14
Kensaleyre ... 77 B 11
Kentallen ... 72 E 13
Kentford ... 30 V 27
Kentisbeare ... 7 K 31
Kentmere ... 48 L 20
Kenton ... 4 J 32
Kents Bank ... 48 L 21
Keoldale ... 84 F 8
Keresley ... 28 P 26
Kerrera ... 65 D 14
Kerry ... 26 K 26
Kersey ... 30 W 27
Kershader ... 82 A 9
Kershopefoot ... 55 L 18
Kesgrave ... 31 X 27
Kessingland ... 31 Z 26
Keswick ... 54 K 20
Kettering ... 28 R 26
Kettleness ... 50 R 20
Kettleshulme ... 43 N 24
Kettletoft ... 87 M 6
Kettlewell ... 49 N 21
Ketton ... 37 S 26
Kew ... 21 T 29
Kewstoke ... 18 L 29
Kexbrough ... 43 P 23
Kexby ... 44 R 23
Keyingham ... 45 T 22
Keymer ... 11 T 31
Keynsham ... 18 M 29
Keyworth ... 36 Q 25
Kibworth Harcourt ... 36 R 26
Kidderminster ... 27 N 26
Kidmore Lodge ... 79 G 10
Kidlington ... 20 Q 28
Kidsgrove ... 35 N 24
Kidstones ... 49 N 21
Kidwelly / Cydweli ... 15 H 28
Kielder ... 55 M 18
Kielder Forest ... 55 M 18
Kielder Reservoir ... 55 M 18
Kiiphedir ... 85 I 9
Kilamarsh ... 44 Q 24
Kilbarchan ... 60 G 16
Kilbirnie ... 60 F 16
Kilbrannan Sound ... 59 D 17

Kilbride ... 65 D 14
Kilburn *Amber Valley* ... 36 P 24
Kilburn *Hambleton* ... 50 Q 21
Kilchattan ... 59 E 16
Kilchenzie ... 59 C 17
Kilcheran ... 65 D 14
Kilchiaran ... 58 A 16
Kilchoan ... 71 B 13
Kilchoman ... 58 A 16
Kilchrenan ... 65 E 14
Kilconquhar ... 69 L 15
Kilcreggan ... 66 F 16
Kildale ... 50 Q 20
Kildary ... 79 H 10
Kildavanan ... 59 E 16
Kildonan ... 59 E 17
Kildonan Lodge ... 85 I 9
Kildrummy ... 74 L 12
Kildrummy Castle ... 74 L 12
Kilfinnan ... 72 F 12
Kilgetti ... 15 F 28
Kilham *Berwick-upon-Tweed* ... 63 N 17
Kilham *East Riding of Yorkshire* ... 51 S 21
Kilkhampton ... 6 G 31
Killay ... 15 H 29
Killean ... 59 D 17
Killearn ... 67 G 15
Killen ... 79 H 11
Killerton ... 7 J 31
Killiechronan ... 65 C 14
Killilan ... 78 D 12
Killin ... 67 H 14
Killinghall ... 50 P 21
Killundine ... 71 C 14
Kilmacolm ... 60 G 16
Kilmersdon ... 19 M 30
Kilmington *East Devon* ... 8 K 31
Kilmington *Salisbury* ... 9 N 30
Kilmorack ... 79 G 11
Kilmore ... 71 C 12
Kilmory *Ardnamurchan* ... 71 B 13
Kilmory *Argyll and Bute* ... 65 C 16
Kilmory *I. Rhum* ... 71 A 12
Kilmory *North Ayrshire* ... 59 E 17
Kilmuir ... 77 A 11
Kilmun ... 66 F 16
Kilncadzow ... 61 I 16
Kilninver ... 65 D 14
Kilnsey ... 49 N 21
Kiloran ... 64 B 15
Kilpeck ... 26 L 28
Kilrenny ... 69 L 15
Kilsyth ... 67 H 16
Kilt Rock ... 77 B 11
Kiltarlity ... 79 G 11
Kilvaxter ... 77 A 11
Kilwinning ... 60 F 17
Kimberley *Broxtowe* ... 36 Q 25
Kimberley *South Norfolk* ... 38 X 26
Kimble ... 20 R 28
Kimbolton ... 29 S 27
Kimmeridge ... 9 N 32
Kimpton ... 21 T 28
Kinbrace ... 85 I 9
Kinbuck ... 67 I 15
Kincardine *Fife* ... 67 I 15
Kincardine *Highland* ... 79 G 10
Kincardine *O'Neil* ... 75 L 12
Kinclaven ... 68 J 14
Kincraig ... 73 I 12
Kineton ... 28 P 27
Kinfauns ... 68 J 14
Kingairloch ... 72 D 14
Kingarth ... 59 E 16
Kinghorn ... 68 K 15
Kinglassie ... 68 K 15
King's Bromley ... 35 O 25
King's Cliffe ... 37 S 26
Kings Langley ... 21 S 28
King's Lynn ... 38 V 25
King's Meaburn ... 55 M 20
King's Somborne ... 10 P 30
King's Sutton ... 28 Q 27
King's Walden ... 29 T 28
Kings Worthy ... 10 Q 30
Kingsbarns ... 69 M 15
Kingsburgh ... 77 A 11

Kingsbury Episcopi ... 8 L 31
Kingsclere ... 20 Q 30
Kingscote ... 19 N 29
Kingsdon ... 8 L 30
Kingsdown ... 23 Y 30
Kingsgate ... 23 Y 29
Kingshouse *Highland* ... 72 F 14
Kingshouse *Stirling* ... 67 H 14
Kingskerswell ... 4 J 32
Kingskettle ... 68 K 15
Kingsland ... 26 L 27
Kingsley *East Hampshire* ... 10 R 30
Kingsley *Staffordshire Moorlands* ... 35 O 24
Kingsmuir ... 74 L 14
Kingsnorth ... 12 W 30
Kingsteignton ... 4 J 32
Kingsthorpe ... 28 R 27
Kingston *Devon* ... 4 I 33
Kingston *East Hampshire* ... 69 L 15
Kingston *Moray* ... 80 K 10
Kingston *South Cambridgeshire* ... 29 T 27
Kingston Bagpuize ... 20 P 28
Kingston Deverill ... 9 N 30
Kingston Lacy ... 9 N 31
Kingston Lisle ... 20 P 29
Kingston Seymour ... 18 L 29
Kingston-St. Mary ... 8 K 30
Kingston-upon-Hull ... 45 S 22
Kingston-upon-Thames *London Borough* ... 21 T 29
Kingstone ... 26 L 27
Kingswear ... 4 J 32
Kingswinford ... 27 N 26
Kingswood ... 19 M 29
Kingswood *Powys* ... 34 K 26
Kingswood *South Glos.* ... 18 M 29
Kington ... 26 K 27
Kington Langley ... 19 N 29
Kington-St. Michael ... 19 N 29
Kingussie ... 73 H 12
Kinkell ... 75 M 12
Kinkell Bridge ... 67 I 15
Kinknockie ... 81 O 11
Kinlet ... 27 M 26
Kinloch ... 71 B 12
Kinloch Hourn ... 72 D 12
Kinloch Lodge ... 84 G 8
Kinloch Rannoch ... 73 H 13
Kinlochard ... 67 G 15
Kinlochbervie ... 84 E 8
Kinlocheil ... 72 E 13
Kinlochewe ... 78 E 11
Kinlochleven ... 72 F 13
Kinlochmoidart ... 71 C 13
Kinloss ... 80 J 11
Kinmuck ... 75 N 12
Kinnaird ... 68 K 14
Kinneff ... 75 N 13
Kinnelhead ... 61 J 18
Kinnerley ... 34 L 25
Kinnersley ... 26 L 27
Kinnesswood ... 68 K 15
Kinninvie ... 56 O 20
Kinross ... 68 J 15
Kinrossie ... 68 K 14
Kintbury ... 20 P 29
Kintessack ... 80 I 11
Kintore ... 75 M 12
Kintra ... 58 B 17
Kintyre (Peninsula) ... 59 D 17
Kinver ... 27 N 26
Kippax ... 43 P 22
Kippen ... 67 H 15
Kippford ... 53 I 19
Kirby Bellars ... 36 R 25
Kirby Cross ... 31 X 28
Kirby Hall ... 29 S 26
Kirby Misperton ... 50 R 21
Kirby Muxloe ... 36 Q 26
Kirby Underwood ... 37 S 25
Kirdford ... 11 S 30
Kirk Ella ... 45 S 22
Kirk Ireton ... 35 P 24
Kirk Merrington ... 56 P 19
Kirk Michael ... 46 G 21
Kirk Yetholm ... 63 N 17
Kirkbampton ... 54 K 19
Kirkbean ... 53 J 19
Kirkbride ... 54 K 19
Kirkbuddo ... 69 L 14
Kirkburn ... 51 S 22
Kirkburton ... 43 O 23
Kirkby ... 42 L 23
Kirkby Fleetham ... 50 P 20

Kirkby-in-Ashfield ... 36 Q 24
Kirkby-la-Thorpe ... 37 S 25
Kirkby Lonsdale ... 48 M 21
Kirkby Malham ... 49 N 21
Kirkby Mallory ... 36 Q 26
Kirkby Malzeard ... 49 P 21
Kirkby Overblow ... 50 P 22
Kirkby Stephen ... 49 M 20
Kirkby Thore ... 55 M 20
Kirkbymoorside ... 50 R 21
Kirkcaldy ... 68 K 15
Kirkcolm ... 52 E 19
Kirkconnel ... 60 I 17
Kirkcowan ... 52 G 19
Kirkcudbright ... 53 H 19
Kirkcudbright Bay ... 53 H 19
Kirkfieldbank ... 61 I 16
Kirkgunzeon ... 53 I 19
Kirkham ... 42 L 22
Kirkheaton ... 56 O 18
Kirkhill ... 79 G 11
Kirkhope ... 61 J 18
Kirkinner ... 52 G 19
Kirkintilloch ... 67 H 16
Kirkland *Dumfries and Galloway* ... 53 I 18
Kirkland *Eden* ... 55 M 19
Kirklees ... 43 O 23
Kirklevington ... 50 P 20
Kirklington *North Yorkshire* ... 50 P 21
Kirklington *Nottinghamshire* ... 36 R 24
Kirkliston ... 68 J 16
Kirkmaiden ... 52 F 19
Kirkmichael *Perthshire and Kinross* ... 74 J 13
Kirkmichael *South Ayrshire* ... 60 G 17
Kirkmuirhill ... 61 I 17
Kirknewton *Berwick-upon-Tweed* ... 63 N 17
Kirknewton *West Lothian* ... 61 J 16
Kirkoswald ... 59 F 18
Kirkpatrick Durham ... 53 I 18
Kirkpatrick-Fleming ... 54 K 18
Kirkstone Pass ... 48 L 20
Kirkton *Dumfries and Galloway* ... 53 J 18
Kirkton *Scottish Borders* ... 62 L 17
Kirkton Manor ... 61 K 17
Kirkton of Culsalmond ... 81 M 11
Kirkton of Durris ... 75 M 12
Kirkton of Glenisla ... 74 K 13
Kirkton of Kingoldrum ... 74 K 13
Kirkton of Largo ... 69 L 15
Kirkton of Skene ... 75 N 12
Kirkton of Strathmartine ... 69 K 14
Kirkton of Auchterless ... 81 M 11
Kirktown of Deskford ... 80 L 11
Kirkwall ... 86 L 7
Kirkwhelpington ... 56 N 18
Kirmington ... 45 T 23
Kirn ... 66 F 16
Kirriemuir ... 74 K 13
Kirtlebridge ... 54 K 18
Kirtling ... 28 Q 28
Kirtomy ... 85 H 8
Kirton *Boston* ... 37 T 25
Kirton *Suffolk Coastal* ... 31 X 27
Kirton End ... 37 T 25
Kirton-in-Lindsey ... 44 S 23
Kishorn (Loch) ... 78 D 11
Kislingbury ... 28 R 27
Kitchener Memorial ... 86 J 6
Kiveton ... 44 Q 23
Knaresborough ... 50 P 21
Knarsdale ... 55 M 19
Knebworth ... 29 T 28
Kneesall ... 36 R 24
Kneesworth ... 29 T 27
Knighton / Trefyclawdd ... 26 K 26
Knightshayes Court ... 7 J 31
Kniveton ... 35 O 24
Knock *Argyll and Bute* ... 65 C 14
Knock *Moray* ... 80 L 11
Knock *Western Isles* ... 83 B 9
Knockandhu ... 80 K 12
Knockbrex ... 53 H 19
Knockie Lodge ... 73 G 12
Knockin ... 34 L 25
Knocknaha ... 59 D 17
Knocksharry ... 46 G 21
Knockvennie Smithy ... 53 I 18
Knole ... 22 U 30
Knossington ... 36 R 25

Knottingley ... 44 Q 22
Knowe ... 52 G 18
Knowehead ... 53 H 18
Knowesgate ... 55 N 18
Knowle ... 27 O 26
Knowsley ... 42 L 23
Knoydart ... 72 D 12
Knutsford ... 42 M 24
Kyle Forest ... 60 G 17
Kyle of Durness ... 84 F 8
Kyle of Lochalsh ... 77 C 12
Kyle of Sutherland ... 79 G 10
Kyle of Tongue ... 84 G 8
Kyleakin ... 77 C 12
Kylerhea ... 72 C 12
Kyles Scalpay ... 82 Z 10
Kylestrome ... 84 E 9
Kynance Cove ... 2 E 34
Kyre park ... 26 M 27

L

La Rocque *Jersey I.* ... 5
Laceby ... 45 T 23
Lacey Green ... 20 R 28
Lache ... 34 L 24
Lacock ... 19 N 29
Ladder Hills ... 74 K 12
Laddock ... 3 F 33
Ladybank ... 68 K 15
Ladybower Reservoir ... 43 O 23
Ladyhill ... 55 N 18
Laga ... 65 C 16
Laggan *Argyll and Bute* ... 58 B 16
Laggan *near Invergarry* ... 72 F 12
Laggan *near Newtonmore* ... 73 H 12
Laggan (Loch) ... 73 G 13
Laggan Point ... 58 B 16
Lagganulva ... 64 B 14
Laide ... 78 D 10
Lair ... 78 E 11
Lairg ... 84 G 9
Lake District National Park ... 48 K 20
Lakenheath ... 30 V 26
Lamanva ... 2 E 33
Lamberhurst ... 12 V 30
Lambeth *London Borough* ... 21 T 29
Lambley *Gedling* ... 36 Q 24
Lambley *Tynedale* ... 55 M 19
Lambourn ... 20 P 29
Lamerton ... 3 H 32
Lamington ... 61 J 17
Lamlash ... 59 E 17
Lamlash Bay ... 59 E 17
Lammermuir Hills ... 62 L 16
Lampeter / Llanbedr Pont Steffan ... 15 H 27
Lamplugh ... 54 J 20
Lamport ... 28 R 26
Lanark ... 61 I 16
Lancaster ... 48 L 21
Lanchester ... 56 O 19
Lancing ... 11 T 31
Landmark Visitor Centre ... 79 I 12
Landrake ... 3 H 32
Land's End ... 2 C 33
Landulph ... 3 H 32
Lane End ... 20 R 29
Laneast ... 6 G 32
Lanercost ... 55 L 19
Langar ... 36 R 25
Langavat (Loch) *Lewis* ... 82 Z 9
Langavat (Loch) *South Harris* ... 76 Z 10
Langbank ... 66 G 16
Langcliffe ... 49 N 21
Langdale End ... 51 S 21
Langdale Valley ... 48 K 20
Langdon Beck ... 55 N 19
Langenhoe ... 30 W 28
Langford *Mid Bedfordshire* ... 29 T 27
Langford *West Oxfordshire* ... 19 P 28
Langford Budville ... 8 K 31
Langham ... 36 R 25
Langholm ... 54 L 18
Langleeford ... 63 N 17
Langley ... 21 S 29
Langley Park ... 56 O 19
Langold ... 44 Q 23
Langport ... 8 L 30
Langrick ... 37 T 24
Langrish ... 10 Q 30
Langsett ... 43 O 23
Langshaw ... 62 L 17
Langstrothdale Chase ... 49 N 21

Langthwaite ... 49 O 20
Langtoft ... 51 S 21
Langton ... 50 R 21
Langton Matravers ... 9 O 32
Langwathby ... 55 L 19
Lanhydrock ... 3 F 32
Lanivet ... 3 F 32
Lanlivery ... 3 F 32
Lanreath ... 3 G 32
Lansallos ... 3 G 32
Lanton ... 62 M 17
Lapford ... 7 I 31
Larachbeg ... 71 C 14
Larbert ... 67 I 15
Largs ... 59 F 16
Larkhall ... 61 I 16
Larkhill ... 19 O 30
Larling ... 30 W 26
Lasswade ... 61 K 16
Lastingham ... 50 R 21
Latchingdon ... 22 W 28
Latton ... 19 O 29
Lauder ... 62 L 16
Lauderdale ... 62 L 16
Laugharne ... 15 G 28
Laughton *Wealden* ... 12 U 31
Laughton *West Lindsey* ... 44 R 23
Launcells ... 6 G 31
Launceston ... 6 G 32
Launton ... 28 Q 28
Laurencekirk ... 75 M 13
Laurieston ... 53 H 19
Lauriston Castle ... 68 K 16
Lavendon ... 29 S 27
Lavenham ... 30 W 27
Laverstock ... 9 O 30
Laverstoke ... 20 Q 30
Lawford ... 30 X 28
Lawrenny ... 16 F 28
Lawshall ... 30 W 27
Laxay ... 82 A 9
Laxey ... 46 G 21
Laxey Bay ... 46 G 21
Laxfield ... 31 Y 27
Laxford (Loch) ... 84 E 8
Laxford Bridge ... 84 E 8
Laxo ... 87 Q 2
Laxton *East Riding of Yorkshire* ... 44 R 22
Laxton *Newark and Sherwood* ... 36 R 24
Layer-de-la-Haye ... 30 W 28
Layer Marney ... 22 W 28
Laytham ... 44 R 22
Layton ... 42 K 22
Lazonby ... 55 L 19
Lea *Herefordshire* ... 26 M 28
Lea *North Wiltshire* ... 19 N 29
Lea *West Lindsey* ... 44 R 23
Leaden Roding ... 22 U 28
Leadenham ... 37 S 24
Leadgate *Derwentside* ... 56 O 19
Leadgate *Eden* ... 55 M 19
Leadhills ... 61 I 17
Leaflied ... 20 P 28
Leagrave ... 29 S 28
Lealholm ... 50 R 20
Lealt ... 65 C 15
Leargybreck ... 65 C 16
Leasingham ... 37 S 24
Leathaid Bhuain (Loch an) ... 84 F 9
Leatherhead ... 21 T 30
Leathley ... 49 P 22
Leavening ... 50 R 21
Lebberston ... 51 S 21
Lechlade ... 19 O 28
Lecht Road ... 74 K 12
Leckmelm ... 78 E 10
Leconfield ... 44 S 22
Ledbury ... 27 M 27
Ledmore ... 84 F 9
Ledsham ... 44 Q 22
Lee ... 16 H 30
Lee-on-the-Solent ... 10 Q 31
Leebotwood ... 34 L 26
Leeds *Kent* ... 22 V 30
Leeds *West Yorks.* ... 43 P 22
Leedstown ... 2 D 33
Leek ... 35 N 24
Leek Wootton ... 27 P 27
Leeming Bar ... 50 P 21
Leeswood ... 34 K 24
Legbourne ... 45 U 23
Legerwood ... 62 M 16
Leicester ... 36 Q 26
Leicester Forest East ... 36 Q 26
Leigh ... 42 M 23

A B C D E F G H I J K L M N O P Q R S T U V W X Y Z

A
B
C
D
E
F
G
H
I
J
K
L
M
N
O
P
Q
R
S
T
U
V
W
X
Y
Z

Leigh *Mole Valley* ....21 T 30
Leigh *North Wiltshire* ....19 O 29
Leigh *Sevenoaks* ....22 U 30
Leigh *West Dorset* ....8 M 31
Leigh-on-Sea ....22 V 29
Leigh Sinton ....27 N 27
Leighterton ....19 N 29
Leighton Buzzard ....29 S 28
Leim ....58 C 17
Leintwardine ....26 L 26
Leirinmore ....84 F 8
Leiston ....31 Y 27
Leith ....68 K 16
Leitholm ....62 M 16
Lemreway ....82 A 9
Lendalfoot ....52 F 18
Lenham ....22 W 30
Lennoxtown ....67 H 16
Leominster ....26 L 27
Leonard Stanley ....19 N 28
Lepe ....10 P 31
Lephinmore ....65 E 15
Lerwick ....87 Q 3
Lesbury ....63 P 17
Leslie *Aberdeenshire* ....81 L 12
Leslie *Fife* ....68 K 15
Lesmahagow ....61 I 17
Leswalt ....52 E 19
Letchworth ....29 T 28
Letham *Angus* ....75 L 14
Letham *Fife* ....68 K 15
Letheringsett ....38 X 25
Letterewe Forest ....78 D 10
Letterfearn ....78 D 12
Lettermore ....84 G 8
Letters ....78 E 10
Letterston ....24 F 28
Leuchars ....69 L 14
Leurbost ....82 A 9
Leven
  East Riding of Yorks. ...51 T 22
Leven *Fife* ....69 K 15
Leven (Loch) ....72 E 13
Leven (River) ....72 F 13
Levens ....48 L 21
Levens Hall ....48 L 21
Levenwick ....87 Q 4
Leverington ....37 U 25
Leverton
  with Habblesthorpe ....44 R 24
Levington ....31 X 27
Levisham ....50 R 21
Lewannick ....3 G 32
Lewdown ....6 H 32
Lewes ....11 U 31
Lewis (Isle of) ....82 Z 9
Lewis and Harris (Isle of) ...82 Z 8
Lewisham
  London Borough ....21 T 29
Lewknor ....20 R 28
Leyburn ....49 O 21
Leyland ....42 L 22
Leysdown-on-Sea ....22 W 29
Lezant ....3 G 32
Lhanbryde ....80 K 11
Lhen (The) ....46 G 20
Liathach ....78 D 11
Libberton ....61 J 16
Lichfield ....35 O 25
Liddesdale ....55 L 18
Lidgate ....30 V 27
Lifton ....6 H 32
Ligger or Perran Bay ....2 E 32
Lilbourne ....28 Q 26
Lilleshall ....35 M 25
Lilliesleaf ....62 L 17
Limmerhaugh ....60 H 17
Limpsfield ....21 U 30
Linchmere ....10 R 30
Lincoln ....44 S 24
Lincolnshire Wolds ....45 T 23
Lindfield ....11 T 30
Lindores ....68 K 14
Lingague ....46 F 21
Lingay *near Eriskay* ....70 X 12
Lingay *near Pabbay* ....70 X 13
Lingen ....26 L 27
Lingfield ....21 T 30
Liniclate ....76 X 11
Linlithgow ....67 J 16
Linn of Dee ....74 J 13
Linn of Tummel ....74 I 13
Linneraineach ....84 E 9
Linney Head ....14 E 29
Linnhe (Loch) ....72 D 14
Linslade ....29 R 28
Lintmill ....80 L 10

Linton *Craven* ....49 N 21
Linton *Herefordshire* ....26 M 28
Linton *Scottish Borders* ...62 M 17
Linton
  South Cambridgeshire ...30 U 27
Linton *South Derbyshire* ...35 P 25
Linton-on-Ouse ....50 Q 21
Linwood *Renfrewshire* ......60 G 16
Linwood *West Lindsey* ......45 T 23
Liphook ....10 R 30
Liskeard ....3 G 32
Lismore ....65 D 14
Liss ....10 R 30
Lisset ....51 T 21
Lisvane ....18 K 29
Litcham ....38 W 25
Litchborough ....28 Q 27
Litchfield ....20 P 30
Litherland ....42 L 23
Little-Baddow ....22 V 28
Little-Barningham ....39 X 25
Little Berkhamsted ....21 T 28
Little Brington ....28 Q 27
Little Budworth ....34 M 24
Little Bytham ....37 S 25
Little Chalfont ....21 S 28
Little Clacton ....31 X 28
Little Colonsay ....64 B 14
Little-Coxwell ....19 P 29
Little Cumbrae Island ....59 F 16
Little Dewchurch ....26 L 28
Little Galdenoch ....52 E 19
Little Glenshee ....67 J 14
Little Hadham ....29 U 28
Little Hallingbury ....22 U 28
Little Harrowden ....28 R 27
Little Houghton ....28 R 27
Little Loch Broom ....78 D 10
Little Loch Roag ....82 Z 9
Little Mill ....18 L 28
Little-Milton ....20 Q 28
Little Minch (The) ....76 Z 11
Little Moreton Hall ....35 N 24
Little Ouse (River) ....30 V 26
Little Ouseburn ....50 Q 21
Little-Raveley ....29 T 26
Little Snoring ....38 W 25
Little-Stretton ....26 L 26
Little-Stukeley ....29 T 26
Little Torrington ....6 H 31
Little Urswick ....48 K 21
Little Walsingham ....38 W 25
Little Waltham ....22 V 28
Little Wenlock ....34 M 26
Littleborough ....43 N 23
Littlebourne ....23 X 30
Littlebury ....30 U 27
Littlecote House ....20 P 29
Littleferry ....79 H 10
Littleham ....4 J 32
Littlehampton ....11 S 31
Littlemill ....79 I 11
Littleport ....30 U 26
Littlestone-on-Sea ....12 W 31
Littleton ....10 P 30
Littleworth ....20 P 28
Litton Cheney ....5 M 31
Liverpool ....42 L 23
Liverton ....50 R 20
Livet (Glen) ....80 K 12
Livingston ....61 J 16
Lizard ....2 E 34
Lizard Peninsula ....2 E 33
Llam ....35 O 24
Llan ....33 J 26
Llan-non ....15 H 28
Llan-y-Bri ....15 G 28
Llanarmon-yn-Ial ....34 K 24
Llanarthne ....24 H 28
Llanarthney ....15 H 28
Llanasa ....41 J 23
Llanbadarn Fawr ....25 H 26
Llanbedr ....33 H 25
Llanbedr Pont Steffan /
  Lampeter ....15 H 27
Llanbedrog ....32 G 25
Llanberis ....33 H 24
Llanberis (Pass of) ....33 H 24
Llanbister ....26 K 26
Llanboidy ....15 G 28
Llanbradach ....18 K 29
Llanbrynmair ....33 J 26
Llanddarog ....15 H 28
Llanddeiniol ....25 H 27
Llandderfel ....33 J 25
Llanddeusant ....40 G 22

Llanddewi Brefi ....25 I 27
Llanddewi Ystradenni ....26 K 27
Llanddona ....40 H 23
Llanddowror ....15 G 28
Llanddulas ....41 J 23
Llandegla ....34 K 24
Llandeilo ....15 I 28
Llandenny ....18 L 28
Llandinam ....25 J 26
Llandissilio ....15 F 28
Llandogo ....18 L 28
Llandovery / Llanymddyfri ...25 I 28
Llandrindod Wells ....25 J 27
Llandrinio ....34 K 25
Llandudno ....41 I 23
Llandudno Junction ....41 I 23
Llandwrog ....32 H 24
Llandybie ....15 I 28
Llandyfaelog ....15 H 28
Llandygai ....40 H 23
Llandysul ....15 H 27
Llanegryn ....33 H 26
Llanelian ....34 K 24
Llanellen ....18 L 28
Llanelli ....15 H 28
Llanelltyd ....33 I 25
Llanengan ....32 G 25
Llanerchymedd ....40 G 23
Llanerfyl ....33 J 25
Llanfachraeth ....40 G 23
Llanfaethlu ....40 G 22
Llanfair ....33 H 25
Llanfair-Caereinion ....34 K 26
Llanfair-Pwllgwyngyll ....40 H 23
Llanfair-ym-Muallt /
  Builth Wells ....25 J 27
Llanfair-yn-Neubwll ....40 G 23
Llanfairfechan ....41 I 23
Llanfairynghornwy ....40 G 22
Llanfechell ....40 G 22
Llanferres ....34 K 24
Llanfihangel-ar-arth ....15 H 28
Llanfihangel Glyn Myfyr ......33 J 24
Llanfihangel Nant Bran ......25 J 28
Llanfihangel Rhydithon ....26 K 27
Llanfihangel-y-Creuddyn ...25 I 26
Llanfilo ....26 K 28
Llanfoist ....18 K 28
Llanfrynach ....25 J 28
Llanfwrog ....40 G 23
Llanfyllin ....33 K 25
Llanfynydd *Carmarthenshire /
  Sir Gaerfyrddin* ....15 H 28
Llanfynydd *Flintshire /
  Sir y Fflint* ....34 K 24
Llanfyrnach ....15 G 28
Llangadfan ....33 J 25
Llangadog ....15 I 28
Llangain ....15 G 28
Llangammarch Wells ....25 J 27
Llangarron ....26 L 28
Llangathen ....15 H 28
Llangedwyn ....34 K 25
Llangefni ....40 H 23
Llangeinor ....17 J 29
Llangeitho ....25 H 27
Llangeler ....15 G 27
Llangenith ....15 H 29
Llangennech ....15 H 28
Llangernyw ....33 I 24
Llangoed ....40 H 23
Llangollen ....34 K 25
Llangorse ....26 K 28
Llangorwen ....25 H 26
Llangrannog ....15 G 27
Llangunllo ....26 K 27
Llangunnor ....15 H 28
Llangurig ....25 J 26
Llangwm ....33 J 25
Llangwm *Monmouthshire /
  Sir Fynwy* ....18 L 28
Llangwm *Pembrokeshire /
  Sir Benfro* ....16 F 28
Llangwnnadl ....32 F 25
Llangwyryfon ....25 H 27
Llangybi ....15 H 27
Llangyndeyrn ....15 H 28
Llangynidr ....26 K 28
Llangynog *Carmarthenshire /
  Sir Gaerfyrddin* ....15 G 28
Llangynog *Powys* ....33 J 25
Llangynwyd ....17 J 29
Llangywer ....33 J 25
Llanharan ....17 J 29
Llanharry ....17 J 29
Llanhilleth ....18 K 28
Llanidloes ....25 J 26

Llanilar ....25 H 26
Llanishen ....18 L 28
Llanllwchaiarn ....26 K 26
Llanllyfni ....32 H 24
Llanmadoc ....15 H 29
Llannefydd ....41 J 23
Llanon ....25 H 27
Llanpumsaint ....15 H 28
Llanrhaeadr ....33 J 24
Llanrhaeadr-ym-
  Mochnant ....34 K 25
Llanrhidian ....15 H 29
Llanrhystud ....25 H 27
Llanrug ....33 H 24
Llanrwst ....33 I 24
Llansanffraid Glan Conwy ...41 I 23
Llansannan ....33 J 24
Llansantffraid ....25 H 27
Llansantffraid-ym-Mechain ...34 K 25
Llansawel ....15 H 27
Llansilin ....34 K 25
Llansoy ....18 L 28
Llansteffan ....15 G 28
Llanthony ....26 K 28
Llanthony Priory ....26 K 28
Llantilio Crossenny ....18 L 28
Llantrisant ....17 J 29
Llantwit Major ....17 J 29
Llanuwchllyn ....33 I 25
Llanvetherine ....18 L 28
Llanwddyn ....33 J 25
Llanwenog ....15 H 27
Llanwnda ....32 H 24
Llanwnen ....15 H 27
Llanwnog ....25 J 26
Llanwrda ....15 I 28
Llanwrin ....33 I 26
Llanwrtyd Wells ....25 J 27
Llanwyddelan ....33 J 26
Llanybydder ....15 H 27
Llanychaer ....24 F 28
Llanymawddwy ....33 J 25
Llanymddyfri / Llandovery ...25 I 28
Llanymynech ....34 K 25
Llanynghenedl ....40 G 23
Llanystumdwy ....32 H 25
Llawhaden ....15 F 28
Llechryd ....15 G 27
Lledrod ....25 I 27
Lleyn Peninsula ....32 G 25
Llithfaen ....32 G 25
Llowes ....26 K 27
Llston ....15 H 29
Llwydcoed ....17 J 28
Llwyndafydd ....24 G 27
Llwyngwril ....33 H 25
Llwynmawr ....34 K 25
Llyfnant Valley ....33 I 26
Llyn Brianne ....25 I 27
Llyn Celyn ....33 I 25
Llyn Tegid or Bala Lake ......33 J 25
Llysfaen ....41 I 23
Llyswen ....26 K 27
Llysworney ....17 J 29
Llywel ....25 J 28
Loanhead ....61 K 16
Lochailort ....72 D 13
Lochaline ....65 C 14
Lochans ....52 E 19
Locharbriggs ....53 J 18
Lochassynt Lodge ....84 E 9
Lochawe ....66 E 14
Lochay (Glen) ....67 G 14
Lochboisdale ....70 Y 12
Lochbuie ....65 C 14
Lochcarron ....78 D 11
Lochdonhead ....65 C 14
Lochdrum ....78 F 10
Lochearnhead ....67 H 14
Locheport ....76 Y 11
Lochgair ....65 D 15
Lochfoot ....53 I 18
Lochgarthside ....73 G 12
Lochgelly ....68 K 15
Lochgilphead ....65 D 15
Lochgoilhead ....66 F 15
Lochinver ....84 E 9
Lochluichart ....78 F 11
Lochmaben ....54 J 18
Lochmaddy ....76 Y 11
Lochore ....68 K 15
Lochportain ....76 Y 11
Lochranza ....59 E 16
Lochsie (Glen) ....74 J 13
Lochstack ....84 F 8
Lochton *Aberdeenshire* ...75 M 12
Lochton *South Ayrshire* ...52 F 18
Lochtyn / Ynys ....15 G 27

Lochuisge ....72 D 14
Lochwinnoch ....60 G 16
Lochy (Loch) ....72 F 13
Lockerbie ....54 J 18
Lockerley ....9 P 30
Locking ....18 L 30
Loddington ....28 R 26
Loddon ....39 Y 26
Lode ....30 U 27
Lodsworth ....11 R 31
Lofthouse ....49 O 21
Loftus ....50 R 20
Logan Gardens ....52 F 19
Loggerheads ....35 M 25
Logie Coldstone ....74 L 12
Logiealmond ....67 I 14
Login ....15 F 28
Lomond (Loch) ....66 G 15
Londesborough ....51 R 22
London ....21 T 29
London Colney ....21 T 28
Long (Loch) *Angus* ....68 K 14
Long (Loch)
  Argyll and Bute ....66 F 15
Long Ashton ....18 M 29
Long Bennington ....36 R 25
Long Bredy ....5 M 31
Long Buckby ....28 Q 27
Long Clawson ....36 R 25
Long Crendon ....20 R 28
Long Eaton ....36 Q 25
Long Hanborough ....20 P 28
Long Itchington ....28 P 27
Long Lawford ....28 Q 26
Long Man (The) ....12 U 31
Long Marston ....50 Q 22
Long Marton ....55 M 20
Long Melford ....30 W 27
Long Mountain ....34 K 26
Long Mynd (The) ....26 L 26
Long Preston ....49 N 21
Long Stratton ....31 X 26
Long Sutton *Lincs.* ....37 U 25
Long Sutton *Somerset* ......8 L 30
Long Wittenham ....20 Q 29
Longay ....77 C 12
Longbenton ....56 P 18
Longborough ....27 O 28
Longbridge Deverill ....9 N 30
Longburton ....8 M 31
Longcot ....19 P 29
Longdon ....35 O 25
Longfield ....22 U 29
Longford
  Derbyshire Dales ....35 O 25
Longford *Tewkesbury* ....27 N 28
Longforgan ....68 K 14
Longformacus ....62 M 16
Longham ....38 W 25
Longhirst ....56 P 18
Longhorsley ....56 O 18
Longhoughton ....63 P 17
Longleat House ....19 N 30
Longmanhill ....81 M 11
Longnewton ....50 P 20
Longney ....19 M 28
Longniddry ....69 L 16
Longnor ....35 O 24
Longridge *Ribble Valley* ...42 M 22
Longridge
  South Staffordshire ....35 N 25
Longridge *West Lothian* ...61 I 16
Longside ....81 O 11
Longstanton ....29 U 27
Longton *South Ribble* ......42 L 22
Longton *Stoke-on-Trent* ...35 N 25
Longtown *Carlisle* ....54 L 18
Longtown *Herefordshire* ...26 L 28
Longwick ....20 R 28
Longworth ....20 P 28
Lonmore ....77 A 11
Looe ....3 G 32
Loose ....22 V 30
Loppington ....34 L 25
Lorn ....65 E 14
Lorn (Firth of) ....65 D 14
Lossiemouth ....80 K 10
Lostwithiel ....3 G 32
Lothbeg ....85 I 9
Lothersdale ....49 N 22
Lothmore ....85 I 9
Loudwater ....21 R 29
Loughborough ....36 Q 25
Loughor (River) ....17 H 29
Loughton ....21 U 29
Louth ....45 U 23
Lovington ....8 M 30

Low Bradley ....49 O 22
Low Crosby ....55 L 19
Low Row *Carlisle* ....55 M 19
Low Row *Richmondshire* ...49 N 20
Low Street ....39 Y 25
Lowca ....53 J 20
Lowdham ....36 Q 24
Lower Beeding ....11 T 30
Lower Bentham ....49 M 21
Lower Boddington ....28 Q 27
Lower Broadheath ....27 N 27
Lower Cam ....19 M 28
Lower Diabaig ....78 C 11
Lower Dounreay ....85 I 8
Lower Dunsforth ....50 Q 21
Lower Halstow ....22 W 29
Lower Hardres ....23 X 30
Lower Heyford ....28 Q 28
Lower Killeyan ....58 B 17
Lower Largo ....69 L 15
Lower Mayland ....22 W 28
Lower Peover ....42 M 24
Lower Upham ....10 Q 31
Lower-Whitley ....42 M 24
Lowestoft ....31 Z 26
Lowgill ....49 M 21
Lowick
  Berwick-upon-Tweed ....63 O 17
Lowick
  East Northamptonshire ...29 S 26
Lowick Bridge ....48 K 21
Lowther ....55 L 20
Lowther Hills ....61 J 18
Loxwood ....11 S 30
Loyal (Loch) ....84 G 8
Loyne (Loch) ....72 E 12
Lùb Score ....77 A 10
Lubcroy ....84 F 10
Lubenham ....28 R 26
Lubnaig (Loch) ....67 H 15
Luccombe ....17 J 30
Luce Bay ....52 F 19
Lucker ....63 O 17
Luddesdown ....22 V 29
Ludford *East Lindsey* ....45 T 23
Ludford *South Shropshire* ...26 L 26
Ludgershall *Bucks.* ....20 Q 28
Ludgershall *Wilts.* ....19 P 30
Ludgvan ....2 D 33
Ludham ....39 Y 25
Ludlow ....26 L 26
Lugton ....60 G 16
Luib *Highland* ....77 B 12
Luib *Stirling* ....67 G 14
Luichart (Loch) ....78 F 11
Luing ....65 D 15
Lullington ....35 P 25
Lulsgate Bottom ....18 L 29
Lulworth Cove ....9 N 32
Lumphanan ....75 L 12
Lumsden ....80 L 12
Lunan ....75 M 14
Lunanhead ....74 L 14
Luncarty ....68 J 14
Lund ....51 S 22
Lundie ....68 K 14
Lundie (Loch) ....78 C 11
Lundin Links ....69 L 15
Lundy ....16 G 30
Lunning ....87 Q 2
Lurgainn (Loch) ....84 E 9
Lurgashall ....11 S 30
Luskentyre ....82 Z 10
Luss ....66 G 15
Lusta ....77 A 11
Lustleigh ....4 I 32
Luston ....26 L 27
Luthermuir ....75 M 13
Luthrie ....68 K 14
Luton ....29 S 28
Luton Hoo ....21 S 28
Lutterworth ....28 Q 26
Lutton ....37 U 25
Luxborough ....7 J 30
Lybster ....86 K 9
Lydbury North ....26 L 26
Lydd ....12 W 31
Lydd-on-Sea ....12 W 31
Lydden ....23 X 30
Lydeard-St. Lawrence ....8 K 30
Lydford *Mendip* ....8 M 30
Lydford *West Devon* ....4 H 32
Lydham ....26 L 26
Lydiard Millicent ....19 O 29
Lydiard Park ....19 O 29
Lydiate ....42 L 23
Lydlinch ....9 M 31

Lydney .... 18 M 28
Lydstep .... 15 F 29
Lyme Bay .... 5 L 32
Lyme Park .... 43 N 23
Lyme Regis .... 5 L 31
Lyminge .... 13 X 30
Lymington .... 10 P 31
Lymm .... 42 M 23
Lympne .... 13 X 30
Lympstone .... 4 J 32
Lyndhurst .... 10 P 31
Lyne .... 61 K 17
Lyneham *North Wiltshire* .. 19 O 29
Lyneham
  West Oxfordshire .... 27 P 28
Lynemouth .... 56 P 18
Lyness .... 86 K 7
Lynmouth .... 17 I 30
Lynton .... 17 I 30
Lyon (Glen) .... 73 H 14
Lyonshall .... 26 L 27
Lytchett Matravers .... 9 N 31
Lytchett Minster .... 9 N 31
Lytes Cary .... 8 L 30
Lytham .... 42 L 22
Lytham St. Anne's .... 42 K 22
Lythe .... 51 R 20

M

Maaruig .... 82 Z 10
Mabie .... 53 J 18
Mablethorpe .... 45 U 23
Macaskin (Island) .... 65 D 15
Macclesfield .... 43 N 24
Macduff .... 81 M 10
Machars (The) .... 52 G 19
Machen .... 18 K 29
Machir Bay .... 58 A 16
Machrihanish .... 58 C 17
Machrihanish Bay .... 58 C 17
Machynlleth .... 33 I 26
Madderty .... 67 I 14
Maddiston .... 67 I 16
Maddy (Loch) .... 76 Y 11
Madeley *Staffs* .... 35 M 24
Madeley
  Telford and Wrekin ... 35 M 26
Madingley .... 29 U 27
Madron .... 2 D 33
Maenclochog .... 15 F 28
Maentwrog .... 33 I 25
Maerdy *Conwy* .... 33 J 25
Maerdy
  Rhondda, Cynon, Taf ...... 17 J 28
Maes Howe .... 86 K 7
Maesbrook .... 34 K 25
Maesteg .... 17 J 29
Maghull .... 42 L 23
Magor .... 18 L 29
Maiden Bradley .... 9 N 30
Maiden Castle .... 8 M 31
Maiden Newton .... 8 M 31
Maidenhead .... 20 R 29
Maidens .... 59 F 17
Maidford .... 28 Q 27
Maids Morelon .... 28 R 27
Maidstone .... 22 V 30
Maidwell .... 28 R 26
Mainland *Orkney Islands* .... 86 J 6
Mainland *Shetland Islands* .. 87 R 3
Mainstone .... 26 K 26
Maisemore .... 27 N 28
Malborough .... 4 I 33
Maldon .... 22 W 28
Malham .... 49 N 21
Mallaig .... 71 C 12
Mallory Park Circuit .... 36 P 26
Mallwyd .... 33 I 25
Malmesbury .... 19 N 29
Malpas .... 34 L 24
Maltby .... 44 Q 23
Maltby-le-Marsh .... 45 U 24
Malton .... 50 R 21
Malvern Wells .... 27 N 27
Mamble .... 26 M 26
Mamore Forest .... 72 F 13
Man (Isle of) .... 46 G 21
Manaccan .... 2 E 33
Manaton .... 4 I 32
Manchester .... 43 N 23
Manderston .... 62 N 16
Manea .... 29 U 26
Mangersta .... 82 Y 9
Mangotsfield .... 18 M 29
Manish .... 76 Z 10
Manningford Bruce .... 19 O 30

Mannings Heath .... 11 T 30
Manningtree .... 31 X 28
Manorbier .... 15 F 29
Mansfield .... 36 Q 24
Mansfield Woodhouse .. 36 Q 24
Manstone .... 9 N 31
Manton .... 36 R 26
Manuden .... 30 U 28
Maplebeck .... 36 R 24
Mapledurham .... 20 Q 29
Mappleton .... 45 T 22
Mappowder .... 9 M 31
Mar (Forest of) .... 74 J 12
Marazion .... 2 D 33
March .... 37 U 26
Marcham .... 20 P 29
Marchington .... 35 O 25
Marchwood .... 10 P 31
Marden .... 22 V 30
Maree (Loch) .... 78 D 10
Mareham-le-Fen .... 37 T 24
Maresfield .... 11 U 31
Margam .... 17 I 29
Margaretting .... 22 V 28
Margate .... 23 Y 29
Margnaheglish .... 59 E 17
Marham .... 38 V 26
Marholm .... 37 T 26
Marian-Glas .... 40 H 22
Marishader .... 77 B 11
Mark *Sedgemoor* .... 18 L 30
Mark *South Ayrshire* .... 52 E 18
Market Bosworth .... 36 P 26
Market Deeping .... 37 T 25
Market Drayton .... 34 M 25
Market Harborough ...... 28 R 26
Market Lavington .... 19 O 30
Market Overton .... 36 R 25
Market Rasen .... 45 T 23
Market Weighton .... 44 S 22
Markfield .... 36 Q 25
Markinch .... 68 K 15
Marks Tey .... 30 W 28
Marksbury .... 18 M 29
Markyate .... 21 S 28
Marlborough .... 19 O 29
Marldon .... 4 J 32
Marlesford .... 31 Y 27
Marloes .... 14 E 28
Marlow .... 20 R 29
Marnhull .... 9 N 31
Marple .... 43 N 23
Marros .... 15 G 28
Marsden .... 43 O 23
Marsett .... 49 N 21
Marsh Gibbon .... 28 Q 28
Marsham .... 39 X 25
Marshaw .... 48 M 22
Marshchapel .... 45 U 23
Marshfield
  Casnewydd / Newport .. 18 K 29
Marshfield
  South Gloucestershire .. 19 N 29
Marshwood .... 8 L 31
Marske .... 49 O 20
Marske-by-the-Sea .... 57 Q 20
Marstch .... 20 Q 28
Marston .... 37 R 25
Marston Magna .... 8 M 31
Marston Moretaine .... 29 S 27
Martham .... 39 Y 25
Martin *New Forest* .... 9 O 31
Martin *North Kesteven* .. 37 T 24
Martin (Isle) .... 84 E 10
Martin Mill .... 23 Y 30
Martindale .... 48 L 20
Martinstown .... 5 M 31
Martlesham .... 31 X 27
Martletwy .... 15 F 28
Martley .... 27 M 27
Martock .... 8 L 31
Marton *Harrogate* .... 50 P 21
Marton *Macclesfield* .. 35 N 24
Marvig .... 82 A 9
Marwell Zoological Park .. 10 Q 31
Mary Arden's House ...... 27 O 27
Mary Tavy .... 4 H 32
Marybank .... 79 G 11
Maryburgh .... 79 G 11
Maryculter .... 75 N 12
Maryfield .... 87 Q 3
Marykirk .... 75 M 13
Marypark .... 80 J 11
Maryport *Allerdale* .... 53 J 19
Maryport
  Dumfries and Galloway .... 52 F 19

Marywell *Aberdeenshire* ...... 75 L 12
Marywell *Angus* .... 69 M 14
Masham .... 49 P 21
Matching Green .... 22 U 28
Mathry .... 14 E 28
Matlock .... 36 P 24
Matlock Bath .... 35 P 24
Mattersey .... 44 R 23
Mattingley .... 20 R 30
Mattishall .... 38 X 26
Mauchline .... 60 G 17
Maud .... 81 N 11
Maughold .... 46 H 21
Maughold Head .... 46 H 21
Mawbray .... 54 J 19
Mawnan .... 2 E 33
Maxstoke .... 27 P 26
Maxton .... 62 M 17
Maybole .... 60 F 17
Mayfield *East Sussex* .. 12 U 30
Mayfield *Staffs* .... 35 O 24
Mc Arthur's Head .... 58 B 16
Meadie (Loch) .... 84 G 9
Meal Bank .... 48 L 20
Mealsgate .... 54 K 19
Meare .... 8 L 30
Measach (Falls of) .... 78 E 10
Measham .... 36 P 25
Meavaig .... 82 Z 10
Meavy .... 4 H 32
Medbourne .... 28 R 26
Medmenham .... 20 R 29
Medstead .... 10 Q 30
Medway (River) .... 22 W 29
Meidrim .... 15 G 28
Meifod .... 34 K 25
Meigle .... 68 K 14
Meikleour .... 68 J 14
Melbost .... 83 B 9
Melbourn .... 29 U 27
Melbourne
  East Riding of Yorkshire .. 44 R 22
Melbourne
  South Derbyshire .... 36 P 25
Melbury Osmond .... 8 M 31
Meldon .... 56 O 18
Melfort .... 65 D 15
Melgarve .... 73 G 12
Melksham .... 19 N 29
Melldalloch .... 65 E 16
Mellerstain .... 62 M 17
Melling .... 48 M 21
Mellon Charles .... 78 D 10
Mellon Udrigle .... 78 D 10
Mells .... 19 M 30
Melmerby *Eden* .... 55 M 19
Melmerby *Harrogate* .. 50 P 21
Melrose .... 62 L 17
Meltham .... 43 O 23
Melton .... 31 X 27
Melton Mowbray .... 36 R 25
Melvaig .... 77 C 10
Melvich .... 85 I 8
Memsie .... 81 N 11
Menai Bridge /
  Porthaethwy .... 40 H 23
Menai Strait .... 33 H 24
Mendip Hills .... 18 L 30
Mendlesham .... 31 X 27
Menheniot .... 3 G 32
Mennock .... 61 I 17
Menston .... 43 O 22
Menstrie .... 67 I 15
Menteith Hills .... 67 H 15
Mentmore .... 29 R 28
Meonstoke .... 10 Q 31
Meopham .... 22 V 29
Mepal .... 29 U 26
Mere *Cheshire* .... 42 M 24
Mere *Wilts* .... 9 N 30
Mereworth .... 22 V 30
Meriden .... 27 P 26
Merkland Lodge .... 84 F 9
Mermaid Inn .... 32 H 24
Merrick .... 52 G 18
Merriott .... 8 L 31
Merrylaw .... 62 K 18
Mersey (River) .... 42 M 23
Merthyr Cynog .... 25 J 27
Merthyr Tydfil .... 17 J 28
Merton *Cherwell* .... 20 Q 28
Merton *Devon* .... 7 H 31
Merton *London Borough* .. 7 I 31
Meshaw .... 7 I 31
Messing .... 30 W 28
Messingham .... 44 S 23
Metfield .... 31 Y 26

Metheringham .... 37 S 24
Methil .... 69 K 15
Methlick .... 81 N 11
Methven .... 68 J 14
Methwold .... 38 V 26
Mevagissey .... 3 F 33
Mexborough .... 44 Q 23
Mhór (Loch) .... 73 G 12
Miavaig .... 82 Z 9
Michaelchurch Escley .. 26 L 27
Michaelstow .... 3 F 32
Micheldever .... 10 Q 30
Michelham Priory .... 12 U 31
Micklefield .... 44 Q 22
Mickleover .... 36 P 25
Mickleton *Cotswold* .. 27 O 27
Mickleton *Teesdale* .. 55 N 20
Mid Ardlaw .... 81 N 10
Mid Calder .... 61 J 16
Mid Lavant .... 10 R 31
Mid Sannox .... 59 E 17
Mid Yell .... 87 Q 2
Midbea .... 86 L 6
Middle Barton .... 28 P 28
Middle Rasen .... 45 S 23
Middle Tysoe .... 28 P 27
Middle Wallop .... 9 P 30
Middle Woodford .... 9 O 30
Middlebie .... 54 K 18
Middleham .... 49 O 21
Middlesbrough .... 57 Q 20
Middlestown .... 43 P 23
Middleton *Argyll and Bute* .. 64 Z 14
Middleton
  Berwick-upon-Tweed .. 63 O 17
Middleton *Bradford* .. 49 O 22
Middleton *Gtr. Mches* .. 43 N 23
Middleton *Cheney* .... 28 Q 27
Middleton-in-Teesdale .. 55 N 20
Middleton-on-Sea .... 11 S 31
Middleton on the Wolds .. 51 S 22
Middleton St. George .. 50 P 20
Middleton Tyas .... 49 P 20
Middletown *Powys* .. 34 K 25
Middlewich .... 35 M 24
Midgeholme .... 55 M 19
Midhurst .... 10 R 31
Midlem .... 62 L 17
Midsomer Norton .... 18 M 30
Midtown .... 78 C 10
Miefield .... 53 H 19
Migdale (Loch) .... 79 H 10
Milborne Port .... 8 M 31
Milborne St. Andrew .. 9 N 31
Milbourne .... 56 O 18
Milburn .... 55 M 20
Mildenhall *Forest Heath* .. 30 V 26
Mildenhall *Kennet* .... 19 O 29
Mile End .... 30 W 28
Milfield .... 63 N 17
Milford .... 11 S 30
Milford Haven /
  Aberdaugleddau .... 14 E 28
Milford-on-Sea .... 9 P 31
Milland .... 10 R 30
Millbrook .... 3 H 32
Millhouse .... 59 E 16
Millmeece .... 35 N 25
Millom .... 47 K 21
Millport .... 59 F 16
Milltown
  Dumfries and Galloway .. 54 K 18
Milltown *Highland* .... 78 F 11
Milltown *Moray* .... 80 L 11
Milnathort .... 68 J 15
Milngavie .... 67 H 16
Milnrow .... 43 N 23
Milnthorpe .... 48 L 21
Milovaig .... 76 Z 11
Milton .... 79 H 10
Milton *Cambs* .... 29 U 27
Milton *Carlisle* .... 55 L 19
Milton *Dumfries* .... 53 I 18
Milton *Highland* .... 79 G 11
Milton *Stranraer* .... 52 F 19
Milton Abbas .... 9 N 31
Milton Abbot .... 3 H 32
Milton Bryan .... 29 S 28
Milton Ernest .... 29 S 27
Milton Keynes .... 28 R 27
Milton Libourne .... 19 O 29
Milton of Campsie .... 67 H 16
Milton of Cushnie .... 75 L 12
Milton-on-Stour .... 9 N 30
Miltonduff .... 80 J 11
Miltown of Edinville .. 80 J 11
Miltown of Edinvillie .. 80 K 11
Milverton .... 8 K 30

Milwich .... 35 N 25
Minard .... 65 E 15
Minch (The) .... 83 C 9
Minehead .... 17 J 30
Minety .... 19 O 29
Mingary .... 76 X 12
Minginish .... 77 B 12
Mingulay .... 70 X 13
Minnigaff .... 52 G 19
Minster *near Sheerness* .. 22 W 29
Minster *near Ramsgate* .. 23 X 29
Minsterley .... 34 L 26
Minsterworth .... 19 N 28
Minterne Magna .... 8 M 31
Minting .... 45 T 24
Mintlaw .... 81 O 11
Minto .... 62 L 17
Mirfield .... 43 O 22
Miserden .... 19 N 28
Misson .... 44 R 23
Misterton *Notts* .... 44 R 23
Misterton *Somerset* .. 8 L 31
Mistley .... 31 X 28
Mitcheldean .... 26 M 28
Mitchell .... 2 E 32
Mitford .... 56 O 18
Mitcham .... 21 T 29
Mithian .... 2 E 33
Moaness .... 86 K 7
Mochdre .... 41 I 23
Mochrum .... 52 G 19
Modbury .... 4 I 32
Moelfre .... 40 H 22
Moffat .... 61 J 17
Moidart .... 72 C 13
Moira .... 36 P 25
Mol-Chlach .... 71 B 12
Mold / Yr Wyddgrug .. 34 K 24
Molland .... 7 I 30
Monach Islands .... 76 W 11
Monadhliath Mountains .. 73 H 12
Monar (Loch) .... 78 E 11
Monar Lodge .... 78 F 11
Monaughty Forest .... 80 J 11
Moneydie .... 68 J 14
Moniaive .... 53 I 18
Monifieth .... 69 L 14
Monikie .... 69 L 14
Monk Fryston .... 44 Q 22
Monkland .... 26 L 27
Monkokehampton .... 7 H 31
Monks Eleigh .... 30 W 27
Monksilver .... 7 K 30
Monkton .... 60 G 17
Monmouth / Trefynwy .. 18 L 28
Monreith .... 52 G 19
Montacute .... 8 L 31
Montgarrie .... 75 L 12
Montgomery / Trefaldwyn .. 34 K 26
Montrose .... 75 M 13
Monyash .... 35 O 24
Monymusk .... 75 M 12
Monzie .... 67 I 14
Moonen Bay .... 76 Z 11
Moor Monkton .... 50 Q 21
Moorends .... 44 R 23
Moorfoot Hills .... 61 K 16
Moors (The) .... 52 F 19
Moortown .... 45 S 23
Morar .... 71 C 13
Moray Firth .... 79 H 11
Morchard Bishop .... 7 I 31
Morcott .... 37 S 26
Morden .... 9 N 31
Mordiford .... 26 M 27
More (Loch) .... 65 C 14
More (Loch) *near Kinloch* .. 84 F 9
More (Loch)
  near Westerdale .. 85 J 8
Morebath .... 7 J 30
Morebattle .... 62 M 17
Morecambe .... 48 L 21
Morecambe Bay .... 48 L 21
Moresby .... 53 J 20
Moreton *Epping Forest* .. 22 U 28
Moreton *Purbeck* .... 9 N 31
Moreton-in-Marsh .... 27 O 28
Moreton-on-lugg .... 26 L 27
Moreton Say .... 34 M 25
Moretonhampstead .... 4 I 32
Morfa Nefyn .... 32 G 25
Moricambe Bay .... 54 K 19
Morie (Loch) .... 79 G 10
Moriston (Glen) .... 72 F 12
Morland .... 55 M 20
Morley .... 43 P 22
Morlich (Loch) .... 74 I 12

Morpeth .... 56 O 18
Morriston .... 17 I 29
Morte Bay .... 6 H 30
Mortehoe .... 16 H 30
Mortimer .... 20 Q 29
Morton *near Bourne* .. 37 S 25
Morton
  near Gainsborough .. 44 R 23
Morton
  North East Derbyshire .. 36 P 24
Morton on Swale .... 50 P 21
Morval .... 3 G 32
Morven .... 85 I 9
Morvern .... 71 C 14
Morvich .... 72 D 12
Morville .... 34 M 26
Morwelham .... 3 H 32
Morwenstow .... 6 G 31
Mosborough .... 43 P 24
Moss Bank .... 42 L 23
Mossdale .... 53 H 18
Mossend .... 60 H 16
Mossley .... 43 N 23
Mosstodloch .... 80 K 11
Mostyn .... 41 K 23
Motherwell .... 61 I 16
Moulin .... 74 I 13
Moulton *Forest Heath* .. 30 V 27
Moulton *Lincs* .... 37 T 25
Moulton *Northants* .. 28 R 27
Moulton Chapel .... 37 T 25
Mountain Ash /
  Aberpennar .... 17 J 28
Mount's Bay .... 2 D 33
Mountsorrel .... 36 Q 25
Mousa .... 87 Q 4
Mousehole .... 2 D 33
Mouswald .... 54 J 18
Mow Cop .... 35 N 24
Mowtie .... 75 N 13
Moy .... 79 H 11
Muasdale .... 59 C 17
Much Dewchurch .... 26 L 28
Much Hadham .... 29 U 28
Much Hoole .... 42 L 22
Much Marcle .... 26 M 28
Much Wenlock .... 34 M 26
Muchalls .... 75 N 12
Muchelney .... 8 L 30
Muchrachd .... 78 F 11
Muck .... 71 B 13
Muckle Roe .... 87 P 2
Mucklestone .... 35 M 25
Muddiford .... 7 H 30
Mudford .... 8 M 31
Mugeary .... 77 B 11
Muick (Loch) .... 74 K 13
Muie .... 85 H 9
Muir of Fowlis .... 75 L 12
Muir of Ord .... 79 G 11
Muirdrum .... 69 L 14
Muirhead .... 60 H 16
Muirkirk .... 60 H 17
Muirshearlich .... 72 E 13
Muker .... 49 N 20
Mulbarton .... 39 X 26
Mulben .... 80 K 11
Muldoanich .... 70 X 13
Mull (Isle of) .... 64 B 14
Mull (Sound of) .... 71 C 14
Mull of Galloway .... 52 F 20
Mull of Oa .... 58 A 17
Mullardoch (Loch) .... 78 E 12
Mullardoch House .... 78 F 11
Mullion .... 2 E 33
Mumbles (The) .... 15 H 29
Mumby .... 45 U 24
Mundesley .... 39 Y 25
Mundford .... 30 V 26
Mundham .... 10 R 31
Munlochy .... 79 H 11
Munlochy Bay .... 79 H 11
Munslow .... 26 L 26
Murlaggan .... 72 E 13
Murrayfield .... 68 K 16
Mursley .... 28 R 28
Murton *Easington* .... 57 P 19
Murton *Eden* .... 55 M 20
Musbury .... 5 K 31
Musselburgh .... 68 K 16
Muston .... 51 T 21
Muthill .... 67 I 15
Mwnt .... 15 G 27
Mybster .... 85 J 8
Myddfai .... 25 I 28
Myddle .... 34 L 25

A B C D E F G H I J K L M N O P Q R S T U V W X Y Z

Mydroilyn ....15 H 27
Mynach Falls ....25 I 26
Mynachlog-ddu ....15 F 28
Mynydd Eppynt ....25 J 27
Mynydd Mawr ....32 F 25
Mynydd Preseli ....15 F 28
Myrelandhorn ....86 K 8
Mytchett ....21 R 30
Mytholmroyd ....43 O 22

N

Na Cùiltean ....58 C 16
Naburn ....50 Q 22
Nacton ....31 X 27
Nafferton ....51 S 21
Nailsea ....18 L 29
Nailstone ....36 P 26
Nailsworth ....19 N 28
Nairn ....79 I 11
Nant (Loch) ....65 E 14
Nant-y-Moch Reservoir ...25 I 26
Nant-y-moel ....17 J 29
Nantgwynant Valley ......33 H 24
Nantwich ....34 M 24
Nantyglo ....18 K 28
Napton ....28 Q 27
Narberth / Arberth ....15 F 28
Narborough Blaby ....36 Q 26
Narborough Breckland ....38 V 25
Naseby ....28 R 26
Nash Point ....17 J 29
Nassington ....37 S 26
Nateby ....49 M 20
National Exhibition Centre ..27 O 26
National Motor Museum ...10 P 31
Naunton ....27 O 28
Navenby ....37 S 24
Naver (Loch) ....84 G 9
Nayland ....30 W 28
Naze (The) ....31 X 28
Neap ....87 Q 3
Neath / Castell-nedd .....17 I 29
Neath (River) ....17 I 29
Nebo ....33 I 24
Necton ....38 W 26
Needham Market ....31 X 27
Needingworth ....29 T 27
Needles (The) ....10 P 32
Nefyn ....32 G 25
Neidpath Castle ....61 K 17
Neilston ....60 G 16
Neist Point ....76 Z 11
Nelson
    Caerffili / Caerphilly ..18 K 29
Nelson Pendle ....43 N 22
Nene (River) ....37 T 26
Nenthead ....55 M 19
Nercwys ....34 K 24
Nereabolls ....58 A 16
Ness ....83 B 8
Ness (Loch) ....73 G 12
Nesscliffe ....34 L 25
Nestley Marsh ....10 P 31
Neston ....42 K 24
Nether Broughton ....36 R 25
Nether Kellet ....48 L 21
Nether Langwith ....44 Q 24
Nether Stowey ....8 K 30
Nether Wasdale ....47 J 20
Nether Whitecleuch ......61 I 17
Netheravon ....19 O 30
Netherbrae ....81 M 11
Netherbury ....8 L 31
Netherend ....18 M 28
Netherhampton ....9 O 30
Nethermill ....54 J 18
Netherthong ....43 O 23
Netherton ....63 N 17
Nethertown ....86 K 7
Netherwitton ....56 O 18
Nethy Bridge ....74 J 12
Netley ....10 P 31
Nettlebed ....20 R 29
Nettleham ....44 S 24
Nettleton ....45 T 23
Nevern ....15 F 27
Nevis (Glen) ....72 E 13
Nevis (Loch) ....72 C 12
New Abbey ....53 J 19
New Aberdour ....81 N 11
New Alresford ....10 Q 30
New Buckenham ....31 X 26
New Byth ....81 N 11
New Clipstone ....36 Q 24
New Cumnock ....60 H 17
New Deer ....81 N 11
New Edlington ....44 Q 23

New Forest National Park ..9 P 31
New Galloway ....53 H 18
New Holland ....45 S 22
New Hythe ....22 V 30
New Leeds ....81 N 11
New Luce ....52 F 19
New Marske ....57 Q 20
New Mills ....43 O 23
New Mills Powys ....33 K 26
New Milton ....9 P 31
New Pitsligo ....81 N 11
New Quay / Ceinewydd ...24 G 27
New Rackheat ....39 Y 26
New Radnor ....26 K 27
New Romney ....12 W 31
New Rossington ....44 Q 23
New Sauchie ....67 I 15
New Scone ....68 J 14
New Silksworth ....57 P 19
New Tredegar ....18 K 28
New Waltham ....45 T 23
Newark-on-Trent ....36 R 24
Newbiggin Eden ....55 L 19
Newbiggin Teesdale ......55 N 20
Newbiggin-by-the-Sea ....56 P 18
Newbigging Angus ....69 L 14
Newbigging
    South Lanarkshire .....61 J 16
Newbold Verdon ....36 P 26
Newborough
    East Staffordshire .....35 O 25
Newborough
    Isle of Anglesey ......32 G 24
Newbridge Caerffili /
    Caerphilly ....18 K 29
Newbridge Isle of Wight ..10 P 31
Newbridge-on-Wye ....25 J 27
Newbrough ....55 N 18
Newburgh Aberdeenshire ..81 N 12
Newburgh Fife ....68 K 14
Newburgh Lancashire .....42 L 23
Newburn ....56 O 19
Newbury ....20 Q 29
Newby Bridge ....48 L 21
Newby Hall ....50 P 21
Newcastle Monmouthshire /
    Sir Fynwy ....18 L 28
Newcastle
    South Shropshire .....26 K 26
Newcastle Emlyn /
    Castell Newydd Emlyn ..15 G 27
Newcastle-under-Lyme ....35 N 24
Newcastle-upon-Tyne .....56 P 19
Newcastle-upon-Tyne
    Airport ....56 O 18
Newcastleton ....55 L 18
Newchapel ....15 G 27
Newchurch Carmarthenshire /
    Sir Gaerfyrddin ....15 G 28
Newchurch Isle of Wight ..10 Q 32
Newchurch Powys ....26 K 27
Newchurch Shepway ......12 W 30
Newdigate ....11 T 30
Newent ....27 M 28
Newgale ....14 E 28
Newhall ....34 M 24
Newham Isle of Wight ....63 O 17
Newham London Borough ..21 U 29
Newhaven ....11 U 31
Newick ....11 U 31
Newington ....22 V 29
Newland ....18 M 28
Newlyn ....2 D 33
Newmachar ....75 N 12
Newmains ....61 I 16
Newmarket Isle of Lewis ..82 A 9
Newmarket Suffolk ....30 V 27
Newmill Moray ....80 L 11
Newmill Scottish Borders ..62 L 17
Newmilns ....60 G 17
Newnham Daventry ....28 Q 27
Newnham Glos. ....18 M 28
Newnham Kent ....22 W 30
Newnham Bridge ....26 M 27
Newport Essex ....30 U 28
Newport I.O.W. ....10 Q 31
Newport Pembrokes ......15 F 27
Newport Stroud ....19 M 28
Newport
    Telford and Wrekin ...35 M 25
Newport /
    Casnewydd Newport ...18 L 29
Newport-on-Tay ....69 L 14
Newport Pagnell ....28 R 27
Newquay ....2 E 32
Newsham ....49 O 20
Newstead ....36 Q 24

Newstead Abbey ....36 Q 24
Newton Aberdeenshire ...81 O 11
Newton Argyll and Bute ..65 E 15
Newton Babergh ....30 W 27
Newton Moray ....80 J 11
Newton Ribble Valley ....49 M 22
Newton Rushcliffe ....36 R 25
Newton Abbot ....4 J 32
Newton Arlosh ....54 K 19
Newton-Aycliffe ....56 P 20
Newton Ferrers ....4 H 33
Newton Flotman ....39 X 26
Newton-le-Willows ....42 M 23
Newton Longville ....28 R 28
Newton Mearns ....60 H 16
Newton-on-Rawcliffe ....50 R 21
Newton-on-Trent ....44 R 24
Newton Poppleford ....5 K 31
Newton Reigny ....55 L 19
Newton St. Cyres ....7 J 31
Newton Stewart ....52 G 19
Newton Tracey ....7 H 30
Newton Wamphray ....54 J 18
Newtongrange ....61 K 16
Newtonhill ....75 N 12
Newtonmore ....73 H 12
Newtown Cheshire ....43 N 23
Newtown Heref. ....26 M 27
Newtown Highland ....73 F 12
Newtown Isle of Man .....46 G 21
Newtown /
    Drenewydd Powys .....26 K 26
Newtown Linford ....36 Q 25
Newtown St. Boswells ...62 L 17
Newtyle ....68 K 14
Neyland ....16 F 28
Nicholaston ....15 H 29
Nigg ....79 H 10
Nigg Bay ....79 H 10
Nine Ladies ....35 P 24
Ninebanks ....55 M 19
Ninfield ....12 V 31
Nisbet ....62 M 17
Nith (River) ....53 J 19
Niton ....10 Q 32
Niths ....61 I 18
Nocton ....37 S 24
Nolton ....14 E 28
Nordelph ....38 U 26
Norfolk Broads ....39 Y 25
Norham ....63 N 16
Normanby ....50 R 21
Normandy ....21 S 30
Normanton ....43 P 22
Normanton-on-the-Wolds ..36 Q 25
North Baddesley ....10 P 31
North Ballachulish ......72 E 13
North Berwick ....69 L 15
North Bovey ....4 I 32
North Bradley ....19 N 30
North Brentor ....4 H 32
North Cadbury ....8 M 30
North Cave ....44 S 22
North-Cerney ....19 O 28
North-Charlton ....63 O 17
North Cliffe ....44 R 22
North Cowton ....50 P 20
North Crawley ....29 S 27
North Creake ....38 W 25
North Curry ....8 L 30
North Dalton ....51 S 22
North Deighton ....50 P 22
North Erradale ....77 C 10
North Esk (Riv.) ....75 L 13
North Fearns ....77 B 11
North Foreland ....23 Y 29
North Frodingham ....51 T 22
North Grimston ....51 R 21
North Harris ....82 Z 10
North Hill ....3 G 32
North Hinksey ....20 Q 28
North Holmwood ....21 T 30
North Hykeham ....37 S 24
North Kelsey ....45 S 23
North Kessock ....79 H 11
North Kyme ....37 T 24
North Leigh ....20 P 28
North-Molton ....7 I 30
North Morar ....72 C 13
North Newbald ....44 S 22
North Nibley ....19 M 29
North Otterington ....50 P 21
North Petherton ....8 K 30
North Petherwin ....6 G 31
North Rigton ....50 P 22
North Ronaldsay ....87 M 5
North-Scarle ....36 R 24

North-Shian ....65 D 14
North Shields ....56 P 18
North Shore ....42 K 22
North Sound (The) ......87 L 6
North Stainley ....50 P 21
North Stainmore ....49 N 20
North Sunderland ......63 P 17
North Tamerton ....6 G 31
North-Tawton ....7 I 31
North Thoresby ....45 T 23
North Tidworth ....19 P 30
North Uist ....76 X 11
North Walsham ....39 Y 25
North Warnborough .....20 R 30
North Water Bridge .....75 M 13
North Weald Bassett ....22 U 28
North Wootton ....38 V 25
North York Moors
    National Park ....50 R 20
Northallerton ....50 P 20
Northam ....6 H 30
Northampton ....28 R 27
Northaw ....21 T 28
Northchapel ....11 S 30
Northchurch ....21 S 28
Northfleet ....22 V 29
Northiam ....12 V 31
Northleach ....19 O 28
Northleigh ....5 K 31
Northlew ....7 H 31
Northop ....34 K 24
Northrepps ....39 Y 25
Northton ....76 Y 10
Northumberland
    National Park ....63 N 18
Northwich ....42 M 24
Northwold ....38 V 26
Northwood ....34 L 25
Norton Daventry ....28 Q 27
Norton Doncaster ......44 Q 23
Norton Ryedale ....50 R 21
Norton Tewkesbury ....27 N 28
Norton Disney ....36 R 24
Norton Fitzwarren .....8 K 30
Norton in Hales ....35 M 25
Norton St. Philip ......19 N 30
Norwich ....39 X 26
Norwick ....87 R 1
Noss (Isle of) ....87 Q 3
Noss Head ....86 K 8
Nottingham ....36 Q 25
Nuffield ....20 Q 29
Nunburnholme ....51 R 22
Nuneaton ....28 P 26
Nuneham Courtenay ....20 Q 28
Nunney ....19 M 30
Nunthorpe ....50 Q 20
Nunton ....76 X 11
Nutley ....11 U 30
Nympsfield ....19 N 28

O

Oa (The) ....58 B 17
Oadby ....36 Q 26
Oakamoor ....35 O 24
Oakdale ....18 K 28
Oakengates ....35 M 25
Oakford ....7 J 31
Oakham ....36 R 25
Oakhill ....18 M 30
Oakington ....29 U 27
Oakley Aylesbury Vale ..20 Q 28
Oakley Bedfordshire ....29 S 27
Oakley Fife ....68 J 15
Oaksey ....19 N 29
Oakwoth ....43 O 22
Oare Kennet ....19 O 29
Oare Swale ....22 W 30
Oare West Somerset ....17 I 30
Oathlaw ....74 L 13
Oban ....65 D 14
Occold ....31 X 27
Ochil Hills ....68 I 15
Ochiltree ....60 G 17
Ockbrook ....36 P 25
Ockle ....71 C 13
Ockley ....11 S 30
Odiham ....20 R 30
Odland ....18 M 29
Odstock ....9 O 30
Offa's Dyke Path ....26 K 26
Offord Cluny ....29 T 27
Ogbourne St. Andrew ...19 O 29
Ogbourne St. George ...19 O 29
Ogil ....74 L 13
Ogle ....56 O 18

Ogmore-by-Sea ....17 J 29
Ogmore Vale ....17 J 29
Oich (Loch) ....73 F 12
Oidhche (Loch na h-) ...78 D 11
Oigh-Sgeir ....71 Z 13
Okeford Fitzpaine .....9 N 31
Okehampton ....4 H 31
Old Alresford ....10 Q 30
Old Bolingbroke ....37 U 24
Old Burghclere ....20 Q 30
Old Castleton ....55 L 18
Old Colwyn ....41 I 23
Old Dailly ....59 F 18
Old Deer ....81 N 11
Old Fletton ....37 T 26
Old Harry Rocks ......9 O 32
Old Head ....87 L 7
Old Hurst ....29 T 26
Old Hutton ....48 L 21
Old Kilpatrick ....67 G 16
Old Knebworth ....29 T 28
Old Leake ....37 U 24
Old Man of Hoy ....86 J 7
Old Man of Storr ......77 B 11
Old Radnor ....26 K 27
Old Rayne ....81 M 11
Old' Sarum ....9 O 30
Old Sodbury ....19 M 29
Old Somerby ....37 S 25
Old Warden ....29 S 27
Old Windsor ....21 S 29
Oldany Island ....84 E 9
Oldbury ....27 N 26
Oldbury on Severn .....18 M 29
Oldcotes ....44 Q 23
Oldham ....43 N 23
Oldhamstocks ....69 M 16
Oldmeldrum ....81 N 11
Oldshoremore ....84 E 8
Olgrinmore ....85 J 8
Ollaberry ....87 P 2
Ollach ....77 B 11
Ollay (Loch) ....76 X 12
Ollerton Macclesfield ..42 M 24
Ollerton
    Newark and Sherwood ..36 Q 24
Olney ....28 R 27
Olveston ....18 M 29
Ombersley ....27 N 27
Once Brewed ....55 M 19
Onchan ....46 G 21
Onecote ....35 O 24
Onich ....72 E 13
Onllwyn ....17 I 28
Onston ....83 O 10
Orchy (Glen) ....66 F 14
Ord ....71 C 12
Ordie ....74 L 12
Orford ....31 Y 27
Orford Ness ....31 Y 27
Orkney Islands 87
Orleton ....26 L 27
Ormesby ....50 Q 20
Ormesby St. Margaret ..39 Z 25
Ormiston ....62 L 16
Ormskirk ....42 L 23
Oronsay ....64 B 15
Orosay near Fuday .....70 X 12
Orosay near Lochboisdale ..70 X 12
Orphir ....86 K 7
Orrin (Glen) ....78 F 11
Orrin Reservoir ....78 F 11
Orsay ....58 A 16
Orsett ....22 V 29
Orston ....36 R 25
Orton ....48 M 20
Orwell ....29 T 27
Orwell (River) ....31 X 28
Osborne House ....10 Q 31
Osdale ....77 A 11
Osgaig (Loch) ....83 E 9
Osgodby ....45 S 23
Oskaig ....77 B 11
Osmington ....9 M 32
Ossett ....43 P 22
Ossington ....36 R 24
Oswaldtwistle ....42 M 22
Oswestry ....34 K 25
Otford ....22 U 30
Othery ....8 L 30
Otley Suffolk ....31 X 27
Otley West Yorks ....49 O 22
Otterbourne ....10 P 30
Otterburn ....55 N 18
Otternish ....76 Y 10
Otterswick ....87 Q 2
Otterton ....5 K 32

Ottery St. Mary ....5 K 31
Ottringham ....45 T 22
Oulton Broad ....39 Z 26
Oulton Park Circuit ....34 M 24
Oundle ....29 S 26
Ouse (River)
    English Channel ....11 T 30
Ouse (River) North Sea ..50 Q 21
Out-Rawcliffe ....42 L 22
Out Skerries ....87 R 2
Outer Hebrides ....82 Y 9
Outhgill ....49 M 20
Outwell ....38 U 26
Over ....29 U 27
Over Compton ....8 M 31
Overseal ....35 P 25
Overstrand ....39 Y 25
Overton Hants. ....20 Q 30
Overton Lancs. ....48 L 21
Overton Wrexham .....34 L 25
Overtown ....61 I 16
Ower ....10 P 31
Owermoigne ....9 N 32
Owlswick ....20 R 28
Owlsebury ....10 Q 30
Owston ....36 R 26
Owston Ferry ....44 R 23
Oxburgh Hall ....38 V 26
Oxen Park ....48 K 21
Oxenhope ....43 O 22
Oxford ....20 Q 28
Oxnam ....62 M 17
Oxted ....21 T 30
Oxton
    Newark and Sherwood ..36 Q 24
Oxton Scottish Borders ..62 L 16
Oxwich ....15 H 29
Oxwich Bay ....15 H 29
Oykel (Glen) ....84 F 9
Oykel Bridge ....84 F 10
Oyne ....81 M 12

P

Pabay ....77 C 12
Pabbay near Harris .....76 Y 10
Pabbay near Mingulay ..70 X 13
Pabbay (Sound of) .....76 Y 10
Packington ....36 P 25
Padbury ....28 R 28
Paddock Wood ....22 V 30
Paddockhole ....54 K 18
Padiham ....42 N 22
Padstow ....3 F 32
Pagham ....10 R 31
Paignton ....4 J 32
Pailton ....28 Q 26
Painscastle ....26 K 27
Painswick ....19 N 28
Paisley ....60 G 16
Pakefield ....31 Z 26
Palnackie ....53 I 19
Pamber End ....20 Q 30
Pandy
    Monmouthshire / Sir Fynwy ..26 L 28
Pandy Powys ....33 J 26
Pangbourne ....20 Q 29
Pant ....34 K 25
Pantymenyn ....15 F 28
Papa Stour ....87 O 3
Papa Westray ....87 L 5
Papplewick ....36 Q 24
Paps of Jura ....65 B 16
Papworth Everard .....29 T 27
Parbh (The) ....84 F 8
Parbold ....42 L 23
Parc Cefn Onn ....18 K 29
Parham House ....11 S 31
Park Gate ....10 Q 31
Park of Pairc ....82 A 9
Parkeston ....31 X 28
Parkgate ....53 J 18
Parkhurst ....10 Q 31
Parnham House ....8 L 31
Parracombe ....17 I 30
Parrett (River) ....8 K 30
Parson Drove ....37 U 26
Partney ....37 U 24
Parton Copeland ......54 J 20
Parton
    Dumfries and Galloway ..53 H 18
Partridge Green ....11 T 31
Parwich ....35 O 24
Pateley Bridge ....49 O 21
Path of Condie ....68 J 15
Pathhead ....62 L 16
Patna ....60 G 17

Patrick .....46 F 21
Patrington .....45 T 22
Patrixbourne .....23 X 30
Patterdale .....48 L 20
Pattingham .....35 N 26
Pattishall .....28 Q 27
Paulerspury .....28 R 27
Paull .....45 T 22
Paulton .....18 M 30
Paxton .....63 N 16
Peacehaven .....11 T 31
Peak District
   National Park .....43 O 23
Pearsie .....74 K 13
Peasedown St. John .....19 M 30
Peasemore .....20 P 29
Peasenhall .....31 Y 27
Peaslake .....21 S 30
Peasmarsh .....12 W 31
Peat Inn .....69 L 15
Peatknowe .....81 M 11
Pebmarsh .....30 W 28
Pebworth .....27 O 27
Peebles .....61 K 17
Peel .....46 F 21
Peel Fell .....62 M 18
Pegswood .....56 P 18
Pegwell Bay .....23 Y 30
Peinchorran .....77 B 12
Peldon .....22 W 28
Pelton .....56 P 19
Pelynt .....3 G 32
Pembrey .....15 H 28
Pembridge .....26 L 27
Pembroke / Penfro .....16 F 28
Pembroke Dock /
   Doc Penfro .....16 F 28
Pembrokeshire Coast
   National Park .....15 F 29
Pembury .....12 V 30
Pen-y-bont / Bridgend .....17 J 29
Pen-y-groes .....32 H 24
Penalun .....15 F 29
Penarth .....18 K 29
Pencader .....15 H 27
Pencaitland .....62 L 16
Pencarrow .....3 F 32
Penclawdd .....15 H 29
Pencombe .....26 M 27
Penderyn .....17 J 28
Pendine .....15 G 28
Pendine Sands .....15 G 28
Pendlebury .....42 N 23
Pendoylan .....17 J 29
Penelewey .....2 E 33
Penfro / Pembroke .....16 F 28
Pengethley .....26 M 28
Penhow .....18 L 29
Penicuik .....61 K 16
Penifiler .....77 B 11
Peninver .....59 D 17
Penistone .....43 P 23
Penketh .....42 L 23
Penkridge .....35 N 25
Penley .....34 L 25
Penmaen .....15 H 29
Penmaenmawr .....41 I 23
Penmaenpool .....33 I 25
Penmark .....17 J 29
Penmon .....40 H 23
Pennal .....33 I 26
Pennant .....33 J 26
Pennerley .....34 L 26
Pennines (The) .....49 N 20
Pennyghael .....65 B 14
Penpont .....53 I 18
Penrhiwpal .....15 G 27
Penrhyn .....40 H 23
Penrhyn Bay .....41 I 23
Penrhyndeudraeth .....33 H 25
Penrith .....55 L 19
Penruddock .....55 L 20
Penryn .....2 E 33
Pensarn .....41 J 23
Penshaw .....56 P 19
Penshurst .....22 U 30
Pensilva .....3 G 32
Pentewan .....3 F 33
Pentire Point .....3 F 32
Pentland Firth .....86 K 7
Pentland Hills .....61 J 16
Pentland Skerries .....87 L 7
Pentraeth .....40 H 23
Pentre-Berw .....40 H 23
Pentre-Celyn .....34 K 24
Pentrebeirdd .....34 K 25
Penwith .....2 D 33

Penybont .....26 K 27
Penysarn .....40 H 22
Penzance .....2 D 33
Pernhyn-Coch .....25 I 26
Perranworthal .....2 E 33
Perranporth .....2 E 32
Perranzabuloe .....2 E 33
Pershore .....27 N 27
Pertenhall .....29 S 27
Perth .....68 J 14
Peterborough .....37 T 26
Peterculter .....75 N 12
Peterhead .....81 O 11
Peterlee .....57 P 19
Petersfield .....10 R 30
Peterstone Wentlooge .....18 K 29
Peterstow .....26 M 28
Petham .....23 X 30
Petrockstowe .....7 H 31
Pett .....12 V 31
Pettaugh .....31 X 27
Petworth .....11 S 31
Pevensey Bay .....12 V 31
Pewsey .....19 O 29
Pickering .....50 R 21
Picklescott .....34 L 26
Picton Castle .....16 F 28
Piddlehinton .....9 M 31
Piddletrenthide .....9 M 31
Piercebridge .....49 O 20
Pierowall .....86 L 6
Pilgrims Hatch .....22 U 29
Pillerton Hersey .....28 P 27
Pillerton Priors .....27 P 27
Pilley .....43 P 23
Pilling .....48 L 22
Pilning .....18 M 29
Pilton .....8 M 30
Pinchbeck .....37 T 25
Pinchbeck-West .....37 T 25
Pinhoe .....4 J 31
Pinmore Mains .....52 F 18
Pinner .....21 S 29
Pinvin .....27 N 27
Pinwherry .....52 F 18
Pinxton .....36 Q 24
Pirbright .....21 S 30
Pirnmill .....59 D 17
Pirton .....29 T 28
Pishill .....20 R 29
Pitcaple .....81 M 12
Pitcombe .....8 M 30
Pitcur .....68 K 14
Pitlochry .....74 I 13
Pitmedden .....81 N 11
Pitminster .....8 K 31
Pitscottie .....69 L 15
Pitsford .....28 R 27
Pittentrail .....85 H 10
Pittenween .....69 L 15
Pladda .....59 E 17
Plaistow .....11 S 30
Plas Newydd Anglesey .....33 H 24
Plas Newydd
   Denbighshire .....34 K 25
Plean .....67 I 15
Pleasington .....42 M 22
Pleasley .....36 Q 24
Plenmeller .....55 M 19
Plockton .....78 D 11
Pluckley .....22 W 30
Plumbland .....54 K 19
Plumpton .....11 T 31
Plymouth .....4 H 32
Plympton .....4 H 32
Plymstock .....4 H 32
Plymtree .....7 J 31
Plynlimon
   (Pumlumon Fawr) .....25 I 26
Pocklington .....50 R 22
Point Lynas .....40 H 22
Point of Ayr Flintshire .....41 K 22
Point of Ayre Isle of Man .....46 G 20
Polbain .....83 D 9
Pole of Itlaw (The) .....81 M 11
Polebrook .....29 S 26
Polegate .....12 U 31
Polesden Lacey .....21 S 30
Polesworth .....35 P 26
Polkerris .....3 F 32
Polloch .....72 D 13
Pollock House .....60 H 16
Polmont .....67 I 16
Polperro .....3 G 33
Polruan .....3 G 33
Polwarth .....62 M 16
Pondersbridge .....29 T 26

Pont-ar-Gothi .....15 H 28
Pontardawe .....17 I 28
Pontarddulais .....15 H 28
Pontarfynach /
   Devil's Bridge .....25 I 26
Pontargothi .....15 H 28
Pontarsais .....15 H 28
Pontefract .....44 Q 22
Ponteland .....56 O 18
Ponterwyd .....25 I 26
Pontesbury .....34 L 26
Pontlottyn .....18 K 28
Pontlyfni .....32 G 24
Pontneddfechan .....17 J 28
Pontrhydfendigaid .....25 I 27
Pontrhydygroes .....25 I 26
Pontrilas .....26 L 28
Pontsticill .....17 J 28
Pontyates .....15 H 28
Pontyberem .....15 H 28
Pontyclun .....17 J 29
Pontycymer .....17 J 29
Pontypool / Pontypwl .....18 K 28
Pontypridd .....17 J 29
Pontypwl / Pontypool .....18 K 28
Poole .....9 O 31
Poole Bay .....9 O 31
Poolewe .....78 D 10
Pooley Bridge .....55 L 20
Pooltiel (Loch) .....76 Z 11
Porlock .....17 J 30
Port Appin .....65 D 14
Port Askaig .....58 B 16
Port Bannatyne .....59 E 16
Port Carlisle .....54 K 19
Port Charlotte .....58 A 16
Port Driseach .....65 E 16
Port Ellen .....58 B 17
Port Erin .....46 F 21
Port-Eynon .....15 H 29
Port-Eynon Point .....15 H 29
Port Gaverne .....3 F 32
Port Glasgow .....66 F 16
Port Henderson .....77 C 10
Port Isaac .....3 F 32
Port Lamont .....59 E 16
Port Logan .....52 F 19
Port Mór .....71 B 13
Port of Menteith .....67 H 15
Port of Ness .....83 B 8
Port Ramsay .....65 D 14
Port St. Mary .....46 F 21
Port Talbot .....17 I 29
Port William .....52 G 19
Portavadie .....59 E 16
Portchester .....10 Q 31
Portencross .....59 F 16
Portesham .....5 M 31
Portgordon .....80 K 11
Portgower .....85 I 9
Porth .....17 J 29
Porth Neigwl
   or Hell's Mouth .....32 G 25
Porth Tywyn /Burry Port .....15 H 28
Porthaethwy /
   Menai Bridge .....40 H 23
Porthcawl .....17 I 29
Porthcothan .....2 E 32
Porthcurno .....2 D 33
Porthgwarra .....2 C 33
Porthkerry .....17 K 29
Porthleven .....2 E 33
Porthmadog .....33 H 25
Porthtowan .....2 E 33
Porthyrhyd .....15 H 28
Portinnisherrich .....65 E 15
Portishead .....18 L 29
Portknockie .....80 L 10
Portland (Isle of) .....8 M 32
Portlethen .....75 N 12
Portmahomack .....79 I 10
Portmeirion .....33 H 25
Portnacroish .....72 D 14
Portnaguran .....83 B 9
Portnahaven .....58 A 16
Portnalong .....77 A 12
Portobello .....68 K 16
Portpatrick .....52 E 19
Portreath .....2 E 33
Portree .....77 B 11
Portscatho .....3 F 33
Portskerra .....85 I 8
Portskewett .....18 L 29
Portslade .....11 T 31
Portslogan .....52 E 19
Portsmouth .....10 Q 31
Portsoy .....81 L 10
Portuairk .....71 B 13

Postbridge .....4 I 32
Potten End .....21 S 28
Potter Heigham .....39 Y 25
Potter Street .....21 U 28
Potterhanworth .....37 S 24
Potterne .....19 N 30
Potters Bar .....21 T 28
Potton .....29 T 27
Poughill .....6 G 31
Poulshot .....19 N 29
Poulton .....19 O 28
Poulton-le-Fylde .....42 L 22
Poundstock .....6 G 31
Powburn .....63 O 17
Powerstock .....8 L 31
Powick .....27 N 27
Powis .....34 K 26
Powmill .....68 J 15
Poynings .....11 T 31
Poynton .....43 N 23
Praa Sands .....2 D 33
Prawle Point .....4 I 33
Praze-an-Beeble .....2 E 33
Prees .....34 M 25
Preesall .....48 L 22
Prendwick .....63 O 17
Prescot .....42 L 23
Prestatyn .....41 J 22
Prestbury Cheltenham .....27 N 28
Prestbury Macclesfield .....43 N 24
Presteigne .....26 K 27
Preston
   East Riding of Yorks. .....45 T 22
Preston Kent .....23 X 30
Preston Lancs. .....42 L 22
Preston Rutland .....36 R 26
Preston West Sussex .....11 S 31
Preston Candover .....10 Q 30
Preston Capes .....28 Q 27
Prestonpans .....69 L 16
Prestwich .....42 N 23
Prestwick .....60 G 17
Prestwood .....20 R 28
Prickwillow .....30 V 26
Priest Island .....83 D 10
Priest Weston .....34 K 26
Princes Risborough .....20 R 28
Princethorpe .....28 P 26
Princetown .....4 I 32
Priors Marston .....28 Q 27
Probus .....3 F 33
Prosen (Glen) .....74 K 13
Prudhoe .....56 O 19
Puckeridge .....29 U 28
Pucklechurch .....19 M 29
Pucks Gutter .....23 X 30
Puddletown .....9 M 31
Pudsey .....43 P 22
Pulborough .....11 S 31
Pulford .....34 L 24
Pulham .....9 M 31
Pulham Market .....31 X 26
Punchardon .....7 H 30
Puncheston .....24 F 28
Purbeck (Isle of) .....9 N 32
Purbrook .....10 Q 31
Puriton .....8 L 30
Purleigh .....22 V 28
Purley .....20 Q 29
Purse Caundle Manor .....9 M 31
Purston Jaglin .....43 P 22
Purton .....19 O 29
Putsborough .....6 H 30
Pwllheli .....32 G 25
Pyecombe .....11 T 31
Pyle .....17 I 29
Pylle .....8 M 30

Q
Quainton .....28 R 28
Quantock Hills .....8 K 30
Quarff .....87 Q 3
Quarr .....10 Q 31
Quatt .....27 M 26
Quedgeley .....19 N 28
Queen Camel .....8 M 30
Queen Elizabeth
   Forest Park .....67 G 15
Queenborough .....22 W 29
Queensbury .....43 O 22
Queensferry .....34 K 24
Quenborough .....30 U 28
Quenington .....19 O 28
Quinag .....84 E 9
Quines's Hill .....46 G 21
Quinish Point .....71 B 14
Quiraing .....77 B 11

Quoich (Loch) .....72 E 12
Quorndon .....36 Q 25
Quothquan .....61 J 17

R
Raasay (Island of) .....77 B 11
Raasay (Sound of) .....77 B 11
Raasay Ho .....77 B 11
Rachub .....33 H 24
Rackenford .....7 J 31
Rackwick .....86 J 7
Radcliffe .....42 N 23
Radcliffe-on-Trent .....36 Q 25
Radlett .....21 T 28
Radley .....20 Q 28
Radnor Forest .....26 K 27
Radstock .....18 M 30
Radyr .....18 K 29
Rafford .....80 J 11
Raglan .....18 L 28
Ragley Hall .....27 O 27
Rainford .....42 L 23
Rainham .....22 V 29
Rainworth .....36 Q 24
Rait .....68 K 14
Ramasaig .....76 Z 11
Rampisham .....8 M 31
Rampside .....47 K 21
Rampton .....44 R 24
Ramsbottom .....42 N 23
Ramsbury .....19 P 29
Ramsey Cambs. .....29 T 26
Ramsey Isle of Man .....46 G 21
Ramsey Bay .....46 G 21
Ramsey Island .....14 D 28
Ramsey St. Mary's .....29 T 26
Ramsgate .....23 Y 29
Ramsgill-in-Nidderdale .....49 O 21
Ranby .....44 Q 24
Ranfurly .....60 G 16
Rangeworthy .....18 M 29
Ranish .....82 A 9
Rankinston .....60 G 17
Rannoch (Loch) .....73 H 13
Rannoch Moor .....73 F 14
Rannoch Sta .....73 G 13
Ranskill .....44 Q 23
Ranton .....35 N 25
Ranworth .....39 Y 25
Rapness .....87 L 6
Rappach .....84 F 10
Ratby .....36 Q 26
Rathen .....81 O 11
Rathmell .....49 N 21
Ratho .....68 J 16
Ratlinghope .....34 L 26
Rattlesden .....30 W 27
Rattray .....68 K 14
Rattray Head .....81 O 11
Raunds .....29 S 26
Ravenglass .....47 J 20
Ravenscar .....51 S 20
Ravensthorpe .....28 Q 27
Ravenstone .....36 P 25
Ravenstonedale .....49 M 20
Ravensworth .....49 O 20
Rawcliffe .....44 R 22
Rawmarsh .....44 P 23
Rawtenstall .....42 N 22
Rayleigh .....22 V 29
Rayne .....30 V 28
Read .....42 M 22
Reading .....20 R 29
Rearsby .....36 Q 25
Reay .....85 I 8
Reay Forest .....84 F 9
Reculver .....23 X 29
Red Wharf Bay .....40 H 23
Redbourn .....21 S 28
Redbourne .....44 S 23
Redbridge
   London Borough .....21 U 29
Redcar .....57 Q 20
Redcliff Bay .....18 L 29
Reddding .....67 I 16
Redditch .....27 O 27
Redesmouth .....55 N 18
Redford .....69 L 14
Redhill North Somerset .....18 L 29
Redhill
   Reigate and Banstead .....21 T 30
Redisham .....31 Y 26
Redmarley d'Abitot .....27 M 28
Redmarshall .....57 P 20
Redmire .....49 O 21
Redpoint .....77 C 11
Redruth .....2 E 33

Redwick .....18 L 29
Reedham .....39 Y 26
Reekie Linn .....74 K 13
Reepham .....45 S 24
Reeth .....49 O 20
Regarby .....46 G 20
Reiff .....83 D 9
Reigate .....21 T 30
Reighton .....51 T 21
Reiss .....86 K 8
Relubbus .....2 D 33
Rempstone .....36 Q 25
Rendcomb .....19 O 28
Rendham .....31 Y 27
Renfrew .....60 G 16
Renish Point .....76 Z 10
Renishaw .....44 P 24
Rennington .....63 O 17
Renton .....66 G 16
Renwick .....55 M 19
Repton .....36 P 25
Rescobie .....75 L 14
Resipole .....72 C 13
Resolven .....17 I 28
Resort (Loch) .....82 Z 9
Restalrig .....68 K 16
Reston .....63 N 16
Restormel Castle .....3 G 32
Retford .....44 R 24
Rettendon .....22 V 29
Reynoldston .....15 H 29
Rhaeadr / Rhayader .....25 J 27
Rhaeadr Ddu .....33 I 25
Rhandirmwyn .....25 I 27
Rhayader / Rhaeadr .....25 J 27
Rheidol (Vale of) .....25 I 26
Rhenigidale .....82 Z 10
Rhian .....84 G 9
Rhiconich .....84 F 8
Rhigos .....17 J 28
Rhilochan .....85 H 9
Rhinns of Galloway (The) .....52 E 19
Rhinns of Kells .....53 G 18
Rhondda .....17 J 29
Rhoose .....17 J 29
Rhos .....17 I 28
Rhoscolyn .....40 G 23
Rhoscrowther .....14 E 28
Rhosllanerchrugog .....34 K 24
Rhosmaen .....25 I 28
Rhosneigr .....40 G 23
Rhossili .....15 H 29
Rhostyllen .....34 K 24
Rhosybol .....40 G 22
Rhu .....66 F 16
Rhuddlan .....41 J 23
Rhum .....71 A 13
Rhuthun / Ruthin .....34 K 24
Rhyd-Ddu .....33 H 24
Rhydaman / Ammanford .....15 I 28
Rhydcymerau .....15 H 28
Rhydd .....27 N 27
Rhyddhywel .....25 J 26
Rhydowen .....15 H 27
Rhyl .....41 J 23
Rhymmi / Rhymney .....18 K 28
Rhymney / Rhymmi .....18 K 28
Rhynie .....80 L 12
Ribble (River) .....49 N 22
Ribblesdale .....49 N 21
Ribchester .....42 M 22
Riber Castle .....36 P 24
Riccall .....44 Q 22
Riccarton .....60 G 17
Richards Castle .....26 L 27
Richborough .....23 X 30
Richmond .....49 O 20
Richmond-upon-Thames
   London Borough .....21 T 29
Rickarton .....75 N 13
Rickmansworth .....21 S 29
Ridgeway Cross .....27 M 27
Ridgeway Path (The) .....20 P 29
Ridsdale .....55 N 18
Rievaulx Abbey .....50 Q 21
Rigg .....77 B 11
Rigside .....61 I 17
Rillington .....51 R 21
Rimington .....49 N 22
Rimsdale (Loch) .....85 H 9
Ringford .....53 H 19
Ringmer .....11 U 31
Ringshall .....30 W 27
Ringstead
   East Northamptonshire .....29 S 26
Ringstead King's Lynn
   and West Norfolk .....38 V 25

A B C D E F G H I J K L M N O P Q R S T U V W X Y Z

Ringwood .... 9 O 31
Ringwould .... 23 Y 30
Rinnes (Glen) .... 80 K 11
Rinns of Islay .... 58 A 16
Rinns Point .... 58 A 16
Ripe .... 12 U 31
Ripley *Derbs.* .... 36 P 24
Ripley *North Yorks.* .. 50 P 21
Ripley *Surrey* .... 21 S 30
Riplingham .... 44 S 22
Ripon .... 50 P 21
Rippingale .... 37 S 25
Ripponden .... 43 O 22
Risabus .... 58 B 17
Risby .... 30 V 27
Risca .... 18 K 29
Risegate .... 37 T 25
Riseley .... 29 S 27
Rishton .... 42 M 22
Risplith .... 50 P 21
Ristol (Isle) .... 83 D 9
Roadside of Kinneff .. 75 N 13
Roag .... 77 A 11
Roag (Loch) .... 82 Z 9
Roan of Graigoch .... 60 F 18
Roberton
    Dumfries and Galloway .... 61 I 17
Roberton
    Scottish Borders .... 62 L 17
Robertsbridge .... 12 V 31
Robin Hood's Bay .... 51 S 20
Roby .... 42 L 23
Rocester .... 35 O 25
Rochdale .... 43 N 23
Roche .... 3 F 32
Rochester .... 22 V 29
Rochester
    Northumberland .... 63 N 18
Rochford .... 22 W 29
Rock .... 3 F 32
Rockcliffe *Cumbria* .. 54 K 19
Rockcliffe
    Dumfries and Galloway .... 53 I 19
Rockfield .... 18 L 28
Rockingham .... 28 R 26
Rode .... 19 N 30
Rode Heath .... 35 N 24
Rodel .... 76 Z 10
Rodmel .... 11 U 31
Rodney Stoke .... 18 L 30
Rogart .... 85 H 9
Rogerstone .... 18 K 29
Rogiet .... 18 L 29
Rokeby Hall .... 49 O 20
Rolleston *Notts.* .... 36 R 24
Rolleston-on-Dove *Staffs.* .. 35 P 25
Rolvenden .... 12 V 30
Romannobridge .... 61 J 16
Romiley .... 43 N 23
Romney Marsh .... 12 W 30
Romsey .... 10 P 31
Romsley .... 27 N 26
Rona (Island of) ..... 77 C 11
Ronaldsway .... 46 G 21
Ronas Voe .... 87 P 2
Ronay .... 76 Y 11
Rookhope .... 55 N 19
Roos .... 45 T 22
Rootpark .... 61 I 16
Ropley .... 10 Q 30
Ropsley .... 37 S 25
Rora .... 81 O 11
Rora Head .... 86 J 7
Rosedale Abbey ...... 50 R 20
Rosehearty .... 81 N 10
Rosemarket .... 16 F 28
Rosemarkie .... 79 H 11
Rosewell .... 61 K 16
Rosgill .... 48 L 20
Roshven .... 71 C 13
Rosley .... 54 K 19
Roslin .... 61 K 16
Rosliston .... 35 P 25
Rosneath .... 66 F 15
Ross
    Berwick-upon-Tweed ...... 63 O 17
Ross
    Dumfries and Galloway .... 53 H 19
Ross of Mull .... 64 B 15
Ross-on-Wye .... 26 M 28
Rossall Point .... 48 K 22
Rossett .... 34 L 24
Rosudgeon .... 2 D 33
Rosyth .... 68 J 15
Rothbury .... 63 O 18
Rothbury Forest ...... 63 O 18
Rotherfield .... 12 U 30

Rotherham .... 43 P 23
Rotherthorpe .... 28 R 27
Rothes .... 80 K 11
Rothesay .... 59 E 16
Rothienorman .... 81 M 11
Rothiesholm .... 87 M 6
Rothwell *Leeds.* .... 43 P 22
Rothwell *Northamp.* .. 28 R 26
Rottingdean .... 11 T 31
Roughburn .... 73 F 13
Roughsike .... 55 L 18
Roughton .... 39 X 25
Rounton .... 50 P 20
Rousay .... 86 K 6
Rousdon .... 5 L 31
Routh .... 45 S 22
Rowardennan Lodge ... 66 G 15
Rowington .... 27 O 27
Rowland's Castle ..... 10 R 31
Rowland's Gill .... 56 O 19
Rownhams .... 10 P 31
Rowsley .... 35 P 24
Roxburgh .... 62 M 17
Roxwell .... 22 V 28
Roy (Glen) .... 72 F 13
Royal Leamington Spa .. 28 P 27
Royal Military Academy .. 20 R 29
Royal Tunbridge Wells .. 12 U 30
Roybridge .... 72 F 13
Roydon *Essex* ...... 21 U 28
Roydon *Norfolk* .... 31 X 26
Royston *Herts.* .... 29 T 27
Royston *South Yorks.* .. 43 P 23
Royton .... 43 N 23
Ruabon .... 34 K 25
Ruan High Lanes ..... 3 F 33
Ruan Minor .... 2 E 34
Ruardean .... 18 M 28
Rubha na Faing ...... 58 A 16
Rubha a' Mhail ...... 64 B 16
Rubha Còigeach ...... 83 D 9
Rubha Dubh .... 70 Z 14
Rubha Hunish .... 77 A 10
Rubha na h-Easgainne .. 71 B 12
Rubha Réidh .... 77 C 10
Rubha Suisnish ...... 71 B 12
Rubh'an Dùnain ...... 71 A 12
Rudbaxton .... 24 F 28
Ruddington .... 36 Q 25
Rudgeway .... 18 M 29
Rudgwick .... 11 S 30
Rudha Ban .... 70 Y 12
Rudston .... 51 T 21
Rufford Old Hall ..... 42 L 23
Rufforth .... 50 Q 22
Rugby .... 28 Q 26
Rugeley .... 35 O 25
Rumburgh .... 31 Y 26
Rumney .... 18 K 29
Runcorn .... 42 L 23
Runswick Bay .... 50 R 20
Runtaleave .... 74 K 13
Runwell .... 22 V 29
Rushall .... 19 O 30
Rushden .... 29 S 27
Ruskington .... 37 S 24
Rusland .... 48 K 21
Rusper .... 11 T 30
Ruspidge .... 18 M 28
Rustington .... 11 S 31
Ruswarp .... 51 S 20
Rutherglen .... 60 H 16
Ruthin / Rhuthun .... 34 K 24
Ruthven *Aberdeenshire* .. 80 L 11
Ruthven *Angus* ..... 74 K 14
Ruthven *Highland* .. 79 I 11
Ruthven (Loch) ...... 79 H 12
Ruthven Barracks .... 73 H 12
Ruthwell .... 54 J 19
Rutland Water .... 37 S 26
Ruyton
    of the Eleven Towns .. 34 L 25
Ryal .... 56 O 18
Ryan (Loch) .... 52 E 19
Rycote .... 20 Q 28
Rydal .... 48 L 20
Ryde .... 10 Q 31
Rye .... 12 W 31
Ryhall .... 37 S 25
Ryhill .... 43 P 23
Ryhope .... 57 P 19
Ryton .... 56 O 19

S

Sabden .... 42 M 22
Sacriston .... 56 P 19

Sadberge .... 50 P 20
Saddell .... 59 D 17
Saddell Bay .... 59 D 17
Sadgill .... 48 L 20
Saffron Walden ...... 30 U 27
Saham Toney .... 38 W 26
St. Abbs .... 63 N 16
St. Abb's Head ...... 63 N 16
St. Agnes .... 2 E 33
St. Albans .... 21 T 28
St. Aldhelm's Head .. 9 N 32
St. Andrews .... 69 L 14
St. Ann's .... 54 J 18
St. Ann's Head ...... 14 E 28
St. Arvans .... 18 L 29
St. Asaph .... 41 J 23
St. Athan .... 17 J 29
St. Austell .... 3 F 32
St. Bees .... 47 J 20
St. Bees Head .... 47 J 20
St. Blazey .... 3 F 32
St. Boswells .... 62 M 17
St. Breock .... 3 F 32
St. Breward .... 3 F 32
St. Briavels .... 18 M 28
St. Brides .... 14 E 28
St. Bride's Bay ..... 14 E 28
St. Brides Major .... 17 J 29
St. Brides-Super-Ely .. 17 K 29
St. Bridge-Wentlooge .. 18 K 29
St. Buryan .... 2 D 33
St. Catherine's Point .. 10 Q 32
St. Clears / Sanclêr .. 15 G 28
St. Cleer .... 3 G 32
St. Columb Major .... 3 F 32
St. Combs .... 81 O 11
St. Cyrus .... 75 M 13
St. David's / Tyddewi .. 14 E 28
St. David's Head .... 14 D 28
St. Day .... 2 E 33
St. Dennis .... 3 F 32
St. Dogmaels .... 15 F 27
St. Dominick .... 3 H 32
St. Donats .... 17 J 29
St. Endellion .... 3 F 32
St. Erth .... 2 D 33
St. Ewe .... 3 F 33
St. Fagans .... 18 K 29
St. Fergus .... 81 O 11
St. Fillans .... 67 H 14
St. Florence .... 15 F 28
St. Gennys .... 6 G 31
St. Germans .... 3 H 32
St. Giles .... 7 H 31
St. Giles-on-the-Heath .. 6 H 31
St. Govan's Head .... 16 F 29
St. Harmon .... 25 J 26
St. Helen Auckland .. 56 O 20
St. Helens *I.O.W.* .. 10 Q 31
St. Helens *Merseyside* .. 42 L 23
St. Helier *Jersey* .. 5
St. Ishmael's .... 14 E 28
St. Issey .... 3 F 32
St. Ive .... 3 G 32
St. Ives *Cambs.* ... 29 T 27
St. Ives *Cornwall* .. 2 D 33
St. John's .... 46 G 21
St. John's Chapel ... 55 N 19
St. John's Loch ..... 86 J 8
St. Jude .... 46 G 20
St. Just .... 2 C 33
St. Just in Roseland .. 2 F 33
St. Keverne .... 2 E 33
St. Kew .... 3 F 32
St. Leonards *Dorset* .. 9 O 31
St. Leonards *East Sussex* .. 12 V 31
St. Mabyn .... 3 F 32
St. Magnus Bay ...... 87 P 2
St. Margaret's at Cliffe .. 23 Y 30
St. Margaret's Bay .. 23 Y 30
St. Margaret's Hope .. 87 L 7
St. Mark's .... 46 G 21
St. Martin's .... 34 K 25
St. Mary in the Marsh .. 12 W 30
St. Mary's *Orkney Islands* .. 86 L 7
St. Mary's
    Perth and Kinross .. 73 I 14
St. Mary's-Bay ...... 13 W 30
St. Mary's-Hoo ...... 22 V 29
St. Mary's Loch ..... 61 K 17
St. Mawes .... 2 E 33
St. Mawgan .... 3 F 32
St. Mellion .... 3 H 32
St. Mellons .... 18 K 29
St. Merryn .... 3 F 32
St. Michael Penkevil .. 2 E 33
St. Michael's Mount .. 2 D 33

St. Michaels-on-Wyre .. 42 L 22
St. Minver .... 3 F 32
St. Monans .... 69 L 15
St. Neot .... 3 G 32
St. Neots .... 29 T 27
St. Nicholas *Pembrokes* .. 14 E 28
St. Nicholas
    Vale of Glamorgan .. 17 K 29
St. Nicholas-at-Wade .. 23 X 29
St. Ninian's Isle ... 87 P 4
St. Osyth .... 23 X 28
St. Patrick's Isle .. 46 F 21
St. Paul's Walden ... 29 T 28
St. Peter Port *Guernsey* .. 5
St. Peter's .... 23 Y 29
St. Pool .... 4 I 33
St. Stephen .... 3 F 32
St. Teath .... 3 F 32
St. Tudwal's Islands .. 32 G 25
St. Tudy .... 3 F 32
St. Vigeans .... 69 M 14
St. Wenn .... 3 F 32
St. Weonards .... 26 L 28
Salcombe .... 4 I 33
Salcombe Regis ...... 5 K 31
Sale .... 42 N 23
Salehurst .... 12 V 31
Salen *Argyll and Bute* .. 65 C 14
Salen *Highland* .... 71 C 13
Salford .... 42 N 23
Salfords .... 21 T 30
Salhouse .... 39 Y 25
Saline .... 68 J 15
Salisbury .... 9 O 30
Salisbury Plain ..... 19 O 30
Salisbury
    Ben More Assybt .. 84 G 9
Sallachy
    near Kyle of Lochalsh .. 78 D 12
Saltash .... 3 H 32
Saltburn .... 79 H 10
Saltburn-by-the-Sea .. 57 R 20
Saltcoats .... 59 F 17
Salter .... 48 M 21
Saltfleet .... 45 U 23
Saltford .... 18 M 29
Salthouse .... 38 X 25
Saltney .... 34 L 24
Salton .... 50 R 21
Samala .... 76 X 11
Samlesbury Old Hall .. 42 M 22
Sampford Courtenay .. 7 I 31
Sampford Peverell ... 7 J 31
Sanaigmore .... 58 A 16
Sanclêr / St. Clears .. 15 G 28
Sancreed .... 2 D 33
Sancton .... 44 S 22
Sand Side .... 47 K 21
Sanda Island .... 59 D 18
Sanday *Highland* ... 71 A 12
Sanday *Orkney Islands* .. 87 M 6
Sandbach .... 35 M 24
Sandbank .... 66 F 16
Sandbanks .... 9 O 31
Sandend .... 80 L 10
Sandford *Eden* ..... 49 M 20
Sandford *Mid Devon* .. 7 J 31
Sandford *North Somerset* .. 18 L 30
Sandford
    South Lanarkshire .. 60 H 17
Sandford Orcas ...... 8 M 31
Sandgate .... 13 X 30
Sandgreen .... 53 H 19
Sandhaven .... 81 N 10
Sandhead .... 52 F 19
Sandhurst *Berks.* .. 20 R 29
Sandhurst *Kent* .... 12 V 30
Sandleigh .... 20 Q 28
Sandlins .... 31 Y 27
Sandness .... 87 P 3
Sandon
    North Hertfordshire .. 29 T 28
Sandon *Stafford* ... 35 N 25
Sandown .... 10 Q 32
Sandray .... 70 X 13
Sandridge .... 21 T 28
Sandringham House ... 38 V 25
Sandsend .... 51 R 20
Sandwell .... 27 O 26
Sandwich .... 23 Y 30
Sandwick *Eden* ..... 48 L 20
Sandwick *Eilean Siar* .. 76 Y 11
Sandwick *Shetland Islands* .. 87 Q 4
Sandwood Loch .... 84 E 8
Sandy .... 29 T 27
Sandygate .... 46 G 20
Sandyhills .... 53 I 19

Sanna .... 71 B 13
Sanquhar .... 61 I 17
Santon Downham ...... 30 W 26
Santon Head .... 46 G 21
Sapperton .... 19 N 28
Saracen's Head ...... 37 T 25
Sarclet .... 86 K 8
Sarisbury .... 10 Q 31
Sark *Channel I.* ... 5
Sarn Meyllteyrn ..... 32 G 25
Sarre .... 23 X 29
Satley .... 56 O 19
Satterthwaite .... 48 K 21
Sauchen .... 75 M 12
Saughall .... 42 L 24
Saughtree .... 62 L 18
Saundersfoot .... 15 F 28
Saunderton .... 20 R 28
Sawbridgeworth ...... 21 U 28
Sawrey .... 48 L 20
Sawston .... 29 U 27
Sawtry .... 29 T 26
Saxby .... 36 R 25
Saxilby .... 44 S 24
Saxlingham Nethergate .. 39 X 26
Saxmundham .... 31 Y 27
Saxted Green .... 31 X 27
Scadavay (Loch) ..... 76 Y 11
Scaddle (Glen) ...... 72 D 13
Scafell Pikes .... 47 K 20
Scagglethorpe .... 50 R 21
Scalasaig .... 64 B 15
Scalby .... 51 S 21
Scaleby .... 55 L 19
Scalford .... 36 R 25
Scalloway .... 87 Q 3
Scalpay *Highland* .. 77 C 12
Scalpay *Western Isles* .. 77 A 10
Scampton .... 44 S 24
Scaniport .... 79 H 11
Scapa Flow .... 86 K 7
Scarba .... 65 C 15
Scarborough .... 51 S 21
Scarcliffe .... 44 Q 24
Scardroy .... 78 F 11
Scarfskerry .... 86 K 8
Scarinish .... 64 Z 14
Scarp .... 82 Y 9
Scavaig (Loch) ...... 71 B 12
Scawby .... 44 S 23
Schiehallion .... 73 H 13
Scilly (Isles of) ... 2 B 34
Scone Palace .... 68 J 14
Scopwick .... 37 S 24
Scoraig .... 83 D 10
Scorton .... 50 P 20
Scotby .... 55 L 19
Scotch-Corner .... 49 P 20
Scothern .... 45 S 24
Scotlandwell .... 68 K 15
Scotney .... 12 V 30
Scotstown .... 72 D 13
Scotter .... 44 S 23
Scotton *Harrogate* .. 50 P 21
Scotton *Richmondshire* .. 49 O 20
Scottow .... 39 Y 25
Scourie .... 84 E 8
Scousburgh .... 87 Q 4
Scrabster .... 85 J 8
Scraptoft .... 36 Q 26
Scredington .... 37 S 25
Scridain (Loch) ..... 64 B 14
Scruton .... 50 P 21
Sculthorpe .... 38 W 25
Scunthorpe .... 44 S 23
Sea Palling .... 39 Y 25
Seaford .... 12 U 31
Seaforth (Loch) ..... 82 Z 10
Seaforth Head .... 82 A 9
Seagrave .... 36 Q 25
Seaham .... 57 P 19
Seahouses .... 63 O 17
Seale .... 21 R 30
Sealga (Loch na) .... 78 D 10
Seamer *Hambleton* .. 50 Q 20
Seamer *Scarborough* .. 51 S 21
Seamill .... 59 F 16
Seascale .... 47 J 20
Seaton *East Devon* .. 5 K 31
Seaton Carew .... 57 Q 20
Seaton Delaval ...... 56 P 18
Seaton Delaval Hall .. 56 P 18
Seaton Ross .... 44 R 22
Seaton Sluice .... 56 P 18

Seave Green .... 50 Q 20
Seaview .... 10 Q 31
Sebergham .... 54 L 19
Sedbergh .... 49 M 21
Sedgebrook .... 36 R 25
Sedgley .... 27 N 26
Sedlescombe .... 12 V 31
Seend .... 19 N 29
Seething .... 39 Y 26
Seighford .... 35 N 25
Seil (Isle of) ...... 65 D 15
Seilich (Loch an t-) .. 73 H 13
Selattyn .... 34 K 25
Selborne .... 10 R 30
Selby .... 44 Q 22
Selker Bay .... 47 J 21
Selkirk .... 62 L 17
Sellindge .... 13 W 30
Selmeston .... 12 U 31
Selsey .... 10 R 31
Selston .... 36 Q 24
Selworthy .... 17 J 30
Semley .... 9 N 30
Senghenydd .... 18 K 29
Sennen .... 2 C 33
Sennybridge .... 25 J 28
Sessay .... 50 Q 21
Settle .... 49 N 21
Seven Sisters
    East Sussex ...... 12 U 31
Seven Sisters
    Neath and Port Talbot .. 17 I 28
Sevenhampton .... 27 O 28
Sevenoaks .... 22 U 30
Severn (River) ...... 27 M 28
Severn Bridge .... 18 M 29
Severn Stoke .... 27 N 27
Sgiabacleit (Loch) .. 82 A 9
Sgiwen .... 17 I 29
Sgurr Mór .... 78 E 10
Shader .... 82 A 8
Shaftesbury .... 9 N 30
Shalbourne .... 20 P 29
Shaldon .... 4 J 32
Shalfleet .... 10 P 31
Shalford .... 21 S 30
Shandon .... 66 F 15
Shanklin .... 10 Q 32
Shap .... 48 L 20
Shapinsay .... 87 L 6
Shapwick .... 8 L 30
Shardlow .... 36 P 25
Sharlston .... 43 P 23
Sharnbrook .... 29 S 27
Sharnford .... 28 Q 26
Sharperton .... 63 N 18
Sharpness .... 18 M 28
Shavington .... 34 M 24
Shaw *Gtr. Mches.* .. 43 N 23
Shaw *West Berkshire* .. 20 Q 29
Shaw *Wilts.* .... 19 N 29
Shawbost .... 82 Z 9
Shawbury .... 34 M 25
Shawford .... 10 Q 30
Shawhead .... 53 I 18
Sheepwash .... 6 H 31
Sheepy Magna .... 36 P 26
Sheering .... 22 U 28
Sheerness .... 22 W 29
Sheffield .... 43 P 23
Sheffield Park ...... 11 T 30
Shefford .... 29 S 27
Sheldon .... 19 N 29
Sheldon Manor .... 19 N 29
Sheldwich .... 22 W 30
Shell or Sealg (Loch) .. 82 A 9
Shelley .... 43 O 23
Shellingford .... 20 P 29
Shelsley Beauchamp .. 27 M 27
Shelton *Rushcliffe* .. 36 R 25
Shelton *South Norfolk* .. 31 X 26
Shelton Lock .... 36 P 25
Shelve .... 34 L 26
Shenley Church End .. 28 R 27
Shenstone .... 27 O 26
Shenval .... 80 K 11
Shepley .... 43 O 23
Sheppey (Isle of) ... 22 W 29
Shepreth .... 29 U 27
Shepshed .... 36 Q 25
Shepton Mallet ...... 18 M 30
Sherborne *Cotswold* .. 19 O 28
Sherborne *West Dorset* .. 8 M 31
Sherborne St. John .. 20 Q 30
Sherburn *Durham* ... 56 P 19

A B C D E F G H I J K L M N O P Q R S T U V W X Y Z

Strathearn	67 I 14
Stratherrick	73 G 12
Strathkinness	69 L 14
Strathmashie	73 H 13
Strathmiglo	68 K 15
Strathmore	75 M 13
Strathnairn	79 H 11
Strathnaver	85 H 8
Strathpeffer	79 G 11
Strathrannoch	79 F 10
Strathspey	80 J 11
Strathvaich Lodge	78 F 10
Strathy	85 I 8
Strathy Point	85 H 8
Strathyre	67 H 15
Stratton Cornwall	6 G 31
Stratton Glos.	19 O 28
Stratton West Dorset	5 M 31
Stratton Audley	28 Q 28
Stratton-on-the-Fosse	18 M 30
Stratton-St. Margaret	19 O 29
Streatley	20 Q 29
Street	8 L 30
Strensall	50 Q 21
Stretford	42 N 23
Stretham	30 U 26
Stretton Cheshire	42 M 23
Stretton Staffs.	35 N 25
Stretton-on-Dunsmore	28 P 26
Strichen	81 N 11
Striven (Loch)	66 E 16
Stroma (Island of)	86 K 7
Stromeferry	78 D 11
Stromemore	78 D 11
Stromness	86 K 7
Stronachlachar	66 G 15
Stronchreggan	72 E 13
Stronchrubie	84 F 9
Strone	66 F 16
Stronmilchan	66 F 14
Stronsay	87 M 6
Stronsay Firth	87 L 6
Strontian	72 D 13
Stroud	19 N 28
Strumble Head	14 E 27
Stuart Castel	79 H 11
Stuartfield	81 N 11
Stubbington	10 Q 31
Studland	9 O 32
Studley Warw.	27 O 27
Studley Wilts.	19 N 29
Studley Royal Gardens	50 P 21
Stuley	76 Y 12
Sturminster Marshall	9 N 31
Sturminster Newton	9 N 31
Sturry	23 X 30
Sturton-le-Steeple	44 R 23
Suainaval (Loch)	82 Z 9
Sudbourne	31 Y 27
Sudbury Derbs.	35 O 25
Sudbury Suffolk	30 W 27
Sudbury Hall	35 O 25
Sudeley Castle	27 O 28
Sùil Ghorm	71 A 13
Sulby	46 G 21
Sulgrave	28 Q 27
Sulhamstead	20 Q 29
Sullom	87 P 2
Sullom Voe	87 P 2
Sully	18 K 29
Sumburgh	87 Q 4
Sumburgh Roost	87 P 4
Summer Island	83 D 9
Summerbridge	49 O 21
Summercourt	3 F 32
Sunart	72 D 13
Sunart (Loch)	71 C 13
Sunbury	21 S 29
Sunderland	57 P 19
Sunderland Bridge	56 P 19
Sunk Island	45 T 23
Sunningdale	21 S 29
Sunninghill	21 S 29
Surfleet	37 T 25
Surlingham	39 Y 26
Sutterton	37 T 25
Sutton Bassetlaw	44 R 23
Sutton Cambs.	29 U 26
Sutton Guildford	21 S 30
Sutton London Borough	21 T 29
Sutton Shrops.	34 M 25
Sutton Bank	50 Q 21
Sutton Benger	19 N 29
Sutton Bonington	36 Q 25
Sutton Bridge	37 U 25
Sutton Cheney	36 P 26
Sutton Coldfield	35 O 26

Sutton Courtenay	20 Q 29
Sutton-in-Ashfield	36 Q 24
Sutton-on-Hull	45 T 22
Sutton-on-Sea	45 U 24
Sutton-on-the-Forest	50 Q 21
Sutton-on-the-Hill	35 P 25
Sutton-on-Trent	36 R 24
Sutton Scotney	10 P 30
Sutton St. Edmund	37 U 25
Sutton St. James	37 U 25
Sutton-St. Nicholas	26 L 27
Sutton under Whitestonecliffe	50 Q 21
Sutton Valence	22 V 30
Sutton Veny	9 N 30
Swadlincote	36 P 25
Swaffham	38 W 26
Swaffham Bulbeck	30 U 27
Swainby	50 Q 20
Swainswick	19 M 29
Swale (River)	50 P 21
Swale (The)	22 W 29
Swale Dale	49 O 20
Swallow	45 T 23
Swallow Falls	33 I 24
Swallowcliffe	9 N 30
Swallowfield	20 R 29
Swanage	9 O 32
Swanbridge	18 K 29
Swanland	44 S 22
Swanley	22 U 29
Swannery	5 M 32
Swanscombe	22 U 29
Swansea / Abertawe	17 I 29
Swanton Abbot	39 Y 25
Swanton Morley	38 W 25
Swanwick	36 P 24
Swarbacks Minn	87 P 2
Swavesey	29 T 27
Sway	9 P 31
Swaythling	10 P 31
Swimbridge	7 I 30
Swinbrook	19 P 28
Swinderby	36 R 24
Swindon Cheltenham	27 N 28
Swindon Swindon	19 O 29
Swinefleet	44 R 22
Swineshead	37 T 25
Swinford	28 Q 26
Swingfield	23 X 30
Swinton Rotherham.	44 Q 23
Swinton Scottish Borders	63 N 16
Swynnerton	35 N 25
Sydenham	20 R 28
Syderstone	38 W 25
Sydling St. Nicholas	8 M 31
Sykehouse	44 Q 23
Symbister	87 Q 2
Symington South Ayrshire	60 G 17
Symington South Lanarkshire	61 J 17
Symonds Yat	18 M 28
Symonds Yat Rock	18 M 28
Symondsbury	5 L 31
Syresham	28 Q 27
Syston	36 Q 25
Sywell	28 R 27

T

Tackley	28 Q 28
Tadcaster	44 Q 22
Taddington	43 O 24
Tadley	20 Q 29
Tadmarton	28 P 27
Tadworth	21 T 30
Takeley	30 U 28
Tal-y-bont Dyfed	25 I 26
Tal-y-Bont Gwynedd	33 H 25
Tal-y-Cafn	41 I 23
Tal-y-Llyn Lake	33 I 25
Talacre	41 K 22
Talgarreg	15 H 27
Talgarth	26 K 28
Talisker	77 A 12
Talke	35 N 24
Talladale	78 D 10
Tallaminnock	60 G 18
Talley	25 I 28
Talsarnau	33 H 25
Talwrn	40 H 23
Talybont-on-Usk Powys	26 K 28
Talywern	33 I 26

Tamanavay (Loch)	82 Y 9
Tamar (River)	6 G 31
Tamerton Foliot	4 H 32
Tamworth	35 O 26
Tan Hill	49 N 20
Tan-y-pistill	33 J 25
Tanera Beg	83 D 9
Tanera Mór	83 D 9
Tangley	20 P 30
Tangmere	11 R 31
Tannach	86 K 8
Tannadice	74 L 13
Tantallon Castle	69 M 15
Taransay	82 Y 10
Taransay (Sound of)	82 Z 10
Tarbat Ness	79 I 10
Tarbert Argyll and Bute	59 D 16
Tarbert Gigha Island	65 C 16
Tarbert Western Isles	82 Z 10
Tarbert (Loch)	65 C 16
Tarbet Argyll and Bute	66 F 15
Tarbet Highland	72 D 13
Tarbolton	60 G 17
Tardy Gate	42 L 22
Tarfside	74 L 13
Tarland	74 L 12
Tarleton	42 L 22
Tarn (The)	48 L 20
Tarporley	34 M 24
Tarrant Gunville	9 N 31
Tarrant Hinton	9 N 31
Tarrant Keyneston	9 N 31
Tarrington	26 M 27
Tarskavaig	71 C 12
Tarskavaig Point	71 B 12
Tarves	81 N 11
Tarvin	34 L 24
Tathwell	45 T 24
Tattersett	38 W 25
Tattershall	37 T 24
Tatton Hall	42 M 24
Taunton	8 K 30
Taunton Deane	7 K 30
Taverham	39 X 25
Tavernspite	15 G 28
Tavistock	4 H 32
Taw (River)	7 I 31
Tay (Firth of)	68 K 14
Tay (Loch)	67 H 14
Tay Road Bridge	69 L 14
Taynton	27 M 28
Taynuilt	65 E 14
Tayport	69 L 14
Tayvallich	65 D 15
Teacuis (Loch)	71 C 14
Tealby	45 T 23
Teangue	71 C 12
Tebay	48 M 20
Tebdurn St. Mary	4 I 31
Teddington	27 N 28
Tees (River)	50 P 20
Teesdale	55 N 20
Teifi (River)	15 G 27
Teignmouth	4 J 32
Telford	34 M 25
Teme (River)	27 M 27
Templand	54 J 18
Temple	61 K 16
Temple Ewell	23 X 30
Temple Grafton	27 O 27
Temple Sowerby	55 M 20
Templeton	15 F 28
Tempsford	29 T 27
Tenbury Wells	26 M 27
Tenby / Dinbych-y-pysgod	15 F 28
Tendring	31 X 28
Tenterden	12 W 30
Terling	22 V 28
Tern Hill	34 M 25
Terrington St. Clement	38 U 25
Test (River)	20 P 30
Tetbury	19 N 29
Tetford	45 T 24
Tetney	45 T 23
Tetsworth	20 Q 28
Tettenhall	35 N 26
Tewin	21 T 28
Tewkesbury	27 N 28
Texa	58 B 17
Teynham	22 W 30
Thakeham	11 S 31
Thame	20 R 28
Thame (River)	20 R 28
Thames (River)	20 Q 29
Thanet (Isle of)	23 Y 29
Thankerton	61 J 17
Thatcham	20 Q 29

Thaxted	30 V 28
Theale Berks.	20 Q 29
Theale Somerset	18 L 30
Theddlethorpe St. Helen	45 U 23
Thetford	30 W 26
Theviothead	62 L 17
Theydon Bois	21 U 28
Thirlestane	62 L 16
Thirlspot	48 K 20
Thirsk	50 P 21
Thistleton	37 S 25
Thixendale	51 R 21
Thompson	38 W 26
Thomshill	80 K 11
Thoralby	49 N 21
Thoresway	45 T 23
Thorganby	44 R 22
Thornaby-on-Tees	50 Q 20
Thornborough	28 R 28
Thornbury Heref.	26 M 27
Thornbury South Glos.	18 M 29
Thornbury Torridge	6 H 31
Thornby	28 Q 26
Thorncombe	8 L 31
Thorne	44 R 23
Thorner	43 P 22
Thorney	37 T 26
Thornford	8 M 31
Thornham	38 V 25
Thornhill Dumfries and Galloway	61 I 18
Thornhill Stirling	67 H 15
Thornton Fife	68 K 15
Thornton Lancs.	42 K 22
Thornton Curtis	45 S 23
Thornton-in-Craven	49 N 22
Thornton-le-Dale	51 R 21
Thornton-le-Moor	69 M 16
Thornyhive Bay	75 N 13
Thorpe Derbs.	35 O 24
Thorpe Essex	22 W 29
Thorpe-le-Soken	31 X 28
Thorpe-on-the-Hill	37 S 24
Thorpe Thewles	57 P 20
Thorpeness	31 Y 27
Thorrington	31 X 28
Thorverton	7 J 31
Thrapston	29 S 26
Threapwood	34 L 24
Three Cocks	26 K 27
Three Crosses	15 H 29
Threekingham	37 S 25
Threlkeld	54 K 20
Thringstone	36 P 25
Throckley	56 O 19
Thropton	63 O 18
Throwleigh	4 I 31
Thrumster	86 K 8
Thruxton Circuit	20 P 30
Thrybergn	44 Q 23
Thundersley	22 V 29
Thurcroft	44 Q 23
Thurgarton	36 R 24
Thurgoland	43 P 23
Thurlby	37 S 25
Thurlestone	4 I 33
Thurlow	30 V 27
Thurlton	39 Y 26
Thurmaston	36 Q 25
Thurne	39 Y 25
Thurnham	22 V 30
Thurnscoe	44 Q 23
Thursby	54 K 19
Thurso	85 J 8
Thurstaston	42 K 23
Thurstonfield	54 K 19
Thurton	39 Y 26
Thwaite	49 N 20
Thwing	51 T 21
Tibbermore	68 J 14
Tibberton Glos.	27 M 28
Tibberton Salop	34 M 25
Tibberton Wychavon	27 N 27
Tibshelf	36 P 24
Ticehurst	12 V 30
Tickhill	44 Q 23
Tiddington	20 Q 28
Tidenham	18 M 29
Tideswell	43 O 24
Tigerton	75 L 13
Tigharry	76 X 11
Tighnabruaich	65 E 16
Tilbury	22 V 29
Tillathrowie	80 L 11
Tillicoultry	67 I 15
Tillington	11 S 31
Tilney St. Lawrence	38 U 25

Tilshead	19 O 30
Tilstock	34 L 25
Tilt (Glen)	73 I 13
Tilton-on-the-Hill	36 R 26
Timberscombe	7 J 30
Timsbury	18 M 30
Timsgarry	82 Y 9
Tingewick	28 Q 28
Tingwall (Loch)	87 P 3
Tintagel	6 F 32
Tintern Abbey	18 L 28
Tintinhull	8 L 31
Tintwistle	43 O 23
Tinwald	53 J 18
Tipton	27 N 26
Tipton-St. john	5 K 31
Tiptree	22 W 28
Tirabad	25 J 27
Tiree	64 Z 14
Tirga Mór	82 Z 10
Tirley	27 N 28
Tiroran	65 B 14
Tisbury	9 N 30
Titchfield	10 Q 31
Titchmarsh	29 S 26
Tiumpan Head	83 B 9
Tiverton Chester	34 L 24
Tiverton Mid Devon	7 J 31
Tobermory	71 B 14
Toberonochy	65 D 15
Tobson	82 Z 9
Tockwith	50 Q 22
Todber	9 N 31
Toddington	29 S 28
Todenham	27 P 27
Todmorden	43 N 22
Toe Head	76 Y 10
Togston	63 P 18
Tokavaig	71 C 12
Toll of Birness	81 O 11
Toller Porcorum	8 M 31
Tollerton	50 Q 21
Tollesbury	22 W 28
Tolleshunt d'Arcy	22 W 28
Tolpuddle	9 N 31
Tolquhon Castle	81 N 11
Tolsta	83 B 8
Tolsta Chaolais	82 Z 9
Tolsta Head	83 B 8
Tomatin	79 I 11
Tombreck	79 H 11
Tomcrasky	72 F 12
Tomdoun	72 E 12
Tomich	78 F 12
Tomintoul	74 J 12
Tomnavoulin	80 K 12
Tomsléibhe	65 C 14
Tonbridge	22 U 30
Tondu	17 J 29
Tong	82 A 9
Tongham	20 R 30
Tongland	53 H 19
Tongue	84 G 8
Tongwynlais	18 K 29
Tonna	17 I 28
Tonypandy	17 J 29
Tonyrefail	17 J 29
Topcliffe	50 P 21
Topsham	4 J 31
Tor Ness	86 K 7
Torbay	4 J 32
Torcross	4 I 33
Torksey	44 R 24
Torlundy	72 E 13
Tormarton	19 N 29
Tornapress	78 D 11
Tornaveen	75 M 12
Torness	79 G 12
Torphichen	67 J 16
Torphins	75 M 12
Torpoint	3 H 32
Torquay	4 J 32
Torran	62 L 16
Torridon (Loch)	77 C 11
Torrin	71 B 12
Torrisdale Bay	85 H 8
Torthorwald	53 J 18
Tortworth	19 M 29
Torver	48 K 20
Toscaig	77 C 11
Totaig Loch Alsh	78 D 12
Totaig Loch Dunvegan	77 A 11
Totland	10 P 31
Totley	43 P 24
Totnes	4 I 32
Toton	36 Q 25
Totscore	77 A 11

Totternhoe	29 S 28
Totton	10 P 31
Tournaig	78 D 10
Tow Law	56 O 19
Towcester	28 R 27
Tower Hamlets London Borough	21 T 29
Towie	74 L 12
Town Yetholm	62 N 17
Towneley Hall	43 N 22
Townhead	53 H 19
Townhead of Greenlaw	53 I 19
Tradespark	79 I 11
Trallwng / Welshpool	34 K 26
Tranent	69 L 16
Trapp	25 I 28
Traquair House	61 K 17
Trawden	43 N 22
Trawsfynydd	33 I 25
Trealaval (Loch)	82 A 9
Trearddur Bay	40 G 23
Trecastle	25 J 28
Trecwn	24 F 28
Tredington	27 P 27
Treen	2 D 33
Trefaldwyn / Montgomery	34 K 26
Trefeglwys	25 J 26
Treffynnon / Holywell	41 K 23
Trefil	18 K 28
Trefnant	41 J 23
Trefonen	34 K 25
Trefor	40 G 23
Trefyclawdd / Knighton	26 K 26
Trefynwy / Monmouth	18 L 28
Tregaron	25 I 27
Tregony	3 F 33
Tregynon	33 J 26
Treharris	18 K 29
Treherbert	17 J 28
Treig (Loch)	73 F 13
Trelawnyd	41 J 23
Trelech	15 G 28
Trelech a'r Betws	15 G 28
Trelissick Gardens	2 E 33
Trelleck	18 L 28
Tremadog	33 H 25
Tremadog Bay	32 H 25
Trenance	2 E 32
Trengwainton Garden	2 D 33
Trent	8 M 31
Trent (River)	36 R 24
Trentham	35 N 25
Treorchy	17 J 29
Trerice	2 E 32
Treshnish Isles	64 A 14
Treshnish Point	71 A 14
Tressait	73 I 13
Tretower	26 K 28
Treuddyn	34 K 24
Trevine	14 E 28
Trevone	3 F 32
Trevor	32 G 25
Trevose Head	2 E 32
Trewithen	3 F 33
Trimdon	56 P 19
Trimley Heath	31 X 28
Trimsaran	15 H 28
Tring	21 R 28
Trispen	2 E 33
Trochry	67 J 14
Troedyrhiw	17 J 28
Trollamarig (Loch)	82 Z 10
Tromie (Glen)	73 H 12
Troon	60 G 17
Trossachs (The)	67 G 15
Trotternish	77 B 11
Troutbeck Eden	54 L 20
Troutbeck South Lakeland	48 L 20
Trowbridge	19 N 30
Trudoxhill	19 M 30
Truim (Glen)	73 H 13
Trull	8 K 31
Trumpington	29 U 27
Trunch	39 Y 25
Truro	2 E 33
Trusthorpe	45 U 24
Trwyn Cilan	32 G 25
Tuath (Loch)	64 B 14
Tuddenham Forest Heath	30 V 27
Tuddenham Suffolk Coastal	31 X 27
Tudhoe	56 P 19
Tudweiliog	32 G 25
Tugford	26 M 26
Tulla (Loch)	66 F 14
Tullibardine	67 I 15

Tullibody ...... 67 I 15
Tullymurdoch ...... 74 K 14
Tumble ...... 15 H 28
Tummel (Loch) ...... 73 I 13
Tunstall
  East Riding of Yorkshire ...45 T 22
Tunstall *Staffs.* ...... 35 N 24
Tunstall *Suffolk* ...... 31 Y 27
Tur Langton ...... 36 R 26
Turnberry ...... 59 F 18
Turnditch ...... 35 P 24
Turret
  (Loch and Reservoir) ...... 67 I 14
Turriff ...... 81 M 11
Turvey ...... 29 S 27
Tusker Rock ...... 17 I 29
Tutbury ...... 35 O 25
Tuxford ...... 44 R 24
Twatt ...... 86 K 6
Tweed (River) ...... 61 J 17
Tweeddale ...... 61 J 17
Tweedmouth ...... 63 N 16
Tweedsmuir Hills ...... 61 J 17
Twemlow Green ...... 35 N 24
Twickenham ...... 21 S 29
Two Dales ...... 35 P 24
Twyford *Berks.* ...... 20 R 29
Twyford *Hants.* ...... 10 Q 30
Twyford *Leics.* ...... 36 R 25
Twynholm ...... 53 H 19
Twynllanan ...... 25 I 28
Tydd-St. Giles ...... 37 U 25
Tydd St. Mary ...... 37 U 25
Tyddewi / St. David's ...... 14 E 28
Tyldesley ...... 42 M 23
Tylorstown ...... 17 J 29
Tyne (River) ...... 56 P 19
Tynehead ...... 62 L 16
Tynemouth ...... 56 P 18
Tynewydd ...... 17 J 28
Tynron ...... 53 I 18
Tythegston ...... 17 J 29
Tytherington ...... 18 M 29
Tywardreath ...... 3 F 32
Tywi (River) ...... 25 I 27
Tywyn ...... 33 H 26

U

Ubiey ...... 18 L 30
Uckfield ...... 11 U 31
Uddingston ...... 60 H 16
Udimore ...... 12 V 31
Uffculme ...... 7 K 31
Uffington ...... 37 S 26
Ufford ...... 31 Y 27
Ugadale Bay ...... 59 D 17
Ugborough ...... 4 I 32
Ugbrooke House ...... 4 J 32
Ugthorpe ...... 50 R 20
Uig *Highland* ...... 77 A 11
Uig *Western Isles* ...... 82 Y 9
Uisg (Loch) ...... 65 C 14
Uiskevagh (Loch) ...... 76 Y 11
Ulbster ...... 86 K 8
Ulceby *East Lindsey* ...... 45 U 24
Ulceby *North Lincolnshire* ...45 T 23
Ulcombe ...... 22 V 30
Uldale ...... 54 K 19
Uley ...... 19 N 28
Ulgham ...... 56 P 18
Ullapool ...... 78 E 10
Ulleskelf ...... 44 Q 22
Ullesthorpe ...... 28 Q 26
Ullinish ...... 77 A 11
Ullock ...... 54 J 20
Ullswater ...... 48 L 20
Ulpha ...... 47 K 21
Ulsta ...... 87 Q 2
Ulva ...... 64 B 14
Ulverston ...... 48 K 21
Unapool ...... 84 E 9
Union Mills ...... 46 G 21
Unst ...... 87 R 1
Upavon ...... 19 O 30
Upchurch ...... 22 V 29
Uphall ...... 68 J 16
Uphill ...... 18 L 30
Upleadon ...... 27 M 28
Uplyme ...... 5 L 31
Upottery ...... 8 K 31
Upper Arley ...... 27 M 26
Upper Badcall ...... 84 E 9
Upper Beeding ...... 11 T 31
Upper Bighouse ...... 85 I 8
Upper Broughton ...... 36 R 25
Upper Chapel ...... 25 J 27
Upper Chute ...... 20 P 30

Upper Dicker ...... 12 U 31
Upper Hale ...... 20 R 30
Upper Heyford ...... 28 Q 28
Upper Hindhope ...... 62 M 17
Upper Knockando ...... 80 J 11
Upper Loch Torridon ...... 78 D 11
Upper Poppleton ...... 50 Q 22
Upper Sandaig ...... 72 D 12
Upper Tean ...... 35 O 25
Uppertown ...... 86 K 7
Uppingham ...... 36 R 26
Upton *Dorset* ...... 9 N 31
Upton *Notts.* ...... 36 R 24
Upton *Vale of White Horse* ...20 Q 29
Upton *Wakefield* ...... 44 Q 23
Upton *West Somerset* ...... 7 J 30
Upton Grey ...... 20 Q 30
Upton House ...... 28 P 27
Upton Magna ...... 34 M 25
Upton Noble ...... 9 M 30
Upton Scudamore ...... 19 N 30
Upton-upon-Severn ...... 27 N 27
Upwell ...... 38 U 26
Upwood ...... 29 T 26
Urchfont ...... 19 O 30
Ure (River) ...... 50 Q 21
Urigill (Loch) ...... 84 F 9
Urmston ...... 42 M 23
Urquhart ...... 80 K 11
Urquhart (Glen) ...... 79 G 11
Urquhart Castle ...... 79 G 12
Urrahag (Loch) ...... 82 A 8
Ushaw Moor ...... 56 P 19
Usk / Brynbuga ...... 18 L 28
Usk (River) ...... 18 K 28
Uttoxeter ...... 35 O 25
Uyea ...... 87 R 2
Uyeasound ...... 87 R 1

V

Vallay Strand ...... 76 X 11
Valle Crucis ...... 34 K 25
Valley ...... 40 G 23
Valtos ...... 82 Z 9
Vatersay ...... 70 X 13
Vatten ...... 77 A 11
Ve Skerries ...... 87 O 2
Venachar (Loch) ...... 67 H 15
Ventnor ...... 10 Q 32
Verham Dean ...... 20 P 30
Verulamium ...... 21 S 28
Verwood ...... 9 O 31
Veryan ...... 3 F 33
Veyatie (Loch) ...... 84 E 9
Vindolanda ...... 55 M 19
Voe ...... 87 Q 2
Voil (Loch) ...... 67 G 14
Vowchurch ...... 26 L 27
Vyrnwy (Lake) ...... 33 J 25

W

Waddesdon ...... 20 R 28
Waddingham ...... 44 S 23
Waddington *Lancs.* ...... 42 M 22
Waddington *Lincs.* ...... 37 S 24
Wadebridge ...... 3 F 32
Wadhurst ...... 12 U 30
Wag ...... 85 I 9
Wainfleet All Saints ...... 38 U 24
Wainstalls ...... 43 O 22
Wakefield ...... 43 P 22
Wakerley ...... 37 S 26
Wakes Colne ...... 30 W 28
Walberswick ...... 31 Y 27
Walcott ...... 37 T 24
Walden Head ...... 49 N 21
Walderslade ...... 22 V 29
Waldringfield ...... 31 X 27
Waldron ...... 12 U 31
Walesby ...... 44 R 24
Walford ...... 34 L 25
Walgherton ...... 34 M 24
Walgrave ...... 28 R 26
Walkden ...... 42 M 23
Walkeringham ...... 44 R 23
Walkern ...... 29 T 28
Walkerith ...... 44 R 23
Wall ...... 35 O 26
Wallace Monument ...... 67 I 15
Wallasey ...... 42 K 23
Wallend ...... 22 W 29
Wallingford ...... 20 Q 29
Wallington House ...... 56 O 18
Walls ...... 87 P 3
Wallyford ...... 69 K 16
Walney (Isle of) ...... 47 K 21
Walpole ...... 31 Y 27

Walpole St. Andrew ...... 38 U 25
Walpole St. Peter ...... 38 U 25
Walsall ...... 35 O 26
Walsden ...... 43 N 22
Walsham le Willows ...... 30 W 27
Walshford ...... 50 P 22
Walston ...... 61 J 16
Waltham *Kent* ...... 23 X 30
Waltham *North East Lincs.* ...45 T 23
Waltham Abbey ...... 21 U 28
Waltham Forest
  London Borough ...... 21 T 29
Waltham-on-the-Wolds ...... 36 R 25
Walton *Carlisle* ...... 55 L 19
Walton *Leeds* ...... 50 Q 22
Walton *Powys* ...... 26 K 27
Walton-East ...... 24 F 28
Walton-in-Gordano ...... 18 L 29
Walton-le-Dale ...... 42 M 22
Walton-on-Thames ...... 21 S 29
Walton-on-the-Naze ...... 31 X 28
Walton-Upon-Trent ...... 35 O 25
Walworth ...... 49 P 20
Wanborough ...... 19 O 29
Wandsworth
  London Borough ...... 21 T 29
Wangford ...... 31 Y 26
Wanlockhead ...... 61 I 17
Wansford
  East Riding of Yorkshire ...51 S 22
Wansford *Peterborough* ...37 S 26
Wanstrow ...... 9 M 30
Wantage ...... 20 P 29
Wappenham ...... 28 Q 27
Warboys ...... 29 T 26
Warbstow ...... 6 G 31
Warcop ...... 49 M 20
Wardington ...... 28 Q 27
Wardour Castle ...... 9 N 30
Ware ...... 21 T 28
Wareham ...... 9 N 31
Wargrave ...... 20 R 29
Wark *near Coldstream* ...63 N 17
Wark *near Hexham* ...55 N 18
Wark Forest ...... 55 M 18
Warkworth ...... 63 P 17
Warley ...... 27 O 26
Warlingham ...... 21 T 30
Warmington
  East Northamptonshire ...29 S 26
Warmington
  Stratford-on-Avon ...28 P 27
Warminster ...... 19 N 30
Warmsworth ...... 44 Q 23
Warmwell ...... 9 M 31
Warnborough ...... 20 R 30
Warnford ...... 10 Q 30
Warnham ...... 11 S 30
Warren ...... 43 N 24
Warren (The) ...... 13 X 30
Warrington ...... 42 M 23
Warsash ...... 10 Q 31
Warslow ...... 35 O 24
Warsop ...... 36 Q 24
Warter ...... 51 R 22
Warton *Alnwick* ...... 63 O 18
Warton *near Morecambe* ...48 L 21
Warton *near Preston* ...42 L 22
Warwick ...... 27 P 27
Warwick Bridge ...... 55 L 19
Warwickshire ...... 27 P 27
Wasbister ...... 86 K 6
Wasdale Head ...... 47 K 20
Wash (The) ...... 38 U 25
Washington
  Tyne and Wear ...... 56 P 19
Washington *West Sussex* ...11 S 31
Wast Water ...... 47 K 20
Watchet ...... 17 K 30
Watchfield ...... 19 P 29
Watchgate ...... 48 L 20
Water Orton ...... 27 O 26
Waterbeach ...... 30 U 27
Waterbeck ...... 54 K 18
Watergate Bay ...... 2 E 32
Waterhead ...... 74 L 13
Waterhouses ...... 35 O 24
Wateringbury ...... 22 V 30
Waterlooville ...... 10 Q 31
Waternish Point ...... 77 A 11
Waters Upton ...... 34 M 25
Waterside ...... 60 G 17
Waterstein ...... 76 Z 11
Watford *Daventry* ...28 Q 27
Watford *Watford* ...... 21 S 29
Wath ...... 50 P 21
Wath-upon-Dearne ...... 44 P 23
Watlington ...... 20 Q 29

Watten ...... 85 K 8
Watton *Breckland* ...... 38 W 26
Watton
  East Riding of Yorkshire ...51 S 22
Watton at Stone ...... 29 T 28
Waunfawr ...... 33 H 24
Waveney (River) ...... 31 Y 26
Waverton *Allerdale* ...... 54 K 19
Waverton *Chester* ...... 34 L 24
Wawne ...... 45 S 22
Wear (River) ...... 56 O 20
Weardale ...... 55 N 19
Weasenhan St. Peter ...... 38 W 25
Weaver (River) ...... 34 M 24
Weaverthorpe ...... 51 S 21
Wedmore ...... 18 L 30
Wednesbury ...... 35 N 26
Wednesfield ...... 35 N 26
Weedon-Bec ...... 28 Q 27
Week St. Mary ...... 6 G 31
Weeley ...... 31 X 28
Weeting ...... 30 V 26
Weeton ...... 42 L 22
Welburn ...... 50 R 21
Welby ...... 37 S 25
Welcombe ...... 6 G 31
Welford *Daventry* ...28 Q 26
Welford *Stratford-on-Avon* ...27 O 27
Welford *West Berkshire* ...20 P 29
Welham Green ...... 21 T 28
Well ...... 50 P 21
Welland ...... 27 N 27
Welland (River) ...... 37 T 25
Wellesbourne ...... 27 P 27
Wellingborough ...... 29 R 27
Wellington
  Herefordshire ...... 26 L 27
Wellington *Salop* ...... 34 M 25
Wellington *Somerset* ...... 8 K 31
Wellow
  Bath and North East ...19 M 30
Wellow
  Newark and Sherwood ...36 R 24
Wells ...... 18 M 30
Wells-next-the-Sea ...... 38 W 25
Wells of Ythan ...... 81 M 11
Welney ...... 38 U 26
Welsh Newton ...... 26 L 28
Welshampton ...... 34 L 25
Welshpool / Trallwng ...... 34 K 26
Welton *Allerdale* ...... 54 K 19
Welton *Daventry* ...... 28 Q 27
Welton *West Lindsey* ...44 S 24
Welton-le-Wold ...... 45 T 23
Welwyn ...... 21 T 28
Welwyn Garden City ...... 21 T 28
Wem ...... 34 L 25
Wembdon ...... 8 K 30
Wembley ...... 21 T 29
Wembsyedale ...... 49 O 21
Wembury ...... 4 H 33
Wembworthy ...... 7 I 31
Wemyss Bay ...... 59 F 16
Wendens Ambo ...... 30 U 27
Wendlebury ...... 28 Q 28
Wendover ...... 20 R 28
Wendron ...... 2 E 33
Wenlock Edge ...... 26 L 26
Wennington ...... 48 M 21
Wensley ...... 49 O 21
Wensleydale ...... 49 O 21
Wentbridge ...... 44 Q 23
Wentnor ...... 26 L 26
Wentworth ...... 43 P 23
Wenvoe ...... 18 K 29
Weobley
  Hereford and Worcester ...26 L 27
Wereham ...... 38 V 26
Werrington ...... 6 G 32
West Alvington ...... 4 I 33
West Auckland ...... 56 O 20
West-Barns ...... 69 M 16
West Bay ...... 8 M 32
West Bergholt ...... 30 W 28
West-Bradenham ...... 38 W 26
West Bridgford ...... 36 Q 25
West Bromwich ...... 27 O 26
West-Buckland
  North Devon ...... 7 I 30
West-Buckland
  Taunton Deane ...... 8 K 31
West Butterwick ...... 44 R 23
West Calder ...... 61 J 16
West Camel ...... 8 M 30
West Charleton ...... 4 I 33
West Chevington ...... 63 P 18
West Chiltington ...... 11 S 31

West-Chinnock ...... 8 L 31
West Coker ...... 8 L 31
West Dean ...... 9 P 30
West-Dereham ...... 38 V 26
West Down ...... 7 H 30
West End ...... 10 Q 31
West Farleigh ...... 22 V 30
West-Felton ...... 34 L 25
West-Firle ...... 11 U 31
West Geirinish ...... 76 X 11
West-Grinstead ...... 11 T 31
West Hanningfield ...... 22 V 28
West Harptree ...... 18 M 30
West Heath ...... 20 R 30
West Heslerton ...... 51 S 21
West-Hill ...... 5 K 31
West Hoathly ...... 11 T 30
West-Huntspill ...... 18 L 30
West Kilbride ...... 59 F 16
West Kingsdown ...... 22 U 29
West Kirby ...... 41 K 22
West Langwell ...... 85 H 9
West Lavington ...... 19 O 30
West Linton ...... 61 J 16
West Loch Roag ...... 82 Z 9
West Loch Tarbert
  Argyll and Bute ...... 59 D 16
West Loch Tarbert
  Western Isles ...... 82 Z 10
West Looe ...... 3 G 32
West Lulworth ...... 9 N 32
West Lutton ...... 51 S 21
West Malling ...... 22 V 30
West Malvern ...... 27 M 27
West Meon ...... 10 Q 30
West Mersea ...... 22 W 28
West Moors ...... 9 O 31
West-Overton ...... 19 O 29
West Putford ...... 6 G 31
West-Quantoxhead ...... 8 K 30
West Rainton ...... 56 P 19
West Runton ...... 39 X 25
West-Stafford ...... 9 M 31
West Strathan ...... 84 G 8
West Tanfield ...... 50 P 21
West-Tarbert ...... 59 D 16
West Thorney ...... 10 R 31
West Town ...... 18 L 29
West-Tytherley ...... 9 P 30
West Walton ...... 37 U 25
West Wellow ...... 9 P 31
West Wickam ...... 21 T 29
West Winch ...... 38 V 25
West Wittering ...... 10 R 31
West Witton ...... 49 O 21
West Woodburn ...... 55 N 18
West Wycombe ...... 20 R 29
Westbourne ...... 10 R 31
Westbury *Cheshire* ...... 34 L 25
Westbury *Wilts.* ...... 19 N 30
Westbury-on-Severn ...... 19 M 28
Westcliff ...... 22 W 29
Westcott ...... 21 S 30
Westenhanger ...... 13 X 30
Wester Ross ...... 78 D 11
Westerdale *Highland* ...85 J 8
Westerdale *Scarborough* ...50 R 20
Westerham ...... 21 U 30
Westerleigh ...... 19 M 29
Western Cleddau ...... 24 E 28
Western *Highland* ...... 85 J 8
Westfield *Rother* ...... 12 V 31
Westfield *West Lothian* ...67 I 16
Westgate-on-Sea ...... 23 Y 29
Westham ...... 12 U 31
Westhoughton ...... 42 M 23
Westleton ...... 31 Y 27
Westmeston ...... 11 T 31
Westmill ...... 29 T 28
Westnewton ...... 54 J 19
Weston *Devon* ...... 8 K 31
Weston
  North Hertfordshire ...29 T 28
Weston *South Holland* ...37 T 25
Weston
  South Northamptonshire ...28 Q 27
Weston *Staffs.* ...... 35 N 25
Weston-by-Welland ...... 28 R 26
Weston Favell ...... 28 R 27
Weston-on-the-Green ...... 28 Q 28
Weston-on-Trent ...... 36 P 25
Weston Rhyn ...... 34 K 25
Weston-super-Mare ...... 18 L 29
Weston Turville ...... 20 R 28
Weston-under-Lizard ...... 35 N 25
Weston-under-Penyard ...26 M 28
Westonbirt ...... 19 N 29

Westonzoyland ...... 8 L 30
Westray ...... 86 K 6
Westruther ...... 62 M 16
Westward ...... 54 K 19
Westward Ho ...... 6 H 30
Westwood ...... 19 N 30
Wetheral ...... 55 L 19
Wetherby ...... 50 P 22
Wetheringsett ...... 31 X 27
Wethersfield ...... 30 V 28
Wetwang ...... 51 S 22
Wey (River) ...... 10 R 30
Weybourne ...... 39 X 25
Weybridge ...... 21 S 29
Weyhill ...... 20 P 30
Weymouth ...... 8 M 32
Whaddon ...... 28 R 28
Whaley Bridge ...... 43 O 24
Whalley ...... 42 M 22
Whalsay ...... 87 R 2
Whalton ...... 56 O 18
Whaplode ...... 37 T 25
Whaplode Drove ...... 37 T 25
Wharfe (River) ...... 44 Q 22
Wharfedale ...... 49 O 22
Whatlington ...... 12 V 31
Whatsandwell ...... 36 P 24
Whauphill ...... 52 G 19
Whaw ...... 49 N 20
Wheathampstead ...... 21 T 28
Wheatley *Notts.* ...... 44 R 23
Wheatley *Oxon.* ...... 20 Q 28
Wheatley Hill ...... 56 P 19
Wheaton Aston ...... 35 N 25
Wheldrake ...... 50 R 22
Whepstead ...... 30 W 27
Whernside ...... 49 M 21
Wherwell ...... 10 P 30
Whickham ...... 56 O 19
Whimple ...... 7 J 31
Whipsnade ...... 21 S 28
Whissendine ...... 36 R 25
Whissonsett ...... 38 W 25
Whitburn South Tyneside ...57 P 19
Whitburn *West Lothian* ...61 I 16
Whitby ...... 51 S 20
Whitchurch
  Basingstoke and Deane ...20 P 30
Whitchurch
  Bath and N.E. Somerset ...18 M 29
Whitchurch *Bucks.* ...... 28 R 28
Whitchurch
  Caerdydd / Cardiff ...18 K 29
Whitchurch *Devon* ...... 4 H 32
Whitchurch
  Heref. and Worc. ...18 M 28
Whitchurch *Oxon.* ...... 20 Q 29
Whitchurch *Salop* ...... 34 L 25
White Coomb ...... 61 K 17
White Horse Hill ...... 20 P 29
White Scarcaves ...... 49 M 21
White Waltham ...... 20 R 29
Whitebridge ...... 73 G 12
Whitecairns ...... 75 N 12
Whitchurch Canonicorum ...5 L 31
Whitefield ...... 42 N 23
Whitehall ...... 87 M 6
Whitehaven ...... 47 J 20
Whitehill ...... 10 R 30
Whitehills ...... 81 M 10
Whitehouse
  Aberdeenshire ...... 75 M 12
Whitehouse
  Argyll and Bute ...... 59 D 16
Whitekirk ...... 69 M 15
Whiten Head ...... 84 G 8
Whiteness Sands ...... 79 I 10
Whiteparish ...... 9 P 30
Whiterashes ...... 81 N 12
Whiteness ...... 79 I 11
Whitesand Bay *Cornwall* ...2 C 33
Whitesand Bay
  Pembrokes ...... 14 E 28
Whiteshill ...... 19 N 28
Whiteside ...... 55 M 18
Whitewell ...... 49 M 22
Whitewreath ...... 80 K 11
Whitfield *Dover* ...... 23 X 30
Whitfield
  South Northamptonshire ...28 Q 27
Whitfield *Tynedale* ...55 M 19
Whitgift ...... 44 R 22
Whithorn ...... 52 G 19
Whiting Bay ...... 59 E 17
Whitland ...... 15 G 28
Whitley ...... 20 R 29
Whitley Bay ...... 56 P 18

A B C D E F G H I J K L M N O P Q R S T U V W X Y Z

A B C D E F G H I J K L M N O P Q R S T U V W X Y Z

Whitley Bridge ...44 Q 22
Whitley Chapel ...55 N 19
Whitminster ...19 N 28
Whitmore ...35 N 25
Whitnash ...28 P 27
Whitsand Bay ...3 H 32
Whitstable ...23 X 29
Whitstone ...6 G 31
Whittingham ...63 O 17
Whittington Derbs. ...43 P 24
Whittington King's Lynn
   and West Norfolk ...38 V 26
Whittington Lancaster ...48 M 21
Whittington Shrops. ...34 L 25
Whittle le Woods ...42 M 22
Whittlebury ...28 R 27
Whittlesey ...37 T 26
Whittlesford ...29 U 27
Whitton North Lincolnshire ...44 S 22
Whitton Powys ...26 K 27
Whitton Suffolk ...31 X 27
Whittonstall ...56 O 19
Whitwell Derbs. ...44 Q 24
Whitwell I.O.W. ...10 Q 32
Whitwell-on-the-Hill ...50 R 21
Whitwick ...36 P 25
Whitworth ...43 N 23
Whixall ...34 L 25
Whygate ...55 M 18
Wiay Highland ...77 A 11
Wiay Western Isles ...76 Y 11
Wibtoft ...28 Q 26
Wick Bro Morgannwg /
   The Vale of Glamorgan ...17 J 29
Wick Highland ...86 K 8
Wick South Glos. ...19 M 29
Wicken Cambs. ...28 R 27
Wicken Northants. ...30 U 27
Wickenby ...45 S 24
Wickersley ...44 Q 23
Wickford ...22 V 29
Wickham ...10 Q 31
Wickham Market ...31 Y 27
Wickhambrook ...30 V 27
Wickwar ...19 M 29
Widdrington ...63 P 18
Wide Open ...56 P 18
Widecombe-in-the-Moor ...4 I 32
Wideford Hill Cairn ...86 K 7
Widemouth Bay ...6 G 31
Widford ...21 U 28
Widnes ...42 L 23
Wigan ...42 M 23
Wiggenhall
   St. Mary Magdalen ...38 V 25
Wigglesworth ...49 N 21
Wight (Isle of) ...10 P 32
Wighton ...38 W 25
Wigmore Herefordshire ...26 L 27
Wigmore Medway ...22 V 29
Wigston ...36 Q 26
Wigton ...54 K 19
Wigtown ...52 G 19

Wigtown Bay ...53 H 19
Wilberfoss ...50 R 22
Wilcot ...19 O 29
Wild Animal Kingdom ...29 S 28
Wilkhaven ...79 I 10
Wilkieston ...61 J 16
Willand ...7 J 31
Willenhall Coventry ...28 P 26
Willenhall Walsall ...35 N 26
Willerby ...45 S 22
Willersey ...27 O 27
Willingdon ...12 U 31
Willingham ...29 U 27
Willingham Forest ...45 T 23
Willington Beds. ...29 S 27
Willington Derbs. ...35 P 25
Willington Durham ...56 O 19
Williton ...7 K 30
Willoughby ...28 Q 27
Wilmcote ...27 O 27
Wilmington East Essex ...12 U 31
Wilmington Kent ...22 U 29
Wilmslow ...43 N 24
Wiloughby ...45 U 24
Wilpshire ...42 M 22
Wilsford ...37 S 25
Wilstead ...29 S 27
Wilton ...9 O 30
Wimbledon ...21 T 29
Wimblington ...29 U 26
Wimborne Minster ...9 O 31
Wimborne St. Giles ...9 O 31
Wincanton ...9 M 30
Wincham ...42 M 24
Winchburgh ...68 J 16
Winchcombe ...27 O 28
Winchelsea ...12 W 31
Winchester ...10 Q 30
Winchfield ...20 R 30
Wincle ...35 N 24
Windermere ...48 L 20
Windhill ...79 G 11
Windlesham ...21 S 29
Windrush ...19 O 28
Windrush (River) ...19 O 28
Windsor ...21 S 29
Windsor Great Park ...21 S 29
Windygates ...68 K 15
Winestead ...45 T 22
Winfarthing ...31 X 26
Winford ...18 M 29
Winforton ...26 K 27
Winfrith Newburgh ...9 N 32
Wing ...28 R 28
Wingate ...57 P 19
Wingerworth ...36 P 24
Wingfield near Alfreton ...36 P 24
Wingfield
   near Chesterfield ...36 P 24
Wingham ...23 X 30
Wingrave ...28 R 28
Winkfield ...21 R 29
Winkleigh ...7 I 31

Winksley ...50 P 21
Winmarleigh ...48 L 22
Winnersh ...20 R 29
Winscombe ...18 L 30
Winsford Cheshire ...34 M 24
Winsford Somerset ...7 J 30
Winsham ...8 L 31
Winshill ...35 P 25
Winslow ...28 R 28
Winster Derbyshire Dales ...35 P 24
Winster South Lakeland ...48 L 20
Winston ...49 O 20
Winstone ...19 N 28
Winterborne Kingston ...9 N 31
Winterborne Stickland ...9 N 31
Winterborne Whitechurch ...9 N 31
Winterbourne ...18 M 29
Winterbourne Abbas ...5 M 31
Winterbourne Dauntsey ...9 O 30
Winterbourne Monkton ...19 O 29
Winterbourne Stoke ...9 O 30
Winteringham ...44 S 22
Winterton ...44 S 23
Winterton-on-Sea ...39 Z 25
Winton ...49 N 20
Wintringham ...51 S 21
Winwick ...29 S 26
Wirksworth ...35 P 24
Wirral ...42 K 24
Wisbech ...37 U 25
Wisbech-St. Mary ...37 U 26
Wisborough Green ...11 S 30
Wishaw ...61 I 16
Wisley ...21 S 30
Wissey (River) ...38 V 26
Wistanstow ...26 L 26
Wistanswick ...34 M 25
Wistaston ...34 M 24
Wiston
   Dumfries and Galloway ...61 J 17
Wiston Pembrokeshire /
   Sir Benfro ...16 F 28
Wistow ...44 Q 22
Witchampton ...9 N 31
Witchford ...30 U 26
Witham ...22 V 28
Witham (River) ...37 T 24
Witham Friary ...9 M 30
Witheridge ...7 I 31
Withern ...45 U 24
Withernsea ...45 U 22
Withernwick ...45 T 22
Withington Cotswold ...19 O 28
Withington Herefordshire ...26 M 27
Withnell ...42 M 22
Withycombe ...4 J 32
Withypool ...7 J 30
Witley ...11 S 30
Witney ...20 P 28
Witsome ...63 N 16
Wittering ...37 S 26
Wittersham ...12 W 30
Witton le Wear ...56 O 19

Wiveliscombe ...7 K 30
Wivelsfield ...11 T 31
Wivenhoe ...30 W 28
Woburn ...29 S 28
Woburn Abbey ...29 S 28
Woburn Sands ...29 S 27
Woking ...21 S 30
Wokingham ...20 R 29
Wold Newton ...45 T 23
Woldingham ...21 T 30
Wollaston ...29 S 27
Wollaton Hall ...36 Q 25
Wolsingham ...56 O 19
Wolston ...28 P 26
Wolvercote ...20 Q 28
Wolverhampton ...35 N 26
Wolverton ...28 R 27
Wolvey ...28 P 26
Wolviston ...57 Q 20
Wombleton ...50 R 21
Wombourne ...27 N 26
Wombwell ...43 P 23
Womersley ...44 Q 22
Wonersh ...21 S 30
Wood Dalling ...39 X 25
Woodborough ...36 Q 24
Woodbridge ...31 X 27
Woodbury ...4 J 31
Woodchurch ...12 W 30
Woodcote ...20 Q 29
Woodford Halse ...28 Q 27
Woodhall Spa ...37 T 24
Woodham Ferrers ...22 V 29
Woodhouse ...43 P 23
Woodhouse Eaves ...36 Q 25
Woodingdean ...11 T 31
Woodland ...56 O 20
Woodlands ...9 O 31
Woodley ...20 R 29
Woodnesborough ...23 X 30
Woodseaves ...35 N 25
Woodsetts ...44 Q 23
Woodsford ...9 M 31
Woodstock ...20 P 28
Woodton ...39 Y 26
Woody Bay ...17 I 30
Wookey ...18 L 30
Wookey Hole ...18 L 30
Wool ...9 N 31
Woolacombe ...16 H 30
Wooler ...63 N 17
Woolfardisworthy ...6 G 31
Woolhampton ...20 Q 29
Woolpit ...30 W 27
Woolsthorpe ...36 R 25
Wooperton ...63 O 17
Woore ...35 M 25
Wootton Bedford ...29 S 27
Wootton Northampton ...28 R 27
Wootton Bassett ...19 O 29
Wootton Brige ...10 Q 31
Wootton Courtenay ...17 J 30
Wootton Rivers ...19 O 29

Wootton-Wawen ...27 O 27
Worcester ...27 N 27
Workington ...53 J 20
Worksop ...44 Q 24
Worle ...18 L 29
Wormbridge ...26 L 28
Wormingford ...30 W 28
Worminghall ...20 Q 28
Wormit ...69 L 14
Worms Head ...15 H 29
Wormsley ...26 L 27
Worplesdon ...21 S 30
Worsbrough ...43 P 23
Worsley ...42 M 23
Worsthorne ...43 N 22
Worthen ...34 L 26
Worthenbury ...34 L 24
Worthing ...11 S 31
Wortley ...43 P 23
Worton ...19 N 30
Wortwell ...31 Y 26
Wotton-under-Edge ...19 M 29
Wrafton ...6 H 30
Wragby East Lindsey ...45 T 24
Wragby Wakefield ...43 P 23
Wrangle ...37 U 24
Wrawby ...44 S 23
Wray ...48 M 21
Wrea Green ...42 L 22
Wreay ...55 L 19
Wrecsam / Wrexham ...34 L 24
Wrekenton ...56 P 19
Wremtham ...31 Z 26
Wrenbury ...34 M 24
Wrestlingworth ...29 T 27
Wrexham / Wrecsam ...34 L 24
Wrington ...18 L 29
Writtle ...22 V 28
Wroot ...44 R 23
Wrotham ...22 U 30
Wroughton ...19 O 29
Wroxall ...10 Q 32
Wroxham ...39 Y 25
Wroxton ...28 P 27
Wyberton ...37 T 25
Wyche ...27 M 27
Wye ...22 W 30
Wye (River) ...26 M 28
Wykeham ...51 S 21
Wylam ...56 O 19
Wylye ...9 O 30
Wymeswold ...36 Q 25
Wymondham Leics. ...36 R 25
Wymondham Norfolk ...39 X 26
Wyre ...87 L 6
Wysall ...36 Q 25
Wyvis Lodge ...79 G 10

Y

Y-Fenni / Abergavenny ...18 L 28
Y Ffor ...32 G 25
Y Llethr ...33 I 25

Y Rhiw ...32 G 25
Yafforth ...50 P 20
Yalding ...22 V 30
Yapton ...11 S 31
Yardley Gobion ...28 R 27
Yardley Hastings ...28 R 27
Yare (River) ...38 W 26
Yarm ...50 P 20
Yarmouth ...10 P 31
Yarnton ...20 Q 28
Yarrow ...62 K 17
Yate ...19 M 29
Yateley ...20 R 29
Yatton ...18 L 29
Yatton Keynell ...19 N 29
Yaxham ...38 W 26
Yaxley ...29 T 26
Yeadon ...43 O 22
Yealand Conyers ...48 L 21
Yealmpton ...4 I 32
Yedingham ...51 S 21
Yelden ...29 S 27
Yell ...87 Q 1
Yelvertoft ...28 Q 26
Yelverton ...4 H 32
Yeolmbridge ...6 G 32
Yeovil ...8 M 31
Yeovilton ...8 M 30
Yesnaby ...86 J 6
Yetminster ...8 M 31
Yetts o' Muckhart ...68 J 15
Yielden ...29 S 27
Ynys / Lochtyn ...15 G 27
Ynysddu ...18 K 29
Ynyslas ...25 H 26
Ynysybwl ...17 J 29
Yockenthwaite ...49 N 21
Yockleton ...34 L 25
York ...50 Q 22
Yorkletts ...23 X 30
Yorkley ...18 M 28
Yorkshire Dales
   National Park ...49 N 21
Yorkshire Wolds ...51 S 21
Youlgreave ...35 O 24
Yoxall ...35 O 25
Yoxford ...31 Y 27
Yr Wyddfa / Snowdon ...33 H 24
Yr Wyddgrug / Mold ...34 K 24
Ysbyty Ifan ...33 I 24
Ystalyfera ...17 I 28
Ystrad-Aeron ...25 H 27
Ystrad Mynach ...18 K 29
Ystradfellte ...17 J 28
Ystradgynlais ...17 I 28
Ystradowen ...17 J 29
Ystwyth (River) ...25 H 26

Z

Zennor ...2 D 33

A

Aasleagh	105	D 7
Abbert	106	F 7
Abbey	100	G 8
Abbeydorney	93	C 10
Abbeyfeale	93	E 10
Abbeylara	107	J 6
Abbeyleix / Mainistir Laoise	101	J 9
Abbeyshrule	107	J 7
Abington	94	G 10
Achill	104	C 6
Achill Head	110	B 6
Achill Island	104	C 6
Achill Sound	104	C 6
Achillbeg Island	104	C 6
Achonry	112	G 5
Aclare	112	F 5
Acoose (Lough)	89	C 11
Adamstown	96	L 10
Adare	94	F 10
Adrigole	89	C 12
Aghaboe	101	J 9
Aghabullogue	90	F 12
Aghada	90	H 12
Aghadiffin	106	F 6
Aghadoe	89	D 11
Aghadoon	110	B 5
Aghadowey	118	M 2
Aghagallon	114	N 4
Aghagower	105	D 6
Aghalane	113	J 5
Aghalee	114	N 4
Aghamore Leitrim	107	I 6
Aghamore Mayo	105	F 6
Aghamuck	106	H 6
Aghavannagh	103	M 9
Aghavas	107	I 6
Aghaville	89	D 13
Aghinlig	114	M 4
Aghla Mountain	116	H 3
Aghleam	110	B 5
Aghnablaney	113	I 4
Aghnacliff	107	J 6
Aghnamullen	108	L 5
Aghowle	96	M 9
Agivey	118	M 2
Aglish Tipperary	100	H 8
Aglish Waterford	91	I 11
Agnew's Hill	115	O 3
Ahakista	89	D 13
Ahalia (Loughs)	105	D 7
Ahascragh	106	G 7
Ahenny	95	J 10
Aherla	90	F 12
Aherlow	94	H 10
Aherlow (Glen of)	95	H 10
Ahoghill	118	M 3
Aillwee Cave	99	E 8
Ailt an Chorráin / Burtonport	116	G 3
Aird Mhór / Ardmore	91	I 12
Akeragh Lough	93	C 10
Aldergrove	115	N 4
Allaghaun	93	E 10
Allen	102	L 8
Allen (Bog of)	102	K 8
Allen (Lough)	112	H 5
Allenwood	102	L 8
Allihies	88	B 13
Allistragh	114	L 4
Alloon Lower	106	G 7
Allow	94	F 11
Allua (Lough)	89	E 12
Altagowlan	112	H 5
Altan Lough	117	H 2
Altnamackan	114	M 5
Altnapaste	117	I 3
An Blascaod Mór / Blasket Islands	92	A 11
An Bun Beag / Bunbeg	116	H 2
An Caisleán Nua / Newcastle West	93	E 10
An Caisleán Riabhach / Castlerea	106	G 6
An Chathair / Caher	95	I 10
An Cheathrú Rua / Carraroe	98	D 8
An Chloich Mhóir /	104	C 6
An Clochán / Clifden	104	B 7
An Clochán / Cloghan Donegal	117	I 3
An Clochán Liath / Dungloe	116	G 3
An Cloigeann / Cleegan	104	B 7
An Cóbh / Cobh	90	H 12
An Coimín / Commeen	117	I 3
An Coireán / Waterville	88	B 12
An Corrán / Currane	104	C 6
An Creagán / Mount Bellew	106	G 7
An Daingean / Dingle	92	B 11
An Dúchoraidh / Doocharry	116	H 3
An Fál Carrach / Falcarragh	117	H 2
An Fhairche / Clonbur	105	D 7
An Geata Mór	110	B 5
An Gleann Garbh / Glengarriff	89	D 12
An Gort / Gort	99	F 8
An Gort Mór / Gortmore	105	D 7
An Leacht / Lahinch	98	D 9
An Longfort / Longford	107	I 6
An Mám / Maam Cross	105	D 7
An Mhala Raithní / Mulrany	104	C 6
An Móta / Moate	101	I 7
An Muileann gCearr / Mullingar	107	J 7
An Nás / Naas	102	M 8
An Ráth / Charleville	94	F 10
An Ros / Rush	109	N 7
An Sciobairín / Skibbereen	89	E 13
An Seanchaisleán / Oldcastle	108	K 6
An Spidéal / Spiddal	99	E 8
An tAonach / Nenagh	100	H 9
An Teampall Mór / Templemore	101	I 9
An Tearmann / Termon	117	I 2
An tInbhear Mór / Arklow	97	N 9
An Tulach / Tullow	102	L 9
An Uaimh / Navan	108	L 7
Anascaul	92	B 11
Anayalla	114	L 5
Anglesborough	94	H 10
Anglesey Bridge	95	H 9
Annacarriga	99	G 9
Annacarty	95	H 10
Annaclone	115	N 5
Annacloy	115	O 4
Annacotty	94	G 9
Annadorn	115	O 5
Annagary	116	H 2
Annagassan	109	M 6
Annageeragh (River)	98	D 9
Annagh Head	110	B 5
Annagh Island	110	C 6
Annaghdown	105	E 7
Annaghmore Lough	106	H 6
Annahilt	115	N 4
Annalee	107	J 5
Annalong	109	O 5
Annamoe	103	N 8
Annes Grove Gardens	94	G 11
Annestown	91	K 11
Annfield	95	I 9
Annie Brady Bridge	111	C 5
Annsborough	115	O 5
Antrim	115	N 3
Antrim (Glens of)	119	N 2
Antrim Coast	119	O 2
Antrim Mountains	119	N 2
Anure (Lough)	116	H 3
Araglin	95	H 11
Árainn Mhór / Aran or Aranmore Island	116	G 2
Aran Islands / Oileáin Árainn	98	C 8
Archdale (Castle)	113	I 4
Archerstown	108	K 7
Ard	104	C 8
Ardagh Donegal	117	J 3
Ardagh Limerick	93	E 10
Ardan	101	J 8
Ardanairy	103	N 9
Ardanew	108	L 7
Ardara	116	G 3
Ardattin	96	L 9
Ardboe	114	M 4
Ardcath	109	M 7
Ardcloon	105	F 7
Ardcrony	100	H 9
Ardea	89	C 12
Arderin	101	J 8
Ardfert	93	C 11
Ardfield	89	F 13
Ardfinnan	95	I 11
Ardgehane	90	F 13
Ardglass	115	P 5
Ardglass	90	H 11
Ardgroom	88	C 12
Ardgroom Harbour	88	C 12
Ardkeen	115	P 4
Ardlea	101	J 9
Ardlougher	107	J 5
Ardmillan	115	O 4
Ardmoney	113	J 5
Ardmore Derry	117	K 3
Ardmore Galway	104	C 8
Ardmore Point Antrim	114	N 4
Ardmore Point Craigavon	114	M 4
Ardmore Point Dunganstown East	103	N 9
Ardmoy	106	G 6
Ardnageeragh	104	B 7
Ardnasodan	105	F 7
Ardpatrick	94	G 10
Ardrahan	99	F 8
Ardreagh	118	M 2
Adress House	114	M 4
Ards Forest Park	117	I 2
Ards Peninsula	115	P 4
Ardscull	102	L 8
Ardshankill	113	I 4
Ardstraw	113	J 3
Argideen	89	F 13
Argory (The)	114	M 4
Arigna	112	H 5
Arinagh	112	F 5
Arless	102	K 9
Armagh	114	M 4
Armaghbrague	114	M 5
Armoy	118	N 2
Arney	113	I 5
Arra Mountains	100	G 9
Arrow (Lough)	106	H 5
Arryheernabin	117	J 2
Artane	103	N 7
Arthurstown	96	L 11
Articlave	118	L 2
Artigarvan	117	J 3
Arvagh	107	J 6
Asdee	93	D 10
Ashbourne	109	M 7
Ashford Glenealy	103	N 8
Ashford Limerick	93	E 10
Ashford Castle	105	E 7
Ashleam Bay	104	B 6
Ashton	90	F 12
Askamore	97	M 9
Askanagap	103	M 9
Askeaton	94	F 10
Askill	112	H 4
Atedaun (Lough)	99	E 9
Áth Cinn / Headford	105	E 7
Athassel Abbey	95	I 10
Athboy	108	L 7
Athea	93	E 10
Athgarvan	102	L 8
Athlacca	94	G 10
Athleague	106	H 7
Athnid	95	I 9
Athy / Baile Átha Í	102	L 9
Atlantic Drive (The)	104	C 6
Atorick (Lough)	99	G 8
Attanagh	101	J 9
Attavally	111	C 5
Attical	109	N 5
Attymass	111	E 5
Attymon	99	G 8
Aucloggen	105	F 7
Audley's Castle	115	P 4
Aughacasla	92	C 11
Aughagault	117	I 3
Aughamullan	114	M 4
Augher	114	K 4
Aughils	92	C 11
Aughinish	99	E 8
Aughinish Island	93	E 10
Aughkeely	117	I 3
Aughnacleagh	118	M 3
Aughnacloy	114	L 4
Aughnanure Castle	105	E 7
Aughnasheelan	107	I 5
Aughrim Galway	100	H 8
Aughrim Wicklow	103	N 9
Aughris	112	F 5
Aughris Head	112	F 5
Aughrus More	104	B 7
Avoca	103	N 9
Avoca (River)	103	N 9
Avoca (Valle of)	103	N 9
Avonbeg	103	M 9
Avondale Forest Park	103	N 9
Avonmore (River)	103	N 9
Awbeg	94	G 11

B

Baginbun Head	96	L 11
Baile an Fheirtéaraigh / Ballyferriter	92	A 11
Baile an Mhóta / Ballymote	112	G 5
Baile an Róba / Ballinrobe	105	E 7
Baile an Sceilg / Ballinskelligs	88	B 12
Baile Átha an Rí / Athenry	99	F 8
Baile Átha Cliath / Dublin	103	N 8
Baile Átha Fhirdhia / Ardee	108	M 6
Baile Átha Luain / Athlone	107	I 7
Baile Átha Troim / Trim	108	L 7
Baile Brigín / Balbriggan	109	N 7
Baile Chláir / Claregalway	99	F 7
Baile Locha Riach / Loughrea	99	G 8
Baile Mhic Andáin / Thomastown	96	K 10
Baile Mhistéala / Mitchelstown	94	H 11
Baile na Finne / Fintown	117	H 3
Baile na Lorgan / Castleblayney	108	L 5
Baile Uí Fhiacháin / Newport	105	D 6
Baile Uí Mhatháin / Ballymahon	107	I 7
Baileysmill	115	O 4
Balbriggan	103	N 7
Balla	105	E 6
Ballaba	99	F 8
Ballagan Point	109	N 5
Ballagh Fermanagh	113	J 5
Ballagh Galway	106	F 7
Ballagh Limerick	93	E 10
Ballagh near Curraghroe	107	H 6
Ballagh near Nahara	106	H 7
Ballagh Tipperary	95	I 10
Ballagh (Neck of the)	112	G 3
Ballaghaderreen / Bealach an Doirín	106	G 6
Ballaghbeama Gap	89	C 12
Ballaghbehy	93	E 10
Ballaghisheen Pass	88	C 12
Ballaghkeen	97	M 10
Ballaghmore	101	I 9
Ballaghnatrillick	112	G 4
Ballard	97	M 9
Ballardiggan	99	F 8
Balleen	101	J 9
Ballickmoyler	102	K 9
Balliggan	115	P 4
Ballina	99	G 9
Ballina / Béal an Átha	111	E 5
Ballinaboy	104	B 7
Ballinabrackey	102	K 7
Ballinabranagh	102	L 9
Ballinaclash	103	N 9
Ballinacor	103	N 9
Ballinadee	90	G 12
Ballinafad Aghanagh	106	G 5
Ballinafad Galway	104	C 7
Ballinagar	101	J 8
Ballinagleragh	113	H 5
Ballinakill	101	K 9
Ballinalack	107	J 7
Ballinalea	103	N 8
Ballinalee	107	J 6
Ballinamallard	113	J 4
Ballinamara	95	J 9
Ballinameen	106	H 6
Ballinamore Bridge	106	G 7
Ballinamuck	107	I 6
Ballinascarty	90	F 12
Ballinaspick	91	I 11
Ballinclashet	90	G 12
Ballinclea	103	M 9
Ballincloher	93	C 10
Ballincollig	90	G 12
Ballincrea	96	K 11
Ballincurrig	90	H 12
Ballindaggan	96	L 10
Ballindarragh	113	J 5
Ballinderreen	99	F 8
Ballinderry Terryglass	100	H 8
Ballinderry Wicklow	103	N 9
Ballinderry Bridge	114	M 4
Ballindine	105	F 6
Ballindrait	117	J 3
Ballineanig	92	A 11
Ballineen	89	F 12
Ballingarrane	94	F 10
Ballingarry Galway	100	H 8
Ballingarry Limerick	94	F 10
Ballingarry Tipperary	95	J 10
Ballingeary / Béal Átha an Ghaorthaidh	89	E 12
Ballingurteen	89	E 12
Ballinhassig	90	G 12
Ballinkillin	96	L 10
Ballinlea	118	M 2
Ballinleeny	94	F 10
Ballinloghig	92	B 11
Ballinlough Meath	108	K 6
Ballinlough Roscommon	106	G 6
Ballinluska	90	H 12
Ballinruan	99	F 9
Ballinskelligs Bay	88	B 12
Ballinspittle	90	G 12
Ballintober	106	G 6
Ballintogher	112	G 5
Ballintotty	100	H 9
Ballintoy	118	M 2
Ballintra Donegal	112	H 4
Ballintra near Leabgarrow	116	G 3
Ballintubber	105	E 6
Ballinunty	95	I 10
Ballinure (River)	100	H 9
Ballinvarry	96	L 10
Ballitore	102	L 8
Ballivor	108	L 7
Ballon	96	L 9
Balloo Cross Roads	115	O 4
Balloughter	97	M 10
Ballure	112	H 4
Ballyagran	94	F 10
Ballyallinan	94	F 10
Ballyalton	115	P 5
Ballyard	113	J 4
Ballybannon	102	L 9
Ballybay near Carrickmacross	108	L 5
Ballybay near Castleblayney	108	L 5
Ballybeg	95	I 11
Ballyboghil	109	N 7
Ballyboy	101	I 8
Ballybrack Dublin	103	N 8
Ballybrack Kerry	88	B 12
Ballybrittas	101	K 8
Ballybrommel	96	L 9
Ballybrood	94	G 10
Ballybrophy	101	J 9
Ballybryan	101	K 7
Ballybunnion	93	D 10
Ballycahill	95	I 9
Ballycallan	95	J 10
Ballycanew	97	N 10
Ballycarney	97	M 10
Ballycarry	115	O 3
Ballycastle Mayo	111	D 5
Ballycastle Moyle	119	N 2
Ballycastle Bay	119	N 2
Ballyclare Newtonabbey	115	N 3
Ballyclare Roscommon	107	I 6
Ballyclerahan	95	I 10
Ballyclery	99	F 8
Ballyclogh	94	F 11
Ballycolla	101	J 9
Ballycommon	100	H 9
Ballyconneely	104	B 7
Ballyconneely Bay	104	B 7
Ballyconnell Cavan	113	J 5
Ballyconnell Sligo	112	G 4
Ballycorick	99	E 9
Ballycotton	91	H 12
Ballycotton Bay	91	H 12
Ballycrossaun	100	H 8
Ballycrovane Harbour	88	C 12
Ballycroy	110	C 5
Ballycuirke Lough	99	E 8
Ballycullane	96	L 11
Ballycullen	103	N 8
Ballycumber	101	I 8
Ballydangan	100	H 7
Ballydavid Galway	100	G 8
Ballydavid Kilmalkedar	92	A 11
Ballydavid Head	92	A 11
Ballydavis	101	K 8
Ballydehob	89	D 13
Ballydesmond	93	E 11
Ballydonegan	88	B 13
Ballydonegan Bay	88	B 13
Ballyduff Dingle	92	B 11
Ballyduff Kerry	93	D 10
Ballyduff Waterford	91	H 11
Ballyduff Wexford	97	M 10
Ballyeaston	115	O 3
Ballyeighter Loughs	99	F 9
Ballyfad	97	N 9
Ballyfair	102	L 8
Ballyfarnagh	105	F 6
Ballyfarnan	106	H 5
Ballyfasy	96	K 10
Ballyfeard	90	G 12
Ballyferis Point	115	P 4
Ballyfin	101	J 8
Ballyfinboy	100	H 8
Ballyforan	106	H 7
Ballyfore	102	K 8
Ballyfoyle	96	K 9
Ballygalley	119	O 3
Ballygalley Head	119	O 3
Ballygar	106	H 7
Ballygarrett	97	N 10
Ballygarries	105	E 6
Ballygarvan	90	G 12
Ballygawley Dungannon	114	K 4
Ballygawley Sligo	112	G 5
Ballyglass near Cornanagh	105	E 6
Ballyglass near Kilmovee	106	G 6
Ballygorman	117	K 1
Ballygowan Ards	115	O 4
Ballygowan Newry-Mourne	109	N 5
Ballygriffin	95	I 10
Ballyhack	96	L 11
Ballyhacket	102	L 9
Ballyhaght	94	G 10
Ballyhahill	93	E 10
Ballyhaise	107	K 5
Ballyhalbert	115	P 4
Ballyhale Galway	105	E 7
Ballyhale Kilkenny	96	K 10
Ballyhar	93	D 11
Ballyhaunis / Béal Átha hAmhnais	106	F 6
Ballyhean	105	E 6
Ballyhear	105	E 7
Ballyheelan	107	J 6
Ballyheerin	117	I 2
Ballyheige	93	C 10
Ballyheige Bay	93	C 10
Ballyhillin	117	J 1
Ballyhoe Bridge	118	N 2
Ballyhoge	96	M 10
Ballyhooly	94	G 11
Ballyhornan	115	P 5
Ballyhoura Mountains	94	G 11
Ballyhuppahane	101	J 8
Ballyjamesduff	107	K 6
Ballykean	101	K 8
Ballykeefe	95	J 10
Ballykeel	115	N 4
Ballykeeran	107	I 7
Ballykelly	118	K 2
Ballykilleen	102	K 8
Ballykinler	115	O 5
Ballyknockan	103	M 8
Ballylacy	97	N 9
Ballylaghnan	99	G 9
Ballylanders	94	G 10
Ballylaneen	91	J 11
Ballylesson	115	O 4
Ballylickey	89	D 12
Ballyliffin	117	J 2
Ballylintagh	118	L 2
Ballylongford	93	D 10
Ballylongford Bay	93	D 10
Ballylooby	95	I 11
Ballyloughbeg	118	M 2
Ballylynan	102	K 9
Ballymacarbry	95	I 11
Ballymacaw	96	K 11
Ballymachugh	107	K 6
Ballymack	96	K 10
Ballymackey	100	H 9
Ballymackilroy	114	K 4
Ballymacoda	91	I 12
Ballymacrevan	115	N 4
Ballymacurly	106	H 6
Ballymacward	106	G 7
Ballymadog	91	I 12
Ballymagan	117	J 2
Ballymagaraghy	118	K 2
Ballymagorry	117	J 3
Ballymakeagh	91	I 12

A
B
C
D
E
F
G
H
I
J
K
L
M
N
O
P
Q
R
S
T
U
V
W
X
Y
Z

A B C D E F G H I J K L M N O P Q R S T U V W X Y Z

Ballymakeery /
Baile Mhic Íre ....89 E 12
Ballymakenny ....109 M 6
Ballymartin ....109 O 5
Ballymartle ....90 G 12
Ballymena ....119 N 3
Ballymoe ....106 G 6
Ballymoney *Ballymoney* ....118 M 2
Ballymoney *Limavady* ....118 K 3
Ballymore *Donegal* ....117 I 2
Ballymore *Westmeath* ....107 I 7
Ballymore Eustace ....103 M 8
Ballymore Lough ....111 E 5
Ballymurphy ....96 L 10
Ballymurragh ....93 E 10
Ballymurray ....106 H 7
Ballynabola ....96 L 10
Ballynacallagh ....88 B 13
Ballynacally ....99 E 9
Ballynacarrick ....116 H 3
Ballynacarriga ....89 E 12
Ballynacarrigy ....107 J 7
Ballynacarrow ....112 G 5
Ballynaclogh ....100 H 9
Ballynacorra ....90 H 12
Ballynacourty ....91 J 11
Ballynadrumny ....102 L 7
Ballynafid ....107 J 7
Ballynagaul ....91 J 11
Ballynagoraher ....105 D 6
Ballynagore ....101 J 7
Ballynagree ....90 F 12
Ballynaguilkee ....95 I 11
Ballynahinch ....115 O 4
Ballynahinch Lake ....104 C 7
Ballynahow ....88 A 12
Ballynahow *Kilcummin* ....98 D 8
Ballynahown *Westmeath* ..101 I 7
Ballynakill *Carlow* ....96 L 9
Ballynakill *Offaly* ....101 K 8
Ballynakill *Westmeath* ....107 I 7
Ballynakill Harbour ....104 B 7
Ballynakilla ....88 C 13
Ballynakilly Upper ....88 C 11
Ballynamallaght ....117 K 3
Ballynamona ....90 G 11
Ballynamult ....95 I 11
Ballynana ....92 A 11
Ballynare ....103 M 7
Ballynashannagh ....117 J 2
Ballynaskeagh ....114 N 5
Ballynaskreena ....93 C 10
Ballynastangford ....105 E 6
Ballynastraw ....97 M 10
Ballynchatty ....113 K 4
Ballyneaner ....118 K 3
Ballyneety ....94 G 10
Ballyneill ....95 J 10
Ballynoe *Cork* ....90 H 11
Ballynoe *Down* ....115 O 5
Ballynure ....115 O 3
Ballyorgan ....94 G 11
Ballypatrick ....95 J 10
Ballypatrick Forest ....119 N 2
Ballyporeen ....95 H 11
Ballyquin ....92 B 11
Ballyquintin Point ....115 P 5
Ballyragget ....101 J 9
Ballyrashane ....118 M 2
Ballyreagh *Dungannon* ....114 L 4
Ballyreagh *Fermanagh* ....113 J 4
Ballyroan ....101 K 9
Ballyroddy ....106 H 6
Ballyroebuck ....97 M 10
Ballyronan ....114 M 3
Ballyroney ....115 N 5
Ballyroon ....88 C 13
Ballysadare ....112 G 5
Ballysadare Bay ....112 G 5
Ballyshannon *Donegal* ....112 H 4
Ballyshannon *Kildare* ....102 L 8
Ballysloe ....95 J 10
Ballysteen ....94 F 10
Ballyteige Bay ....96 L 11
Ballytoohy ....104 C 6
Ballyvaughan ....99 E 8
Ballyvaughan Bay ....99 E 8
Ballyvester ....115 P 4
Ballyvoge /
Baile Uí Bhuaigh ....89 E 12
Ballyvoneen ....106 G 7
Ballyvourney /
Baile Bhuirne ....89 E 12
Ballyvoy ....119 N 2
Ballyvoyle Head ....91 J 11
Ballywalter ....115 P 4
Ballyward ....115 N 5

Ballywilliam ....96 L 10
Balnamore ....118 M 2
Balrath ....108 M 7
Balrothery ....109 N 7
Balscaddan ....109 N 7
Baltimore ....89 D 13
Baltray ....109 N 6
Banada ....106 F 5
Banagher ....101 I 8
Banagher Forest ....118 L 3
Banbridge ....114 N 4
Bandon River ....89 F 12
Bangor *Mayo* ....111 C 5
Bangor North-Down ....115 O 4
Bangor Trail ....111 C 5
Bann (River)
Lough Neagh ....115 N 5
Bann (River) *River Slaney* ...97 M 10
Banna ....93 C 10
Banna Strand ....93 C 11
Bannow ....96 L 11
Bannow Bay ....96 L 11
Bansha ....95 H 10
Banteer ....94 F 11
Bantry / *Beanntraí* ....89 D 12
Bantry Bay ....89 C 13
Barefield ....99 F 9
Barley Cove ....88 C 13
Barna *Limerick* ....94 H 10
Barna *Offaly* ....101 I 9
Barnaderg ....106 F 7
Barnesmore ....113 H 3
Barnesmore Gap ....113 I 3
Barnmeen ....115 N 5
Barnycarroll ....105 F 6
Baronscourt Forest ....113 J 3
Barr na Trá / Barnatra ....110 C 5
Barrack Village ....101 K 9
Barraduff ....89 D 11
Barrigone ....93 E 10
Barringtonsbridge ....94 G 10
Barrow (River) ....102 K 8
Barrow Harbour ....93 C 11
Barry ....107 I 7
Barry's Point ....90 F 13
Batterstown ....108 M 7
Baunskeha ....96 K 10
Bauntlieve ....99 E 9
Baurtregaum ....93 C 11
Bawn Cross Roads ....94 F 11
Bawnboy ....113 I 5
Beagh *Galway* ....105 F 7
Beagh *Roscommon* ....112 H 5
Beagh (Lough) ....117 I 7
Beagh (Slieve) ....113 K 4
Beal ....93 D 10
Béal an Átha / Ballina ....111 E 5
Béal an Átha Mhóir /
Ballinamore ....107 I 5
Béal an Mhuirthead /
Belmullet ....110 C 5
Béal Átha an Ghaorthaidh /
Ballingeary ....89 E 12
Béal Átha na Muice /
Swinford ....105 F 6
Béal Átha na Sluaighe /
Ballinasloe ....100 H 8
Béal Deirg / Belderrig ....111 D 5
Beal Point ....93 D 10
Béal Tairbirt / Belturbet ....107 J 5
Bealach Conglais /
Baltinglass ....102 L 9
Bealach Féich /
Ballybofey ....117 I 3
Bealaclugga / New Quay ...99 E 8
Bealad Cross Roads ....89 F 13
Bealadangan ....105 D 8
Bealaha ....98 D 9
Bealalaw Bridge ....88 C 12
Bealanabrack ....104 C 7
Bealin ....107 I 7
Bealnablath ....90 F 12
Beara ....88 C 12
Bearna / Barna ....99 E 8
Beaufort ....89 D 11
Bective ....108 L 7
Beehive Huts ....92 A 11
Beenmore ....88 B 11
Beennaskehy ....90 G 11
Beenoskee ....92 B 11
Beg (Lough) *Antrim* ....114 N 4
Beg (Lough) *River Bann* ...114 M 3
Beginish Island ....88 B 12

Behy ....88 C 11
Bekan ....105 F 6
Belcarra ....105 E 6
Belclare ....105 F 7
Belcoo ....113 I 5
Belderg Harbour ....111 D 5
Belfarsad ....104 C 6
Belfast ....115 O 4
Belfast Lough ....115 O 3
Belgooly ....90 G 12
Belhavel Lough ....112 H 5
Belladrihid ....112 G 5
Bellagarvaun ....110 C 6
Bellacorick ....111 D 5
Belladrihid ....112 G 5
Bellagarvaun ....110 C 6
Bellaghy ....114 M 3
Bellahy ....106 F 6
Bellameeny ....106 H 7
Bellanagare ....106 G 6
Bellanaleck ....113 J 5
Bellanamore ....117 H 3
Bellanamullia ....107 H 7
Bellanagh ....107 J 6
Bellanode ....114 K 5
Bellarena ....118 L 2
Bellavary ....105 E 6
Belleek ....114 M 5
Belleek ....113 H 4
Bellewstown ....109 M 7
Belmont ....101 I 8
Belmore Mountain ....113 I 5
Beltra *Croaghmoyle* ....105 D 6
Beltra *Sligo* ....112 G 5
Beltra Lough ....105 D 6
Belvelly ....90 H 12
Belview Port ....96 K 11
Belville ....111 D 5
Ben Gorm ....104 C 7
Benbane Head ....118 M 2
Benbaun ....104 C 7
Benbo ....112 H 5
Benbrack ....113 I 5
Benbreen ....104 C 7
Benbulben ....112 G 4
Benburb ....114 L 4
Bencroy or
Gubnaveagh ....113 I 5
Bendooragh ....118 M 2
Benettsbridge ....96 K 10
Benmore ....111 D 5
Benmore or Fair Head ...119 N 2
Bennacunneen ....105 D 7
Benwee Head ....111 C 4
Beragh ....114 K 4
Bere Haven ....88 C 13
Bere Island ....88 C 13
Bernish Rock ....114 M 5
Berrings ....90 F 12
Bertraghboy Bay ....104 C 7
Bessbrook ....114 M 5
Bettystown ....109 N 6
Big Dog Forest ....113 I 4
Big Island ....100 H 8
Big Trosk ....119 N 2
Bilboa ....102 K 9
Bilboa (River) ....95 H 10
Billis Bridge ....108 K 6
Bills Rocks ....104 B 6
Binevenagh ....118 L 2
Binn Éadair / Howth ....103 N 7
Biorra / Birr ....101 I 8
Birdhill ....99 G 9
Birreencorragh ....105 D 6
Bishops Court ....115 P 5
Black *Galway* ....105 E 7
Black (River) *Longford* ....107 I 6
Black Ball Head ....88 B 13
Black Bull ....103 M 7
Black Gap (The) ....113 I 4
Black Head *Clare* ....99 E 8
Black Head *Larne* ....115 O 3
Black Lion ....101 J 8
Black Rock ....110 B 5
Blacklion ....113 I 5
Blackpool ....94 G 10
Blackrock *Cork* ....90 G 12
Blackrock *Louth* ....109 M 6
Blackrock *Rathdown* ....103 N 8
Blackskull ....114 N 4
Blacksod Bay ....110 B 5
Blacksod Point ....110 B 5
Blackwater ....97 M 10
Blackwater (River) *Cork* ...89 F 11

Blackwater (River)
Lough Neagh ....114 L 4
Blackwater (River)
River Boyne ....108 L 6
Blackwater Bridge
Innfield ....102 L 7
Blackwater Bridge *Tahilla* ..88 C 12
Blackwater Harbour ....97 N 10
Blackwatertown ....114 L 4
Blanchardstown ....103 M 7
Blane Bridge ....93 E 10
Blaney ....113 I 4
Blarney ....90 G 12
Blasket Sound ....92 A 11
Bleach ....99 G 8
Bleach Lake ....94 F 10
Blennerville ....93 C 11
Blessington ....103 M 8
Bloody Foreland ....116 H 2
Blue Ball ....101 J 8
Blue Stack Mountains ....113 H 3
Blueford ....93 E 11
Boa Island ....113 I 4
Boardmills ....115 O 4
Boderg (Lough) ....107 I 6
Bodyke ....99 G 9
Bofeenaun ....105 E 6
Bofin (Lough) *Galway* ....105 D 7
Bofin (Lough)
Roscommon ....107 I 6
Bogay ....117 J 3
Boggan *Meath* ....108 L 6
Boggan *Tipperary* ....95 J 9
Boggaun ....101 I 9
Boggeragh Mountains ....89 F 11
Bohateh ....99 G 9
Bohaun ....105 D 6
Boheeshil ....88 C 12
Boher ....94 G 10
Boheraphuca ....101 I 8
Boherbue ....93 E 11
Boheren ....94 G 10
Boherlahan ....95 I 10
Bohermeen ....108 L 7
Boherquill ....107 J 6
Boho ....113 I 4
Bohola ....105 E 6
Bola (Lough) ....104 C 7
Bolea ....118 L 2
Boleran ....118 L 2
Boley ....102 L 8
Bolinglanna ....104 C 6
Boliska Lough ....99 E 8
Bolton's Cross Roads ....93 D 10
Bolus Head ....88 A 12
Bonet ....112 H 5
Boola ....91 I 11
Boolakennedy ....95 J 11
Boolattin ....95 J 11
Boolteens ....93 C 11
Boolyduff ....99 E 9
Boolyglass ....96 K 10
Borris ....96 L 10
Borris in Ossory ....101 J 9
Borrisoleigh ....100 I 9
Boston ....99 F 8
Bottlehill ....90 G 11
Bouladuff ....95 I 9
Boviel ....118 L 3
Bow ....99 G 9
Boyerstown ....108 L 7
Boyle (River) ....106 H 6
Boyne (River) ....102 K 7
Brackagh ....101 K 8
Brackley Lough ....113 I 5
Bracklin ....108 K 7
Brackloon *Mayo* ....106 F 6
Brackloon *Roscommon* ....106 G 6
Bracknagh *Offaly* ....102 K 8
Bracknagh *Roscommon* ....106 G 6
Brackwanshagh ....111 E 5
Brandon Bay ....92 B 11
Brandon Head ....92 B 11
Brandon Hill ....96 L 10
Brannock Islands ....98 C 8
Bray Head *Kerry* ....88 A 12
Bray Head *Wicklow* ....103 N 8
Bré / Bray ....103 N 8
Breaghva ....98 C 10
Breaghwy ....105 E 6
Bree ....96 M 10
Breenagh ....117 I 3
Brickeens ....105 F 6
Bricklieve Mountains ....106 G 5
Bride *Cork* ....89 F 12

Bride *River Blackwater* ....91 I 11
Bridebridge ....90 H 11
Brideswell *Ballyellis* ....97 M 9
Brideswell *Ballynamona* ....106 H 7
Bridge End ....117 J 2
Bridgeland ....103 M 9
Bridget Lough ....99 G 9
Bridgetown
Cannock Chase ....96 M 11
Bridgetown *Clare* ....99 G 9
Bridgetown *Donegal* ....112 H 4
Briensbridge ....99 G 9
Brittas *Limerick* ....94 G 10
Brittas *Saggart* ....103 M 8
Brittas Bay ....103 N 9
Britway ....90 H 11
Broad Haven ....110 C 5
Broad Meadow ....109 N 7
Broadford *Clare* ....99 G 9
Broadford *Limerick* ....94 F 10
Broadway ....97 M 11
Brookeborough ....113 J 5
Broomfield ....108 L 5
Brosna ....93 E 11
Brosna (River) ....101 I 8
Broughal ....101 I 8
Broughane Cross Roads ...93 D 11
Brougher Mount ....113 J 4
Broughshane ....119 N 3
Brow Head ....88 C 13
Brown Flesk ....93 D 11
Brownstown ....96 K 11
Brownstown Head ....96 K 11
Bruckless ....112 G 4
Bruff ....94 G 10
Bruree ....94 G 10
Bryansford ....115 O 5
Buckna ....119 N 3
Buckode ....112 H 4
Buiríos Uí Chéin /
Borrisokane ....100 H 9
Bulgaden ....94 G 10
Bull (The) ....88 B 13
Bull Point ....119 N 2
Bullaba ....117 I 3
Bullaun ....99 G 8
Bull's Head ....92 B 11
Bun Cranncha / Buncrana 117 J 2
Bun Dobhráin / Bundoran .112 H 4
Bun na hAbhna /
Bunnahowen ....110 C 5
Bun na Leaca / Brinlack ....116 H 2
Bunaclugga Bay ....93 D 10
Bunacurry ....110 C 6
Bunatrahir Bay ....111 D 5
Bunaveela Lough ....111 D 5
Bunaw ....88 C 12
Bunbrosna ....107 J 7
Bunclody ....96 M 10
Bunlahy ....107 J 6
Bunmahon ....91 J 11
Bunnafollistran ....105 E 7
Bunnaglass ....99 F 8
Bunnahown ....104 C 7
Bunnanaddan ....112 G 5
Bunny (Lough) ....99 F 8
Bunnyconnellan ....111 E 5
Bunowen ....104 C 7
Bunratty ....99 F 9
Burnchurch ....96 K 10
Burncourt ....95 H 11
Burnfoot *Birdstown* ....117 J 2
Burnfoot *Limavady* ....118 L 3
Burnfort ....90 G 11
Burr Point ....115 P 4
Burren *Clare* ....99 E 8
Burren *Cork* ....90 F 12
Burren *Mayo* ....105 E 6
Burren (The) ....99 E 8
Burren Centre Kifenora ....99 E 8
Burrenfadda ....99 E 8
Burrishoole Abbey ....105 D 6
Burrow ....97 M 11
Burtown ....102 L 9
Bush ....118 M 2
Bush (The) *Dungannon* ...114 L 4
Bush (The) *Rathcor* ....109 N 6
Bushfield ....100 G 9
Bushmills ....118 M 2
Butler's Bridge ....107 J 5
Butlerstown ....90 F 13
Buttevant ....94 F 11
Butts (The) ....101 K 9
Bweeng ....90 F 11

Cadamstown *Kildare* ....102 L 7
Cadamstown *Offaly* ....101 J 8
Caddy ....114 N 3
Caggan ....105 D 7
Caha Mountains ....89 C 12
Caha pass ....89 D 12
Caher *Clare* ....99 G 9
Caher *Mayo* ....104 B 6
Caher Island ....104 B 6
Caher Roe's Den ....96 L 10
Caheradrine ....99 F 8
Caheragh ....89 E 13
Caherbarnagh
Corcaigh / Cork ....89 E 11
Caherbarnagh *Kerry* ....88 B 12
Caherconlish ....94 G 10
Caherconnel ....99 E 8
Caherconree ....92 C 11
Caherdaniel ....88 B 12
Caherea ....99 E 9
Caherlistrane ....105 E 7
Cahermore *Cork* ....88 B 13
Cahermore *Galway* ....99 F 8
Cahermurphy ....98 D 9
Cahernahallia ....95 H 10
Cahore Point ....97 N 10
Caiseal / Cashel ....95 I 10
Caisleán an Bharraigh /
Castlebar ....105 E 6
Caisleán an Chomair /
Castlecomer ....101 K 9
Calafort Ros Láir /
Rosslare Harbour ....97 M 11
Caledon ....114 L 4
Calf Islands ....89 D 13
Callaghansmills ....99 F 9
Callainn / Callan ....95 J 10
Callow *Galway* ....104 B 7
Callow *Mayo* ....105 E 6
Callow *Roscommon* ....106 G 6
Caltra ....106 G 7
Caltraghlea ....100 H 7
Calverstown ....102 L 8
Cam Forest ....118 L 2
Camlin (River) ....107 I 6
Camlough ....114 M 5
Camoge ....94 G 10
Camolin ....97 M 10
Camowen ....113 K 4
Camp ....92 C 11
Campile ....96 L 11
Campsey ....118 K 2
Camross ....101 J 8
Camus Bay ....105 D 8
Canglass Point ....88 B 12
Canningstown ....108 K 6
Canon Island ....99 E 9
Cappagh *Dungannon* ....114 L 4
Cappagh *Limerick* ....94 F 10
Cappagh *River* ....100 G 8
Cappagh White ....95 H 10
Cappaghmore ....99 F 8
Cappalinnan ....101 J 9
Cappamore ....94 G 10
Cappanacreha ....105 D 7
Cappanrush ....100 G 8
Cappataggle ....100 G 8
Cappeen ....89 F 12
Car (Slieve) ....111 D 5
Caragh (Lough) ....88 C 11
Caragh (River) ....89 C 12
Caragh Bridge ....92 C 11
Caragh Lake ....92 C 11
Carbery's Hundred Isles ...89 D 13
Carbury ....102 L 7
Cardy ....115 P 4
Cargan ....119 N 3
Carhan House ....88 B 12
Cark ....117 I 3
Cark Mountain ....117 I 3
Carland ....114 L 4
Carlanstown ....108 L 6
Carlingford ....109 N 5
Carlingford Lough ....109 N 5
Carn ....113 I 4
Carna ....104 C 8
Carnageer ....119 O 3
Carnaghan ....117 J 2
Carnalbanagh Sheddings .119 N 3
Carnanelly ....114 L 3
Carnanreagh ....118 K 3
Carnaross ....108 L 6
Carnaween ....112 H 3
Carncastle ....119 O 3
Carndonagh /
Carn Domhnach ....118 K 2
Carnduff ....119 N 2

C
Cabragh ....114 L 4

Carne .....97 M 11
Carneatly .....119 N 2
Carnew .....97 M 9
Carney *Sligo* .....112 G 4
Carney *Tipperary* .....100 H 9
Carnlough .....119 O 3
Carnlough Bay .....119 O 3
Carnmore .....99 F 8
Carnoneen .....105 F 7
Carnowen .....117 J 3
Carnsore Point .....97 M 11
Carnteel .....114 L 4
Carntogher .....118 L 3
Carra (Lough) .....105 E 6
Carracastle .....106 F 6
Carragh .....102 L 8
Carraholly .....105 D 6
Carraig Airt / Carrigart .....117 I 2
Carraig Mhachaire Rois /
  Carrickmacross .....108 L 6
Carraig na Siúire /
  Carrick-on-Suir .....95 J 10
Carran .....99 E 8
Carrantuohill .....89 C 11
Carrick *Wexford* .....96 L 11
Carrick / An Charraig
  Donegal .....112 G 4
Carrick-a-Rede
  Rope Bridge .....118 M 2
Carrick-on-Shannon /
  Cora Droma Rúisc .....107 H 6
Carrickaboy .....107 K 6
Carrickashedoge .....108 L 6
Carrickboy .....107 I 7
Carrickfergus .....115 O 3
Carrickhugh .....118 K 2
Carrickmore .....114 K 4
Carrickroe .....114 K 4
Carrig .....94 G 11
Carrig Island .....93 D 10
Carrigadrohid .....90 F 12
Carrigafoyle Castle .....93 D 10
Carrigagulla .....90 F 11
Carrigaholt .....93 C 10
Carrigaholt Bay .....93 C 10
Carrigahorig .....100 H 8
Carrigaline .....90 G 12
Carrigallen .....107 J 6
Carrigan .....107 J 6
Carrigan Head .....112 F 4
Carriganimmy .....89 E 12
Carrigans .....117 J 3
Carrigatogher .....100 H 9
Carrigfadda .....89 E 13
Carrigglass Manor .....107 I 6
Carriggower .....103 N 8
Carrigkerry .....93 E 10
Carrignavar .....90 G 12
Carrigrohane .....90 G 12
Carrigtohill .....90 H 12
Carrowbehy .....106 G 6
Carrowdore .....115 P 4
Carrowkeel *Donegal* .....117 J 2
Carrowkeel *Galway* .....99 G 8
Carrowkennedy .....105 D 6
Carrowmore *Galway* .....99 F 8
Carrowmore *Kilmacowen* .....112 G 5
Carrowmore
  near Cloonacool .....112 F 5
Carrowmore
  near Crossboyne .....105 E 6
Carrowmore
  near Killasser .....105 F 6
Carrowmore
  near Killogeary .....111 E 5
Carrowmore Lake .....110 C 5
Carrowmore Point .....98 D 9
Carrowmoreknock .....105 E 7
Carrownacon .....105 E 6
Carrowneden .....112 F 5
Carrownisky .....104 C 6
Carrowntanlis .....105 F 7
Carrowreagh
  Roscommon .....100 H 7
Carrowreagh *Sligo* .....112 F 5
Carrowrory .....107 I 7
Carry Bridge .....113 J 5
Carrybeg .....95 J 10
Carryduff .....115 O 4
Casheen bay .....98 C 8
Cashel *Donegal* .....117 I 2
Cashel *Mayo* .....104 C 6
Cashel
  near Glennamaddy .....106 G 7
Cashel / An Caiseal
  Galway .....104 C 7
Cashel (Rock of) .....95 I 10

Cashelgarran .....112 G 4
Cashelmore .....117 I 2
Cashen River .....93 D 10
Cashla .....99 F 8
Cashla Bay .....98 D 8
Cashleen .....104 B 7
Casla / Costelloe .....98 D 8
Casltepollard .....107 K 6
Cassagh .....96 L 10
Castle Carry .....118 K 2
Castle Coole .....113 J 4
Castle Gardens .....90 F 13
Castle Haven .....89 E 13
Castle Island .....89 D 13
Castle Point .....98 C 10
Castlebaldwin .....112 G 5
Castlebar (River) .....105 E 6
Castlebellingham .....109 M 6
Castleblakeney .....106 G 7
Castlebridge .....97 M 10
Castlecaulfield .....114 L 4
Castleconnell .....99 G 9
Castleconor .....111 E 5
Castlecor .....94 F 11
Castlecove .....88 B 12
Castlecuffe .....101 J 8
Castledawson .....114 M 3
Castlederg .....113 J 3
Castledermot .....102 L 9
Castlefinn .....117 J 3
Castlefreke .....89 F 13
Castlegal .....112 G 4
Castlegar .....99 E 8
Castlegregory .....92 B 11
Castlehill *Ballycroy South* ..110 C 6
Castlehill
  near Rake Street .....111 D 5
Castlejordan .....102 K 7
Castleknock .....103 M 7
Castlellis .....97 M 10
Castlelyons .....90 H 11
Castlemaine .....93 C 11
Castlemaine Harbour .....92 C 11
Castlemartyr .....90 H 12
Castleplunket .....106 G 6
Castlequin .....88 B 12
Castlerahan .....108 K 6
Castlerock .....118 L 2
Castleroe .....118 M 2
Castleshane .....114 L 5
Castletown *Clare* .....99 E 8
Castletown *Cork* .....89 F 12
Castletown *Laois* .....101 J 9
Castletown *Limerick* .....94 F 10
Castletown *Meath* .....108 L 6
Castletown *near Finnea* .....107 K 6
Castletown *Westmeath* .....107 J 7
Castletown *Wexford* .....97 N 9
Castletown House .....103 M 7
Castletownbere .....88 C 13
Castletownroche .....94 G 11
Castletownshend .....89 E 13
Castleville .....105 E 7
Castleward House .....115 P 4
Castlewarren .....96 K 9
Castlewellan .....115 O 5
Castlewellan Forest Park ..115 O 5
Cathair na Mart /
  Westport .....105 D 6
Cathair Saidhbhín /
  Cahersiveen .....88 B 12
Cathedral Rocks .....104 B 6
Causeway .....93 C 10
Causeway Head .....118 M 2
Cavan / An Cabhán .....107 J 6
Cavanagarvan .....114 L 5
Cavangarden .....112 H 4
Cé Bhréanainn / Brandon ..92 B 11
Ceanannas / Ceanannus Mór
  (Kells) .....108 L 6
Ceann Toirc / Kanturk .....94 F 11
Ceapach Choinn /
  Cappoquin .....91 I 11
Ceatharlach / Carlow .....102 L 9
Ceathrú Thaidhg /
  Carrowteige .....111 C 5
Cecilstown .....94 F 11
Celbridge .....103 M 7
Chanonrock .....108 M 6
Chapeltown *Down* .....115 P 5
Chapeltown
  near Portmagee .....88 A 12
Chapeltown *near Tralee* .....93 C 11
Charlemont .....114 L 4
Charlestown *Craigavon* .....114 M 4
Charlestown *Mayo* .....106 F 6
Cheekpoint .....96 K 11

Cherryville .....102 L 8
Chesney's Corner .....114 M 3
Church Ballee .....115 P 5
Church Cross .....89 D 13
Church Hill *Donegal* .....117 I 3
Church Hill *Fermanagh* .....113 I 4
Church Quarter .....119 N 2
Church Town .....117 J 3
Church Village .....105 E 6
Churchstreet .....106 G 6
Churchtown *Cookstown* .....114 L 3
Churchtown *Cork* .....90 H 12
Churchtown *Wexford* .....96 L 11
Churchtown Point .....114 M 3
Cill Airne / Killarney .....89 D 11
Cill Chainnigh / Kilkenny .....96 K 10
Cill Chaoi / Kilkee .....98 D 9
Cill Dalua / Killaloe .....99 G 9
Cill Dara / Kildare .....102 L 8
Cill Mhantáin / Wicklow ..103 N 9
Cill Mocheallóg /
  Kilmallock .....94 G 10
Cill Orglan / Killorglin .....93 C 11
Cill Rois / Kilrush .....93 D 10
Cill Rónáin / Kilronan .....98 C 8
Cionn tSáile / Kinsale .....90 G 12
City Walls .....96 K 11
Clabby .....113 J 4
Cladagh .....113 I 5
Claddagh .....106 F 7
Claddaghduff .....104 B 7
Clady *Antrim* .....115 N 4
Clady *Magherafelt* .....118 M 3
Clady *Strabane* .....117 J 3
Clady (River) .....116 H 2
Clady Milltown .....114 M 5
Claggan *Donegal* .....117 J 2
Claggan *Mayo* .....104 C 6
Clamper Cross .....93 E 11
Clanabogan .....113 J 4
Clane .....102 L 8
Clár Chlainne Mhuiris /
  Claremorris .....105 F 6
Clara *Antrim* .....103 N 9
Clara (Valle of) .....103 N 9
Clarahill .....101 J 8
Clare *Armagh* .....114 M 5
Clare *Craigavon* .....114 N 4
Clare (River) .....105 F 7
Clare Island .....104 B 6
Clarecastle .....99 F 9
Clareen .....101 I 8
Clarina .....94 F 10
Clarinbridge .....99 F 8
Clark's Cross Roads .....107 J 7
Clash .....100 H 9
Clash North .....93 E 10
Clashmore .....91 I 11
Claudy .....118 K 3
Cleggan / An Cloigeann ...104 B 7
Cleggan Bay .....104 B 7
Cléire (Oilean) /
  Clear Island .....89 D 13
Cleristown .....96 M 11
Clew Bay .....104 C 6
Clifden Bay .....104 B 7
Cliff .....112 H 4
Clifferna .....108 K 6
Cliffony .....112 G 4
Clogga *Kilkenny* .....96 K 11
Clogga *Wicklow* .....97 N 9
Clough *Ballymena* .....119 N 3
Clogh *Kilkenny* .....101 K 9
Clogh *Laois* .....101 J 9
Clogh *Wexford* .....97 M 10
Cloghan *Offaly* .....101 I 8
Cloghan *Westmeath* .....107 K 7
Cloghane .....92 B 11
Cloghaneely .....117 H 2
Clogharinka .....102 K 7
Cloghaun .....105 F 7
Cloghboley .....112 G 4
Cloghbrack *Cloonbur* .....105 D 7
Cloghbrack *Meath* .....108 K 7
Clogheen .....95 I 11
Clogher *Dungannon* .....113 K 4
Clogher *Kerry* .....93 D 11
Clogher
  near Carrownacon .....105 E 6
Clogher *near Westport* .....105 D 6
Clogher *Roscommon* .....107 H 6
Cloghera .....99 G 9
Clogherhead .....109 N 6

Cloghjordan .....100 H 9
Cloghmacoo .....108 L 6
Cloghoge .....109 M 5
Cloghroe *Cork* .....90 G 12
Cloghroe *Donegal* .....117 I 3
Cloghy .....115 P 4
Cloghy Bay .....115 P 4
Clohamon .....96 M 10
Clohernagh .....96 K 11
Cloich na Coillte /
  Clonakilty .....89 F 13
Clóirtheach / Clara .....101 J 7
Clomantagh .....95 J 9
Clonakenny .....101 I 9
Clonakilty Bay .....90 F 13
Clonalis House .....106 G 6
Clonalvy .....109 M 7
Clonard .....108 K 7
Clonaslee .....101 J 8
Clonavoe .....101 K 8
Clonbern .....106 G 7
Clonbullogue .....102 K 8
Cloncagh .....94 F 10
Clonco Bridge .....100 G 8
Cloncrave .....108 K 7
Cloncullen .....107 I 7
Cloncurry .....102 L 7
Clondalkin .....103 M 8
Clondaw .....97 M 10
Clonderalaw Bay .....93 E 10
Clondulane .....90 H 11
Clonea .....95 J 11
Clonea Bay .....91 J 11
Clonee .....103 M 7
Cloneen .....95 J 10
Clonegall .....96 M 9
Clonelly .....113 I 4
Clonevin .....97 N 10
Clonfert .....100 H 8
Clonfert Cross Roads .....100 H 8
Clonkeevy .....112 G 5
Clonleigh .....117 J 3
Clonlost .....107 K 7
Clonmacnoise .....101 I 8
Clonmany .....117 J 2
Clonmellon .....108 K 7
Clonmore *Carlow* .....103 M 9
Clonmore *Tipperary* .....101 I 9
Clonmult .....90 H 12
Clonony .....101 I 8
Clonoulty .....95 I 10
Clonroche .....96 L 10
Clonsilla .....103 M 7
Clontarf .....103 N 7
Clontibret .....114 L 5
Clonycavan .....108 L 7
Clonygowan .....101 K 8
Cloon Lake .....88 C 12
Cloonacleigha Lake .....112 G 5
Cloonacool .....112 F 5
Cloonagh Lough .....106 F 6
Cloonaghlin Lough .....88 C 12
Cloonaghmore .....111 D 5
Cloonboo .....105 E 7
Cloondaff .....105 D 6
Cloondara .....107 I 6
Cloone .....107 I 6
Cloone Grange .....107 I 6
Cloonee Loughs .....89 C 12
Clooneen .....107 J 6
Clooney .....116 G 3
Cloonfad *Kiltullagh* .....106 F 6
Cloonfad *near Old Town* ...100 H 8
Cloonfallagh .....105 F 6
Cloonfinish .....105 F 6
Cloonfower .....106 G 6
Cloonfree Lough .....106 H 6
Cloonkeen *Kerry* .....89 E 12
Cloonkeen *Mayo* .....105 D 6
Cloonkeen *Roscommon* .....106 G 6
Cloonlara .....99 G 9
Cloonloogh .....106 G 6
Cloonlusk .....94 H 10
Cloonmore .....106 F 6
Cloonoon .....100 H 8
Cloonteen .....94 H 10
Cloontia .....106 G 6
Cloonties .....88 C 12
Cloonymorris .....100 G 8
Cloonyquin .....106 H 6
Cloran .....108 L 7
Clough .....115 O 5
Cloughmills .....118 N 3
Cloverhill *Cavan* .....107 J 5
Cloverhill *Galway* .....105 E 7
Cloyfin .....118 M 2

Cloyne .....90 H 12
Cluain Eois / Clones .....113 K 5
Cluain Meala / Clonmel .....95 I 10
Cluainín / Manorhamilton ..112 H 5
Clydagh .....105 E 6
Clynacantan .....88 A 12
Coachford .....90 F 12
Coagh .....114 M 4
Coalbrook .....95 J 10
Coalisland .....114 L 4
Coan .....101 K 9
Cod's Head .....88 B 13
Coill an Chollaigh /
  Bailieborough .....108 L 6
Colbinstown .....102 L 8
Coldwood .....99 F 8
Colebrooke .....113 J 5
Colehill .....107 I 7
Coleraine .....118 L 2
Colgagh .....112 G 5
Colgagh Lough .....112 G 5
Colligan (River) .....95 I 11
Collin Top .....119 N 3
Collinstown .....107 K 7
Collon .....109 M 6
Collooney .....112 G 5
Colly .....88 C 12
Colmanstown .....106 G 7
Comber .....115 O 4
Comeragh Mountains .....95 J 11
Commeen .....117 H 3
Commons .....95 J 10
Conay Island .....112 G 5
Cong / Conga .....105 E 7
Conlig .....115 O 4
Conn (Lough) .....111 E 5
Conna .....90 H 11
Connagh .....100 G 9
Connemara .....104 C 7
Connemara
  National Park .....104 C 7
Connolly .....99 E 9
Connonagh .....89 E 13
Connor .....115 N 3
Connor Pass .....92 B 11
Convoy .....117 I 3
Coogue .....105 F 6
Cookstown .....114 L 4
Coola .....112 G 5
Coolagarry .....106 H 7
Coolaney .....112 G 5
Coolattin .....97 M 9
Coolbaun .....101 K 9
Coolbawn .....100 H 9
Coolboy .....97 M 9
Coolcull .....96 L 11
Coolderry .....101 I 8
Coole (Castle) .....113 J 4
Coole Abbey .....90 H 11
Coolea / Cúil Aodha .....89 E 12
Coolearagh .....102 L 8
Cooley Point .....109 N 6
Coolgrange .....96 K 10
Coolgreany .....97 N 9
Coolkeeragh .....117 K 2
Coolkellure .....89 E 12
Coolmeen .....93 E 10
Coolmore .....112 H 4
Coolnareen .....101 J 9
Coolrain .....101 J 9
Coolroebeg .....96 K 10
Coolshaghtena .....107 H 6
Coolteige .....106 H 6
Coomacarrea .....88 B 12
Coomakesta Pass .....88 B 12
Coomasaharn Lake .....88 C 12
Coomhola .....89 D 12
Coomhola Bridge .....89 D 12
Coonagh .....94 F 10
Cooraclare .....98 D 9
Coorleagh .....96 K 9
Coornagillagh .....89 C 12
Cootehall .....106 H 6
Copany .....113 H 4
Copeland Island .....115 P 3
Coppanagh .....108 L 6
Cora Droma Rúisc /
  Carrick-on-Shannon ...107 H 6
Corbally
  Castleconor West .....111 E 5
Corbally *Clare* .....98 D 9
Corbally *Kildare* .....102 L 8
Corbay Upper .....107 I 6
Corbet Milltown .....115 N 4
Corcaigh / Cork .....90 G 12
Corclogh .....110 B 5
Corcomroe Abbey .....99 E 8

Cordal .....93 D 11
Cordarragh .....105 D 6
Corduff .....109 N 7
Cork Harbour .....90 H 12
Corkey .....119 N 2
Corkscrew Hill .....99 E 8
Corlea .....107 I 7
Corlee .....105 E 5
Corlis Point .....93 D 10
Corn Hill .....107 I 6
Cornafulla .....101 H 7
Cornagillagh .....117 I 3
Cornamona .....105 D 7
Cornanagh .....105 E 6
Corracloona .....113 H 4
Corrakyle .....99 G 9
Corraleehan .....113 I 5
Corran Cross Roads .....114 M 5
Corrandulla .....105 F 7
Corranny .....113 K 5
Corraree .....106 H 7
Corraun Peninsula .....104 C 6
Corraun Point .....110 B 5
Corrawaleen .....107 I 5
Correllstown .....107 K 7
Corrib (Lough) .....105 E 7
Corries .....96 L 11
Corriga .....107 I 6
Corrigeenroe .....106 H 5
Corrofin .....99 E 9
Corronoher .....94 F 10
Corroy .....111 E 5
Corry .....112 H 5
Corstown .....95 J 10
Cortowm .....108 L 6
Corvally .....108 L 6
Corvoley .....111 D 5
Cottoners .....89 C 11
Coulagh Bay .....88 B 12
Coumfea .....95 J 11
Courtmacsherry .....90 F 13
Courtmacsherry Bay .....90 G 13
Courtown .....97 N 10
Cousane Gap .....89 E 12
Craanford .....97 M 9
Craffield .....103 M 9
Crag Cave .....93 D 11
Craggaunowen
  Megalithic Centre .....99 F 9
Craig .....118 K 3
Craigantlet .....115 O 4
Craigavad .....115 O 4
Craigavon .....114 M 4
Craignamaddy .....114 K 3
Craigs .....118 M 3
Crana .....117 J 2
Cranagh .....114 K 3
Cranfield Point .....109 N 5
Cranford .....117 I 2
Crannogeboy .....116 G 3
Cranny .....99 E 9
Cratloe .....99 F 9
Craughwell .....99 F 8
Crawfordsburn .....115 O 4
Crazy Corner .....107 K 7
Creagh .....113 J 4
Creagh (The) .....114 M 3
Creaghanroe .....114 L 5
Crean's Cross Roads .....90 F 12
Crecora .....94 F 10
Creegh .....98 D 9
Creeslough .....117 I 2
Creevagh .....111 D 5
Creevagh Head .....111 E 5
Creeves .....93 E 10
Creevykeel .....112 G 4
Cregg *Clare* .....99 E 8
Cregg *Cork* .....89 E 13
Cregg *Galway* .....105 E 7
Cregg *Sligo* .....112 G 5
Creggan *Armagh* .....108 M 5
Creggan *Dungannon* .....114 K 4
Cregganbaun .....104 C 6
Creggaun .....94 F 10
Creggs .....106 G 7
Crilly .....114 L 4
Crindle .....118 L 2
Crinkill .....101 I 8
Croagh *Donegal* .....112 G 3
Croagh *Limerick* .....94 F 10
Croagh Patrick .....105 C 6
Croaghaun .....110 B 6
Croaghmoyle .....105 D 6
Croaghnageer .....113 I 3
Croaghnakeela Island .....104 C 8
Croaghrimbeg .....105 D 6

A
B
C
D
E
F
G
H
I
J
K
L
M
N
O
P
Q
R
S
T
U
V
W
X
Y
Z

Croan (Lough) ...... 106 H 7
Croangar (Lough) ...... 116 H 3
Crockaneel ...... 119 N 2
Crockets Town ...... 111 E 5
Crockmore ...... 113 I 4
Crocknasmug ...... 118 L 2
Croghan *Offaly* ...... 101 K 7
Croghan *Roscommon* ...... 106 H 6
Croghan Mountain ...... 103 N 9
Crohane ...... 89 D 12
Crohy Head ...... 116 G 3
Crois Mhaoiliona /
  Crossmolina ...... 111 E 5
Croithlí / Crolly ...... 116 H 2
Cromane ...... 92 C 11
Cromoge ...... 101 J 9
Croob (Slieve) ...... 115 N 4
Crookedwood ...... 107 K 7
Crookhaven ...... 88 C 13
Crookstown *Kildare* ...... 102 L 8
Crookstown *Moviddy* ...... 90 F 12
Croom ...... 94 F 10
Croos ...... 106 H 7
Cross *Cong* ...... 105 E 7
Cross *Waterford* ...... 91 I 11
Cross (River) ...... 105 D 7
Cross Barry ...... 90 G 12
Cross Keys *Cavan* ...... 107 K 6
Cross Keys *Meath* ...... 108 K 6
Cross Keys *Meath* ...... 108 M 7
Cross Roads ...... 117 I 3
Crossabeg ...... 97 M 10
Crossakeel ...... 108 K 6
Crossboyne ...... 105 E 6
Crossconnell ...... 100 H 8
Crossdoney ...... 107 J 6
Crossea ...... 107 J 7
Crosserlough ...... 107 K 6
Crossgar ...... 115 O 4
Crossgare ...... 118 L 2
Crosshaven ...... 90 H 12
Crossmaglen ...... 108 M 5
Crossna ...... 106 H 5
Crossooha ...... 99 F 8
Crosspatrick *Kilkenny* ...... 101 J 9
Crosspatrick *Wicklow* ...... 97 M 9
Crosswell ...... 106 G 7
Crove ...... 112 G 3
Crow Head ...... 88 B 13
Crownarad ...... 112 G 4
Cruit Island ...... 116 G 2
Crumlin *Antrim* ...... 115 N 4
Crumlin *Cong* ...... 105 D 7
Crusheen ...... 99 F 9
Crutt ...... 101 K 9
Cúil an tSúdaire /
  Portarlington ...... 101 K 8
Cuilcagh ...... 113 I 5
Cuilkillew ...... 111 E 5
Cuilmore ...... 105 F 6
Culdaff ...... 118 K 2
Culdaff Bay ...... 118 K 2
Culfadda ...... 106 G 5
Culfin ...... 104 C 7
Culky ...... 113 J 5
Cullahill ...... 101 J 9
Cullane ...... 94 G 10
Cullaun ...... 94 H 10
Cullaville ...... 108 M 5
Culleens ...... 111 F 5
Cullen *Cork* ...... 94 H 10
Cullen *Tipperary* ...... 93 E 11
Cullenagh (River) ...... 99 E 9
Cullenstown
  near Duncormick ...... 96 L 11
Cullenstown
  near Newbawn ...... 96 L 10
Cullin ...... 105 E 6
Cullin (Lough) ...... 105 E 6
Cullybackey ...... 118 M 3
Cullyhanna ...... 108 M 5
Culmore ...... 117 K 2
Culnady ...... 118 M 3
Cummeragh ...... 88 B 12
Cunningburn ...... 115 P 4
Curlew Mountains ...... 106 G 6
Curracloe ...... 97 M 10
Curragh ...... 91 I 12
Curragh (The) ...... 102 L 8
Curragh Camp ...... 102 L 8
Curragh West ...... 106 G 7
Curragha ...... 109 M 7
Curraghbonaun ...... 106 H 7
Curraghboy ...... 106 H 7
Curraghmore Gardens ...... 95 J 11
Curraghroe ...... 107 H 6
Curraglass ...... 91 H 11

Currahchase Forest Park ...... 94 F 10
Curran ...... 114 M 3
Currane (Lough) ...... 88 B 12
Currans ...... 93 D 11
Curraun ...... 105 D 7
Curreel (Lough) ...... 104 C 7
Curreeny ...... 100 H 9
Currow ...... 93 D 11
Curry ...... 105 E 6
Curryglass ...... 88 C 12
Curryskeskin ...... 118 M 2
Cushendall ...... 119 N 2
Cushendun ...... 119 N 2
Cusher ...... 114 M 5
Cushina ...... 101 K 8
Cut (The) ...... 101 J 8
Cutra (Lough) ...... 99 F 8

D

Dahybaun (Lough) ...... 111 D 5
Daingean ...... 101 K 8
Dalgan ...... 105 F 7
Dalkey ...... 103 N 8
Damastown ...... 109 N 7
Damerstown ...... 101 K 9
Damhead ...... 118 M 2
Dan (Lough) ...... 103 N 8
Danesfort *Kilkenny* ...... 96 K 10
Danesfort *Longford* ...... 107 I 6
Dangan *Cork* ...... 91 H 12
Dangan *Waterford* ...... 96 K 11
Darby's Gap ...... 97 M 10
Dargle ...... 103 N 8
Dark Hedges (The) ...... 118 M 2
Darkley ...... 114 L 5
Darragh ...... 99 E 9
Dartry Mountains ...... 112 G 4
Davagh Forest Park ...... 114 L 3
Davidstown ...... 103 M 9
Dawros ...... 104 C 7
Dawros Head ...... 116 G 3
Dead ...... 94 H 10
Dealagh ...... 98 D 9
Dee ...... 108 L 6
Deel *Limerick* ...... 94 F 10
Deel *Mayo* ...... 111 D 5
Deel *Westmeath* ...... 108 K 7
Deel Bridge ...... 111 D 5
Deele (River) ...... 117 I 3
Deelish ...... 89 E 12
Deenish Island ...... 88 B 12
Delamont ...... 115 O 4
Delgany ...... 103 N 8
Delphi ...... 104 C 7
Delvin (River) ...... 109 N 7
Dennet (Burn) ...... 117 J 3
Derg (Lough) ...... 113 J 3
Derg (Lough)
  near Donegal ...... 113 I 4
Derg (Lough)
  near Nenagh ...... 100 H 9
Dergalt ...... 117 J 3
Dernagree ...... 93 E 11
Derravaragh (Lough) ...... 107 J 7
Derreen
  near Ballynagoraher ...... 105 D 6
Derreen near Cloghmore ...... 104 C 6
Derreen near Formoyle ...... 99 E 8
Derreen near Lahinch ...... 98 D 9
Derreen Gardens ...... 89 C 12
Derreendarragh ...... 89 C 12
Derreeny ...... 88 C 12
Derreeny Bridge ...... 89 E 13
Derriana Lough ...... 88 C 12
Derries ...... 101 J 8
Derry ...... 112 G 5
Derryadd ...... 114 M 4
Derryanvil ...... 114 M 4
Derrybeg ...... 116 H 2
Derryboye ...... 115 O 4
Derrybrien ...... 99 G 8
Derryclare Lough ...... 104 C 7
Derrycooly ...... 101 I 8
Derrycraff ...... 105 D 6
Derrydruel ...... 116 G 3
Derryerglinna ...... 105 D 7
Derryfadda ...... 101 J 9
Derrygolan ...... 101 J 8
Derrygonnelly ...... 113 I 4
Derrygoolin ...... 100 G 9
Derrygrogan ...... 101 J 8
Derrykeevan ...... 114 M 4
Derrykeighan ...... 118 M 2
Derrylea ...... 104 C 7
Derrylin ...... 113 J 5
Derrylough ...... 116 G 3

Derrymore ...... 93 C 11
Derrymore Island ...... 93 C 11
Derrynane ...... 88 B 12
Derrynane House ...... 88 B 12
Derrynasaggart Mountains ...... 89 E 11
Derrynawilt ...... 113 K 5
Derryneen ...... 104 C 7
Derrynoose ...... 114 L 5
Derryrush ...... 104 C 7
Derrytrasna ...... 114 M 4
Derryveagh Mountains ...... 117 H 3
Derryvohy ...... 105 E 6
Derrywode ...... 106 G 6
Dervock ...... 118 M 2
Desertmartin ...... 114 L 3
Devenish Island ...... 113 J 4
Devilsbit ...... 101 I 9
Devilsmother ...... 105 D 7
Diamond (The) *Antrim* ...... 114 N 4
Diamond (The)
  Cookstown ...... 114 M 4
Diamond (The) *Omagh* ...... 113 J 4
Dingle / Daingean Uí Chúis ...... 92 B 11
Dingle Bay ...... 92 B 11
Dingle Harbour ...... 92 B 11
Divis ...... 115 N 4
Doagh *Newtownabbey* ...... 115 N 3
Doagh *Rosguill* ...... 117 I 2
Doagh Beg /
  Dumhaigh Bhig ...... 117 J 2
Doagh Isle ...... 117 J 2
Dodder ...... 103 M 8
Doe Castle ...... 117 I 2
Dolla ...... 100 H 9
Dollingstown ...... 114 N 4
Domhnach Phádraig /
  Donaghpatrick ...... 108 L 6
Donabate ...... 109 N 7
Donacarney ...... 109 N 6
Donadea ...... 102 L 7
Donagh ...... 113 J 5
Donaghadee ...... 115 P 4
Donaghaguy ...... 109 N 5
Donaghcloney ...... 114 N 4
Donaghey ...... 114 L 4
Donaghmore ...... 114 L 4
Donaghmore *Meath* ...... 109 M 7
Donard *Wexford* ...... 96 L 10
Donard *Wicklow* ...... 103 M 8
Donard (Slieve) ...... 115 O 5
Donaskeagh ...... 95 I 10
Donegal / Dún na nGall ...... 113 H 4
Donegal Airport ...... 116 G 2
Donegal Bay ...... 112 G 5
Donegal Point ...... 98 D 9
Doneraile ...... 94 G 11
Donohill ...... 95 H 10
Donore ...... 109 M 6
Donoughmore ...... 90 F 12
Doo (Lough) ...... 99 E 9
Doo Lough ...... 104 C 7
Doo Lough Pass ...... 104 C 7
Dooagh ...... 110 B 6
Doobehy ...... 111 D 5
Doocastle ...... 106 G 5
Dooega Head ...... 104 B 6
Dooey Point ...... 116 G 3
Doogary ...... 107 J 5
Dooghbeg ...... 104 C 6
Dooghort ...... 110 B 5
Doohooma ...... 110 C 5
Dooish Mount ...... 117 J 3
Doolough Point ...... 110 C 5
Doon *Galway* ...... 100 G 7
Doon *Limerick* ...... 94 H 10
Doon Lough ...... 99 F 9
Doona ...... 110 C 5
Doonaha ...... 93 D 10
Doonbeg ...... 98 D 9
Doonloughan ...... 104 B 7
Doonmanagh ...... 92 B 11
Doorin Point ...... 112 H 4
Dooyork ...... 110 C 5
Dore ...... 116 H 2
Dorrusawillin ...... 107 H 5
Dough ...... 88 C 13
Douglas ...... 90 G 12
Douglas Bridge ...... 113 J 3
Doulus Bay ...... 88 A 12
Doulus Head ...... 88 A 12
Dowdallshill ...... 109 M 5
Dowling ...... 96 K 10
Downhill ...... 118 L 2
Downpatrick ...... 115 O 5
Downpatrick Head ...... 111 D 5
Downs (The) ...... 107 K 7
Dowra ...... 113 H 5

Dowth ...... 109 M 6
Drains Bay ...... 119 O 3
Drangan ...... 95 J 10
Draperstown ...... 114 L 3
Dreen ...... 118 K 3
Dreenagh ...... 92 C 10
Drimoleague ...... 89 E 12
Drinagh *Cork* ...... 89 E 13
Drinagh *Wexford* ...... 97 M 11
Drinaghan ...... 111 E 5
Dring ...... 107 J 6
Dripsey ...... 90 F 12
Dripsey (River) ...... 90 F 11
Drishaghaun ...... 105 D 7
Drishane Bridge ...... 89 D 13
Droichead Átha /
  Drogheda ...... 109 M 6
Droichead na Bandan /
  Bandon ...... 90 F 12
Drom ...... 101 I 9
Dromahair ...... 112 H 5
Dromara ...... 115 N 4
Dromcolliher ...... 94 F 10
Dromin *Limerick* ...... 94 G 10
Dromin *Louth* ...... 109 M 6
Dromina ...... 94 F 11
Dromineer ...... 100 H 9
Dromiskin ...... 109 M 6
Dromkeen ...... 94 G 10
Drommahane ...... 90 F 11
Dromod ...... 107 I 6
Dromoland Castle ...... 99 F 9
Dromore *Banbridge* ...... 115 N 4
Dromore *Omagh* ...... 113 J 4
Dromore Lake ...... 94 F 10
Dromore West ...... 112 F 5
Dromtrasna ...... 93 E 10
Drones (The) ...... 118 M 2
Drowes ...... 112 H 4
Drum *Monaghan* ...... 108 K 5
Drum *Roscommon* ...... 101 H 7
Drum *Sligo* ...... 112 G 5
Drum Hills ...... 91 I 11
Drum Manor
  Forest Park ...... 114 L 4
Drumahoe ...... 117 K 3
Drumandoora ...... 99 F 8
Drumaness ...... 115 O 4
Drumanoo Head ...... 112 G 4
Drumatober ...... 100 G 8
Drumbane ...... 95 I 10
Drumbeg *Feddyglass* ...... 117 J 3
Drumbeg *Lisburn* ...... 115 O 4
Drumbo ...... 115 O 4
Drumbologe ...... 117 I 3
Drumcar ...... 109 M 6
Drumcard ...... 113 I 5
Drumcliff ...... 112 G 5
Drumcliff Bay ...... 112 G 5
Drumcondra ...... 108 M 6
Drumcong ...... 107 I 5
Drumcree ...... 108 K 7
Drumcullen ...... 114 M 3
Drumduff ...... 113 J 4
Drumena Cashel ...... 115 O 5
Drumfea ...... 96 L 10
Drumfin ...... 112 G 5
Drumfree ...... 117 J 2
Drumgoft ...... 103 M 9
Druminte ...... 109 M 5
Drumkeary ...... 99 G 8
Drumkeen ...... 117 I 3
Drumkeeran ...... 112 H 5
Drumlaheen Lough ...... 107 I 5
Drumlea ...... 107 I 5
Drumlegagh ...... 113 J 4
Drumlish ...... 107 I 6
Drumlosh ...... 101 I 7
Drummannon ...... 114 M 4
Drummin ...... 96 L 10
Drummullin ...... 106 H 6
Drumnakilly ...... 114 K 4
Drumone ...... 108 K 6
Drumquin ...... 113 J 4
Drumraney ...... 107 I 7
Drumreagh ...... 110 B 5
Drumshanbo ...... 107 H 5
Drumsna ...... 107 H 6
Drumsurn ...... 118 L 3
Duagh ...... 93 D 10
Dually ...... 95 I 10
Dublin Bay ...... 103 N 7
Duff ...... 112 H 4
Duffy ...... 102 L 7
Duleek ...... 109 M 7
Dumha Éige / Dooega ...... 104 B 6
Dún Aengus ...... 98 C 8

Dún A'Rí Forest Park ...... 108 L 6
Dún Chaoin / Dunquin ...... 92 A 11
Dún Dealgan / Dundalk ...... 109 M 5
Dún Garbhán /Dungarvan ...... 91 J 11
Dun Laoghaire ...... 103 N 8
Dún Mánmhaí /
  Dunmanway ...... 89 E 12
Dún Mór / Dunmore ...... 106 F 7
Dún na nGall / Donegal ...... 113 H 4
Dunabrattin Head ...... 91 K 11
Dunadry ...... 115 N 3
Dunaff ...... 117 J 2
Dunaff Head ...... 117 J 2
Dunaghy ...... 118 M 2
Dunagree Point ...... 118 L 2
Dunamase (Rock of) ...... 101 K 8
Dunamon ...... 106 H 7
Dunany ...... 109 N 6
Dunany Point ...... 109 N 6
Dunbel ...... 96 K 10
Dunboyne ...... 103 M 7
Dunbrody Abbey ...... 96 L 11
Dunbulcaun Bay ...... 99 F 8
Duncannon ...... 96 L 11
Duncormick ...... 96 M 11
Dundalk Bay ...... 109 N 6
Dunderrow ...... 90 G 12
Dunderry ...... 108 L 7
Dundonald ...... 115 O 4
Dundrod ...... 115 N 4
Dundrum *Down* ...... 115 O 5
Dundrum *Dublin* ...... 103 N 8
Dundrum *Tipperary* ...... 95 H 10
Dundrum Bay ...... 115 O 5
Dunfanaghy ...... 117 I 2
Dungannon ...... 114 L 4
Dunganstown ...... 96 L 10
Dungarvan Harbour ...... 91 J 11
Dungiven ...... 118 L 3
Dungloe /
  An Clochán Liath ...... 116 G 3
Dungonnell Dam ...... 119 N 3
Dungourney ...... 90 H 12
Dunguaire Castle ...... 99 F 8
Dunhill ...... 91 K 11
Duniry ...... 100 G 8
Dunkellin ...... 99 F 8
Dunkerrin ...... 101 I 9
Dunkineely ...... 112 G 4
Dunkitt ...... 96 K 11
Dunlavin ...... 102 L 8
Dunleer ...... 109 M 6
Dunlewy ...... 117 H 2
Dunloe (Gap of) ...... 89 D 11
Dunloy ...... 118 M 2
Dunluce Castle ...... 118 M 2
Dunmanus ...... 89 D 13
Dunmanus Bay ...... 88 C 13
Dunmore ...... 109 O 5
Dunmore Cave ...... 96 K 9
Dunmore East ...... 96 L 11
Dunmore Head *Dunquin* ...... 92 A 11
Dunmore Head
  near Culdaff ...... 118 K 2
Dunmore Head
  near Portnoo ...... 116 G 3
Dunmurry ...... 115 N 4
Dunnamaggan ...... 96 K 10
Dunnamanagh ...... 117 K 3
Dunnamore ...... 114 L 3
Dunnycove Bay ...... 89 F 13
Dunowen Head ...... 89 F 13
Dunree Head ...... 117 J 2
Dunsany ...... 108 M 7
Dunshaughlin ...... 108 M 7
Dunworly Bay ...... 90 F 13
Durlas / Thurles ...... 95 I 9
Durrow ...... 101 J 9
Durrus ...... 89 D 13
Dursey Head ...... 88 B 13
Dursey Island ...... 88 B 13
Duvillaun Beg ...... 110 B 5
Duvillaun More ...... 110 B 5
Dyan ...... 114 L 4
Dysart ...... 107 J 7
Dysart O'Dea ...... 99 E 9

E

Éadan Doire / Édenderry ...... 102 K 7
Eagle (Mount) ...... 92 A 11
Eagle Island ...... 110 B 5
Eagles Hill ...... 88 B 12
Eany ...... 112 H 3
Eanymore ...... 112 H 3
Easky ...... 111 F 5
Easky Lough ...... 112 F 5
East Ferry ...... 90 H 12

East Town ...... 116 H 2
Eddy Island ...... 99 F 8
Eden ...... 115 O 3
Ederny ...... 113 J 4
Edgeworthstown ...... 107 J 6
Edgeworthstown /
  Meathas Troim ...... 107 J 6
Egish (Lough) ...... 108 L 5
Eglinton ...... 118 K 2
Eglish ...... 114 L 4
Eighter ...... 108 K 6
Eleven Lane Ends ...... 114 M 5
Ellistrin ...... 117 I 3
Elly Bay ...... 110 B 5
Elphin ...... 106 H 6
Elton ...... 94 G 10
Elva (Slieve) ...... 99 E 8
Emlagh Point ...... 104 C 6
Emly ...... 94 G 10
Emmoo ...... 106 H 7
Emo ...... 101 K 8
Emo Court ...... 101 K 8
Emyvale ...... 114 L 4
Ennel (Lough) ...... 107 J 7
Ennis / Inis ...... 99 F 9
Enniscorthy /
  Inis Córthaidh ...... 97 M 10
Enniskean ...... 89 F 12
Enniskerry ...... 103 N 8
Enniskillen ...... 113 J 4
Ennistimon / Inis Díomáin ...... 99 E 9
Eochaill / Youghal ...... 91 I 12
Erne (Lower Lough) ...... 113 I 4
Erne (River) ...... 107 J 6
Erne (Upper Lough) ...... 113 J 5
Erra ...... 107 I 6
Errew Abbey ...... 111 E 5
Erriff (River) ...... 105 D 7
Errigal Mountain ...... 117 H 2
Erril ...... 101 I 9
Erris Head ...... 110 B 5
Errisbeg ...... 104 C 7
Errislannan ...... 104 B 7
Errit Lough ...... 106 F 6
Ervey Cross Roads ...... 118 K 3
Eshnadarragh ...... 113 K 5
Eshnadeelada ...... 113 K 5
Eske ...... 113 H 3
Eske (Lough) ...... 113 H 3
Esker ...... 99 F 8
Esker South ...... 107 I 6
Eskeragh ...... 111 D 5
Eskragh ...... 113 K 4
Eyeries ...... 88 C 12
Eyrecourt ...... 100 H 8

F

Faha ...... 91 J 11
Fahamore ...... 92 B 11
Fahan ...... 117 J 2
Fahy ...... 100 H 8
Fahy Lough ...... 110 C 5
Fair Green ...... 99 F 9
Fair Head ...... 88 C 13
Fairyhouse ...... 108 M 7
Fairymount ...... 106 G 6
Fallmore ...... 110 B 5
Fanad ...... 117 I 2
Fanad Head ...... 117 J 2
Fane River ...... 108 M 5
Fanore ...... 99 E 8
Farahy ...... 94 G 11
Fardrum ...... 101 I 7
Fardurris Point ...... 98 D 8
Farmer's Bridge ...... 93 D 11
Farnagh ...... 101 I 7
Farnaght ...... 107 I 6
Farnanes Cross Roads ...... 90 F 12
Farnoge ...... 96 K 10
Farran ...... 90 F 12
Farran Forest Park ...... 90 F 12
Farrancassidy
  Cross Roads ...... 112 H 4
Farranfore ...... 93 D 11
Fastnet Rock ...... 89 D 13
Faughan ...... 118 K 3
Fawney ...... 117 K 3
Fea (Lough) ...... 114 L 3
Feagarrid ...... 95 I 11
Feakle ...... 99 G 9
Feale (River) ...... 93 D 10
Fearn Hill ...... 113 J 3
Fedamore ...... 94 G 10
Fee (Lough) ...... 104 C 7
Feeagh (Lough) ...... 105 D 6
Feeard ...... 93 C 10
Feenagh ...... 94 F 10

A B C D E F G H I J K L M N O P Q R S T U V W X Y Z

Feeny 118 K3
Feevagh 106 H7
Fenagh 107 I5
Fenit 92 C11
Fennagh 96 L9
Fennor 91 K11
Feohanagh *Kerry* 92 A11
Feohanagh *Limerick* ..94 F10
Feohanagh (River) ..92 B11
Ferbane 101 I8
Fergus (River) 99 E9
Fern (Lough) 117 I2
Ferns 97 M10
Ferry Bridge 94 F10
Ferrybank 97 N9
Ferrycarrig 97 M10
Ferta 88 B12
Fethard 96 L11
Fews 95 J11
Feystown 119 O3
Fiddown 96 K10
Fieries 93 D11
Finavarra 99 E8
Finglas 93 N7
Finglass 89 C11
Finn (Lough) 117 H3
Finn (River) 117 J3
Finnea 107 J6
Finnisglin 104 C7
Fintona 113 K4
Fintragh Bay 112 G4
Finuge 93 D10
Finvoy 118 M2
Fiodh Ard / Fethard ..95 I10
Fionnaithe / Finny ..105 D7
Firkeel 88 B13
Fisherhill 105 E6
Five Corners 115 N3
Fivealley 101 I8
Fivemilebridge 90 G12
Fivemiletown 113 K4
Flagmount *Corlea* ..99 G9
Flagmount *Kilkenny* ..96 K10
Flat Head 90 G12
Flesk 89 D11
Florence Court 113 I5
Florence Court
   Forest Park 113 I5
Foaty Island/Fota Island ..90 H12
Foilycleara 95 H10
Folk Park 99 F9
Fontstown 102 L8
Forbes (Lough) ...107 I6
Fordstown 108 L6
Fore 107 K6
Forkill 109 M5
Forlorn Point 96 M11
Formoyle *Lonford* ..107 I7
Formoyle *Mayo* ..104 C6
Formoyle
   near Ballivaghan ..99 E8
Formoyle *near Inagh* ..99 E9
Formoyle (Lough) ..105 D7
Fort Stewart 117 J2
Forthill 107 I7
Fota Island 90 H12
Foul Sound 98 D8
Foulksmills 96 L11
Fountain Cross ...99 E9
Four Mile House ..106 H6
Four Roads 106 H7
Fourknocks 109 N7
Foxford 105 E6
Foxhall 105 E7
Foyle (Lough) 118 K2
Foynes 93 E10
Foynes Island 93 E10
Francis' Gap 99 G8
Freemount 94 F11
Frenchpark 106 G6
Freshford 95 J9
Freynestown 102 L8
Frosses 112 H3
Frower Point 90 G12
Fuerty 106 H7
Funshin More 99 F8
Funshinagh (Lough) ..106 H7
Funshion 94 G11
Furbogh 99 E8
Furnace 105 D7
Furnace Lough ...105 D6
Furness 103 M8
Fyagh (Slieve) 111 D5

G

Gabriel (Mount) 89 D13
Gaddagh 89 C11

Gaillimh / Galway 99 E8
Gainestown 107 K7
Galbally *Dungannon* ..114 L4
Galbally *Limerick* ..94 H10
Galbally *Wexford* ..96 M10
Galbolie 108 K6
Galey 93 D10
Galgorm 118 N3
Gallarus Oratory ..92 A11
Galley Head 89 F13
Gallion (Slieve) ...114 L3
Galmoy 101 J9
Galty Mountains ..95 H10
Galtymore Mountain ..95 H10
Galway Bay 98 D8
Galways Bridge ...89 D12
Gaoth Dobhair /
   Gweedore 116 H2
Gaoth Sáile / Geesala ..110 C5
Gap (The) 95 I11
Gara (Lough) 106 G6
Garadice 102 L7
Garadice Lough ...107 I5
Garbally 100 H8
Garinish Island 88 C12
Garnavilla 95 I10
Garnish Point 88 B13
Garrane 89 E12
Garranlahan 106 G6
Garraun *Clare* 98 D9
Garraun *Galway* ..100 G8
Garraun (Mount) ..104 C7
Garries Bridge 89 D12
Garrison 112 H4
Garristown 109 M7
Garron Point 119 O2
Garrycloonagh 111 E5
Garrycullen 96 L11
Garryduff 118 M2
Garryfine 94 F10
Garrykennedy 100 G9
Garryspillane 94 G10
Garryvoe 91 H12
Gartan Lough 117 I3
Gartree Point 114 N4
Garty Lough 107 J6
Garvagh *Coleraine* ..118 L3
Garvagh *Rowan* ..107 I6
Garvaghy 114 K4
Garvary 113 J4
Gattabaun 101 J9
Gearagh (The) 90 F12
Gearha Bridge 88 C12
Geashill 101 K8
Geevagh 112 H5
George (Lough) ...99 F9
Gerahies 89 D13
Giant's Causeway ..118 M2
Giles Quay 109 N6
Gilford 114 M4
Gill (Lough) *near Sligo* ..112 G5
Gill (Lough) *nearTralee* ..92 B11
Glanaruddery Mountains ..93 D11
Glandore 89 E13
Glandore Harbour ..89 E13
Glangevlin 113 I5
Glanmire 90 G12
Glanmore Lake 89 C12
Glanoe 93 D10
Glantane 90 F11
Glanworth 94 G11
Glarryford 118 M3
Glasdrumman 109 O5
Glaslough 114 L5
Glasmullan 117 J2
Glassan 107 I7
Glasshouse Lake ..107 J5
Glassillaun 104 C6
Glastry 115 P4
Gleann Cholm Cille /
   Glencolumbkille ..112 F3
Gleann Domhain /
   Glendowan 117 I3
Gleann na Muaidhe /
   Glenamoy 111 C5
Glen 117 I2
Glen (River) *Cork* ..90 F11
Glen (River) *Donegal* ..112 G3
Glen Bay 112 F3
Glen Head 112 F3
Glen Lough *Donegal* ..117 I2
Glen Lough *Westmeath* 107 J7
Glenaan 119 N2
Glenade 112 H4
Glenade Lough ...112 H4
Glenamoy (River) ..111 D5
Glenariff 119 N2
Gortin Glen Forest Park ..113 K3

Glenariff Forest Park 119 N2
Glenariff or Waterfoot ..119 N2
Glenarm 119 O3
Glenavy 115 N4
Glenballyemon 119 N2
Glenbeg Lough 88 C12
Glenbeigh 92 C11
Glenboy 112 H5
Glenbridge Lodge ..103 M8
Glenbrohane 94 G10
Glenbrook 90 G12
Glencar 88 C12
Glencar Lough 112 G4
Glencloy 119 O3
Glencolmcille Folk Village ..112 F3
Glencree 103 N8
Glencullen 103 N8
Glendalough *Brockagh* 103 M8
Glendalough *Waterford* ..95 J11
Glenderry 92 C10
Glendorragha 116 G3
Glendovan Mountains ..117 H3
Glendree 99 F9
Glendum 119 N2
Glenealy 103 N9
Gleneely *near Ballybofey* ..113 I3
Gleneely *near Cardonagh* ..118 K2
Glenelly 114 K3
Glenelly Valley 114 K3
Glenfarne 113 I5
Glenflesk 89 D11
Glengad Head 118 K1
Glengarriff (River) ..89 D12
Glengarriff Harbour ..89 D12
Glengesh Pass 112 G3
Glengormley 115 O3
Glenhead 118 K2
Glenhull 114 K3
Glenicmurrin Lough ..98 D8
Glenmacnass 103 M8
Glenmalur 103 M9
Glenmore *Clare* ..99 E9
Glenmore *Kilkenny* ..96 K10
Glennagevlagh 105 D7
Glennamaddy 106 G7
Glennascaul 99 F8
Glenoe 115 O3
Glenshane Pass ..118 L3
Glenshesk 119 N2
Glentaisie 119 N2
Glentane 106 G7
Glenties 116 H3
Glentogher 118 K2
Glentrasna 105 D7
Glenvale 118 M3
Glenvar / Gleann Bhairr ..117 J2
Glenveagh National Park ..117 I2
Glenville 90 G11
Glin 93 E10
Glin Castle 93 E10
Glinsce / Glinsk 104 C7
Glinsk *Donegal* ..117 I2
Glinsk *Mayo* 111 D5
Glounthaune 90 G12
Glyde (River) 108 M6
Glynn *Carlow* 96 L10
Glynn *Larne* 115 O3
Gneevgullia 93 E11
Gob an Choire /
   Achill Sound 104 C6
Gobbins (The) 115 O3
Gokane Point 89 E13
Gola Island / Gabhla ..116 G2
Golagh Lough 113 H4
Golam Head 98 C8
Golden 95 I10
Golden Vale 95 H10
Goleen 88 C13
Goold's Cross 95 I10
Goresbridge 96 K10
Gorey / Guaire 97 N9
Gormanston 109 N7
Gort an Choirce /
   Gortahork 117 H2
Gortaclare 113 K4
Gortahill 113 I5
Gortaleam 106 F7
Gortarevan 100 H8
Gortaroo 91 I12
Gortaway 117 J2
Gorteen 106 G6
Gorteen Bridge 101 J8
Gorteeny 100 G8
Gortgarriff 88 C12
Gortgarrigan 112 H5
Gortin 113 K3

Gortletteragh 107 I6
Gortmore *near Ballycastle* ..111 D5
Gortmore *near Bangor* ..111 C5
Gortmullan 113 J5
Gortnadeeve 106 G7
Gortnahoo 95 J9
Gortnasillagh 106 G6
Gortree 117 J3
Gortymadden 100 G8
Gorumna Island ...98 C8
Gosford Forest Park ..114 M5
Gougane Barra
   Forest Park 89 D12
Gougane Barra Lake ..89 E12
Gouladoo 89 C13
Gowla 104 C7
Gowlaun 104 C7
Gowlin 96 L10
Gowna (Lough) 107 J6
Gowran 96 K10
Gracehill 118 N3
Graffy 116 H3
Gráig na Manach /
   Graiguenamanagh ..96 L10
Graigue 102 L9
Graigue Hill 96 L9
Graigue More 96 M10
Graigues 88 B12
Granabeg 103 M8
Gránard / Granard ..107 J6
Grand Canal 101 I8
Graney 102 L9
Graney (Lough) 99 G9
Graney (River) 99 G9
Grange *Kildare* ..102 K7
Grange *Kilkenny* ..96 K10
Grange *Louth* 109 N5
Grange *Sligo* 112 G4
Grange *Waterford* ..91 I12
Grange (River) 106 F7
Grange Con 102 L9
Grangebellew 109 M6
Grangeford 102 L9
Grangegeeth 108 M6
Granias Gap 117 K2
Grannagh 99 F8
Gransha 115 O3
Granville 114 L4
Greagh 107 I6
Great Blasket Island ..92 A11
Great Island 90 H12
Great Newtown Head ..96 K11
Great Skellig 88 A12
Great Sugar Loaf ..103 N8
Greatman's Bay ...98 D8
Greenan 103 N9
Greenanstown 109 N7
Greencastle *Donegal* ..118 L2
Greencastle
   Newry-Mourne ..109 N5
Greencastle *Omagh* ..114 K3
Greenfield 105 E7
Greenisland 115 O3
Greenore 109 N5
Greenore Point 97 N11
Gregans Castle 99 E8
Gregory's Sound ..98 D8
Grenagh 90 G11
Grey Abbey 115 P4
Grey Point 115 O3
Greysteel 118 K2
Greystone 114 L4
Greystones 114 L4
Grianan of Aileach ..117 J2
Grogan 101 I8
Groomsport 115 P3
Gubaveeny 113 I5
Gubbaroe Point ...113 I4
Gulladoo Lough ...107 J6
Gulladuff 118 M3
Gullion (Slieve) ...109 M5
Gur (Lough) 94 G10
Gurteen *Cappalusk* ..99 G7
Gurteen *Leitrim* ..112 H5
Gusserane 96 L11
Gwebarra Bridge ..116 H3
Gweebarra 116 H3
Gweebarra Bay 116 G3
Gweestin 93 D11
Gweestion 105 E6
Gyleen 90 H12

H

Hacketstown 103 M8
Hags Head 98 D9
Hamiltonsbawn 114 M4
Hand Cross Roads (The) ..99 E9
Hannahstown 115 N4

Hare Island 89 D13
Harristown 96 K10
Harrow (The) 97 M10
Healy Pass 89 C12
Helen's Bay 115 O3
Helvick Head 91 J11
Herbertstown 94 G10
High Island 104 B7
Highwood 112 H5
Hill Street 107 H6
Hillsborough 115 N4
Hilltown *Harristown* ..96 L11
Hilltown
   Newry and Mourne ..115 N5
Hind 106 H7
Hog's Head 88 B12
Holeopen Bay West ..90 G13
Hollyford 95 H10
Hollyfort 97 M9
Hollymount 105 E7
Hollywood 103 M8
Holy Cross 95 I10
Holycross 94 G10
Holywell 113 I5
Holywell Hill 117 J2
Holywood 115 O4
Hook Head 96 L11
Hore Abbey 95 I10
Horn Head 117 I2
Horse and Jockey ..95 I10
Horse Island 89 D13
Horseleap 101 J7
Hospital 94 G10
Hugginstown 96 K10
Hungry Hill 88 C12
Hurlers Cross 99 F9
Hurley 109 M7
Hyne (Lough) 89 E13

I

Ilen 89 E13
Illaunstookagh 92 C11
Illauntannig 92 B11
Illies 117 J2
Illnacullin 89 D12
Inagh 99 E9
Inagh (Lough) 104 C7
Inch 92 C11
Inch *Donegal* 117 J2
Inch *near Whitegate* ..90 H12
Inch *near Youghal* ..91 I12
Inch *Tipperary* ...95 H9
Inch *Wexford* 97 N9
Inch Abbey 115 O4
Inch Island 117 J2
Inchagoill 105 E7
Inchamore Bridge ..108 L7
Inchbeg 96 J9
Inchcleraun 107 H7
Inchee Bridge 89 D12
Inchicronan Lough ..99 F9
Inchigeelagh 89 E12
Inchiquin 105 E7
Inchiquin Lough *Clare* ..99 E9
Inchiquin Lough *Kerry* ..89 D12
Inchmore 107 I7
Inchnamuck 95 H11
Inchydoney Island ..90 F13
Indreabhán / Inveran ..98 D8
Inis / Ennis 99 F9
Inis Bó Finne / Inishbofin ..117 H2
Inis Meáin / Inishmaan ..98 D8
Inis Mór / Inishmore ..98 D8
Inis Oírr / Inisheer ..98 D8
Inishannon 90 G12
Inisharbra 98 C8
Inishbiggle 110 C6
Inishbofin 104 B7
Inishcarra 90 G12
Inishcarra Reservoir ..90 F12
Inishcrone 111 E5
Inishdoorus 105 D7
Inishfarnard 88 B12
Inishfree Bay 116 G2
Inishfree Upper ...116 G3
Inishglora 110 B5
Inishkea North 110 B5
Inishkea South 110 B5
Inishmaine Island ..105 E7
Inishmicatreer 105 E7
Inishmurray 112 G4
Inishnabro 92 A11
Inishnee 104 C7
Inishowen 117 J2
Inishowen Head ...118 L2
Inishshark 104 B7

Inishtooskert 92 A11
Inishtrahull 118 K1
Inishtrahull Sound ..118 K1
Inishturk 104 B6
Inishvickillane 92 A11
Inistioge 96 K10
Innfield 102 L7
Innisfree 112 G5
Inniskeen 108 M5
Inny (River) 107 J6
Inver *Donegal* ...112 H4
Inver *Mayo* 110 C5
Inver Bay 112 H4
Ireland's Eye 103 N7
Irish Agricultural
   Museum 97 M11
Irishtown 105 F7
Iron (Lough) 107 J7
Iron Mountains ...113 I5
Irvinestown 113 J4
Island Lake 106 F6
Island Reavy (Lough) ..115 N5
Islandmagee 115 O3
Islandmore 115 P4
Iveragh 88 B12

J

J. F. Kennedy Park ..96 L11
Jamestown *Cloonteem* ..107 H6
Jamestown *Laois* ..101 K8
Japanese Gardens ..102 L8
Jerpoint Abbey ...96 K10
Jerrettspass 114 M5
Johnstown *Kildare* ..103 M8
Johnstown *Kilkenny* ..101 J9
Johnstown *Meath* ..108 M7
Johnstown *near Arklow* ..103 N9
Johnstown
   near Coolgreany ..97 N9
Johnstown Bridge ..107 I6
Johnstownbridge ..102 L7
Jonesborough 109 M5
Joyce 105 D7
Julianstown 109 N6

K

Kanturk Castle 94 F11
Katesbridge 115 N5
Keadew 107 H5
Keady 114 L5
Keady Mountain ..118 L2
Kealduff 89 C12
Kealkill 89 D12
Kearney 115 P4
Kearney Point 115 P4
Keeagh 99 E8
Keel 110 B6
Keel (Lough) 117 I2
Keel Lough 110 B6
Keeloges 106 G7
Keem Strand 110 B6
Keenagh *Longford* ..107 I7
Keenagh *Mayo* ..111 D5
Keeraunnagark 98 D8
Keereen 91 I11
Keimaneigh (The pass of) ..89 E12
Kells *Ballymena* ..115 N3
Kells *Kerry* 88 B12
Kells *Kilkenny* ...96 K10
Kells (Ceanannus Mor) /
   Ceanannas *Meath* ..108 L6
Kells Bay 88 B11
Kells Priory 96 K10
Kellysgrove 100 H8
Kenmare River 88 B12
Kentstown 108 M7
Kerry (Ring of) 88 B12
Kerry Head 92 C10
Kesh *Fermanagh* ..113 I4
Kesh Toomour 106 G5
Keshcarrigan 107 I5
Key (Lough) 106 H5
Kid Island 110 C5
Kilbaha 93 C10
Kilbaha Bay 93 C10
Kilbane 99 G9
Kilbarry 89 E12
Kilbeacanty 99 F8
Kilbeggan 101 J7
Kilbehenny 94 H11
Kilbennan 105 F7
Kilberry *Bert* 102 K8
Kilberry *Kildare* ..102 K8
Kilbreedy 94 F10
Kilbrickan 105 D7
Kilbricken 101 J9
Kilbride *near Blessington* ..103 M8

A B C D E F G H I J **K** **L** M N O P Q R S T U V W X Y Z

Kilbride *near Ratoah* 103 M7
Kilbride *near Trim* 108 L7
Kilbride *near Wicklow* 103 N9
Kilbrien 95 J11
Kilbrittain 90 F12
Kilcaimin 99 F8
Kilcar 112 G4
Kilcarn 108 L7
Kilcatherine Point 88 B12
Kilcavan 101 J8
Kilchreest 99 G8
Kilclaran 99 G9
Kilclief 115 P5
Kilcloher 93 C10
Kilclonfert 101 J8
Kilclooney 116 G3
Kilcock 102 L7
Kilcogy 107 J6
Kilcolgan 99 F8
Kilcolman *Cashel* 90 F12
Kilcolman *Dunmoylan East* 93 E10
Kilcoltrim 96 L10
Kilcomin 101 I9
Kilcommon *near Caher* 95 I10
Kilcommon *near Milestone* 95 H9
Kilcon 111 E5
Kilconly *Galway* 105 F7
Kilconly *Kerry* 93 D10
Kilcoo 115 N5
Kilcoole 103 N8
Kilcormac 101 I8
Kilcotty 97 M10
Kilcredan 91 I12
Kilcredaun Point 93 C10
Kilcrohane 89 C13
Kilcrow 100 H8
Kilcullen 102 L8
Kilcummin *Kerry* 92 B11
Kilcummin *Mayo* 111 E5
Kilcummin Farmhill 93 D11
Kilcurly 109 M5
Kilcurry 109 M5
Kildalkey 108 L7
Kildangan 102 K8
Kildavin 96 L9
Kilderry 96 K9
Kildoney Point 112 H4
Kildorrery 94 G11
Kildress 114 L4
Kildrum 115 N3
Kilfeakle 95 H10
Kilfearagh 98 D10
Kilfenora 99 E9
Kilfinnane 94 G10
Kilfinny 94 F10
Kilflyn 93 D10
Kilgarvan 89 D12
Kilglass *Galway* 106 G7
Kilglass *Sligo* 111 E5
Kilglass Lough 107 H6
Kilgobnet *Kerry* 89 C11
Kilgobnet *Waterford* 91 J11
Kilgory Lough 99 F9
Kilgowan 102 L8
Kiljames 96 K10
Kilkea 102 L9
Kilkeary 100 H9
Kilkeasy 96 K10
Kilkeel 109 N5
Kilkeeran High Crosses 95 J10
Kilkenny West 107 I7
Kilkerrin 106 G7
Kilkieran / Cill Chiaráin 104 C8
Kilkieran Bay 104 C7
Kilkiernan 96 K9
Kilkinamurry 115 N5
Kilkinlea 93 E10
Kilkishen 99 F9
Kill *Cavan* 108 K5
Kill *Waterford* 91 J11
Killabunane 89 D12
Killaclug 94 H11
Killacolla 94 F10
Killadangan 105 D6
Killadeas 113 I4
Killadoon 104 C6
Killadysert 99 E9
Killafeen 99 F8
Killag 96 M11
Killagan Bridge 118 M2
Killaghteen 93 E10
Killahy 95 J9
Killakee 103 N8
Killala 111 E5

Killala Bay 111 E5
Killallon 108 K6
Killaloo 118 K3
Killamery 95 J10
Killane 102 K8
Killanena 99 F9
Killann 96 L10
Killard 98 D9
Killard Point 115 P5
Killarga 112 H5
Killarney National Park 89 D11
Killarone 105 E7
Killary Harbour 104 C7
Killashandra 107 J5
Killashee 107 I6
Killasser 105 F6
Killavally *Mayo* 105 D6
Killavally *Westmeath* 101 J7
Killavil 106 G5
Killavullen 94 G11
Killea *Donegal* 117 J3
Killea *Tipperary* 101 I9
Killeagh 91 H12
Killealy 115 N3
Killeany 98 D3
Killedmond 96 L10
Killeedy 93 E10
Killeen *Ardamullivan* 99 F9
Killeen *Armagh* 114 M4
Killeen *Dungannon* 114 M4
Killeenaran 99 F8
Killeeneenmore 99 F8
Killeenleagh Bridge 88 B12
Killeevan 113 K5
Killeigh 101 J8
Killen 113 J3
Killenagh 97 N10
Killenaule 95 I10
Killeshil 101 K8
Killeshin 102 K9
Killeter 113 I3
Killeter Forest 113 I3
Killevy 109 M5
Killevy Churches 109 M5
Killilan Bridge 99 G8
Killimer 93 D10
Killimor 100 H8
Killinaboy 99 E9
Killinaspick 96 K10
Killinchy 115 O4
Killincooly 97 N10
Killiney *Dublin* 103 N8
Killiney *Kerry* 92 B11
Killiney Bay 103 N8
Killinick 97 M11
Killinierin 97 N9
Killinkere 108 K6
Killinny 99 F8
Killinthomas 102 K8
Killinure Lough 107 I7
Killiskey 103 N8
Killkelly 105 F6
Killmuckbridge 97 N10
Killogeary 111 E5
Killogeenaghan 101 I7
Killonecaha 88 B12
Killoran 100 G8
Killoscobe 106 G7
Killough 115 P5
Killough 103 N8
Killowen 109 N5
Killucan 108 K7
Killukin 107 H6
Killurin 96 M10
Killurly 88 B12
Killusty 95 J10
Killwaughter 115 O3
Killyclogher 113 K4
Killyclug 117 I3
Killycolpy 114 M4
Killygar 107 J5
Killygordon 117 I3
Killykeen Forest Park 107 J5
Killylea 114 L4
Killyleagh 115 P4
Killyon 101 I8
Kilmacanoge 103 N8
Kilmacduagh Monastery 99 F8
Kilmacoo 103 N9
Kilmacow 96 K11
Kilmacrenan 117 I2
Kilmacteige 111 F5
Kilmacthomas 95 J11
Kilmactranny 106 H5
Kilmacurragh 103 N9
Kilmaganny 96 K10

Kilmaine 105 E7
Kilmainham Wood 108 L6
Kilmakilloge Harbour 88 C12
Kilmaley 99 E9
Kilmalkedar 92 B11
Kilmanagh 95 J10
Kilmeadan 96 K11
Kilmeage 102 L8
Kilmeedy 94 F10
Kilmeelickin 105 D7
Kilmeena 105 D6
Kilmessan 108 M7
Kilmichael *near Castletownbere* 88 B13
Kilmichael *near Macroom* 89 E12
Kilmichael Point 97 N9
Kilmihil 98 E9
Kilmona 90 G12
Kilmoon 89 D13
Kilmore *Armagh* 114 M4
Kilmore *Clare* 99 G9
Kilmore *Down* 115 O4
Kilmore *Mayo* 105 E6
Kilmore *Roscommon* 107 H6
Kilmore *Wexford* 96 M11
Kilmore Quay 96 M11
Kilmorna 93 D10
Kilmorony 102 L9
Kilmovee 106 F6
Kilmurry *Cork* 90 F12
Kilmurry *Limerick* 94 G10
Kilmurry *near Kilkishen* 99 F9
Kilmurry *near Milltown* 98 D9
Kilmurry *Wicklow* 102 L9
Kilmurry Mac Mahon 93 E10
Kilmurvy 98 C8
Kilmyshall 96 M10
Kilnagross 107 I6
Kilnalag 106 G6
Kilnaleck 107 K6
Kilnamanagh 97 M10
Kilnamona 99 E9
Kiltown 115 N4
Kilpatrick 90 F12
Kilpeacan Cross Roads 88 B12
Kilpedder 103 N8
Kilquigguin 97 M9
Kilraghts 118 M2
Kilrane 97 M11
Kilrea 118 M3
Kilrean 116 H3
Kilreekill 100 G8
Kilroghter 99 E8
Kilross *Donegal* 117 I3
Kilross *Tipperary* 94 H10
Kilruddery 103 N8
Kilsallagh *Galway* 106 G7
Kilsallagh *Mayo* 104 C6
Kilsallaghan 103 N7
Kilsally 114 M4
Kilsaran 109 M6
Kilshanchoe 102 L7
Kilshannig 92 B11
Kilshanny 99 E9
Kilsheelan 95 J10
Kilskeer 108 L6
Kilskeery 113 J4
Kiltealy 96 L10
Kilteel 103 M8
Kilteely 94 G10
Kiltegan 103 M9
Kilternan 103 N8
Kiltimagh 105 E6
Kiltober 101 J7
Kiltoom 107 H7
Kiltormer 100 H8
Kiltullagh 99 G8
Kiltyclogher 113 H4
Kilvine 105 F7
Kilworth 94 H11
Kilworth Mountains 94 H11
Kinale (Lough) 107 J6
Kinard 93 E10
Kinawley 113 J5
Kincasslagh 116 G2
Kindrohid 117 J2
Kindrum 117 I2
Kingarrow 117 H3
Kings River 95 J10
Kingscourt 108 L6
Kingsland 106 G6
Kingsmill 114 M4
Kingstown 104 B7
Kinlough 112 H4
Kinnadoohy 104 C6
Kinnagoe Bay 118 K2
Kinnegad 108 K7

Kinnitty 101 I8
Kinsale (Old Head of) 90 G13
Kinsale Harbour 90 G12
Kinsalebeg 91 I12
Kinsaley 103 N7
Kinvarra *near Camus Bay* 105 D7
Kinvarra *near Kinvarra Bay* 99 F8
Kinvarra Bay 99 F8
Kippure 103 N8
Kircubbin 115 P4
Kirkhills 118 M2
Kirkistown 115 P4
Kishkeam 93 E11
Kitconnell 100 G8
Knappagh 105 D6
Knappogue Castle 99 F9
Knight's Town 88 B12
Knock *Clare* 93 E10
Knock *Mayo* 105 F6
Knock *Tipperary* 101 I9
Knockaderry 94 F10
Knockadoon Head 91 I12
Knockainy 94 G10
Knockalla Mount 117 J2
Knockalongy 112 F5
Knockalough 99 E9
Knockanaffrin 95 J11
Knockananna 103 M9
Knockanevin 94 G11
Knockanillaun 111 E5
Knockanimpaha 93 E10
Knockanure 93 D10
Knockaunalour 90 G11
Knockaunavoher 94 G10
Knockaunnaglashy 92 C11
Knockboy *near Dungarvan* 95 I11
Knockboy *near Waterford* 96 K11
Knockboy (Mount) 89 D12
Knockbrack 117 I3
Knockbrandon 97 M9
Knockbride 108 L6
Knockbridge 109 M6
Knockbrit 95 I10
Knockcloghrim 114 M3
Knockcroghery 106 H7
Knockdrin 107 K7
Knockerry 98 D10
Knockferry 105 E7
Knocklayd 119 N2
Knocklofty 95 I10
Knocklomena 89 C12
Knocklong 94 G10
Knockmealdown 95 I11
Knockmealdown Mountains 95 H11
Knockmore 104 B6
Knockmore (Mount) 104 C6
Knockmourne 90 H11
Knockmoy Abbey 106 F7
Knocknaboul Cross 93 E11
Knocknacarry 119 N2
Knocknacree 102 L9
Knocknadobar 88 B12
Knocknagantee 88 C12
Knocknagashel 93 D11
Knocknagree 93 E11
Knocknahilan 90 F12
Knocknalina 110 C5
Knocknalower 110 C5
Knockowen 89 C12
Knockraha 90 G12
Knocks *Cork* 89 F12
Knocks *Fermanagh* 113 J5
Knocks *Laois* 101 J8
Knockshanahullion 95 H11
Knockskagh 89 F12
Knocktopher 96 K10
Knocktown 96 M11
Knockundervaul 93 D10
Knockvicar 106 H5
Knowth 108 M6
Kylemore 100 H8
Kylemore Abbey 104 C7
Kylemore Lough 104 C7

L

Laban 99 F8
Labasheeda 93 E10
Lack 113 J4
Lackagh 102 K8
Lackan *Carlow* 96 K9
Lackan *Wicklow* 103 M8
Lackan bay 111 E5
Lackareagh 89 F12

Laconnell 116 G3
Ladies View 89 D12
Lady's Island Lake 97 M11
Ladysbridge 90 H12
Ladywell 96 K10
Laffansbridge 95 I10
Lag 117 K2
Lagan (River) 115 N4
Lagan Valley 115 O4
Lagavara 118 M2
Lagganstown 95 I10
Laghey Corner 114 L4
Laghtnafrankee 95 J11
Laghy 113 H4
Lahardaun 111 E5
Lakyle 93 E10
Lambay Island 109 N7
Lambeg 115 N4
Lamb's Head 88 B12
Lanesborough 107 I6
Laney (River) 89 F12
Laracor 108 L7
Laragh *Kildare* 102 L7
Laragh *Monaghan* 108 L5
Laragh *Wicklow* 103 N8
Largan *Mayo* 111 D5
Largan *Sligo* 111 F5
Largy 112 G4
Largydonnell 112 H4
Larne 115 O3
Larne Lough 115 O3
Lattin 94 H10
Laune (River) 93 C11
Lauragh 88 C12
Laurelvale 114 M4
Laurencetown 100 H8
Lavagh 112 F5
Lavagh More 117 H3
Lawrencetown 114 N4
Leabgarrow 116 G3
League (Slieve) 112 F4
League Point 89 D13
Leamaneh Castle 99 E9
Leamlara 90 H12
Leamore Strand 103 N8
Leane (Lough) 89 D11
Leannan (River) 117 I2
Leap 89 E13
Leap (The) *near Enniscorthy* 96 M10
Leap (The) *near New Ross* 96 L11
Lecale Peninsula 115 O5
Lecarrow *Leitrim* 112 H5
Lecarrow *Roscommon* 107 H7
Leckanarainey 112 H4
Leckanvy 105 C6
Leckaun 112 H5
Leckavrea Mountain 105 D7
Leckemy 118 K2
Lee 93 C11
Lee (River) 90 G12
Lee Reservoir 90 F12
Leek Point 93 C10
Leenane 104 C7
Legan or Lenamore 107 J7
Legananny Dolmen 115 N5
Leggah 107 J6
Legoniel 115 O4
Lehardan 117 J2
Leighlinbridge 96 L9
Leinster (Mount) 96 L10
Leitir Meallán / Lettermullan 98 C8
Leitir Mhic an Bhaird / Lettermacaward 116 H3
Leitrim *Banbridge* 115 O5
Leitrim *Creegh* 98 D9
Leitrim *Leitrim* 107 H6
Leixlip 103 M7
Lemanaghan 101 I8
Lemybrien 91 J11
Lenadoon Point 111 E5
Lenan Head 117 J2
Lene (Lough) 107 K7
Lerrig 93 C10
Leslie Hill 114 L5
Letterbarra 117 I3
Letterbreen 113 I5
Lettercallow 98 C8
Lettercraffroe Lough 105 D7
Letterfinish 88 C12
Letterfrack 104 C7
Letterkelly 99 E9
Letterkenny / Leitir Ceanainn 117 I3
Letterleague 117 I3
Lettermore 98 D8

Lettermore Island 98 C8
Levally 106 F7
Levally Lough 105 E6
Licketstown 96 K11
Liffey (River) 102 M8
Lifford 117 J3
Light House Island 115 P3
Limavady 118 L2
Limerick / Luimneach 94 G10
Limerick Junction 95 H10
Lios Dúin Bhearna / Lisdoonvarna 99 E8
Lios Mór / Lismore 91 I11
Lios Póil / Lispole 92 B11
Lios Tuathail / Listowel 93 D10
Lisacul 106 G6
Lisbane 115 O4
Lisbellaw 113 J5
Lisburn 115 N4
Liscannor 98 D9
Liscannor Bay 98 D9
Liscarney 105 D6
Liscarroll 94 F11
Liscolman 118 M2
Liscooly 117 J3
Lisdoart 114 K4
Lisdowney 101 J9
Lisduff *Cavan* 108 K6
Lisduff *Leitrim* 107 I6
Lisduff *Offaly* 101 I8
Lisgarode 100 H8
Lisgoold 90 H12
Lislea *Magherafelt* 118 M3
Lislea *Newry-Mourne* 114 M5
Lismacaffry 107 J6
Lismoghry 117 J3
Lismoyle 106 H7
Lisnacree 109 N5
Lisnageer 108 K5
Lisnagleer 114 L4
Lisnagry 94 G9
Lisnagunogue 118 M2
Lisnamuck 118 L3
Lisnarrick 113 I4
Lisnaskea 113 J5
Lisnavagh 102 L9
Lispatrick 90 G13
Lisroe 99 E9
Lisronagh 95 I10
Lisryan 107 J6
Lissadell House 112 G4
Lissalway 106 G6
Lissamona 89 D13
Lissatinnig Bridge 88 C12
Lissavaird 89 F13
Lisselton 93 D10
Lissinagroagh 112 H5
Lissiniska 112 H4
Lissycasey 99 E9
Listellick 93 C11
Listerlin 96 K10
Listooder 115 O4
Lisvarrinane 94 H10
Little Bray 103 N8
Little Island 90 G12
Little Skellig 88 A12
Littleton 95 I10
Lixnaw 93 D10
Loanends 115 N4
Lobinstown 108 M6
Loch Garman / Wexford 97 M10
Loghill 93 E10
Lombardstown 94 F11
Londonderry 117 K3
Lonehort Point 88 C13
Long Island 89 D13
Longford 101 I8
Longhill 101 K9
Longwood 108 L7
Loo Bridge 89 D12
Loobagh 94 G10
Loop Head 92 C10
Lorrha 100 H8
Loskeran 91 J11
Losset *Cavan* 107 J6
Losset *Donegal* 117 I2
Lough Bradan Forest 113 J4
Lough Gowna 107 J6
Lough Key Forest Park 106 H6
Lough Navar Forest 113 I4
Loughanavally 107 J7
Loughanillaunmore 98 D8
Loughanure 116 H2
Loughbrickland 114 N5
Lougher 92 C11
Loughermore 118 L3
Loughfad Hill 113 I4

Ireland 145

Loughgall 114 M 4
Loughglinn 106 G 6
Loughguile 119 N 2
Loughinisland 115 O 4
Loughlinstown 103 N 8
Loughmoe 101 I 9
Loughmorne 108 L 5
Loughros More Bay 116 G 3
Loughros Point 116 G 3
Loughsalt Mount 117 I 2
Loughshinny 109 N 7
Louisburgh 104 C 6
Loup (The) 114 M 3
Louth 108 M 6
Lower Ballinderry 114 N 4
Lower Lake 103 N 8
Lowertown 89 D 13
Lowerymore 113 I 3
Lowtown 115 N 5
Lucan 103 M 7
Luggacurren 101 K 9
Lugnaquillia Mountain 103 M 9
Luimneach / Limerick 94 G 10
Lukeswell 96 K 10
Lullymore 102 L 8
Lurgan *Craigavon* 114 N 4
Lurgan *Frenchpark* 106 G 6
Lurganboy *Donegal* 117 J 2
Lurganboy *Leitrim* 112 H 5
Lusk 109 N 7
Lyle 115 N 3
Lyracrumpane 93 D 10
Lyre 90 F 11
Lyrenaglogh 95 H 11

M

Maas 116 G 3
Mac Gregor's Corner 119 N 3
Mac Laughlins Corner 118 M 3
Mac Mahon's Town 114 K 4
Mac Swyne's Bay 112 G 4
Mace 105 D 6
Mace Head 104 C 8
Macgillycuddy's Reeks 89 C 12
Machugh (Lough) 116 G 3
Mackan 113 J 5
Macnean Lower (Lough) 113 I 5
Macnean Upper (Lough) 113 I 5
Macosquin 118 L 2
Macroom/ Maigh Chromtha 89 F 12
Maddan 114 L 5
Maddockstown 96 K 10
Maganey 102 L 9
Maghaberry 115 N 4
Maghanlawaun 89 C 12
Maghera *Clare* 99 F 9
Maghera *Donegal* 116 G 3
Maghera *Down* 115 O 5
Maghera *Magherafelt* 118 L 3
Magherabane 117 J 2
Magherafelt 114 M 3
Magheragall 115 N 4
Magheralin 114 N 4
Magheramason 117 J 3
Magheramorne 115 O 3
Magheraveely 113 K 5
Maghery *near Dungannon* 114 M 4
Maghery *near Dunglow* 116 G 3
Magilligan 118 L 2
Magilligan Point 118 L 2
Magilligan Strand 118 L 2
Maguiresbridge 113 J 5
Mahee Island 115 P 4
Mahon 95 J 11
Mahon (Lough) 90 G 12
Mahoonagh 93 E 10
Maigh Chromtha / Macroom 89 F 12
Maigh Cuilinn / Moycullen 105 E 7
Maigh Nuad / Maynooth 103 M 7
Maigue (River) 94 F 10
Main 118 N 3
Maine (River) 93 C 11
Mainham 102 L 8
Mainistir Fhear Maí / Fermoy 90 H 11
Mainistir na Búille / Boyle 106 H 6
Mainistir na Corann / Midleton 90 H 12
Máistir Gaoithe / Mastergeehy 88 B 12
Mal Bay 98 D 9
Mala / Mallow 94 G 11
Málainn Bhig / Malin Beg 112 F 3
Malin 118 K 2
Malin Bay 112 F 3
Malin Head 117 J 1
Malin More 112 F 3
Mallusk 115 N 3
Mamore (Gap of) 117 J 2
Manger 112 H 4
Mangerton Mountain 89 D 12
Mannin Bay 104 B 7
Mannin Lake 105 F 6
Manorcunningham 117 J 3
Manselstown 95 I 9
Mansfieldstown 109 M 6
Mantua 106 H 6
Manulla 105 E 6
Manulla (River) 105 E 6
Maothail / Mohill 107 I 6
Marble Arch Caves 113 I 5
Marble Hill 117 I 2
Mardyke 95 J 10
Markethill 114 M 5
Marshalstown 96 M 10
Martin 90 G 12
Martinstown *Emlygrennan* 94 G 10
Martinstown *Grennanstown* 108 L 7
Martinstown *South Somerset* 119 N 3
Mask (Lough) 105 D 7
Massford 115 N 4
Masshill 112 F 5
Masterstown 95 I 10
Matehy 90 G 12
Matrix (Castle) 94 F 10
Mattock (River) 108 M 6
Mauherslieve 95 H 9
Maum 105 D 7
Maumakeogh 111 D 5
Maumeen Lough 104 B 7
Maumtrasna 105 D 7
Maumturk Mountains 104 C 7
Mauricesmills 99 E 9
Mayo 105 E 6
Mayo (Plains of) 105 E 6
Mayobridge 114 N 5
Mazetown 115 N 4
Mealagh 89 D 12
Meanus 94 G 10
Meathas Troim / Edgeworthstown 107 J 6
Meela (Lough) 116 G 3
Meelick 100 H 8
Meelin 93 E 11
Meenaclady 116 H 2
Meenacross 116 G 3
Meenanarwa 117 H 3
Meenaneary / Mín na Aoire 112 G 3
Meenatotan 116 H 3
Meenavean 112 F 3
Meencorwick 116 H 3
Meenglass 113 I 3
Meenlaragh 117 H 2
Meenreagh 113 I 3
Meentullynagarn 112 G 3
Meenybraddan 112 H 3
Meeting of the Waters 103 N 9
Mellifont Abbey 109 M 6
Melmore Head 117 I 2
Melvin (Lough) 112 H 4
Menlough 106 G 7
Mew Island 115 P 3
Michelstown Caves 95 H 11
Middletown 116 H 2
Middletown *Armagh* 114 L 5
Midfield 105 F 6
Mile 117 J 2
Milebush 115 O 3
Milehouse 96 M 10
Milemill 102 L 8
Milestone 95 H 9
Milford *Armagh* 114 L 5
Milford *Cork* 94 F 10
Mill Town 114 L 5
Millbay 115 O 3
Millbrook *Derry* 118 K 3
Millbrook *Larne* 115 O 3
Millbrook *Oldcastle* 108 K 6
Milleen 93 E 11
Millford 117 I 2
Millisle 115 P 4
Millroad 96 M 11
Millstreet *Cork* 89 E 11
Millstreet *Waterford* 91 I 11
Milltown *Armagh* 114 L 5
Milltown *Ballymoney* 118 M 2
Milltown *Banbridge* 114 N 5
Milltown *Cavan* 107 J 5
Milltown *Craigavon* 114 M 4
Milltown *Dublin* 103 M 8
Milltown *Kildare* 102 L 8
Milltown *near Dingle* 92 B 11
Milltown *near Mount Bellew* 106 G 7
Milltown *near Tralee* 93 C 11
Milltown *near Tuam* 105 F 7
Milltown *Omagh* 114 K 4
Milltown *Wexford* 97 M 10
Milltownpass 107 K 7
Minane Bridge 90 G 12
Minard Head 92 B 11
Mine Head 91 J 12
Minerstown 115 O 5
Minterburn 114 L 4
Mizen Head 88 C 13
Moanmore 98 D 9
Modelligo 91 I 11
Modreeny 100 H 9
Mogeely 90 H 12
Moglass 95 I 10
Moher (Cliffs of) 98 D 9
Moher Lough 105 D 6
Mohil 96 K 9
Móinteach Mílic / Mountmellick 101 K 8
Moira 115 N 4
Moll's Gap 89 D 12
Monard 95 H 10
Monaseed 97 M 9
Monaster 94 G 10
Monasteraden 106 G 6
Monasteranenagh Abbey 94 G 10
Monasterboice 109 M 6
Monasterevin 102 K 8
Monavullagh Mountains 95 J 11
Mondello Park 102 L 8
Monea 113 I 4
Moneen *Clare* 93 C 10
Moneen *Galway* 105 F 7
Money Point 93 D 10
Moneydig 118 M 3
Moneygall 101 I 9
Moneyglass 114 M 3
Moneygold 112 G 4
Moneylahan 112 G 4
Moneymore 114 L 3
Moneyneany 118 L 3
Moneyreagh 115 O 4
Monilea 107 K 7
Monivea 106 F 7
Monkstown *Cork* 90 G 12
Monkstown *Newtownabbey* 115 O 3
Monroe 107 J 7
Montpelier 99 G 9
Mooncoin 96 K 11
Moone 102 L 9
Moord 91 I 12
Moore Bay 98 C 9
Moorfields 115 N 3
More (Island) 105 D 6
Morenane 94 F 10
Morley's Bridge 89 D 12
Morningstar 94 G 10
Mornington 109 N 6
Mosney 109 N 7
Moss-Side 118 M 2
Mossley 115 O 3
Mothel 95 J 11
Motte Stone 103 N 9
Mount Falcon 111 E 5
Mount Garret 96 L 10
Mount Hamilton or Sperrin 114 K 3
Mount Melleray Monastery 95 I 11
Mount Norris 114 M 5
Mount Nugent 107 K 6
Mount Stewart Gardens 115 P 4
Mount Talbot 106 H 7
Mount Temple 107 I 7
Mount Uniacke 91 H 12
Mount Usher Gardens 103 N 8
Mountbolus 101 J 8
Mountcastle 117 J 3
Mountcharles 112 H 4
Mountcollins 93 E 11
Mountfield 114 K 4
Mounthenry 105 E 7
Mountjoy *Dungannon* 114 M 4
Mountjoy *Omagh* 113 J 4
Mountrath 101 J 8
Mountrivers Bridge 98 D 9
Mountshannon 100 G 9
Mourne (Lough) *near Ballybofey* 113 I 3
Mourne (Lough) *near Carrickfergus* 115 O 3
Mourne Beg 113 I 3
Mourne Mountains 109 N 5
Mourne River 113 J 3
Moveen 98 C 10
Moville / Bun an Phobail 118 K 2
Mowhan 114 M 5
Moy 114 L 4
Moy (River) 111 E 5
Moyagh 117 J 3
Moyallan 114 M 4
Moyard 104 B 7
Moyarget 118 N 2
Moyasta 98 D 9
Moydow 107 I 7
Moygashel 114 L 4
Moyglass 99 G 8
Moylough *Galway* 106 G 7
Moylough *Sligo* 106 F 5
Moynalty 108 L 6
Moynalvy 108 L 7
Moyne *Roscommon* 106 G 6
Moyne *Tipperary* 107 J 6
Moyne *Wicklow* 103 M 9
Moyne Abbey 111 E 5
Moyrus 104 C 7
Moyteoge Head 110 B 6
Moyvally 102 L 7
Moyvore 107 J 7
Moyvoughly 107 I 7
Muck (Isle of) 115 O 3
Muckamore 115 N 3
Muckanagh Lough 99 F 9
Muckish Mountain 117 H 2
Mucklon 102 L 7
Muckno Lake 108 L 5
Muckros Head 112 G 4
Muckross 89 D 11
Muff 117 K 2
Muggort's Bay 91 J 11
Muinchille / Cootehill 108 K 5
Muine Bheag / Bagenalstown 96 L 9
Muineachán / Monaghan 114 L 5
Muing 111 D 5
Muingnabo 111 C 5
Mulhuddart 103 M 7
Mulkear 94 G 10
Mullach Íde / Malahide 103 N 7
Mullagh *Cavan* 108 L 6
Mullagh *Galway* 100 G 8
Mullagh *Mayo* 104 C 6
Mullagh *Meath* 103 M 7
Mullaghanattin 88 C 12
Mullaghanish 89 E 12
Mullaghareirk Mountains 93 E 10
Mullaghash 118 K 3
Mullaghbane 109 M 5
Mullaghboy 115 O 3
Mullaghcarn 113 K 3
Mullaghcleevaun 103 M 8
Mullaghclogha 114 K 3
Mullaghmore *Cliffony North* 112 G 4
Mullaghmore *Magherafelt* 118 L 3
Mullaghmore Head 112 G 4
Mullaghroe 106 G 6
Mullan *Coleraine* 118 L 2
Mullan *Figullar* 114 L 4
Mullany'sCross 111 F 5
Mullartown 109 O 5
Mullenbeg 96 K 10
Mullet Peninsula 110 B 5
Mullinahone 95 J 10
Mullinasole 112 H 4
Mullinavat 96 K 10
Mulroy Bay 117 I 2
Multeen 95 H 10
Multyfarnham 107 J 7
Mungret 94 F 10
Muntervary or Sheep's Head 88 C 13
Murley 113 K 4
Murlough Bay 119 N 2
Murntown 97 M 11
Murreagh 92 A 11
Murrisk 105 D 6
Murroe 94 G 10
Murrough 99 E 8
Musheramore 89 F 11
Mussenden Temple 118 L 2
Mutton Island 98 D 9
Mweelrea Mountains 104 C 7
Mweenish Island 104 C 8
Myshall 96 L 9

N

Na Cealla Beaga / Killybegs 112 G 4
Na Clocha Liatha / Greystones 103 N 8
Na Dúnaibh / Downies 117 I 2
Na Sceirí / Skerries 109 N 7
Nacorra (Lough) 105 D 6
Nacung (Lough) 117 H 2
Nad 90 F 11
Nafooey (Lough) 105 D 7
Nagles Mountains 90 G 11
Nalughraman (Lough) 116 G 3
Naminn (Lough) 117 J 2
Namona (Lough) 88 B 12
Nanny 108 M 7
Narin 116 G 3
Narraghmore 102 L 8
Narrow Water Castle 109 N 5
Naul 109 N 7
Neagh (Lough) 114 M 4
Neale 105 E 7
Nealstown 101 I 9
Neidín / Kenmare 89 D 12
Nenagh 100 H 9
Nephin 111 D 5
Nephin (Glen) 105 D 6
Nephin Beg 111 D 5
Nephin Beg Range 111 C 5
New Birmingham 95 J 10
New Buildings 117 J 3
New Inn *Cavan* 108 K 6
New Inn *Galway* 100 G 8
New Kildimo 94 F 10
New Quay / Bealaclugga 99 E 8
New Twopothouse Village 94 G 11
Newbawn 96 L 10
Newbliss 113 K 5
Newbridge *Fingal* 109 N 7
Newbridge *Limerick* 94 F 10
Newbridge *near Tuomard* 106 G 7
Newbridge / An Droichead Nua 102 L 8
Newcastle *Down* 115 O 5
Newcastle *Dublin* 103 M 8
Newcastle *Galway* 99 F 7
Newcastle *Tipperary* 95 I 11
Newcastle *Wicklow* 103 N 8
Newcestown 90 F 12
Newchapel 95 I 10
Newferry 114 M 3
Newgrange 109 M 6
Newinn 95 I 10
Newmarket *Cork* 93 F 11
Newmarket *Kilkenny* 96 K 10
Newmarket on Fergus 99 F 9
Newmills *Donegal* 117 I 3
Newmills *Dungannon* 114 L 4
Newport *Tipperary* 100 G 9
Newport Bay 105 C 6
Newport Trench 114 M 4
Newry 114 M 5
Newtown *Cork* 94 G 11
Newtown *Galway* 99 F 8
Newtown *Kildare* 102 L 7
Newtown *Laois* 101 K 9
Newtown *Limerick* 94 G 10
Newtown *near Knock* 101 I 9
Newtown *near Nenagh* 100 H 9
Newtown *Offaly* 100 H 8
Newtown *Roscommon* 100 H 7
Newtown *Tipperary* 95 H 10
Newtown *Waterford* 95 J 11
Newtown *Wexford* 96 M 11
Newtown Cashel 107 I 7
Newtown Cloghans 111 E 5
Newtown-Crommelin 119 N 3
Newtown Cunningham 117 J 3
Newtown Forbes 107 I 6
Newtown Gore 107 I 5
Newtown Mount Kennedy 103 N 8
Newtown Sandes 93 D 10
Newtownabbey 115 O 4
Newtownards 115 O 4
Newtownbreda 115 O 4
Newtownbutler 113 J 5
Newtownhamilton 114 M 5
Newtownlow 101 J 7
Newtownlynch 99 E 8
Newtownshandrum 94 F 10
Newtownstewart 113 J 3
Nier 95 J 11
Ninemilehouse 95 J 10
Nobber 108 L 6
Nohaval 90 G 12
Nore 101 J 9
Nore (River) 96 K 10
North Channel 119 O 2
North Ring 90 F 13
North Sound 98 C 8
Nose of Howth 103 N 7
Noughaval *Doora* 99 F 9
Noughaval *Noughaval* 99 E 8
Nowen Hill 89 E 12
Nuns Quarter 115 O 4
Nurney *Carlow* 96 L 9
Nurney *Kildare* 102 L 8
Nutt's Corner 115 N 4

O

Oaghley 93 D 10
Oatfield 99 F 9
Oatquarter 98 C 8
O'Brien's Tower 98 D 9
O'Flynn (Lough) 106 G 6
Oghil *Clare* 100 H 8
Oghil *Galway* 98 C 8
Ogonnelloe 99 G 9
O'Grady (Lough) 99 G 9
Oileán Ciarraí / Castleisland 93 D 11
Oilgate 97 M 10
Oily 112 G 4
Old Court 89 E 13
Old Head *Ballymackean* 90 G 13
Old Head *Louisburgh* 104 C 6
Old Kilcullen 102 L 8
Old Kildimo 94 F 10
Old Ross 96 L 10
Old Town *Donegal* 117 I 3
Old Town *Laois* 101 J 9
Old Town *Roscommon* 100 H 8
Old Town *Wexford* 96 L 10
Old Twopothouse 94 G 11
Oldleighlin 96 K 9
Oldmill Bridge 93 E 10
Oldtown *Dublin* 109 N 7
Oldtown *Roscommon* 101 I 7
Omagh 113 K 4
Omeath 109 N 5
Omey Island 104 B 7
Onaght 98 C 8
Oola 94 H 10
Oorid Lough 105 D 7
Oranmore 99 F 8
Oriel (Mount) 108 M 6
Oristown 108 L 6
Oritor 114 L 4
Ossian's Grave 119 N 2
Oughter (Lough) 107 J 6
Oulart 97 M 10
Ovens 90 G 12
Owel (Lough) 107 J 7
Owenascaul 92 B 11
Owenator 116 H 3
Owenavorragh 97 M 10
Owenbeagh 117 H 3
Owenbeg 111 F 5
Owenbeg (River) 112 G 5
Owenboliska 99 E 8
Owenboy 90 G 12
Owenbristy 99 F 8
Owencarrow 117 I 2
Owendalulleegh 99 G 8
Owenea 116 G 3
Owengarve *Clew Bay* 105 D 6
Owengarve *River Moy* 106 F 5
Owenglin 104 C 7
Oweniny 111 D 5
Owenkillew *Glenelly* 114 K 3
Owenkillew *Lough Swilly* 117 J 2
Owenmore Bridge 105 D 6
Owennacurra 90 H 12
Owenreagh Hill 117 J 3
Owenriff 105 D 7
Owentaraglin 93 E 11
Owentocker 116 H 3
Owenur (River) 106 H 6
Ower 105 E 7
Owning 95 J 10
Owroe Bridge 88 B 12
Owvane 89 D 12
Oysterhaven 90 G 12

P

Palace 96 L 10
Palatine 102 L 9
Pallas 101 J 8
Pallas Cross 100 I 9
Pallas Green 94 G 10
Pallaskenry 94 F 10

A B C D E F G H I J K L M N O P Q R S T U V W X Y Z

A

Paps (The) ... 89 E 11
Park *Bellavary* ... 105 E 6
Park *Derry* ... 118 K 3
Parke's Castle ... 112 H 5
Parkgate ... 115 N 3
Parkmore ... 99 F 8
Parkmore Point ... 92 A 11
Parknasilla ... 88 C 12
Parteen ... 99 G 9
Partry ... 105 E 6
Partry Mountains ... 105 D 7
Passage ... 106 H 7
Passage East ... 96 L 11
Passage West ... 90 G 12
Patrickswell ... 94 F 10
Patterson's Spade Mill ... 115 N 3
Paulstown ... 96 K 9
Peake ... 90 F 12
Peatlands ... 114 M 4
Peterswell ... 99 F 8
Pettigoe ... 113 I 4
Phoenix Park ... 103 M 7
Piercetown ... 97 M 11
Pigeons (The) ... 107 I 7
Pike ... 100 H 8
Pike (The) *near Boola* ... 91 I 11
Pike (The) *near Lamybrien* ... 91 J 11
Pike (The) *Tipperary* ... 100 H 8
Pike Corner ... 108 L 7
Pike of Rush Hall ... 101 J 9
Piltown ... 95 K 10
Pluck ... 117 J 3
Plumbridge ... 113 K 3
Pollagh ... 101 I 8
Pollan Bay ... 117 J 2
Pollatomish ... 111 C 5
Pollnalaght ... 113 J 4
Pollshask ... 106 G 7
Pomeroy ... 114 L 4
Pontoon ... 105 E 6
Port ... 116 F 2
Port Ballintrae ... 118 M 2
Port Durlainne / Porturlin ... 111 C 5
Port Láirge / Waterford ... 96 K 11
Port Laoise / Portlaoise ... 101 K 8
Port Omna / Portumna ... 100 H 8
Portacloy ... 111 C 5
Portadown ... 114 M 4
Portaferry ... 115 P 4
Portaleen ... 118 K 2
Portavogie ... 115 P 4
Portbradden ... 118 M 2
Portglenone ... 118 M 3
Portland ... 100 H 8
Portlaw ... 96 K 11
Portmagee ... 88 A 12
Portmagee Channel ... 88 A 12
Portmarnock ... 103 N 7
Portmuck ... 115 O 3
Portnablagh ... 117 I 2
Portnoo ... 116 G 3
Portrane ... 109 N 7
Portroe ... 100 G 9
Portrush ... 118 M 2
Portsalon ... 117 J 2
Portstewart ... 118 L 2
Poulaphouca Reservoir ... 103 M 8
Poulnamucky ... 95 I 10
Poulnasherry Bay ... 98 D 10
Power Head ... 90 H 12
Power's Cross ... 100 H 8
Powerscourt Demesne ... 103 N 8
Powerstown ... 96 K 10
Poyntz Pass ... 114 M 5
Priesthaggard ... 96 L 11
Prosperous ... 102 L 8
Puckaun ... 100 H 9
Puffin Island ... 88 A 12
Punchestown ... 103 M 8

Q

Quarrytown ... 119 N 3
Querrin ... 93 D 10
Quigley's Point ... 118 K 2
Quilty ... 98 D 9
Quin ... 99 F 9
Quoile ... 115 O 4

R

Rabbit Islands ... 89 E 13
Race End ... 117 I 2
Raffrey ... 115 O 4
Raghly ... 112 G 5
Raghtin More ... 117 J 2
Rahan ... 101 J 8
Rahanagh ... 93 E 10
Rahara ... 106 H 7
Raharney ... 108 K 7
Raheen ... 96 L 10
Raigh ... 105 D 7
Railyard ... 101 K 9
Rake Street ... 111 D 5
Ram Head ... 91 I 12
Ramor (Lough) ... 108 K 6
Ramore Head ... 118 M 2
Rams Island ... 114 N 4
Ramsgrange ... 96 L 11
Randalstown ... 114 N 3
Rapemills ... 101 I 8
Raphoe ... 117 J 3
Rasharkin ... 118 M 3
Rashedoge ... 117 I 3
Rath ... 101 I 8
Ráth Caola / Rathkeale ... 94 F 10
Ráth Droma / Rathdrum ... 103 N 9
Rathangan ... 102 L 8
Rathaspick ... 107 J 7
Rathbrit ... 95 I 10
Rathcabban ... 100 H 8
Rathconrath ... 107 J 7
Rathcool ... 89 F 11
Rathcoole ... 103 M 8
Rathcor ... 109 N 6
Rathcore ... 102 L 7
Rathcormack *near Fermoy* ... 90 H 11
Rathcormack *near Sligo* ... 112 G 5
Rathcroghan ... 106 H 6
Rathdangan ... 103 M 9
Rathdowney ... 101 J 9
Rathduff ... 90 G 11
Rathedan ... 96 L 9
Rathfeigh ... 108 M 7
Rathfriland ... 115 N 5
Rathfylane ... 96 L 10
Rathgarogue ... 96 L 10
Rathgormuck ... 95 J 11
Rathkeevin ... 95 I 10
Rathkenny ... 108 M 6
Rathlackan ... 111 E 5
Rathlee ... 111 E 5
Rathlin Island ... 119 N 2
Rathlin O'Birne Island ... 112 F 4
Rathlin Sound ... 119 N 2
Rathmelton ... 117 J 2
Rathmines ... 103 N 8
Rathmolyon ... 108 L 7
Rathmore ... 89 E 11
Rathmullan ... 117 J 2
Rathnew ... 103 N 9
Rathnure ... 96 L 10
Rathoma ... 111 E 5
Rathowen ... 107 J 7
Rathvilla ... 101 K 8
Rathvilly ... 102 L 9
Ratoath ... 108 M 7
Raven Point (The) ... 97 M 10
Ravensdale ... 109 M 5
Ray *near Dunfanaghy* ... 117 I 2
Ray *near Rathmillan* ... 117 J 2
Ray (River) ... 117 H 2
Rea (Lough) ... 99 G 8
Reaghstown ... 108 M 6
Reananeree / Rae na nDoirí ... 89 E 12
Reanascreena ... 89 E 13
Rear Cross ... 95 H 9
Red Bay ... 119 N 2
Redcastle ... 118 K 2
Redcross ... 103 N 9
Redgate ... 97 M 10
Redhills ... 107 K 5
Ree (Lough) ... 107 I 7
Reelan ... 117 H 3
Reen ... 89 D 12
Reens ... 94 F 10
Reevanagh ... 96 K 9
Relaghbeg ... 108 L 6
Rerrin ... 88 C 13
Rhode ... 101 K 7
Richhill ... 114 M 4
Ridge ... 96 K 9
Ridge Point ... 110 C 5
Rine (River) ... 99 F 9
Rineanna Point ... 99 F 9
Ringabella Bay ... 90 H 12
Ringarogy Island ... 89 D 13
Ringaskiddy ... 90 H 12
Ringboy ... 115 P 4
Ringfad Point ... 115 P 5
Ringsend ... 118 L 2
Ringstown ... 101 J 8
Ringville / An Rinn ... 91 J 11
Rinmore Point ... 117 I 2
Rinn (River) ... 107 I 6
Rinn Lough ... 107 I 6
Rinneen *Clare* ... 98 D 9
Rinneen *Cork* ... 89 E 13
Rinroe Point ... 110 C 5
Rinville ... 99 F 8
Rinvyle ... 104 C 7
Rinvyle Castle ... 104 B 7
Rinvyle Point ... 104 B 7
River ... 110 B 6
Riverchapel ... 97 N 10
Riverstick ... 90 G 12
Riverstown *Cork* ... 90 G 12
Riverstown *Sligo* ... 112 G 5
Riverstown *Tipperary* ... 101 I 8
Riverville ... 93 D 11
Roadford ... 98 D 8
Roaninish ... 116 G 3
Roaringwater Bay ... 89 D 13
Robe ... 105 E 6
Robert's Head ... 90 H 12
Robertstown ... 102 L 8
Robinstown ... 108 L 7
Roche's Point ... 90 H 12
Rochestown ... 96 K 11
Rochfortbridge ... 101 K 7
Rock (The) ... 114 L 4
Rock Island ... 98 C 8
Rockabill ... 109 N 7
Rockchapel ... 93 E 11
Rockcorry ... 108 K 5
Rockhill ... 94 F 10
Rockmills ... 94 G 11
Rodeen ... 107 H 6
Roe ... 118 L 3
Roe Valley ... 118 L 2
Roney Point ... 97 N 10
Rooaun ... 100 H 8
Roonagh Quay ... 104 C 6
Roonah Lough ... 104 C 6
Roosky *Leitrim* ... 112 H 4
Roosky *Mayo* ... 106 F 6
Roosky *Roscommon* ... 107 I 6
Ropefield ... 112 G 5
Ros an Mhil / Rossaveel ... 98 D 8
Ros Comáin / Roscommon ... 106 H 7
Ros Cré / Roscrea ... 101 I 9
Ros Láir / Rosslare ... 97 M 11
Ros Mhic Thriúin / New Ross ... 96 L 10
Rosapenna ... 117 I 2
Rosbercon ... 96 L 10
Rosegreen ... 95 I 10
Rosenallis ... 101 J 8
Rosguill ... 117 I 2
Roskeeragh Point ... 112 F 4
Rosmuck ... 105 D 7
Rosmult ... 95 I 9
Rosnakill ... 117 I 2
Ross *Lough Leane* ... 89 D 11
Ross *Lough Sheelin* ... 107 K 6
Ross Abbey ... 105 E 7
Ross Lake ... 105 E 7
Ross Port ... 111 C 5
Ross West ... 105 E 6
Rossan Point ... 112 F 3
Rossbeg ... 116 G 3
Rossbeigh Creek ... 92 C 11
Rossbrin ... 89 D 13
Rosscahill ... 105 E 7
Rosscarbery ... 89 E 13
Rosscarbery Bay ... 89 E 13
Rosscor ... 113 H 4
Rossdohan Island ... 88 C 12
Rosserk Abbey ... 111 E 5
Rosses (The) ... 116 G 2
Rosses Bay ... 116 G 2
Rosses Point ... 112 G 5
Rossgeir ... 117 J 3
Rossglass ... 115 O 5
Rossinver ... 112 H 4
Rosslare Bay ... 97 M 11
Rosslare Point ... 97 M 11
Rosslea ... 113 K 5
Rossmore *Cork* ... 89 F 12
Rossmore *Laois* ... 102 K 9
Rossmore Forest Park ... 114 L 5
Rossmore Island ... 88 C 12
Rossnowlagh ... 112 H 4
Rostellan ... 90 H 12
Rostrevor ... 109 N 5
Rosturk ... 105 C 6
Rough Point ... 92 B 11
Roughty ... 89 D 12
Roundfort ... 105 E 7
Roundstone ... 104 C 7
Roundwood ... 103 N 8
Roury ... 89 E 13
Rousky ... 114 K 3
Rowallane Gardens ... 115 O 4
Rower (The) ... 96 L 10
Royal Canal ... 107 I 7
Royaloak ... 96 L 9
Ruan ... 99 F 9
Rubane ... 115 P 4
Rue Point ... 119 N 2
Runabay Head ... 119 N 2
Runnabackan ... 106 H 6
Rushen (Slieve) ... 113 J 5
Russborough House ... 103 M 8
Rutland Island ... 116 G 3
Ryefield ... 108 K 6
Ryehill ... 106 F 7
Rylane Cross ... 90 F 12

S

Saddle Head ... 110 B 5
Saggart ... 103 M 8
St. Finan's Bay ... 88 A 12
St. John's Lough ... 107 I 5
St. John's Point ... 115 P 5
St. John's Point ... 112 G 4
St. Johnstown ... 117 J 3
St. Macdara's Island ... 104 C 8
St. Margaret's ... 103 N 7
St. Mochta's House ... 108 M 6
St. Mullin's ... 96 L 10
Saintfield ... 115 O 4
Saleen *Cork* ... 90 H 12
Saleen *Kerry* ... 93 D 10
Salia ... 104 C 6
Sallahig ... 88 B 12
Sallins ... 102 M 8
Sally Gap ... 103 N 8
Sallybrook ... 90 G 12
Sallypark ... 100 H 9
Salrock ... 104 C 7
Saltee Islands ... 96 M 11
Salthill ... 99 E 8
Salt (River) ... 102 L 8
Sandholes ... 114 L 4
Sandyford ... 103 N 8
Santry ... 103 N 7
Saul ... 115 O 4
Sawel Mountain ... 118 K 3
Scardaun *Mayo* ... 105 E 7
Scardaun *Roscommon* ... 106 H 7
Scarnagh ... 97 N 9
Scarriff / An Scairbh ... 99 G 9
Scarriff Island ... 88 B 12
Scartaglin ... 93 D 11
Scarva ... 114 M 5
Scattery Island ... 93 D 10
Schull / Skull ... 89 D 13
Scolban (Lough) ... 113 H 4
Scotch Town ... 114 K 3
Scotshouse ... 113 K 5
Scotstown ... 114 K 5
Scrabo Hill ... 115 O 4
Scramoge ... 107 H 6
Screeb Cross ... 105 D 7
Screen ... 97 M 10
Screggan ... 101 J 8
Scribbagh ... 113 H 4
Scullogue Gap ... 96 L 10
Scur (Lough) ... 107 I 5
Seaforde ... 115 O 5
Seapatrick ... 114 N 4
Seefin ... 95 J 11
Seskinore ... 113 K 4
Seskinryan ... 96 L 9
Seven Heads ... 90 F 13
Seven Hogs or Magharee Islands (The) ... 92 B 11
Shalwy ... 112 G 4
Shanacashel ... 88 C 11
Shanagarry ... 90 H 12
Shanaglish ... 99 F 8
Shanagolden ... 93 E 10
Shanahoe ... 101 J 9
Shanballard ... 99 G 7
Shanbally *Cork* ... 90 G 12
Shanbally *Galway* ... 106 G 7
Shanballymore ... 94 G 11
Shanco ... 114 L 4
Shankill ... 103 N 8
Shanlaragh ... 89 E 12
Shanlis ... 108 M 6
Shannagh (Lough) ... 115 N 5
Shannawona ... 105 D 7
Shannon ... 99 F 9
Shannon (River) ... 100 H 8
Shannon Airport ... 99 F 9
Shannon Harbour ... 101 I 8
Shannonbridge ... 100 H 8
Shanragh ... 101 K 9
Shantonagh ... 108 L 5
Sharavogue ... 101 I 8
Sheddings (The) ... 119 N 3
Sheeanamore ... 103 M 9
Sheeaun ... 99 G 9
Sheeffry Hills ... 105 C 6
Sheehan's Point ... 88 B 12
Sheelin (Lough) ... 107 K 6
Sheep Haven ... 117 I 2
Sheever (Lough) ... 107 K 7
Shehy Mountains ... 89 D 12
Shercock ... 108 L 6
Sherkin Island ... 89 D 13
Sherky Island ... 88 C 12
Sheskin ... 111 D 5
Sheskinapoll ... 117 J 3
Shillelagh ... 97 M 9
Shinrone ... 101 I 9
Shiven ... 106 G 7
Shoptown ... 115 N 3
Shot Head ... 89 C 13
Shranamanragh Bridge ... 110 C 5
Shrule ... 105 E 7
Silent Valley ... 109 O 5
Sillan (Lough) ... 108 L 5
Silver Bridge ... 108 M 5
Silver Strand ... 104 C 6
Silvermine Mountains ... 100 H 9
Silvermines ... 100 H 9
Sinking ... 106 F 7
Sion Mills ... 113 J 3
Six Crosses ... 93 D 10
Six Road Ends ... 115 P 4
Six Towns (The) ... 114 L 3
Sixmilebridge ... 99 F 9
Sixmilecross ... 114 K 4
Skannive (Lough) ... 104 C 8
Skeagh ... 107 J 7
Skehana ... 101 K 9
Skehanagh ... 106 G 7
Skerries (The) ... 118 M 2
Skreen *Meath* ... 108 M 7
Skreen *Sligo* ... 112 F 5
Sky Road ... 104 B 7
Slade ... 96 L 11
Slane ... 108 M 6
Slane (Hill of) ... 108 M 6
Slaney (River) ... 97 M 10
Slat (Lough) ... 92 B 11
Slea Head ... 92 A 11
Slemish Mountain ... 119 N 3
Sliabh na Caillighe ... 108 K 6
Slieve Anierin ... 113 I 5
Slieve Aught Mountains ... 99 G 8
Slieve Bernagh ... 99 G 9
Slieve Bloom Mountains ... 101 J 8
Slieve Gamph or the Ox Mountains ... 111 F 5
Slieve Mish Mountains ... 93 C 11
Slieve Miskish Mountains ... 88 C 13
Slieveanorra ... 119 N 2
Slievecallan ... 99 E 9
Slievefelim Mountains ... 94 H 9
Slievekimalta ... 100 H 9
Slievekirk ... 117 K 3
Slievemore *Dungannon* ... 114 K 4
Slievemore *Mayo* ... 110 B 5
Slievemurry ... 106 G 7
Slievenamon ... 95 J 10
Slieveroe ... 96 K 11
Slievetooey ... 116 G 3
Sligeach / Sligo ... 112 G 5
Sligo Bay ... 112 F 5
Slyne Head ... 104 B 7
Smerwick ... 92 A 11
Smerwick Harbour ... 92 A 11
Smithborough ... 114 K 5
Smithstown ... 101 K 9
Snagh (Slieve) *Derryveagh Mts.* ... 117 H 3
Snaght (Slieve) *Inishowen* ... 117 J 2
Snave ... 89 D 12
Sneem ... 88 C 12
Snave Castle ... 114 N 3
Soldierstown ... 115 N 4
Sord / Swords ... 103 N 7
South Sound ... 98 D 8
Spa ... 93 C 11
Spa (The) ... 115 O 4
Spanish Point *Locality* ... 98 D 9
Spanish Point *Mal Bay* ... 98 D 9
Speenoge ... 117 J 2
Spelga Dam ... 115 N 5
Sperrin Mountains ... 118 K 3
Spink ... 101 K 9
Spittaltown ... 101 J 7
Springfield ... 113 I 4
Springhill ... 114 M 3
Springwell Forest ... 118 L 2
Squires Hill ... 115 O 4
Sraghmore ... 103 N 8
Srah / An tSraith ... 105 E 6
Srahduggaun ... 111 C 6
Srahmore *near Bangor* ... 111 C 5
Srahmore *near Newport* ... 105 D 6
Srahmore *River* ... 105 D 6
Sráid na Cathrach / Milltown Malbay ... 98 D 9
Stabannan ... 109 M 6
Stackallan ... 108 M 6
Stack's Mountains ... 93 D 11
Staffordstown ... 114 M 3
Stags (The) ... 89 E 13
Stags of Broad Haven ... 111 C 4
Staigue Stone Fort ... 88 B 12
Stamullin ... 109 N 7
Stapleston ... 102 L 8
Stepaside ... 103 N 8
Stewartstown ... 114 L 4
Stickstown ... 90 F 12
Stillorgan ... 103 N 8
Stone Bridge ... 113 K 5
Stonyford *Kilkenny* ... 96 K 10
Stonyford *Lisburn* ... 115 N 4
Stormont ... 115 O 4
Strabane ... 117 J 3
Stracashel ... 117 H 3
Stradbally *Kerry* ... 92 B 11
Stradbally *Laois* ... 101 K 8
Stradbally *Waterford* ... 91 J 11
Strade ... 105 E 6
Stradone ... 107 K 6
Stradreagh ... 118 L 2
Straffan ... 103 M 8
Stragar ... 112 G 3
Straid *Donegal* ... 117 J 2
Straid *Larne* ... 115 O 3
Straid *Moyle* ... 118 M 2
Straith Salach / Recess ... 104 C 7
Strand ... 93 E 10
Strandhill ... 112 G 5
Strangford ... 115 P 4
Strangford Lough ... 115 P 4
Stranocum ... 118 M 2
Stranorlar ... 117 I 3
Stratford ... 102 L 9
Stravally ... 112 G 3
Streamstown ... 104 B 7
Streedagh Point ... 112 G 4
Streek Head ... 89 C 13
Street ... 107 J 6
Strokestown ... 106 H 6
Stroove ... 118 L 2
Struell Wells ... 115 O 5
Strule ... 113 J 3
Sturrakeen ... 95 H 10
Suck (River) ... 106 G 6
Suir (River) ... 101 I 9
Summercove ... 90 G 12
Summerhill ... 108 L 7
Suncroft ... 102 L 8
Sunderlin (Lough) ... 107 I 7
Swan ... 101 K 9
Swanlinbar ... 113 I 5
Swan's Cross Roads ... 114 K 5
Swatragh ... 118 L 3
Sweep (The) ... 95 J 10
Swilly (Lough) ... 117 J 2
Swilly (River) ... 117 J 2
Sybil Head ... 92 A 11

T

Table Mountain ... 103 M 8
Tacumshane ... 97 M 11
Tacumshin Lake ... 97 M 11
Taghmon ... 96 M 11
Taghshinny ... 107 I 7
Tagoat ... 97 M 11
Tahilla ... 88 C 12
Talbot Island ... 104 B 7
Talbotstown ... 102 M 9
Tallaght ... 103 M 8
Tallanstown ... 108 M 6
Tallow ... 91 H 11
Tallowbridge ... 91 H 11
Talt (Lough) ... 111 F 5
Tamlaght *Fermanagh* ... 113 J 5

Tamlaght *Magherafelt* ....118 M 3
Tamnamore ....114 M 4
Tandragee ....114 M 4
Tang ....107 I 7
Tangaveane ....116 H 3
Tappaghan Mount ....113 J 4
Tara (Hill of) ....108 M 7
Tarbert ....93 D 10
Tardree Forest ....115 N 3
Tarker (Lough) ....108 L 5
Tarmon ....112 H 5
Tarsaghaunmore ....111 C 5
Tassagh ....114 L 5
Taughblane ....115 N 4
Taur ....93 E 11
Tawin ....99 E 8
Tawin Island ....99 E 8
Tawny ....117 I 2
Tawnyinah ....106 F 6
Tawnylea ....112 H 5
Tay ....95 J 11
Tay (Lough) ....103 N 8
Taylor's Cross ....101 I 8
Tearaght Island ....92 A 11
Tedavnet ....114 K 5
Teelin ....112 G 4
Teemore ....113 J 5
Teeranea ....98 D 8
Teeranearagh ....88 B 12
Teerelton ....89 F 12
Teermaclane ....99 E 9
Teernakill ....105 D 7
Teeromoyle ....88 B 12
Teevurcher ....108 L 6
Temple (The) ....115 O 4
Temple of the Winds ....115 P 4
Templeboy ....112 F 5
Templederry ....100 H 9
Templeglentan ....93 E 10
Templehouse Lake ....112 G 5
Templemartin ....90 F 12
Templenoe ....89 C 12
Templeoran ....101 J 7
Templepatrick ....115 N 3
Templeshanbo ....96 L 10
Templetouhy ....101 I 9
Templetown ....96 L 11
Tempo ....113 J 4
Terenure ....103 N 8
Termon ....98 D 10
Termonbarry ....107 I 6
Termonfeckin ....109 N 6

Terryglass ....100 H 8
Tevrin ....107 K 7
Thomas Street ....106 H 7
Thomastown *Meath* ....108 L 6
Thomastown *Tipperrary* ....95 H 10
Thoor Ballylee ....99 F 8
Three Castle Head ....88 C 13
Three Castles ....96 J 9
Three Rock ....103 N 8
Tiduff ....92 B 11
Tievealehid ....116 H 2
Tievemore ....113 I 4
Tillyvoos ....112 H 4
Tiltinbane ....113 I 5
Timahoe ....102 L 8
Timoleague ....90 F 13
Timolin ....102 L 9
Tinahely ....103 M 9
Tinnahinch ....96 L 10
Tinriland ....102 L 9
Tiobraid Árann / Tipperary ....95 H 10
Tirnaneill ....114 L 5
Tirneevin ....99 F 8
Toames ....89 F 12
Tobar an Choire / Tubbercurry ....112 F 5
Tober ....101 J 7
Toberbeg ....102 M 8
Toberdoney ....118 M 2
Tobermore ....114 L 3
Tobernadarry ....105 E 7
Toberscanavan ....112 G 5
Toe Head ....89 E 13
Toem ....95 H 10
Togher *Cork* ....89 E 12
Togher *Louth* ....109 N 6
Togher *Offaly* ....101 K 8
Tolka ....103 M 7
Tollymore Forest Park ....115 O 5
Tombrack ....97 M 10
Tomdarragh ....103 N 8
Tomhaggard ....97 M 11
Tonabrocky ....99 E 8
Tonakeera Point ....104 C 7
Tonyduff ....108 K 6
Toomaghera ....99 E 8
Toomard ....106 G 7
Toombeola ....104 C 7
Toome ....114 M 3
Toomyvara ....100 H 9
Toor ....100 H 9

Tooraree ....93 E 10
Tooreencahill ....93 E 11
Toorlestraun ....112 F 5
Toormore ....89 D 13
Toormore Bay ....89 D 13
Toornafulla ....93 E 10
Toraigh / Tory Island ....116 H 2
Torc Waterfall ....89 D 11
Torneady Point ....116 G 2
Torr Head ....119 N 2
Tory Sound ....117 H 2
Tourig (River) ....91 I 11
Tower ....90 G 12
Trá Lí / Tralee ....93 C 11
Trá Mhór / Tramore ....96 K 11
Trabane Strand ....112 F 4
Tracton ....90 G 12
Trafrask ....89 D 12
Tragumna ....89 E 13
Tralee Bay ....92 C 11
Tramore Bay ....96 K 11
Tranarossan Bay ....117 I 2
Travara Bridge ....88 C 12
Trawbreaga Bay ....117 K 2
Trawenagh Bay ....116 G 3
Trawmore Bay ....110 C 5
Trean ....105 D 7
Treantagh ....117 I 2
Treehoo ....107 K 5
Trien ....106 G 6
Trillick ....113 J 4
Tristia ....110 C 5
Trory ....113 J 4
Trostan ....119 N 2
Truskmore ....112 G 4
Trust / Tuam ....100 G 7
Tuaim / Tuam ....105 F 7
Tuamgraney ....99 G 9
Tuar Mhic Éadaigh / Tourmakeady ....105 D 7
Tubber ....99 F 8
Tubbrid *Kilkenny* ....95 J 9
Tubbrid *Tipperary* ....95 I 11
Tulach Mhór / Tullamore ....101 J 8
Tulla *near Ennis* ....99 F 9
Tulla *near Gort* ....99 F 8
Tullagh Point ....117 J 2
Tullaghan ....112 G 4
Tullaghan Bay ....110 C 5

Tullaghanstown ....108 L 7
Tullagher ....96 K 10
Tullaghobegly ....117 H 2
Tullaherin ....96 K 10
Tullahought ....95 J 10
Tullakeel ....88 C 12
Tullamore ....93 D 10
Tullaroan ....95 J 10
Tullig ....92 C 11
Tullig Point ....93 C 10
Tullokyne ....105 E 7
Tully
  Lower Lough Erne ....113 I 4
Tully *near Ballyshannon* ....113 H 4
Tully *Upper Lough Erne* ....113 J 5
Tully Cross ....104 C 7
Tully National Stud ....102 L 8
Tullyallen ....109 M 6
Tullyamalra ....108 L 5
Tullycanna ....96 L 11
Tullydush ....117 J 2
Tullyhogue ....114 L 4
Tullylease ....94 F 11
Tullymacreeve ....109 M 5
Tullynaha ....112 H 3
Tullynally Castle ....107 J 6
Tullyroan ....114 M 4
Tullyvin ....108 K 5
Tulrohaun ....105 F 6
Tulsk ....106 H 6
Turlough ....105 E 6
Turloughmore ....105 F 7
Turner's Rock Tunnel ....89 D 12
Turreen ....107 I 7
Tuskar Rock ....97 N 11
Twelve Pins (The) ....104 C 7
Twomileborris ....95 I 9
Tylas ....108 M 7
Tynagh ....100 G 8
Tynan ....114 L 5
Tyrella ....115 O 5
Tyrellspass ....101 J 7

U
Uachtar Ard / Oughterard ....105 E 7
Uaigh / Owey Island ....116 G 2
Ugga Beg (Lough) ....98 D 8
Ulster American Folk Park ....113 J 4
Ulster Folk Museum (The) ....115 O 4

Union Hall ....89 E 13
Unshin ....112 G 5
Upper Ballinderry ....115 N 4
Upper Lake ....103 M 8
Upperchurch ....95 H 9
Upperlands ....118 M 3
Urbalreagh ....117 K 1
Urglin Glebe ....102 L 9
Urlaur ....106 F 6
Urlaur Lough ....106 F 6
Urlingford ....95 J 9

V
Valencia Island ....88 A 12
Valley ....110 C 5
Valleymount ....103 M 8
Vartry Reservoir ....103 N 8
Ventry ....92 A 11
Ventry Harbour ....92 A 11
Vicarstown ....102 K 8
Victoria Bridge ....113 J 3
Villierstown ....91 I 11
Virginia ....108 K 6
Virginia Road ....108 K 6
Vow ....118 M 3

W
Waddingtown ....96 M 11
Walshestown ....97 M 11
Walshtown ....90 H 12
Ward ....103 N 7
Ward (River) ....103 N 7
Waringsford ....115 N 4
Waringstown ....114 N 4
Warrenpoint ....109 N 5
Washing Bay ....114 M 4
Watch Ho.-Village ....96 M 9
Waterfall ....90 G 12
Waterfoot or Glenariff ....119 N 2
Waterford Harbour ....96 L 11
Watergrasshill ....90 G 11
Waterworks ....114 L 3
Wattle Bridge ....113 J 5
Welchtown ....117 I 3
Wellington Bridge ....96 L 11
Wells Cross ....114 M 4
Wesport Bay ....105 C 6
West Town ....116 H 2
Westcove ....88 B 12
Westport House ....105 D 6
Westport Quay ....105 D 6
Wexford Bay ....97 N 10

Wexford Harbour ....97 M 10
Whale Head ....117 J 2
Wheathill ....113 I 5
Whiddy Island ....89 D 12
White *Limerick* ....93 E 10
White *Louth* ....109 M 6
White Castle ....118 K 2
White Hall ....89 D 13
White Island ....113 I 4
White Park Bay ....118 M 2
White Strand ....98 D 9
Whiteabbey ....115 O 3
Whitechurch *Cork* ....90 G 12
Whitechurch *Waterford* ....91 I 11
Whitecross ....114 M 5
Whitegate ....90 H 12
Whitehall *Roscommon* ....107 I 6
Whitehall *Westmeath* ....107 K 7
Whitehead ....115 O 3
Whites Town ....109 N 6
White'sCross ....90 G 12
Whitesides Corner ....114 M 3
Wicklow Gap ....103 M 8
Wicklow Mountains ....103 N 8
Wicklow Way ....103 N 8
Wildfowl and Wetlands Trust ....115 O 4
Wilkinstown ....108 L 6
Willbrook ....99 E 9
Williamstown *Galway* ....106 G 6
Williamstown *Westmeath* ....107 I 7
Windgap ....95 J 10
Windmill ....102 L 7
Windy Gap *Kerry* ....89 D 12
Windy Gap *Louth* ....109 N 5
Windy Gap *Mayo* ....105 E 5
Wolfhill ....101 K 9
Womanagh ....91 I 12
Woodburn ....115 O 3
Woodcock Hill ....99 F 9
Woodenbridge ....103 N 9
Woodford (River) ....99 G 8
Woodstown ....96 L 11

Y
Yellow Furze ....108 M 6
Yganavan (Lough) ....92 C 11
Youghal ....100 H 9
Youghal Bay ....91 I 12

A B C D E F G H I J K L M N O P Q R S T U V W X Y Z

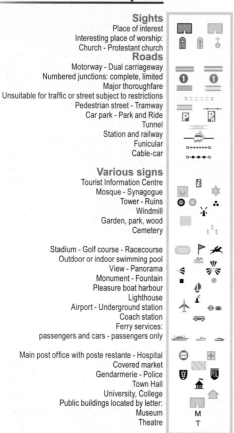

Town plans

Sights
Place of interest
Interesting place of worship:
Church - Protestant church
Roads
Motorway - Dual carriageway
Numbered junctions: complete, limited
Major thoroughfare
Unsuitable for traffic or street subject to restrictions
Pedestrian street - Tramway
Car park - Park and Ride
Tunnel
Station and railway
Funicular
Cable-car

Various signs
Tourist Information Centre
Mosque - Synagogue
Tower - Ruins
Windmill
Garden, park, wood
Cemetery

Stadium - Golf course - Racecourse
Outdoor or indoor swimming pool
View - Panorama
Monument - Fountain
Pleasure boat harbour
Lighthouse
Airport - Underground station
Coach station
Ferry services:
passengers and cars - passengers only

Main post office with poste restante - Hospital
Covered market
Gendarmerie - Police
Town Hall
University, College
Public buildings located by letter:
Museum
Theatre

Plans

Curiosités
Bâtiment intéressant
Édifice religieux intéressant : catholique - protestant
Voirie
Autoroute - Double chaussée de type autoroutier
Échangeurs numérotés : complet - partiels
Grande voie de circulation
Rue réglementée ou impraticable
Rue piétonne - Tramway
Parking - Parking Relais
Tunnel
Gare et voie ferrée
Funiculaire, voie à crémaillère
Téléphérique, télécabine

Signes divers
Information touristique
Mosquée - Synagogue
Tour - Ruines
Moulin à vent
Jardin, parc, bois
Cimetière

Stade - Golf - Hippodrome
Piscine de plein air, couverte
Vue - Panorama
Monument - Fontaine
Port de plaisance
Phare
Aéroport - Station de métro
Gare routière
Transport par bateau :
passagers et voitures, passagers seulement

Bureau principal de poste restante - Hôpital
Marché couvert
Gendarmerie - Police
Hôtel de ville
Université, grande école
Bâtiment public repéré par une lettre :
Musée
Théâtre

Stadtpläne

Sehenswürdigkeiten
Sehenswertes Gebäude
Sehenswerter Sakralbau:Katholische - Evangelische Kirche
Straßen
Autobahn - Schnellstraße
Nummerierte Voll- bzw. Teilanschlussstellen
Hauptverkehrsstraße
Gesperrte Straße oder mit Verkehrsbeschränkungen
Fußgängerzone - Straßenbahn
Parkplatz - Park-and-Ride-Plätze
Tunnel
Bahnhof und Bahnlinie
Standseilbahn
Seilschwebebahn

Sonstige Zeichen
Informationsstelle
Moschee - Synagoge
Turm - Ruine
Windmühle
Garten, Park, Wäldchen
Friedhof

Stadion - Golfplatz - Pferderennbahn
Freibad - Hallenbad
Aussicht - Rundblick
Denkmal - Brunnen
Yachthafen
Leuchtturm
Flughafen - U-Bahnstation
Autobusbahnhof
Schiffsverbindungen:
Autofähre, Personenfähre
Hauptpostamt (postlagernde Sendungen) - Krankenhaus
Markthalle
Gendarmerie - Polizei
Rathaus
Universität, Hochschule
Öffentliches Gebäude, durch einen Buchstaben gekennzeichnet:
Museum
Theater

Plattegronden

Bezienswaardigheden
Interessant gebouw
Interessant kerkelijk gebouw: Kerk - Protestantse kerk

Wegen
Autosnelweg - Weg met gescheiden rijbanen
Knooppunt / aansluiting: volledig, gedeeltelijk
Hoofdverkeersweg
Onbegaanbare straat, beperkt toegankelijk
Voetgangersgebied - Tramlijn
Parkeerplaats - P & R
Tunnel
Station, spoorweg
Kabelspoor
Tandradbaan

Overige tekens
Informatie voor toeristen
Moskee - Synagoge
Toren - Ruine
Windmolen
Tuin, park, bos
Begraafplaats

Stadion - Golfterrein - Renbaan
Zwembad: openlucht, overdekt
Uitzicht - Panorama
Gedenkteken, standbeeld - Fontein
Jachthaven
Vuurtoren
Luchthaven - Metrostation
Busstation
Vervoer per boot:
Passagiers en auto's - uitsluitend passagiers

Hoofdkantoor voor poste-restante - Ziekenhuis
Overdekte markt
Marechaussee / rijkswacht - Politie
Stadhuis
Universiteit, hogeschool
Openbaar gebouw, aangegeven met een letter::
Museum
Schouwburg

Piante

Curiosità
Edificio interessante
Costruzione religiosa interessante: Chiesa - Tempio

Viabilità
Autostrada - Doppia carreggiata tipo autostrada
Svincoli numerati: completo, parziale
Grande via di circolazione
Via regolamentata o impraticabile
Via pedonale - Tranvia
Parcheggio - Parcheggio Ristoro
Galleria
Stazione e ferrovia
Funicolare
Funivia, cabinovia

Simboli vari
Ufficio informazioni turistiche
Moschea - Sinagoga
Torre - Ruderi
Mulino a vento
Giardino, parco, bosco
Cimitero

Stadio - Golf - Ippodromo
Piscina: all'aperto, coperta
Vista - Panorama
Monumento - Fontana
Porto turistico
Faro
Aeroporto - Stazione della metropolitana
Autostazione
Trasporto con traghetto:
passeggeri ed autovetture - solo passeggeri

Ufficio centrale di fermo posta - Ospedale
Mercato coperto
Carabinieri - Polizia
Municipio
Università, scuola superiore
Edificio pubblico indicato con lettera:
Museo
Teatro

Planos

Curiosidades
Edificio interessante
Edificio religioso interessante: católica - protestante

Vías de circulación
Autopista - Autovía
Enlaces numerados: completo, parciales
Vía importante de circulacion
Calle reglamentada o impracticable
Calle peatonal - Tranvía
Aparcamiento - Aparcamientos «P+R»
Túnel
Estación y línea férrea
Funicular, línea de cremallera
Teleférico, telecabina

Signos diversos
Oficina de Información de Turismo
Mezquita - Sinagoga
Torre - Ruinas
Molino de viento
Jardín, parque, madera
Cementerio

Estadio - Golf - Hipódromo
Piscina al aire libre, cubierta
Vista parcial - Vista panorámica
Monumento - Fuente
Puerto deportivo
Faro
Aeropuerto - Estación de metro
Estación de autobuses
Transporte por barco:
pasajeros y vehículos, pasajeros solamente

Oficina de correos - Hospital
Mercado cubierto
Policía National - Policía
Ayuntamiento
Universidad, escuela superior
Edificio público localizado con letra :
Museo
Teatro

Plans de ville
Town plans / Stadtpläne / Stadsplattegronden
Piante di città / Planos de ciudades

GREAT BRITAIN

- Aberdeen 150
- Bath 150
- Birmingham............ 151
- Bournemouth 152
- Brighton and Hove 153
- Bristol 154
- Cambridge.............. 155
- Canterbury............. 156
- Cardiff 157
- Chester 158
- Coventry............... 159
- Dundee................ 159
- Durham................ 160
- Edinburgh 161
- Exeter.................. 162
- Glasgow 163
- Leeds 164
- Leicester 165
- Lincoln................. 165
- Liverpool 166-167
- Greater London 168-169
- London 170-171
- Manchester 172
- Newcastle-upon-Tyne ... 173
- Norwich 174
- Nottingham............. 174
- Oxford 175
- Perth 176
- Plymouth 177
- Portsmouth
  and Southsea 178
- Southampton 179
- Stirling................. 180
- Stratford-upon-Avon 181
- Winchester............. 182
- Windsor................ 183
- York 184

IRELAND

- Belfast 185
- Cork 186
- Galway................. 187
- Dublin 188-189
- Killarney 190
- Limerick 191

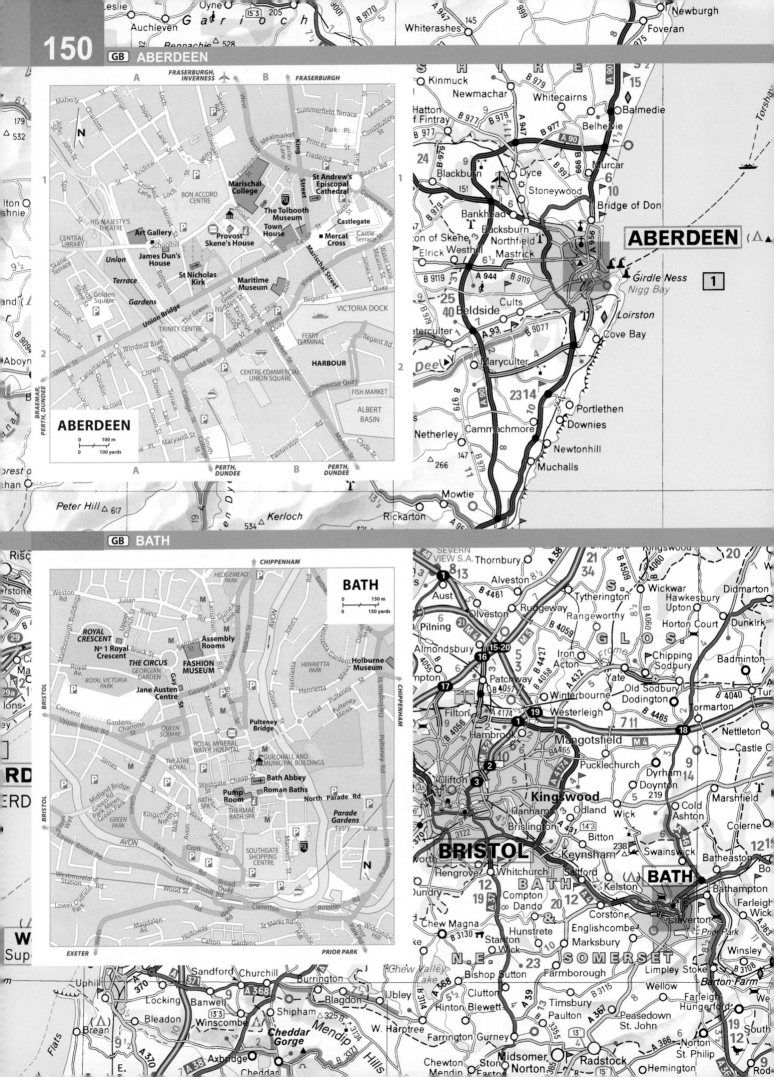

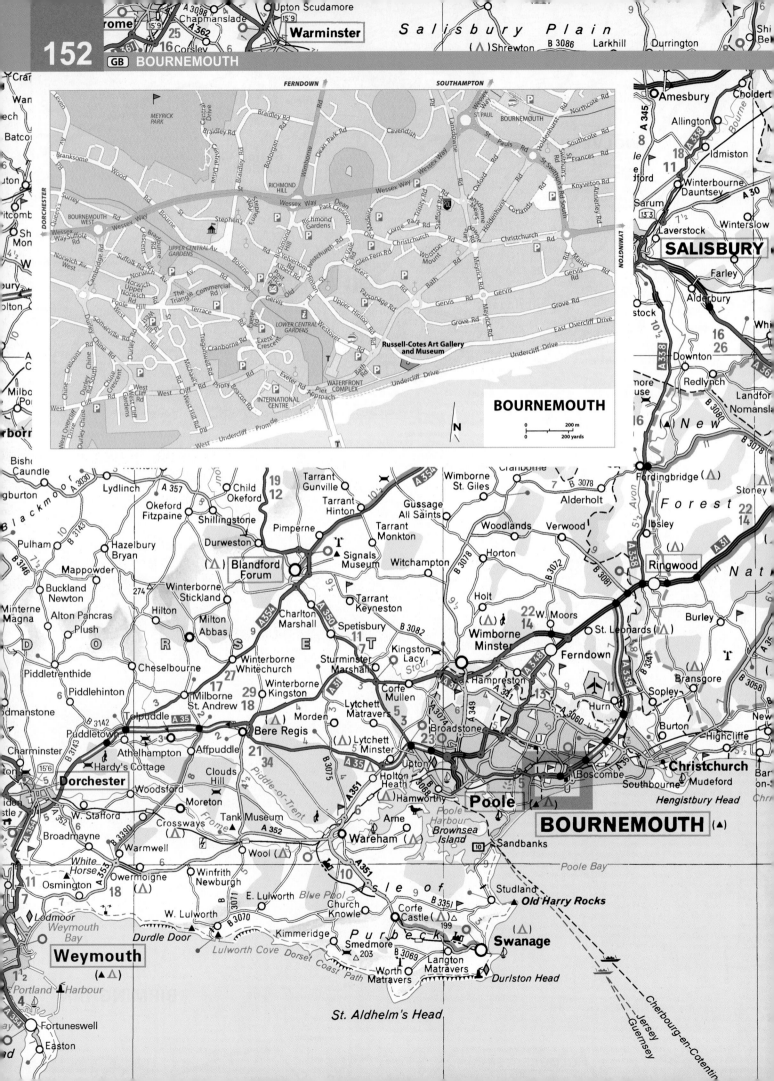

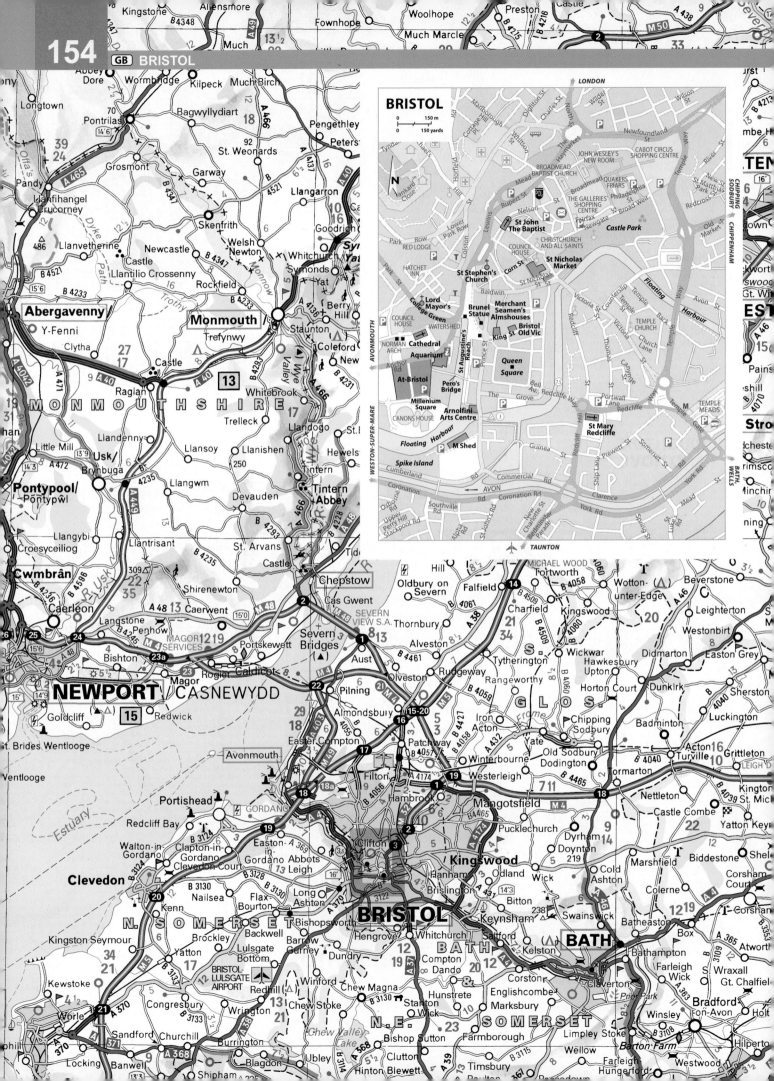

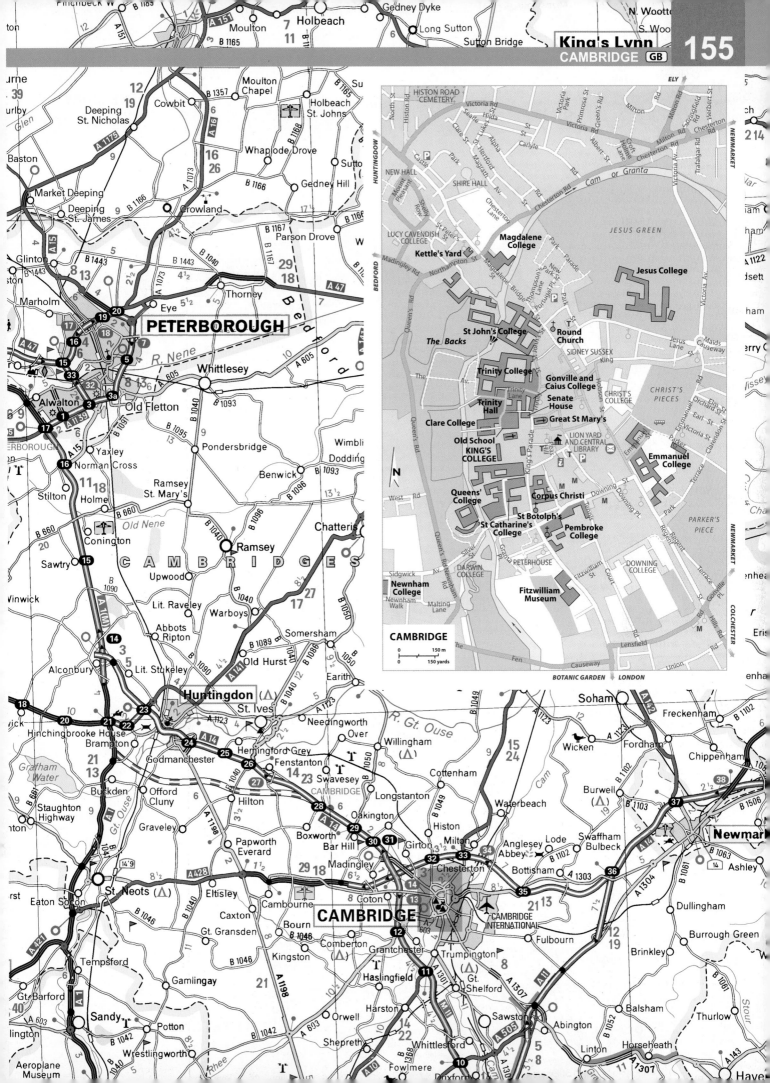

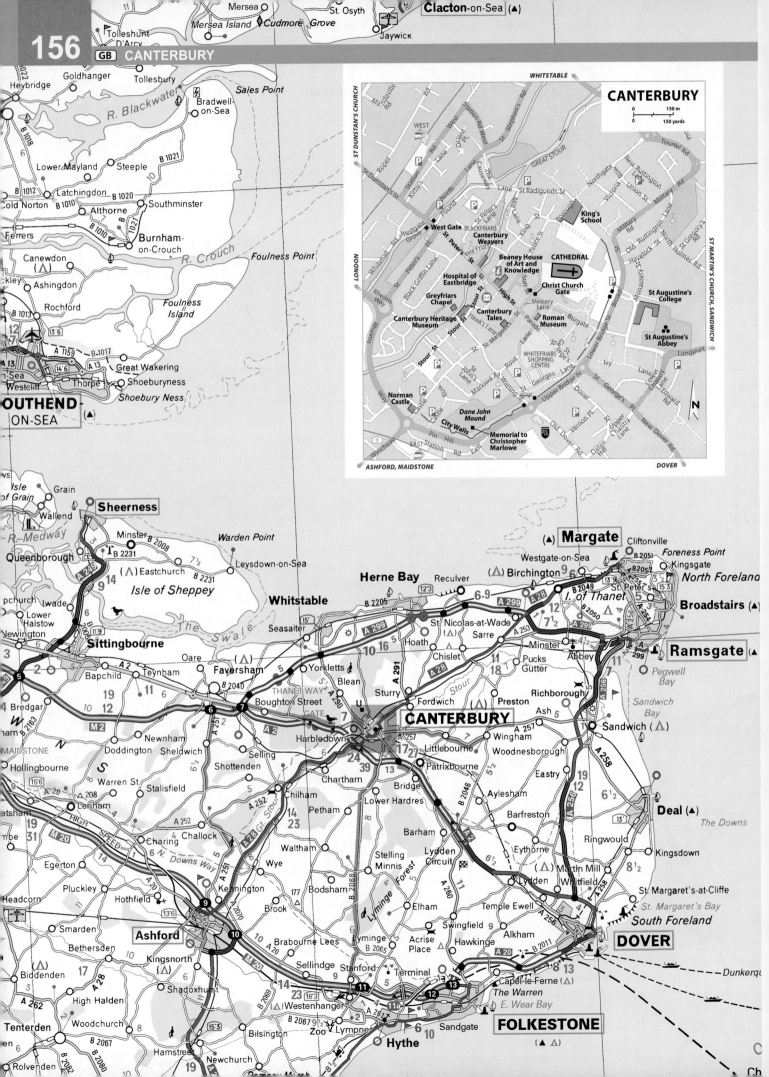

CANTERBURY (inset map)

0 — 150 m
0 — 150 yards

Key locations on inset map: ST DUNSTAN'S CHURCH, WHITSTABLE, St Dunstan's St, Roper Rd, Kirby's Ln, Station Rd West, St Stephens Rd, Tourtel Rd, WEST, North Ln, The Causeway, St Radigunds St, New Ruttington Lane, Union St, Victoria Rd, Military Rd, King's School, West Gate, BLACKFRIARS, Canterbury Weavers, Borough, Northgate, Old Ruttington Lane, North Holmes Rd, St Gregory's, ST MARTIN'S CHURCH, SANDWICH, St Peter's Ln, Beaney House of Art and Knowledge, CATHEDRAL, Havelock St, St Augustine's College, Hospital of Eastbridge, High St, Christ Church Gate, Monastery St, Greyfriars Chapel, Canterbury Tales, Roman Museum, Burgate, Lower Bridge St, St Augustine's Abbey, Canterbury Heritage Museum, Hawk's Lane, Mercery Lane, Parade, St Margaret's, Longport, St George's, Rose Lane, Ivy Lane, Chantry Rd, Edward Rd, WHITEFRIARS SHOPPING CENTRE, Watling St, St Georges Pl, Dover St, Upper Chantry Lane, New Dover Rd, Norman Castle, Castle St, Pin Hill, City Walls, Dane John Mound, Memorial to Christopher Marlowe, Old Dover Rd, Vernon Pl, Upper Bridge St, EAST STATION, Wincheap, ASHFORD, MAIDSTONE, DOVER, N

Mersea, Mersea Island, Cudmore Grove, St. Osyth, **Clacton-on-Sea** (▲), Jaywick, Tolleshunt D'Arcy

Heybridge, Goldhanger, Tollesbury, Sales Point, Bradwell-on-Sea, R. Blackwater

Lower Mayland, Steeple, B 1021, B 1018

B 1012, Latchingdon, B 1020, B 1010, Cold Norton, Althorne, Southminster, Ferrers, Burnham-on-Crouch, R. Crouch, Foulness Point

Canewdon (▲), Ashingdon, Foulness Island, Rochford, B 1013

Hockley, Great Wakering, Shoeburyness, A 1159, B-1017, A 13, Thorpe, Shoebury Ness, Westcliff

SOUTHEND-ON-SEA (▲)

Isle of Grain, Grain, Wallend, R. Medway, **Sheerness**, Minster, B 2008, B 2231, Warden Point, Queenborough, A 249, Eastchurch, B 2231, Leysdown-on-Sea, Isle of Sheppey, **Margate** (▲), Cliftonville, Foreness Point, Westgate-on-Sea, Kingsgate, North Foreland, Birchington, B 2051, St Peter's, I. of Thanet, **Broadstairs** (▲), A 299, A 28, A 2050, A 254, A 256

Upchurch, Iwade, Lower Halstow, Newington, The Swale, Herne Bay, Reculver, Whitstable, B 2205, A 299, St. Nicolas-at-Wade, Sarre, A 253, Minster, Abbey, **Ramsgate** (▲), Pegwell Bay

Sittingbourne, Oare, (▲), Seasalter, Hoath, Chislet, Pucks Gutter, Sandwich Bay

Bredgar, Bapchild, Teynham, Faversham, B 2040, Yorkletts, Blean, A 291, Sturry, Fordwich, Preston, Richborough, Ash, Sandwich (▲)

MAIDSTONE, Newnham, Doddington, Sheldwich, Selling, Boughton Street, THANET WAY, BLEAN, THANET GATE, Harbledown, **CANTERBURY**, Littlebourne, Wingham, Woodnesborough, A 257, A 258

Hollingbourne, Warren St., Stalisfield, Shottenden, Chartham, Patrixbourne, Bridge, Eastry, A 256, **Deal** (▲), The Downs

Lenham, M 20, Charing, Challock, A 252, Chilham, Petham, Lower Hardres, Aylesham, Barfreston, Ringwould, Kingsdown

Egerton, HIGH SPEED, N. Downs Way, Waltham, Wye, Barham, Stelling Minnis, Lydden Circuit, Eythorne, Martin Mill, Lydden, Whitfield, St Margaret's-at-Cliffe

Pluckley, Hothfield, Kennington, Brook, Bodsham, Lyminge Forest, Elham, A 260, Temple Ewell, Alkham, St Margaret's Bay, South Foreland

Headcorn, Smarden, Bethersden, **Ashford**, Brabourne Lees, Lyminge, Swingfield, Hawkinge, A 20, B 2011, **DOVER**, Dunkerque

Biddenden, A 28, Kingsnorth, Sellindge, Stanford, Terminal, Acrise Place, Capel-le-Ferne (▲), The Warren, E. Wear Bay

High Halden, Shadoxhurst, Westenhanger, Zoo, Lympne, **FOLKESTONE**, Sandgate

Tenterden, Woodchurch, A 262, B 2067, Bilsington, Newchurch, Hamstreet, **Hythe** (▲)(▲)

Rolvenden

CARDIFF

Scale: 0 — 200 m / 0 — 200 yards

Points of interest and streets (city inset):

SWANSEA · MERTHYR TYDFIL · CAERPHILLY · BRISTOL · PENARTH · BRIGEND

THOMPSON'S PARK · Bute Park · WELSH OFFICE · UNIVERSITY COLLEGE · TEMPLE OF PEACE · ALEXANDRA GARDENS · OLD COUNTY HALL · National Museum Cardiff · City Hall · Gorsedd Gardens · Law Courts · Cardiff Castle · Military Museums · St John's Church · St David's Shopping Centre · CAPITOL CENTRE · CARDIFF NEW SYNAGOGUE · Cardiff Arms Park · Central Market · The Old Library · Millennium Stadium · Quay St · CARDIFF CENTRAL · QUEEN ST · CALLAGHAN SQUARE · SWAMINARAYANA TEMPLE · SEVENOAKS PARK · Bute East Dock · Ocean Way · GRANGETOWN MUSLIM CULTURAL CENTRE · CARDIFF BAY · THE SALVATION ARMY · BUTETOWN · Coal Exchange · THE RED DRAGON CENTRE · St Cuthbert's · Techniquest · Pierhead Building · Wales Millennium Centre · Y Senedd · MERMAID QUAY · Norwegian Church · HAMADRYAD PARK · CARDIFF BAY WETLANDS RESERVE · CARDIFF YACHT CLUB · LECKWITH WOODS · QUEEN ALEXANDRA DOCK

Street names include: Cardiff Rd · Pen-Hill Rd · Pencisely Rd · Romilly · Pembroke Rd · Cowbridge Rd East · Lansdowne · Leckwith Av · Broadstairs Rd · Broadhaven · Lawrenny · Hadfield Rd · Sloper Rd · Penarth Rd · Corporation Rd · Clare Rd · Ferry Rd · Clive St · Penhevad St · Pentrebane St · Llanmaes St · Fagans St · Bromsgrove St · Holmesdale St · Avondale Rd · Canal Parade · Dumballs Rd · Bute St · Tyndall St · East Moors Rd · Cargo Rd

Surrounding area (lower map):

CAERPHILLY · Pontypridd · Cymmer · Tonyrefail · Senghenydd · Llanbradach · Machen · Risca · Bedwas · Rogerstone · Caerleon · Langstone · Penhow · MAGOR SERVICES · Caerwent · SEVERN VIEW S.A. · Severn Bridges · Aust · Beddau · Caerphilly / Caerffili · Thornhill · Parc Cefn Onn · Bishton · M4 SERVICES · Magor · Pilning · Talbot Green · Llantrisant · Pentyrch · Tongwynlais · Lisvane · Castleton · Marshfield · NEWPORT / CASNEWYDD · Goldcliff · Redwick · Roglet · Caldicot · Almondsbury · Pontyclun · Miskin · Llanishen · Whitchurch · St. Mellons · St. Brides Wentlooge · Avonmouth · Easter Compton · Filton · Llanharry · Hensol · Radyr · St. Fagans · Rumney · Peterstone Wentlooge · Portishead · GORDANO · Hen... · radowen · St-Brides-Super-Ely · Ely · Wenvoe · Dinas Powys · Portishead · Redcliff Bay · Clapton-in-Gordano · Easton-in-Gordano · Abbots Leigh · Clifton · Pendoylan · St. Nicholas · Bonvilston · Walton-in-Gordano · Clevedon Court · Beaupre Castle · Penmark · Clevedon · Kenn · Nailsea · Flax Bourton · Long Ashton · Eglwys Brewis · St. Athan · Penarth · Severn Estuary · N. SOMERSET · Bishopsworth · East-Aberthaw · Rhoose · Porthkerry · CARDIFF AIRPORT · Sully · Swanbridge · Barry / Barri · Kingston Seymour · Brockley · Backwell · Barrow Gurney · Dundry · BRIS... · Flat Holm · Kewstoke · Yatton · Lulsgate Bottom · Winford · Chew Magna · Weston-Super-Mare · Congresbury · Redhill · BRISTOL-LULSGATE AIRPORT · Wrington · Chew Stoke · Hengrove

CARDIFF / CAERDYDD

VALE OF GLAMORGAN

CHESTER

HOYLAKE · ELLESMERE PORT · MANCHESTER, LIVERPOOL

Northgate
The Walls
King Charles' Tower
Kaleyard's Gate
Chester Cathedral
Town Hall
FORUM SHOPPING CENTRE
Eastgate
THE ROWS
Grosvenor Shopping Centre
Dewa Roman Experience
Newgate
Three Old Arches
St John's
Roman Amphitheatre
Stanley Palace
Grosvenor Museum
Bridgegate
CASTLE
Roodee
Grosvenor Park
QUEEN'S PARK

NORTHGATE ARENA

N

CHESTER
0 — 150 m
0 — 150 yards

WREXHAM · CONWY

QUEENSFERRY

SOUTHPORT
Birkdale
Ainsdale
Formby
Halsall
Ormskirk
Skelmersdale
Maghull
Crosby
Litherland
Kirkby
ST. HELENS
Bootle
New Brighton
Knowsley
LIVERPOOL
Roby
Huyton
Wallasey
BIRKENHEAD
Woolton
Farnworth
Widnes
Irby
Pensby
Port Sunlight
Bebington
Bromborough
Eastham
LIVERPOOL JOHN LENNON AIRPORT
Hale
Runcorn
River Mersey
Ellesmere Port
Elton
CHESTER

Rhyl
Prestatyn
Talacre
Point of Ayr
West Kirby
Thurstaston
Heswall
Thornton Hough
Parkgate
Neston
Willaston
Puddington
Whitby
Backford Cross
Stoak
Kinmel Bay
Rhuddlan
Dyserth
Trelawnyd
Llanasa
Mostyn
Holywell / Treffynnon
Greenfield
Flint / Fflint
Connah's Quay
Queensferry
Saughall
Sealand
Upton
Great Barrow
Little Barrow
Bridge Trafford
Pensarn
Castle
Rhualt
Babell
Caerwys
Afon-wen
Halkyn
Bagillt
Northop
Ewloe
Hawarden
Lache
Saltney
CHESTER
Christleton
Waverton
Abergele
Bodelwyddan
St. Asaph
Tremeirchion
Bodfari
Nannerch
Northop Hall
Buckley
Bwcle
Mold
Yr Wyddgrug
Broughton
Handbridge
Huxley
Llannefydd
Trefnant
Henllan
Denbigh / Dinbych
Cilcain
Loggerheads
Nercwys
Penyffordd
CHESHIRE WEST AND CHESTER
Aldford
Tattenhall
Bylchau
Llanrhaeadr
Llandyrnog
Moel Fammau
Llanferres
Leeswood
Waun y llyn
Hope
Burton
Pulford
Handley
Higher Burwardsley
FLINTSHIRE
DENBIGHSHIRE
Ruthin / Rhuthun
Cyffylliog
Clocaenog
Pentre Celyn
Llandegla
Treuddyn
Llanfynydd
Caergwrle
Rossett
Farndon
Bwlchgwyn
Brymbo
Gresford
Holt
Broxton
Clawddnewydd
Llanelidan
Coedpoeth
Wrexham / Wrecsam
Rhostyllen
Erddig
Marchwiel
Malpas
Clocaenog Forest
Llanfihangel Glyn Myfyr
Bettws Gwerfil Goch
Bryneglwys
Rhoslannerchrugog
Worthenbury

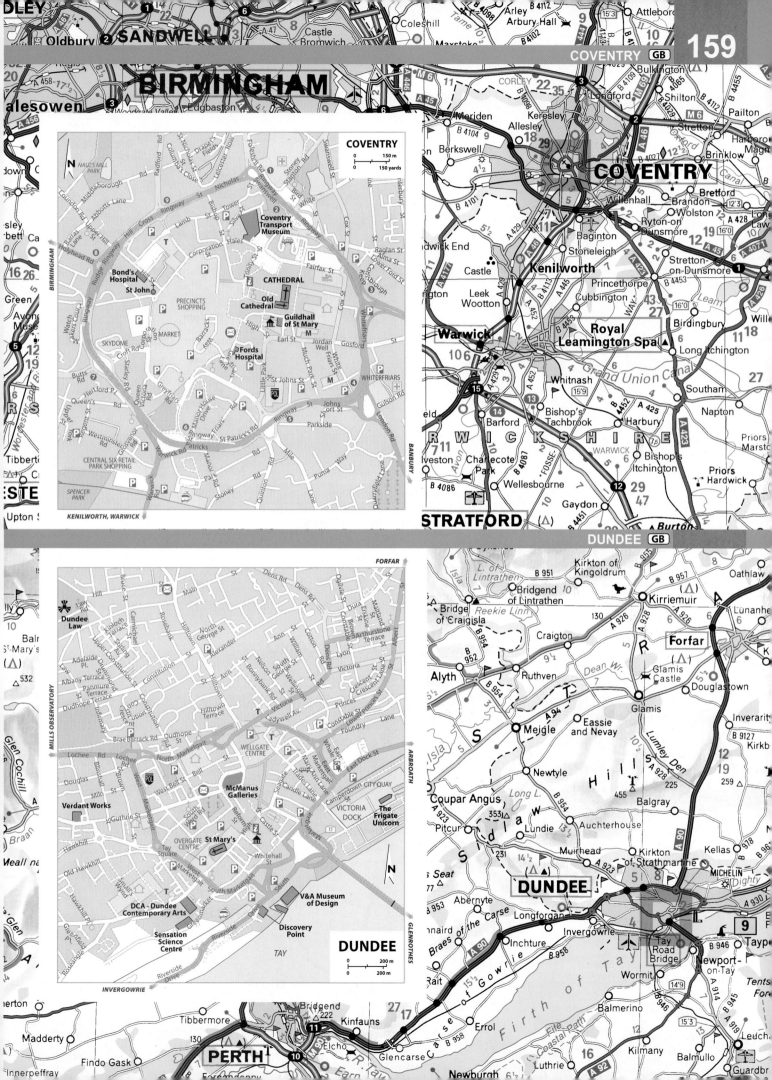

EDINBURGH

0 250 m
0 250 yards

EXETER

0 — 150 m
0 — 150 yards

N

OKEHAMPTON, PLYMOUTH

Inset map labels (Exeter city centre):

Howell Rd · Elm Grove Rd · Hele Rd · New North Rd · Queen St · Richmond Rd · Blackall Rd · York Rd · Howell Rd · Oxford Rd · King William St · Longbrook Terrace · CENTRAL · CASTLE · ROUGEMONT HOUSE · Royal Albert Memorial Museum · HARLEQUINS SHOPPING CENTRE · Bailey St · High St · PRINCESSHAY SHOPPING CENTRE · Cheeke St · Sidwell St · Western Way · David's · Richmond Court · Lower North St · Iron Bridge · GUILDHALL CENTRE · SHIP INN · St Martin's Church · Mol's Coffee House · Dinham Crescent · Dinham Mount · BARNSTAPLE · Bonhay Rd · Bartholomew St West · Guildhall · Cathedral · Gandy St · Dix's Field · Archibald Rd · Athelstan Rd · Barnfield Rd · St Nicholas Priory · Fore St · South St · George St · Real · Cathedral Close · City · Denmark Rd · Southernhay Gardens · TUCKER'S HALL · WHITE HART · King St · Preston St · Market St · Palace Gate · WYNARD'S HOSPITAL · Magdalen Rd · ST MARY STEPS · Frog St · St Western Way · New Bridge St · Tudor St · Western Way · Holloway St · Temple Rd · Fairpark Rd · Magdalen St · Montford Rd · Bull Meadow Rd · Commercial Rd · CUSTOM HOUSE · Quay House Visitor Centre · Edmund St · EXE · Cowick St · Alphington St · Haven Rd · ST THOMAS · HISTORIC QUAYSIDE · Shooting Marsh Stile · Lucky Lane · Colleton Crescent · The Quay · Haven Banks · Topsham Rd · 156

Main regional map labels:

Bishop's Tawton · W. Buckland · E. Buckland · Swimbridge · N. Molton · Hawkridge · Upton · Huish Ch · A 361 · Dane's Brook · Regis · Brushford · Morebath · Exebridge · Shillingford · ith Mill · B 3227 · Bampton · Oakford · Holcombe R · Rackenford · Knightshayes Court · Sampford Peverell · 283 · 286 · defor · cross · Lit. · Petr · Shee · Witheridge · Little Dart · Cheriton Fitzpaine · Bolham · Tiverton · Halberton · Willan · B 3137 · B 3042 · Cullompton · Bickleigh · A 361 · A 373 · 24 · 15 · DEVON · Creedy · Bradninch · Plymtr · A 3072 · Sandford · Thorverton · Silverton · Killerton · B 3181 · Clyst Hydon · Newton St. Cyres · Crediton · A 377 · Stoke Canon · Talato · Whimple · Broadclyst · Spreyton · Tedburn St. Mary · EXETER · Pinhoe · Clyst Honiton · EXETER AIRPORT · A 30 · Okehampton · Sticklepath · S. Tawton · Cheriton Bishop · Ide · Alphington · Venn Ot · Popple · Belstone · S. Zeal · Whiddon Down · Spinster's Rock · Drewsteignton · Dunsford · A 3015 · Topsham · Clyst St Mary · Woodbury · A 3079 · Sourton · Throwleigh · Sandy Park · Castle Drogo · Fingle Bridge · Doddiscombsleigh · Kennford · Exminster · Exton · Yet · High Willhays · 621 · Scorhill · Easton · A 382 · 356 · B 3193 · Lympstone · A La Ronde · Hayes Barton · Withycombe · Lydford · Chagford · B 3206 · Moretonhampstead · Trusham · Kenton · Starcross · Littleha · N. Brentor · Dartmoor Forest · Shovel Down · Christow · Chudleigh · EXMOUTH · Mary Tavy · Cut Hill · Grey Wethers · N. Bovey · Manaton · Lustleigh · Hennock · Ideford · Dartmoor · Becky Falls · Bovey · Wistman's Wood · Postbridge · Widecombe-in-the-Moor · Haytor Rocks · Bovey Tracey · Bishopsteignton · Dawlish · Great Mis Tor · Two Bridges · Ilsington · Kingsteignton · Teignmouth · Tavistock · Dartmoor Prison · Buckland-in-the-Moor · Bickington · Shaldon · Whitchurch · Princetown · Dartmeet · Combeinteignhead · National · River Dart · Newton Abbot · Abbotskerswell · Babbacombe Bay · Ryder's Hill · Ashburton · Maidencombe · Yelverton · Meavy · Holne · Kingskerswell · TORQUAY · Buckland Abbey · Buckfast · Ipplepen · Compton · Babbacombe · Park · Buckfastleigh · Staverton · Marldon · Cockington · TORBAY · Bickleigh · Cornwood · Dartington · Castle · Tor Bay · PLYMOUTH · S. Brent · Berry Pomeroy · Paignton · Plympton · Harberton · Totnes · Stoke Gabriel · Goodrington · Ivybridge · Avonwick · Diptford · Ashprington · Galmpton · Churston Ferrers · Ugborough · Harbertonford · Cornworthy · Brixham · Berry Head · Ermington · Dittisham

GLASGOW

0   450 m
0   450 yards

DUMBARTON   STIRLING   KIRKINTILLOCH

Botanic Gardens

Hunterian Art Gallery   MACKINTOSH HOUSE
Hunterian Museum
University Gilmorehill Building
WESTERN INFIRMARY
Kelvingrove Park
Kelvingrove Art Gallery and Museum
KELVIN HALL
Park Circus

Queen's Cross Church

Tenement House
The National Piping Centre
Beresford
Glasgow School of Art
The Mitchell Library
CCA
Willow Tearoom
Willow Street
Martyr's School
BUCHANAN STREET BUS STATION
BUCHANAN GALLERIES
Merchants' House
Willow Tea Rooms
The Lighthouse
Gallery of Modern Art
Princes Square
City Chambers
George Street
Trades Hall
CATHEDRAL
Necropolis
Provand's Lordship
St Mungo Museum of Religious Life and Art
Royal Infirmary

Scottish Exhibition and Conference Center
EXHIBITION CENTRE STATION
Clyde Auditorium - The "Armadillo"
Glasgow Tower
Science Centre
Imax
BBC Building
La grue Finnieston

CENTRAL STATION
St Enoch
ST ENOCH SHOPPING CENTRE
Tolbooth Steeple
Glasgow Cross
Bridgegate Steeple
The Barras
Saltmarket

Clyde River
Kingston Bridge

Scotland Street School Museum

Glasgow Green
People's Palace
Doulton Fountain
Templeton Business Centre

KILMARNOCK   MOTHERWELL   HAMILTON   KILMARNOCK   EAST KILBRIDE

Greenock
Port Glasgow
Dumbarton
Erskine Bridge
Duntocher
Kilpatrick Hills
Milngavie
Torrance
Kirkintilloch
Cumbernauld
Slamannan
Renton
Langbank
Old Kilpatrick
Bearsden
Lenzie
Muirhead
Condorrat
Riggend
Longriggend
Caldercruix
Bishopton
Kilmacolm
Houston
Clydebank
Renfrew
Stepps
Coatbridge
Stand
Bridge of Weir
Linwood
Airdrie
Chapelhall
Salsburgh
Muirshiel
Heathfield
Ranfurly
Kilbarchan
PAISLEY
GLASGOW
Rutherglen
Holytown
Mossend
Bellshill
Garfin
Newarthill
Johnstone
Howwood
Barrhead
Uddingston
Bothwell
Cambuslang
Blantyre
Cleland
Motherwell
Wishaw
Neilston
Busby
Carmunnock
Hamilton
Newton Mearns
East Kilbride
Eaglesham
Ballageich Hill
Auldhouse
Overtown
Larkhall
Law
Dalserf
Kilbirnie
Beith
Barrmill
Lugton
Dunlop
Dalry

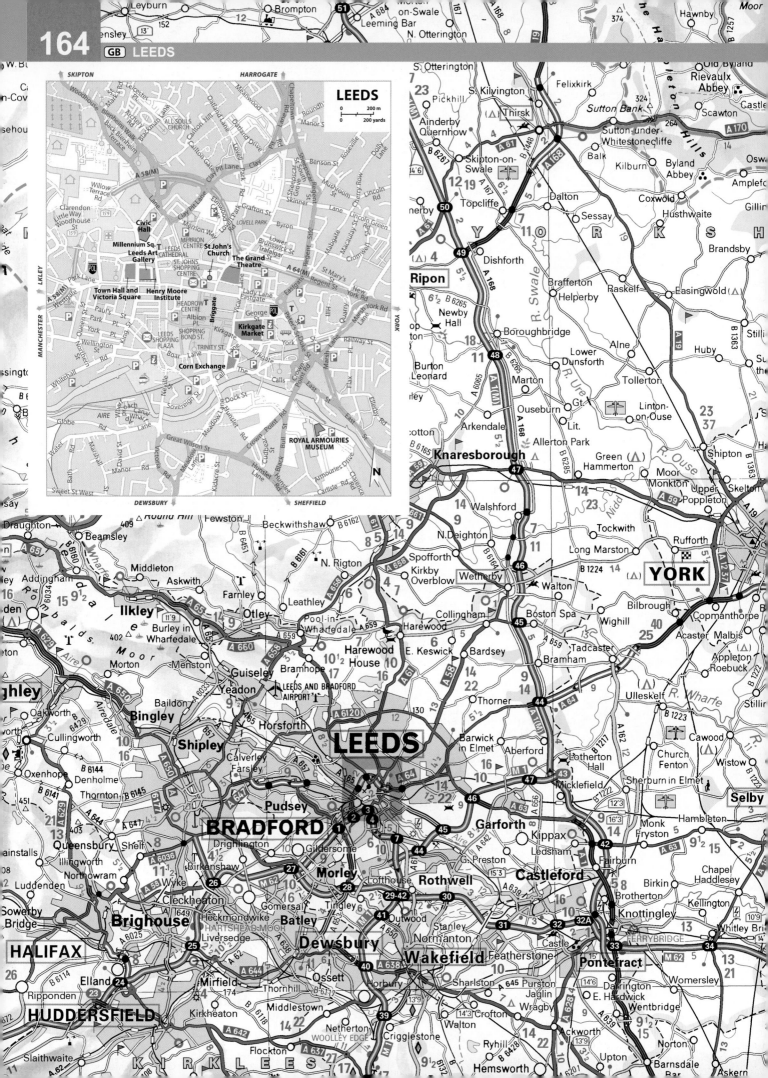

LEEDS

0 — 200 m
0 — 200 yards

SKIPTON   HARROGATE

ALL SOULS CHURCH

Civic Hall

Millennium Sq.
Leeds Art Gallery

Town Hall and Victoria Square

Henry Moore Institute

LEEDS CATHEDRAL
ST. JOHN'S SHOPPING CENTRE

St John's Church

The Grand Theatre

HEADROW CENTRE

MERRION CENTRE

Albion Pl.
SHOPPING BOND ST.

Briggate

Kirkgate

Kirkgate Market

LEEDS SHOPPING PLAZA

Corn Exchange

TRINITY ST.

ROYAL ARMOURIES MUSEUM

MANCHESTER   ILKLEY   YORK

DEWSBURY   SHEFFIELD   N

Leyburn   Brompton   51
on-Swale
Leeming Bar   N. Otterington
Hawnby   Moor

Old Byland
Rievaulx Abbey   Scawton   Castle

S. Otterington
23   Felixkirk
Pickhill   S. Kilvington   Sutton Bank   264
Thirsk   Sutton-under-
Ainderby   Whitestonecliffe
Quernhow   Balk   Kilburn   Byland Abbey
Skipton-on-   Coxwold   Ampleforth
12 19   Swale   Dalton   Husthwaite
50   Topcliffe   Sessay   Brandsby
49   Dishforth   Brafferton
11 O   Helperby   Raskelf   Easingwold
Ripon   A 168   Newby   Alne   Huby
Hall   Lower
18   Boroughbridge   Dunsforth   Tollerton
48   Burton   Marton   Linton-
Leonard   Ouseburn   on-Ouse   23
Arkendale   Lit.   37
Allerton Park   Shipton
Knaresborough   Green   Moor   Skelton
47   Hammerton   Monkton   Upper
14   Poppleton
Walshford   Tockwith   Rufforth
N.Deighton   Long Marston
Spofforth   11   YORK
Kirkby   46   Walton   Bilbrough   Copmanthorpe
Overblow   Wetherby   Boston Spa   Wighill
Collingham   45   Acaster Malbis
Harewood   Bramham   Tadcaster   Appleton
E. Keswick   Bardsey   Roebuck
Harewood   Ulleskelf
House   Thorner   Church   Cawood
Bramhope   44   Fenton   Wistow
LEEDS AND BRADFORD   Barwick   Sherburn in Elmet
AIRPORT   in Elmet   Aberford   Selby
Horsforth   Lotherton   Micklefield
LEEDS   Hall   Monk
Garforth   Fryston
Pudsey   45   Kippax   Fairburn
BRADFORD   Ledsham   42   Hambleton
Drighlington   Garforth   Chapel
Gildersome   44   G. Preston   Castleford   Haddlesey
Morley   Rothwell   Birkin
Lofthouse   Brotherton   Kellington
27   Tingley   Stanley   Knottingley
26   Gomersal   Outwood   Normanton   FERRYBRIDGE
Cleckheaton   41   Castle   32 32A   Whitley Br
Brighouse   Batley   Dewsbury   Wakefield   33   Pontefract
HALIFAX   Heckmondwike   Featherstone   34
Liversedge   Featherstone   Darrington
Elland   25   Mirfield   Ossett   Sharlston   E. Hardwick   Wentbridge
Ripponden   Thornhill   Norbury   Purston   Wragby   Womersley
HUDDERSFIELD   Kirkheaton   Middlestown   Crofton   Jaglin   Norton
Flockton   WOOLLEY EDGE   Netherton   Walton   Barnsdale
Slaithwaite   KIRKLEES   Crigglestone   Ryhill   Hemsworth   Askern

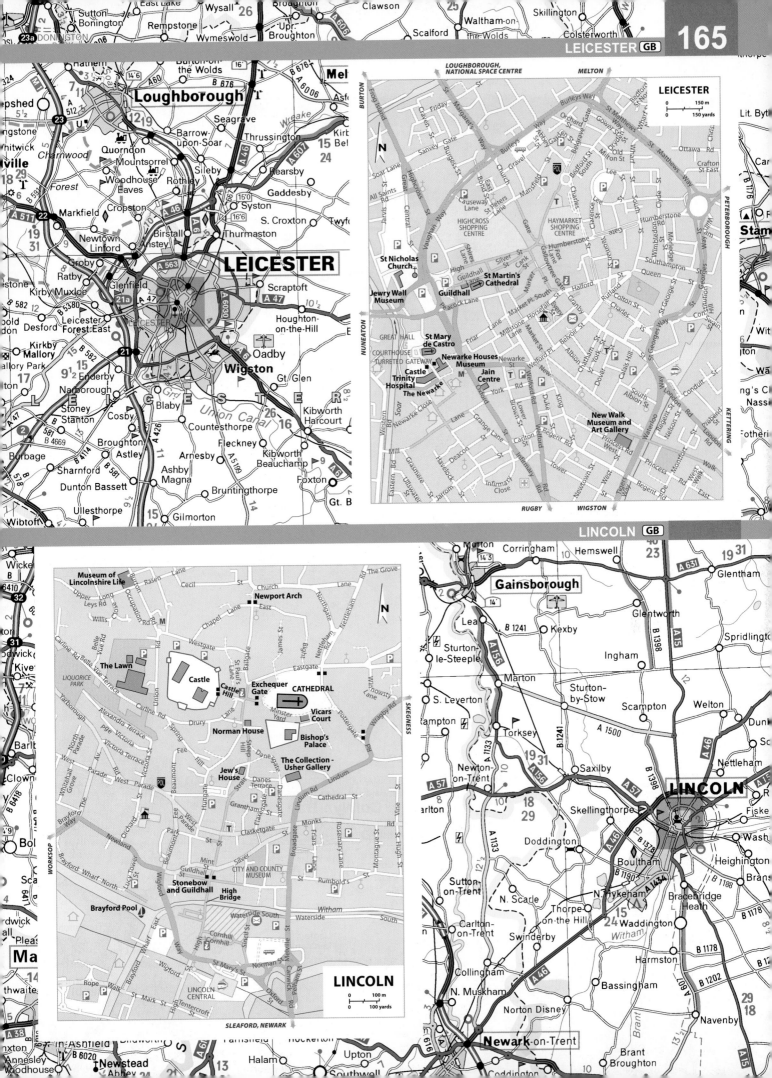

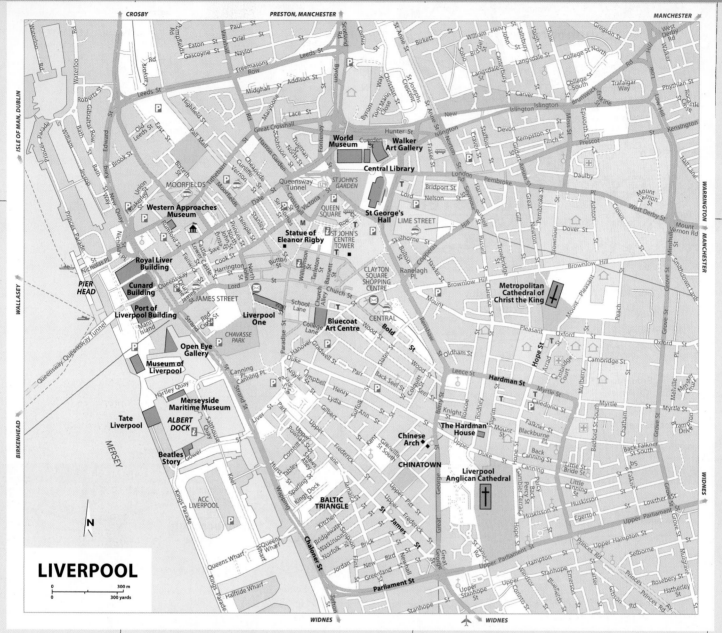

LIVERPOOL

CROSBY — **PRESTON, MANCHESTER** — **MANCHESTER**

ISLE OF MAN, DUBLIN
WALLASEY
PIER HEAD
BIRKENHEAD
MERSEY

World Museum
Walker Art Gallery
Central Library
Western Approaches Museum
St John's Garden
St George's Hall
LIME STREET
Statue of Eleanor Rigby
St John's Centre Tower
Royal Liver Building
Cunard Building
Port of Liverpool Building
Liverpool One
Bluecoat Art Centre
Clayton Square Shopping Centre
CENTRAL
Bold St
Metropolitan Cathedral of Christ the King
Hope St
Hardman St
Open Eye Gallery
Museum of Liverpool
CHAVASSE PARK
Chinese Arch
The Hardman House
Merseyside Maritime Museum
ALBERT DOCK
Tate Liverpool
Beatles Story
CHINATOWN
Liverpool Anglican Cathedral
BALTIC TRIANGLE
ACC LIVERPOOL
Parliament St

N

LIVERPOOL
| 0 | 300 m |
| 0 | 300 yards |

WIDNES — **WIDNES**

Great Orme's Head
Welsh Channel
Llandudno (▲)
Prestatyn
Talacre
Poir of A
Puffin Island
Lit. Ormes Head
Penrhyn Bay (△)
(▲) Rhyl
Penmon
Llangoed
Conwy Bay
Deganwy
Llandudno Junction
Rhos-on-Sea
Colwyn Bay / Bae Colwyn
Kinmel Bay
Llanasa
Castle
Mochdre
Old Colwyn
Llanddulas
Abergele
Pensarn
Rhuddlan
Castle
Dyserth
Trelawnyd
Beaumaris
Conwy
Penmaenmawr
Llansantffraid Glan Conwy
Bodelwyddan
St Asaph
Rhuallt
Bangor
Llanfairfechan
Bodnant Garden
Betws-yn-Rhos
Llanfair Talhaiarn
Trefnant
Abergwyngregyn
Penrhyn
Tal-y-Cafn
Tal-y-Bont
Vale of Conwy
Llannefydd
Henllan
Denbigh
Dinbych
Llandygai
Foel-Fras
Dolgarrog
Llangernyw
Rachub
Bethesda
Carnedd Llewelyn
Llyn Eigiau Resr.
Trefriw
Llansannan
Bylchau
Llanrhaeadr
Landyrnog
Penrhyn Quarries
Carnedd Dafydd
Llyn Cowlyd Resr.
Deiniolen
Llanrwst (△)
Ystrad
Nant Ffrancon

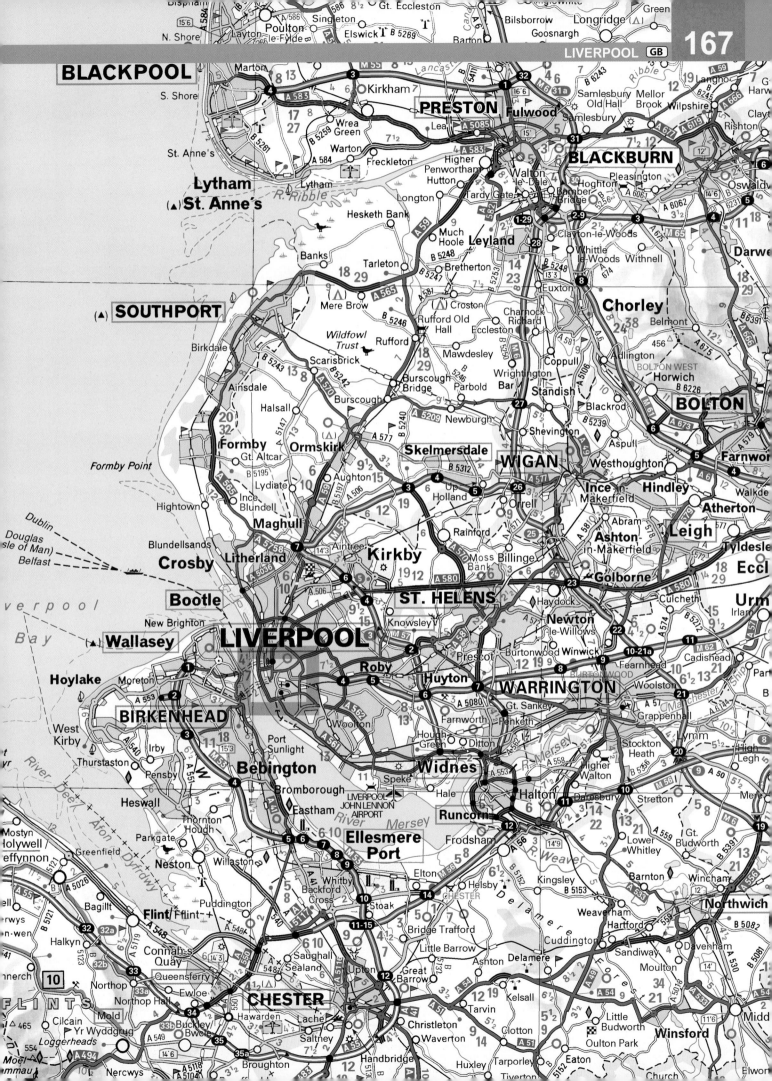

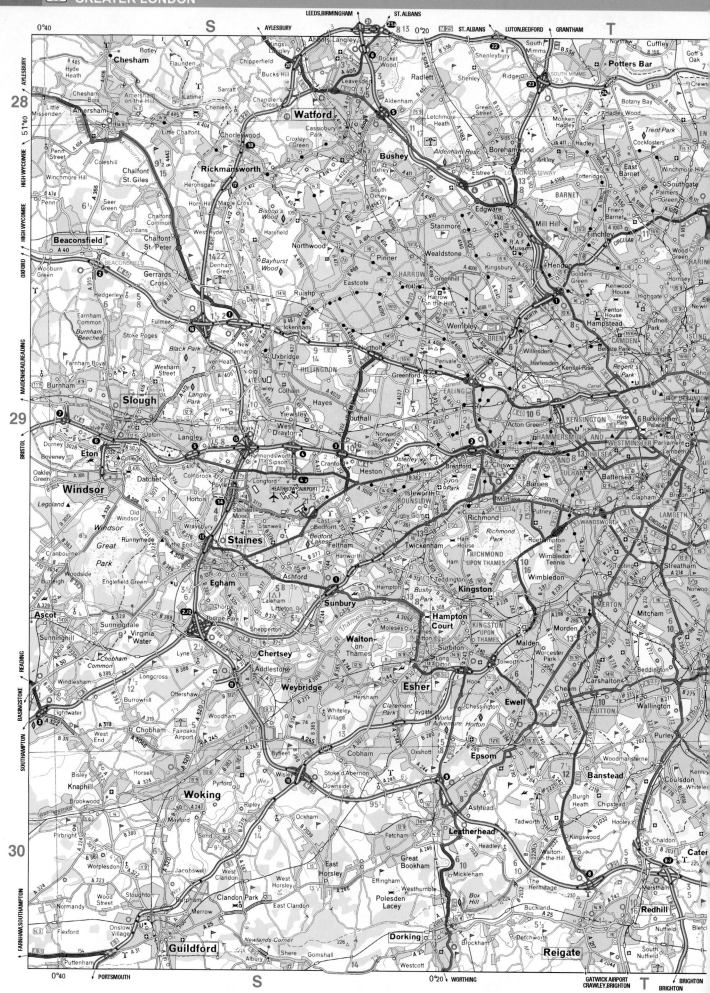

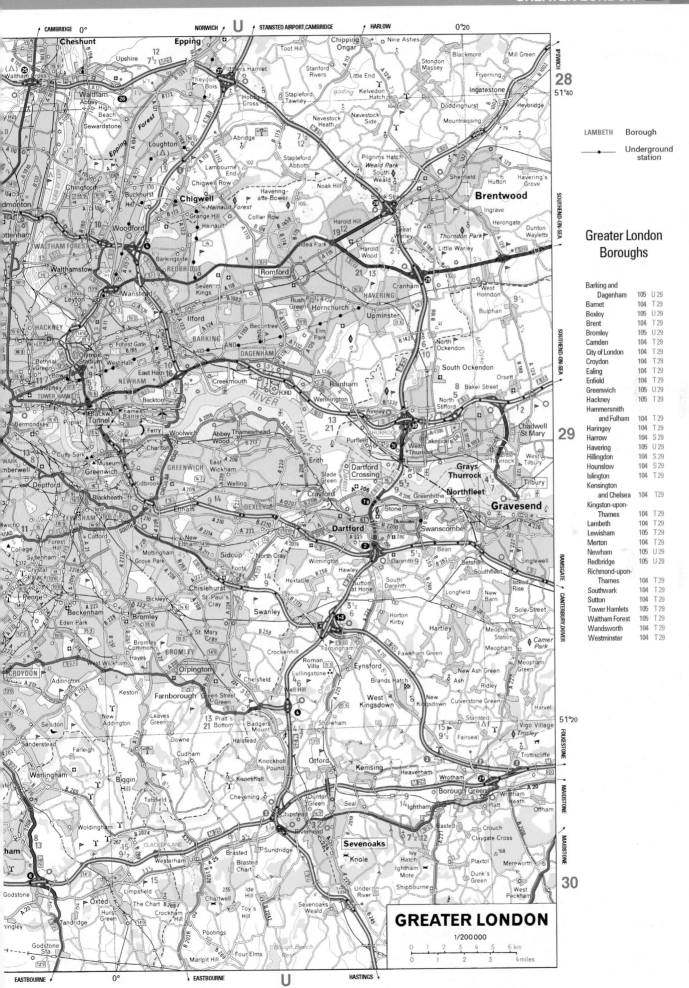

LAMBETH Borough

•——• Underground station

Greater London Boroughs

Barking and Dagenham	105	U 29
Barnet	104	T 29
Bexley	105	U 29
Brent	104	T 29
Bromley	105	U 29
Camden	104	T 29
City of London	104	T 29
Croydon	104	T 29
Ealing	104	T 29
Enfield	104	T 29
Greenwich	105	U 29
Hackney	105	T 29
Hammersmith and Fulham	104	T 29
Haringey	104	T 29
Harrow	104	S 29
Havering	105	U 29
Hillingdon	104	S 29
Hounslow	104	S 29
Islington	104	T 29
Kensington and Chelsea	104	T 29
Kingston-upon-Thames	104	T 29
Lambeth	104	T 29
Lewisham	105	T 29
Merton	104	T 29
Newham	105	U 29
Redbridge	105	U 29
Richmond-upon-Thames	104	T 29
Southwark	104	T 29
Sutton	104	T 29
Tower Hamlets	105	T 29
Waltham Forest	105	T 29
Wandsworth	104	T 29
Westminster	104	T 29

GREATER LONDON

1/200 000

0 1 2 3 4 5 6 km

0 1 2 3 4 miles

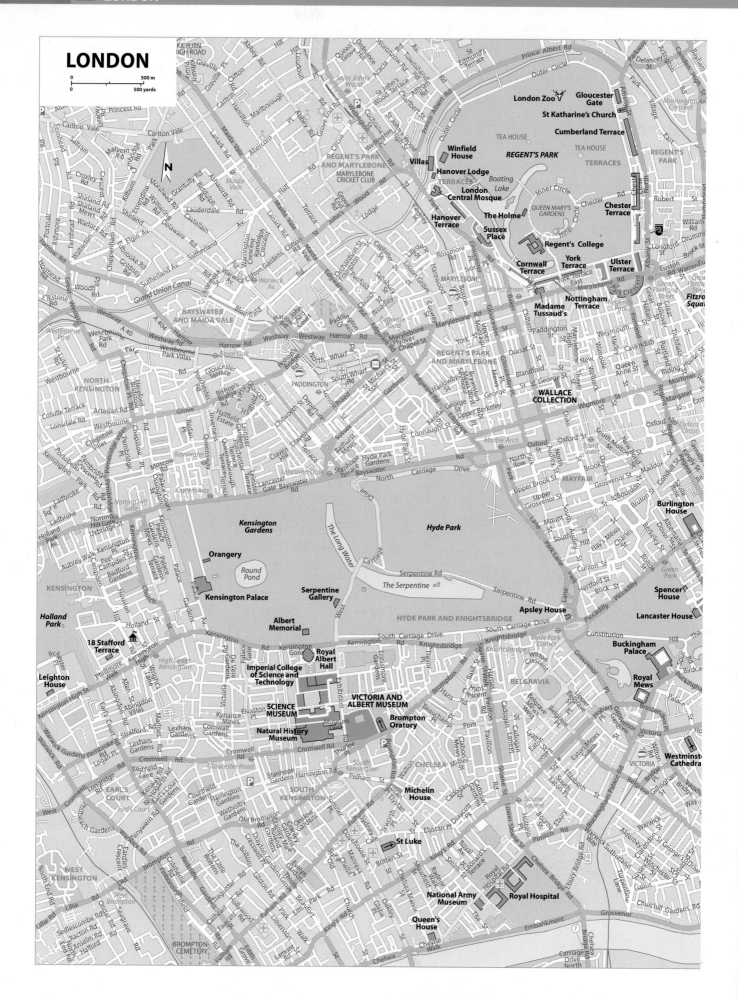

Belsay
Ogle
Stannington
Woods
Seaton Delaval Hall
Milbourne
Seaton Burn
Dudley
Seaton Delaval
Whitley Bay
Ponteland
Dinnington
Wide Open
Earsdon
Stamfordham
Darras Hall
Shiremoor
Priory

NEWCASTLE UPON-TYNE
Wall
Longbenton
Gosforth
TYNEMOUTH
Wallsend
N. Shields
SOUTH SHIELDS
Harlow Hill
Throckley
Heddon-on-the-W
Newburn
Tyne Tunnel
Jarrow
Hebburn
Amsterdam
Horsley
Wylam
Ryton
Crawcrock
Blaydon
Greenside
Whickham
GATESHEAD
Felling
Cleadon
Whitburn
Boldon
Southwick
Prudhoe
Stocksfield
Wrekenton
N O R
Whittonstall
Chopwell
Burnopfield
Beamish Hall
Birtley
Washington
SUNDERLAND
Derwent Walk
Shotley Bridge
Ebchester
WASHINGTON
Penshaw
Herrington
Ryhope
Stanley
Pelton
Shiney Row
New Silksworth
Chester-le-Street
Annfield
Leadgate
Seaham
Murton
Houghton-le-Spring
S. Hetton
Easington
Horden
Shotton Colliery
Thornley
Peterlee
Blackhall
Blackhall Rocks
Wheatley Hill
Hesleden
Wingate
Hart
HARTLEPOOL
Trimdon
Fishburn
Elwick
Seaton Carew
Sedgefield
Tees Bay
Thorpe Thewles
Wolviston
Greatham
Billingham
Bishopton
Redmarshall
Dormanstown
Stockton-on-Tees
MIDDLESBROUGH
Longnewton
Thornaby-on-Tees
Eston
Ormesby
Eaglescliffe
Ingleby Barwick
Nunthorpe
DURHAM TEES VALLEY AIRPORT
Yarm
Kirklevington
Seamer
Gt. Ayton
Longnewton
Stokesley
Crathorne
Appleton Wiske
Hutton Rudby
Gt. Broughton
Moulton
N. Cowton
Carlton

NEWCASTLE UPON TYNE

0   150 m
0   150 yards

EXHIBITION PARK
Clayton Park
Brandling Park
Claremont Rd
Framlington Pl.
Park Terrace
Windsor Terrace
Jesmond
Osborne Terrace
Portland Terrace
Great North Museum : Hancock
Great North Rd
Sandyford
Chester Rd
Richardson
ST JAMES PARK
St James
Haymarket
St Mary's Pl.
College
Laing Art Gallery and Museum
SHOPPING CENTRE
ELDON SQUARE
Grey's Monument
Blackett St
Grainger Street
Grey Street
The Gate
Blackfriars
Bigg Market
Cloth Market
SAINT NICHOLAS CATHEDRAL
All Saints
Black Gate
Bessie Surtees' House
CENTRAL
Castle Keep
Guildhall
Swing Bridge
Sage
INTL. CENTRE FOR LIFE
High Level Bridge
Tyne Bridge
Quayside
Discovery Museum
Life Science Centre
GATESHEAD MILLENNIUM BRIDGE, BALTIC CENTRE
CONSETT, DURHAM
SUNDERLAND
HEXHAM
BLAYDON

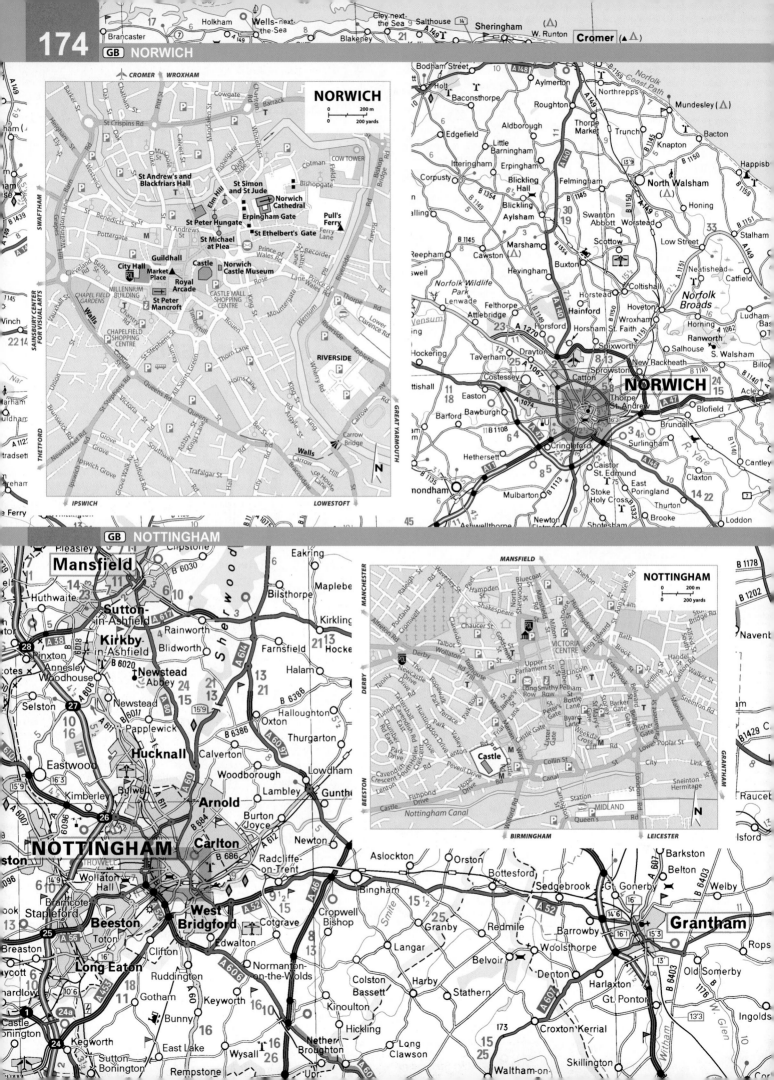

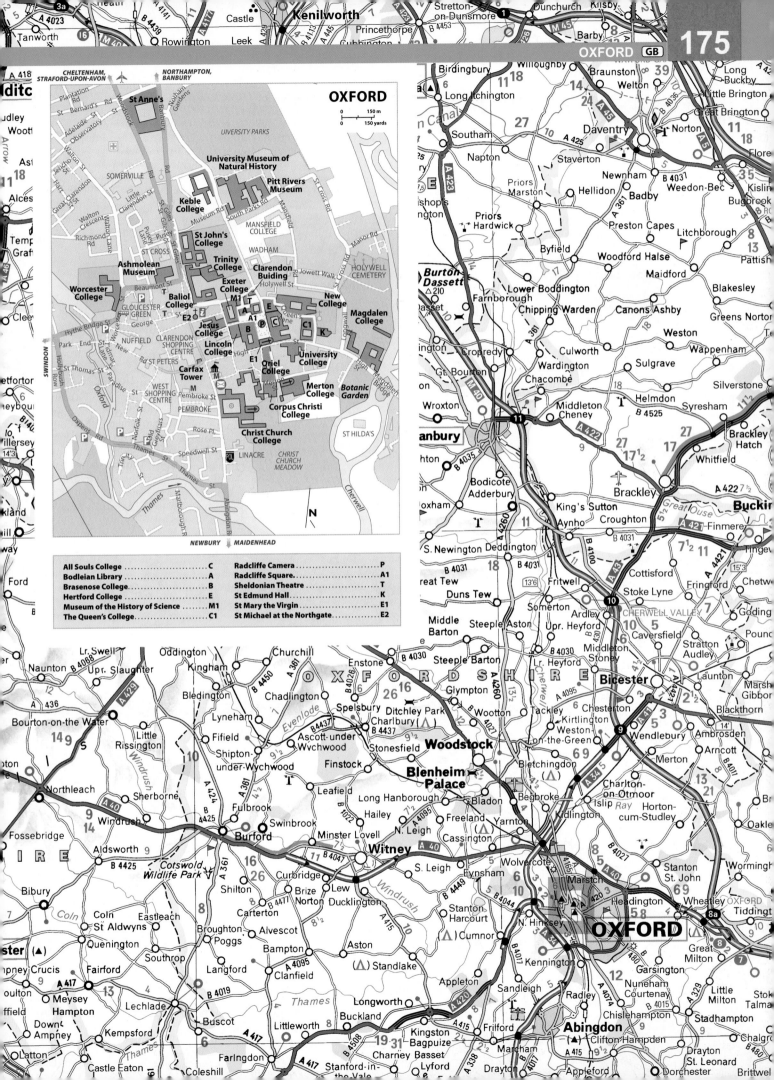

PERTH (inset map)

BRAEMAR, SCONE PALACE — COUPAR ANGUS

0 — 100 m
0 — 100 yards

Black Watch Regimental Museum
BELL'S SPORTS CENTRE
North
Inch
RIVERSIDE PARK
Balhousie Av.
Hay St.
Barrack St.
Dunkeld Rd.
Barossa Place
Nº 10
Rose Terrace
Old Perth Academy
Mill St.
Georgian Terraces
Atholl Crescent
Melville St.
Union Lane
Atholl St.
Charlotte St.
Perth Bridge
St. NINIAN'S CATHEDRAL
Foundry Lane
Charlotte Square
Fair Maids House
Murray St.
TAY
ST. CATHERINE'S RETAIL PARK SHOPPING CENTRE
Lower City Mills
Perth Concert Hall
Perth Museum and Art Gallery
High St.
South Methven St.
Scott St.
St. John's St.
St JOHN'S CENTRE
City Hall
St John's
Maison des Évêques de Dunkeld
Kinnoull St.
Gowrie Commercial St.
York Pl.
Caledonian Rd.
County Pl.
New Row
Canal Crescent
Salutation Hotel
Sheriff Court
Kinnoull Causeway
King James VI Hospital
Alexandra St.
St Exchange
St Lane
Andrew St.
Pomarium St.
Victoria St.
Canal St.
South William St.
Nelson St.
Tay St.
Riverside
Kinnoull Hill
Dundee Rd.
Queen's Bridge
RIVERSIDE PARK
King's Pl.
King James Pl.
South St.
ST. LEONARD'S IN THE FIELDS
Water Works et Fergusson Gallery
South Inch
MONCREIFFE ISLAND
BRANKLYN GARDEN, FRIARTON BRIDGE
INVERNESS, CAITHNESS GLASS
CRIANLARICH, CRIEFF
STIRLING
CHERRYBANK
FORTH ROAD BRIDGE

Main map

Loch Muick
Glas-allt
Socach
920
998
Callater
A 93
Loch Lee
Inchgrundle
Glen
Braedownie
741
691
West Knock
896
Ben Tirran
778
White Hill
Clova
B 955
726
Waterhead
Runtaleave
Glenprosen Village
246
Isla Forest
Cat Law
678
Dykehead
Ogil
Fern
Backwater Resr.
Balintore
Pearsie
Tannadice
Dykends
Kirkton of Kingoldrum
B 955
B 957
Oathlaw
L. of Lintrathen
B 951
Kirriemuir
Lunanhead
Bridgend of Lintrathen
A 926
A 928
A 926
Kingsmuir
Craigisla
Reekie Linn
Craigton
A 926
130
Forfar
B 954
B 952
Ruthven
Glamis Castle
Douglastown
A 94
Mejgle
Eassie and Nevay
Glamis
Inverarity
B 9127
Kirkbuddo
B 978
Newtyle
12 19
259
Dunkeld
Clunie
B 947
Meikleour
A 984
Coupar Angus
Long L.
Balgray
Mor
Inver
Birnam
Caputh
Kinclaven
A 984
A 923
Pitcur
353
Lundie
Auchterhouse
Newbigg
Trochry
Strathbraan
Tay
28 45
B 867
101
Cargill
Burrelton
B 954
231
Muirhead
Kirkton of Strathmartine
Kellas
B 978
B 961
MICHELIN
Bankfoot
B 9099
16
A 94
31
King's Seat
377
Dundee
Little Glenshee
Stanley
132
Guildtown
B 953
Abernyte
Longforgan
Invergowrie
Broughty Ferry
Caorach
623
Logiealmond
Kinrossie
Kinnaird
Braes of the Carse
9
Tayport
Harrietfield
Moneydie
A 93
Balbeggie
Inchture
Tay Road Bridge
Newport-on-Tay
Buchanty
Almond
Luncarty
Scone Palace
Rait
Gowrie
Wormit
Tentsmuir Forest
Fowlis Wester
Methven
Huntingtower Castle
A 85
New Scone
Errol
Firth of Tay
Balmerino
Findo Gask
Tibbermore
Bridgend
222
Kinfauns
27 17
Glencarse
B 958
Kilmany
Balmullo
Leuchars
PERTH
Elcho
R. Tay
Coastal Path
Guardbridge
Forgandenny
10
Newburgh
Luthrie
A 92
Kinkell Bridge
Aberuthven
B 934
Bridge of Earn
9
B 935
Forteviot
A 913
Abernethy
Lindores
Dairsie
Strathkinness
A 91
Dunning
A 912
Pitmedden Forest
Auchtermuchty
Cupar
Craigtoun
A 915
Auchterarder
31 50
B 8062
229
18 11
141
A 91
Howe of Fife
Springfield
15
Hill of Tarvit
Pitscottie
Peat Inn
Steele's Knowe
485
Common of Dunning
Path of Condie
Glenfarg
Ladybank
Scotstarvit Tower
Ceres
Craigrothie
Gateside
Strathmiglo
B 936
Kingskettle
B 939
B 8062
316
497
M90
B 996
11
Lomond Hills
Falkland
Backmuir of New Gilston
Freuchie
Largoward

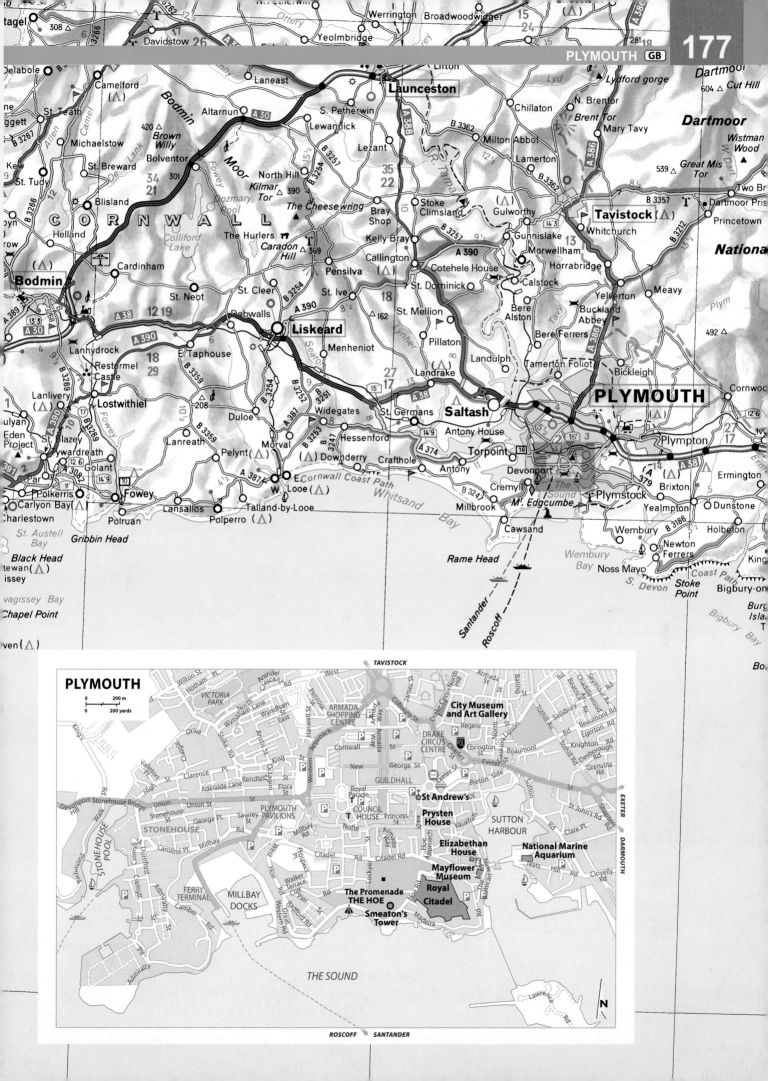

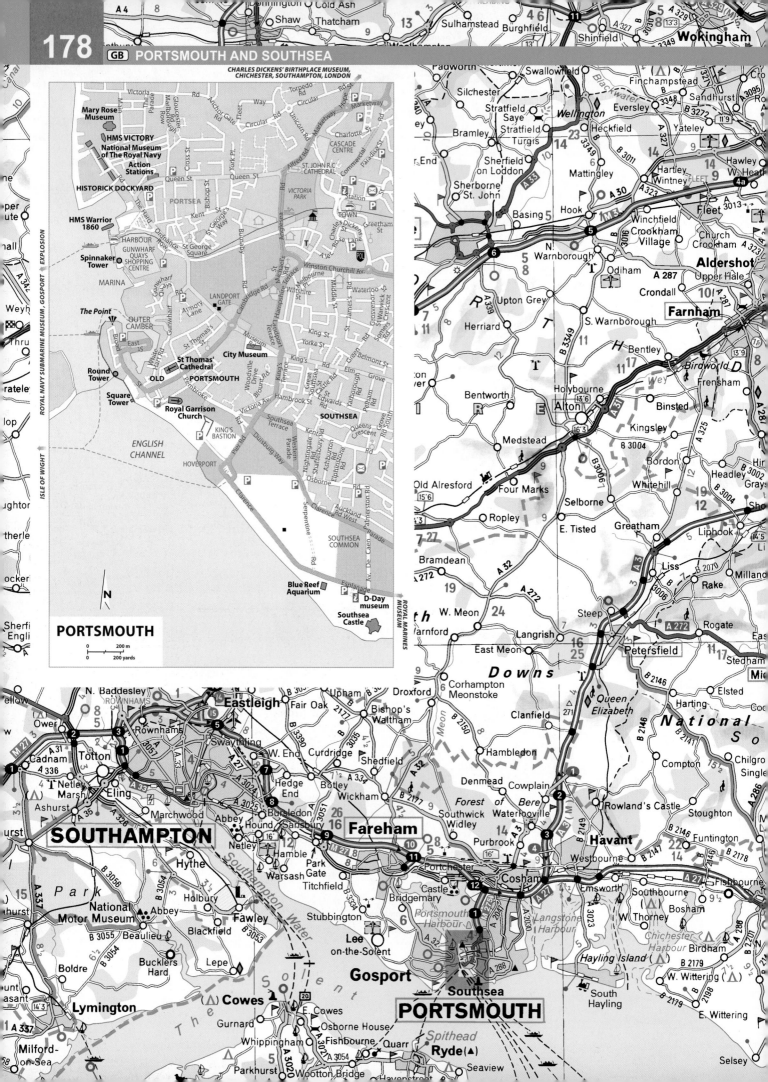

PORTSMOUTH (inset map)

CHARLES DICKENS' BIRTHPLACE MUSEUM, CHICHESTER, SOUTHAMPTON, LONDON

Mary Rose Museum
HMS VICTORY
National Museum of The Royal Navy
Action Stations
HISTORICK DOCKYARD
HMS Warrior 1860
Spinnaker Tower
The Point
Round Tower
Square Tower
Royal Garrison Church
KING'S BASTION
HOVERPORT
ENGLISH CHANNEL

ROYAL NAVY SUBMARINE MUSEUM, GOSPORT, EXPLOSION

ISLE OF WIGHT

St Thomas' Cathedral
OLD PORTSMOUTH
City Museum
SOUTHSEA
Blue Reef Aquarium
D-Day museum
Southsea Castle
ROYAL MARINES MUSEUM

PORTSMOUTH

0   200 m
0   200 yards

N

Regional map

Wokingham
Shaw Thatcham
Sulhamstead Burghfield
Shinfield
Silchester Swallowfield Finchampstead
Stratfield Saye Eversley Sandhurst
Bramley Stratfield Turgis Heckfield Yateley
Sherfield on Loddon Mattingley Hartley Wintney FLEET Hawley W. Heath
Sherborne St. John Fleet
Basing Hook Winchfield Church Crookham
Warnborough Crookham Village Aldershot
N. Warnborough Upper Hale
Upton Grey Odiham **Farnham**
Herriard S. Warnborough Crondall
Bentley Birdworld Frensham
Bentworth Holybourne Binsted
Alton Kingsley Bordon Headley
Medstead Whitehill Grays
Old Alresford Four Marks Selborne Greatham Liphook
Ropley E. Tisted Liss Rake Milland
Bramdean Greatham Steep
W. Meon Langrish Rogate
Warnford East Meon Petersfield Stedham
Corhampton Meonstoke Downs Elsted
Droxford Clanfield Queen Elizabeth Harting
N. Baddesley Ulpham Bishop's Waltham National
Eastleigh Fair Oak Hambledon Compton
Rownhams Curdridge Denmead Cowplain Rowland's Castle Stoughton
Swaythling W. End Shedfield Forest of Bere Waterlooville
Totton Hedge End Botley Wickham Southwick Widley Havant
Cadnam Marchwood Bursledon Fareham Purbrook Westbourne Emsworth Southbourne Fishbourne
Netley Marsh Eling Abbey Hound Netley Portchester Cosham W. Thorney Bosham
Ashurst **SOUTHAMPTON** Hamble Castle Bridgemary Birdham
Hythe Park Gate Titchfield Portsmouth Harbour Hayling Island
National Motor Museum Holbury Warsash Stubbington Langstone Harbour Chichester Harbour
Beaulieu Fawley Bridgemary **Gosport** South Hayling W. Wittering
Boldre Blackfield Lee on-the-Solent **Southsea** E. Wittering
Bucklers Hard Lepe **PORTSMOUTH** Selsey
Lymington Cowes Spithead
Milford-on-Sea Gurnard **Ryde**
Whippingham Fishbourne Quarr Seaview
Parkhurst Wootton Bridge Havenstreet
The Solent
Southampton Water

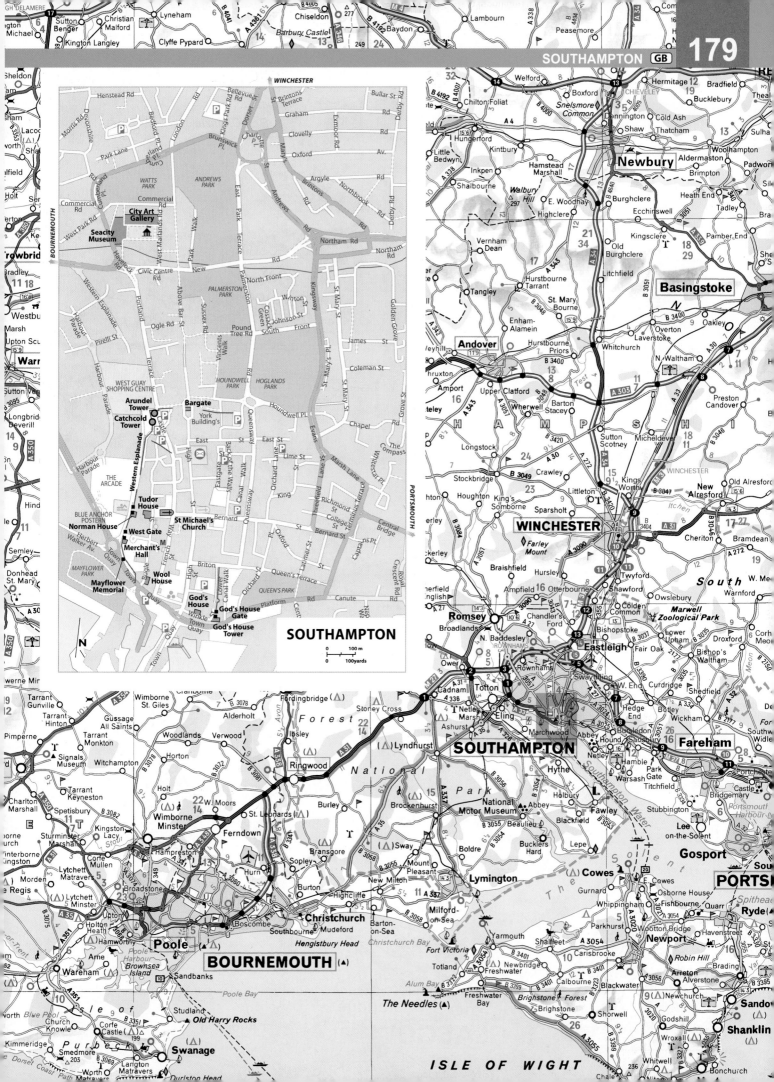

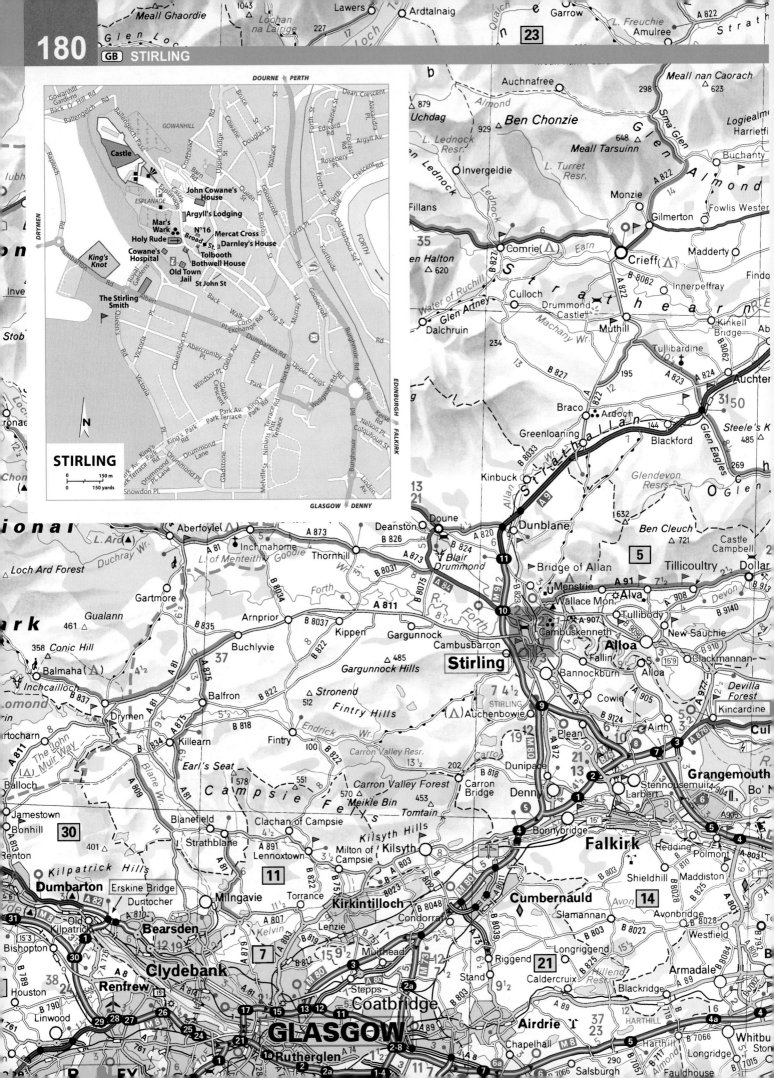

STIRLING

0   150 m
0   150 yards

N

Castle
GOWANHILL
Gowanhill Gardens
Back O' Hill Rd
Ballengeich Rd
Ballengeich Pass
ESPLANADE
Mar's Wark
Holy Rude
Cowane's Hospital
King's Knot
Royal Gardens
The Stirling Smith

John Cowane's House
Argyll's Lodging
N°16
Mercat Cross
Darnley's House
Tolbooth
Bothwell House
Old Town Jail
St John St

DOURNE PERTH

EDINBURGH FALKIRK

GLASGOW DENNY

Meall Ghaordie
Lochan na Lairige
Lawers
Ardtalnaig
Garrow
L. Freuchie
Amulree
Strath
A 822

Auchnafree
Meall nan Caorach
Ben Chonzie
Uchdag
Meall Tarsuinn
Logiealm
Harrietfi
L. Lednock Resr.
Invergeldie
Monzie
Gilmerton
Fowlis Wester
Glen Almond

Fillans
Comrie
Crieff
Madderty
Strathearn

Glen Halton
Culloch
Drummond Castle
Muthill
Innerpeffray
Kinkell Bridge
Findo

Dalchruin
Glen Artney

Braco
Ardoch
Auchter

Greenloaning
Blackford
Steele's K
Glen Eagles

Kinbuck
Glendevon Resrs

Aberfoyle
L. Ard
Deanston
Doune
Dunblane
Ben Cleuch
Castle Campbell
Tillicoultry
Dollar

Inchmahome
L. of Menteith
Thornhill
Blair Drummond
Bridge of Allan
Menstrie
Alva
Devon

Loch Ard Forest
Gartmore
Arnprior
Kippen
Gargunnock
Cambusbarron
Stirling
Wallace Mon.
Cambuskenneth
Tullibody
New Sauchie

Gualann
Conic Hill
Balmaha
Buchlyvie
Gargunnock Hills
Auchenbowie
Bannockburn
Fallin
Alloa
Alloa
Clackmannan

Inchcailloch
Drymen
Balfron
Stronend
Fintry Hills
Cowie
Devilla Forest
Kincardine

Lomond
The John Muir Way
Killearn
Fintry
Endrick Wr.
Carron Valley Resr.
Dunipace
Plean
Airth
Grangemouth
Cul

Balloch
Earl's Seat
Carron Valley Forest
Carron Bridge
Denny
Larbert
Stennousemuir
Bo'

Jamestown
Bonhill
Blanefield
Meikle Bin
Tomtain
Bonnybridge
Redding
Polmont

Renton
Strathblane
Clachan of Campsie
Kilsyth Hills
Milton of Campsie
Falkirk
Shieldhill
Maddiston

Kilpatrick Hills
Dumbarton
Erskine Bridge
Duntocher
Milngavie
Lennoxtown
Kilsyth
Cumbernauld
Longriggend
Armadale

Clydebank
Bearsden
Torrance
Kirkintilloch
Condorrat
Caldercruix
Blackridge
Westfield

Bishopton
Old Kilpatrick
Lenzie
Muirhead
Riggend
Slamannan
Avonbridge

Houston
Linwood
Renfrew
Stepps
Coatbridge
Stand
Airdrie
Harthill

GLASGOW
Rutherglen
Chapelhall
Salsburgh
Fauldhouse

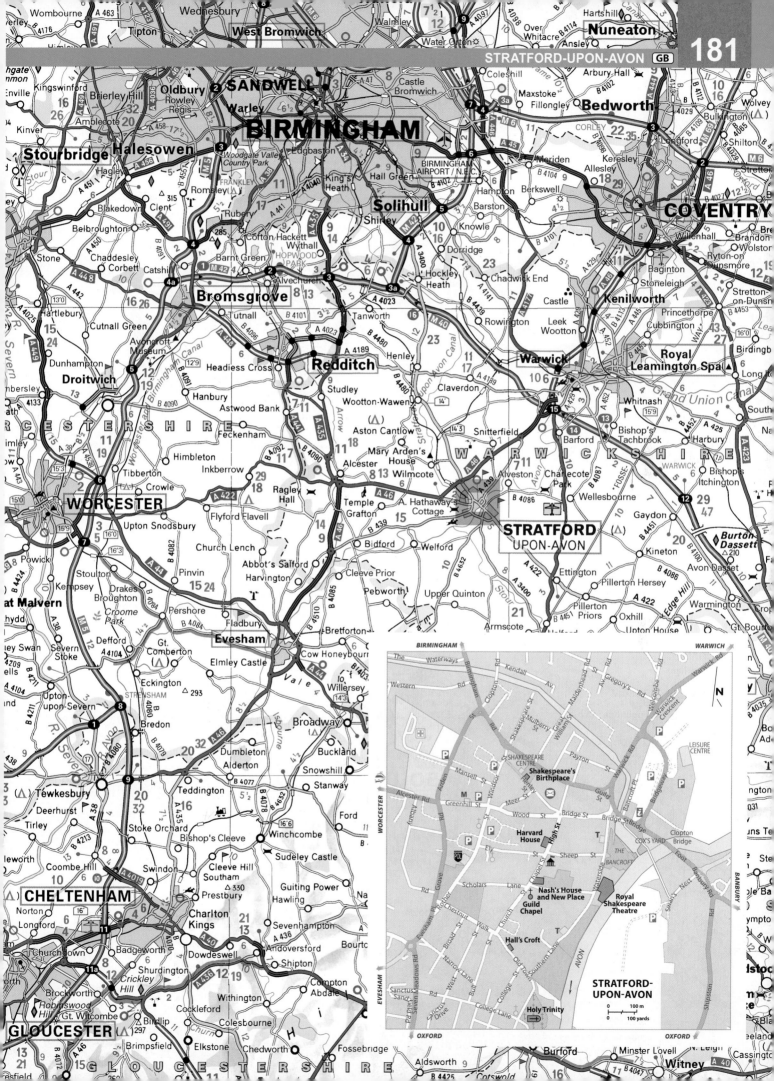

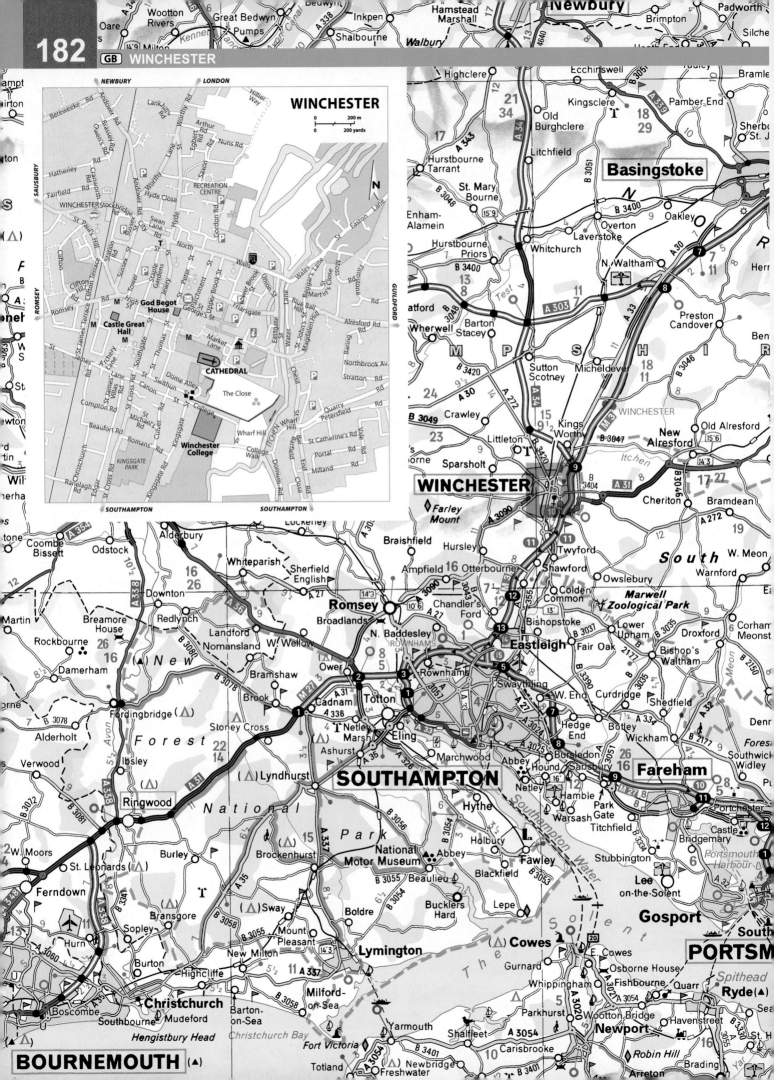

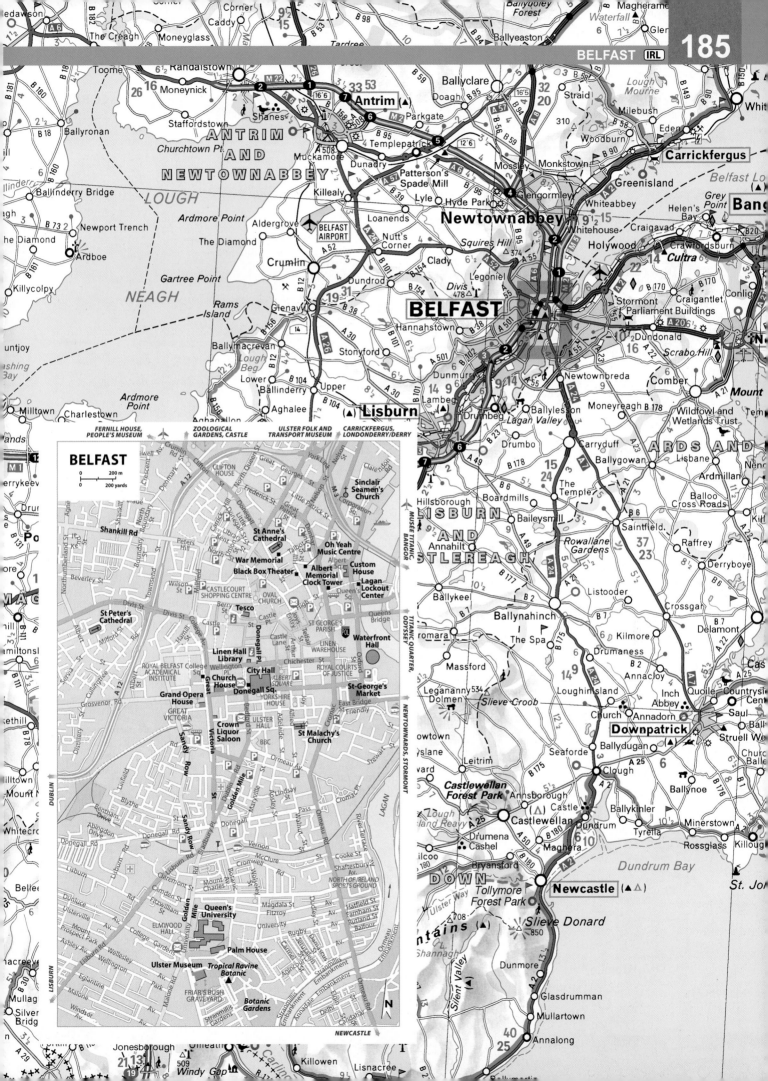

CORK (inset city map)

MALLOW

French's Villas
St Mary and St Anne's Cathedral
Hillgrove Lane
Leitrim
Shandon Court
Lower Richmond
Youghal Rd
St Anne's Shandon
St Patrick's Hill
Sidney Park
Belgrave Av.
Summerhill North
St Vincent's St
Mary Aikenhead Pl.
Dominick St
O'Connell's Sq.
Devonshire St
Wellington
Glanmire
Alfred St
Cork Butter Museum
John St Upper
Carroll's Quay
Maccurtain St
Brian Boru St
Blarney
North Mall
Pope's Quay
Camden Pl.
Penrose Quay
Kyrl's Quay
Lee
Anderson's Quay
Bachelor's Quay
Corn Market St
Merchant's Quay
SHOPPING CENTRE
Opera House
Crawford Art Gallery
Emmet Pl.
St Peter's Cork
Lavitt's Quay
St Patrick St
Parnell Pl.
CHATEAU BAR
Grattan St
Oliver Plunkett St
Albert Quay
Washington St West
Hanover St
English Market
South Mall
Grand Parade
Father Mathew Quay
Beamish Brewery
National Monument
Sullivan's Quay
George's Quay
South Terrace
St Fin Barre's Cathedral
Bishop St
Elizabeth Fort
Red Abbey Tower
Douglas St
Barrack St
Evergreen St
Old Blackrock Rd

0   150 m
0   150 yards

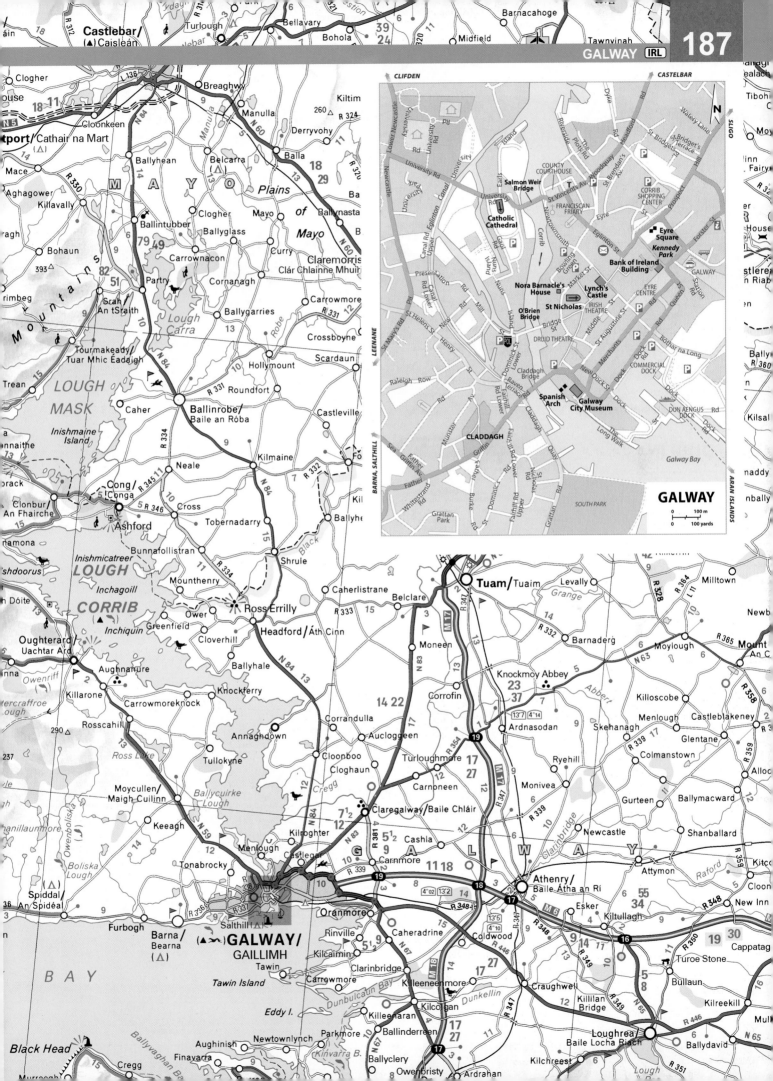

GALWAY

CLIFDEN
CASTELBAR
SLIGO
CLAREGALWAY
CLIFDEN

Salmon Weir Bridge
COUNTY COURTHOUSE
CORRIB SHOPPING CENTER
FRANCISCAN FRIARY
Catholic Cathedral
Eyre Square
Kennedy Park
Bank of Ireland Building
Nora Barnacle's House
Lynch's Castle
EYRE CENTRE
St Nicholas
IRISH THEATRE
O'Brien Bridge
DRUID THEATRE
POL
Claddagh Bridge
COMMERCIAL DOCK
Raleigh Row
DUN AENGUS DOCK
Spanish Arch
Galway City Museum
The Long Walk
CLADDAGH
Galway Bay
SOUTH PARK
Grattan Park
ARAN ISLANDS

GALWAY
0   100 m
0   100 yards

Castlebar/(▲)Caisleán
Turlough
Bellavary
Barnacahoge
Midfield
Tawnvinah
Clogher
Breaghwy
Bohola
Manulla
Kiltim
Derryvohy
Balla
Ballynasta
Northport/Cathair na Mart
Ballyhean
Belcarra
Mace
Aghagower
Killavally
Ballintubber
Clogher
Mayo
Ballyglass
Curry
Claremorris/Clár Chlainne Mhuir
Bohaun
Carrownacon
Cornanagh
Carrowmore
Partry
Ballygarries
Srah/An tSraith
Lough Carra
Tourmakeady/Tuar Mhic Eadaigh
Roundfort
Scardaun
Trean
LOUGH MASK
Caher
Ballinrobe/Baile an Róba
Castleville
Hollymount
Inishmaine Island
Crossboyne
Kilmaine
Neale
Fo
Cong/Conga
Cross
Ballyhe
Clonbur/An Fhairche
Ashford
Tobernadarry
Kil
Ballyhe
Bunnafollistran
Shrule
Inishmicatreer
LOUGH CORRIB
Mounthenry
Caherlistrane
Belclare
Tuam/Tuaim
Levally
Milltown
Inchagoill
Ower
Ross Errilly
Grange
Oughterard/Uachtar Ard
Greenfield
Cloverhill
Headford/Áth Cinn
Moneen
Barnaderg
Moylough
Mount An C
Aughnanure
Ballyhale
Knockmoy Abbey
Killoscobe
Killarone
Knockferry
Corrandulla
Corrofin
Ardnasodan
Menlough
Castleblakeney
Carrowmoreknock
Aucloggeen
Turloughmore
Ryehill
Glentane
Rosscahill
Ross Lake
Tullokyne
Cloonboo Cloghaun
Carnoneen
Monivea
Colmanstown
Moycullen/Maigh Cuilinn
Annaghdown
Alloc
Ballycuirke Lough
Cregg
Claregalway/Baile Chláir
Cashla
Gurteen
Ballymacward
Keeagh
Kilroghter
Carnmore
Newcastle
Shanballard
Boliska Lough
Menlough
Castlegar
Athenry/Baile Átha an Rí
Attymon
Spiddal/An Spidéal
Tonabrocky
Oranmore
Caheradrine
Esker
Kiltullagh
New Inn
Furbogh
Barna/Bearna
GALWAY/GAILLIMH
Rinville
Coldwood
Cappatag
Salthill
Kilcaimin
Clarinbridge
Turoe Stone
Tawin
Killeenmore
Craughwell
Bullaun
BAY
Tawin Island
Carrowmore
Dunbulcaun Bay
Killcolgan
Killilan Bridge
Kilreekill
Eddy I.
Killeenaran
Parkmore
Loughrea/Baile Locha Riach
Ballydavid
Black Head
Aughinish
Newtownlynch
Ballinderreen
Ardrahan
Kilchreest
Mul
Cregg
Finavarra
Kinvarra B.
Ballyclery
Owenbristy

KILLARNEY

KILLARNEY NATIONAL PARK

St Mary's Cathedral

Market Cross

St Mary's Church

Methodist Church

Franciscan Friary

KENMARE ← → GLENGARRIFF

MOUTH OF THE SHANNON

Tullig Point
Breaghva
Querrin
Kilrush
Cill Rois
Kilmurry Mc Mahon
Coolmeen
Killadys

Kilbaha Bridge
Kilbaha
Kilbaha Bay
Kilcloher
Beal Point
Beal
Carrigafoyle
Knock

Leck Point
Kilcredaun Point
Kilconly
Asdee
Ballylc

(Δ) Ballybunnion
Lisselton
Oaghley
Six

Ballynaskreena
Ballyduff
Rattoo
Lixnaw
Finuge

(Δ) Ballyheige
Ballyheige Bay
Lerrig
Ballincloher
Knc

Banna Strand
Banna
Abbeydorney
Kilflyn
Glanoe
Lyracrumpane

Barrow Harbour
Ardfert
Stack's Mountains

Fenit
Chapeltown Spa
Listellick
Reanagowan Cross Roads
Broughane Cross Roads

Tralee / Trá Lí
Blennerville

Derrymore I.
Windmill
Derrymore
Clogher

Baurtregaum
Slieve Mish Mountains
Farmer's Br.
Crag Cave
Rockchapel

Boolteens
Riverville
Currans
Castleisland / Oileán Ciarraí
Knockanefune
Cordal
Taur
Meelin

Castlemaine Harbour
Castlemaine
Fieries
Currow
Knocknaboul Cross
Clamper Cross
Blueford

Knockaunnaglashy
Milltown
Farranfore
Scartaglin
Ballydesmond
Kishkeam
Newr

KERRY

Tullig
Killorglin / Cill Orglan
Ballyhar
Tooreencahill

Caragh Lake
Ballyhar
Kilcummin Farmhill
Gneevgullia
Knocknagree
Cullen
Dernagree

Lough Caragh
Kilgobnet
Aghadoe
KILLARNEY / CILL AIRNE
Rathmore

Shanacashel
Beaufort
Killarney
Lough Leane
National
Barraduff
Caherbarnagh
Millstreet

Carrantuohill
Macgillycuddy's Reeks
Gap of Dunloe
Ross
Muckross
Park
Glenflesk
The Paps
Caherbarnagh

Boheeshil
Maghanlawaun
Upper Lake
Torc Waterfall
Crohane
Garries Bridge
Cloonken
Mullaghanish
Mountains

Ladies View
Galways Br.
Mangerton Mountain
Loo Br.
Derrynasaggart
Carriganimmy

Ballaghbeama Gap
Moll's Gap
Windy Gap
Morley's Br.
Coclea / Cúil Aodha
Ballyvourney / Baile Bhuirne
Garrane

Knocklomena
Kilgarvan
Inchee Br.
Ballymakeery / Baile Mhic Íre
Derreendarragh
Gearha Br.
Kenmare / Neidín
Roughty
Reananeree / Rae na nDoirí
Mac

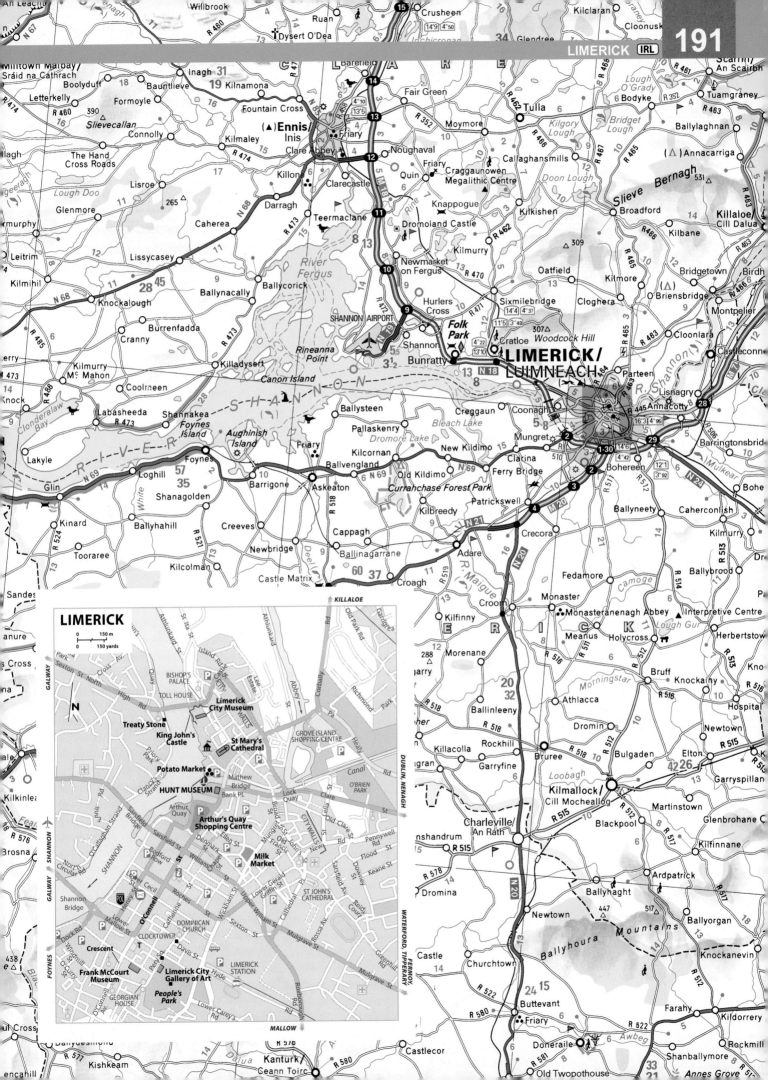

Eochair

Bóithre
Mótarbhealach - Limistéar seirbhíse
Carrbhealach dúbailte le saintréithe mótarbhealaigh
Acomhail mótarbhealaigh: iomlán - teoranta
Vimhreacha ceangail
Líonra idirnáisiúnta agus náisiúnta bóithre
Bóthar idir-réigiúnach nach bhfuil chomh plódaithe
Bóthar nuadheisithe - gan réitiú
Cosán - Conair mharcáilte / Cosán marcaíochta
Mótarbhealach, bóthar á dhéanamh
(an dáta oscailte sceidealta, mas eol)

Leithead bóithre
Carrshlí dhéach
4 lána - 2 leathanlána
2 lána - 2 chunglána

Fad bóthar (iomlán agus meánfhad)
Bhóithre dola ar an mótarbhealach
Saor ó dhola ar an mótarbhealach
i mílte - i gciliméadair
ar an mbóthar

Aicmiú oifigiúil bóithre
Mótarshl - GB: Príomhbhealach
IRL: Bóithre eile ,
Príomhbóithre agus fobhóithre náisiúnta
Ceann scríbe ar ghréasán bóithre priomha

Constaicí
Timpeall - Beamas agus a airde os cionn leibhéal na mara (i méadair)
Fána ghéar (suas treo an gha)
IRL: Bealach deacair nó baolach
Bóthar cúng le hionaid phasála (in Albain)
Crosaire comhréidh: iarnród ag dul, faoi bhóthar, os cionn bóthar
Bóthar toirmeasctha - Bóthar faoi theorannú
Bacainn dola - Bóthar aonsli
(Ar phríomhbóithre agus ar bhóithre réigiúnacha)
Teorainneacha airde (faoi 15'6" IRL, faoi 16'6" GB)
Teorann Mheáchain (faoi 16t)

Iompar
Leithead caighdeánach - Staisiún paisinéirí
Aerfort - Aerpháirc
Longsheirbhísí : (Seirbhísí séasúracha: dearg)
Bád
Fartha (uas - ulach : tonnaí méadracha)
Coisithe agus lucht rothar

Lóistín - Riarachán
Teorainneacha riaracháin
Teorainn na hAlban agus teorainn na Breataine Bige
Teorainn idirnáisiúnta - Custam

Áiseanna Spóirt agus Súgartha
Machaire Gailf - Ráschúrsa
Timpeall rásaíochta - Cuan bád aeraíochta
Láthair champa , láthair charbhán
Conair mharcáilte - Páirc thuaithe
Zú - Tearmannéan mara
IRL: Lascaireacht - Ráschúrsa con Lamród thraein ghaille
Traein cábla
Carr cábla , cathaoir cábla

Amhairc
Príomhradharcanna:
féach AN EOLAÍ UAINE
Bailte nó áiteanna inspéise, baill lóistín
Foirgneamh Eaglasta - Caisleán
Fothrach - Leacht meigiliteach - Pluais
Páirc, Gáirdín - Ionaid eile spéisiúla
IRL: Dunfort - Cros Cheilteach - Cloigtheach
Lánléargas - Cothrom Radhairc - Bealach Aoibhinn

Comharthaí Eile
Cáblashlí thionsclaíoch
Crann teileachumarsáide - Teach solais
Stáisiún Giniúna - Cairéal
Mianach - Tionsclaíocht
Scaglann - Aill
Páirc Fhoraoise Naisiúnta - Páirc Naisiúnta

Allwedd

Ffyrdd
Traffordd - Mannau gwasanaeth
Ffordd ddeuol â nodweddion traffordd
Cyfnewidfeyd: wedi'i chwblhau - cyfyngedig
Rhifau'r cyffyrdd
Ffordd ar rwydwaith rhyngwladol a chenedlaethol
Ffordd rhyngranbarthol a llai prysur
Ffordd ac wyneb iddi - heb wyneb
Llwybr troed - Llwybr troed ag arwyddion / Llwybr ceffyl
Traffordd - ffordd yn cael ei hadeiladu
(Os cyfodi yr achos: dyddiad agor disgwyliedig)

Ffyrdd
ffordd ddeuol
4 lôn - 2 lôn lydan
2 lôn - 2 lôn gul

Pellter (cyfanswm a'r rhyng-bellter)
Tollffyrdd ar y draffordd
Rhan di-doll ar y draffordd
mewn miltiroedd - mewn kilometrau
ar y ffordd

Dosbarthiad ffyrdd swyddogol
Traffordd - GB : Prif ffordd
IRL: Prif ffordd genedlaethol a ffordd eilradd
Ffyrdd eraill
Cylchfan ar rwydwaith y prif ffyrdd

Rhwystrau
Cylchfan - Bwlch a'i uchder uwchlaw lefel y môr (mewn metrau)
Rhiw serth (esgyn gyda'r saeth)
IRL: Darn anodd neu beryglus o ffordd
Yn yr Alban : ffordd gul â mannau pasio
Croesfan rheilffordd: croesfan rheilffordd, o dan y ffordd, dros y ffordd
Ffordd waharddedig - Ffordd a chyfyngiadau arni
Rhwystr Toll - Unffordd
(Ar brif ffyrdd a ffyrdd rhanbarthol)
Terfyn uchder (llai na 15'6" IRL, 16'6" GB)
Terfyn pwysau (llai na 16t)

Cludiant
Lled safonol - Gorsaf deithwyr
Maes awyr - Maes glanio
Llongau ceir: (Gwasanaethau tymhorol: mewn coch)
llong
Fferi (llwyth uchaf: mewn tunelli metrig)
Teithwyr ar droed neu feic yn unig

LIety - Gweinyddiaeth
Ffiniau gweinyddol
Ffin Cymru, ffin yr Alban
Ffin ryngwladol - Tollau

Cyfleusterau Chwaraeon a Hamdden
Cwrs golf - Rasio Ceffylau
Rasio Cerbydau - Harbwr cychod pleser
Leoedd i wersylla
Llwybr troed ag arwyddion - Parc gwlad
Parc saffari, sw - Gwarchodfa natur
IRL: Pysgota - Maes rasio milgwn
Trên twristiaid
Rhaffordd, car cêbl, cadair esgyn

Golygfeydd
Gweler Llyfr Michelin
Rye [▲]
Ergol ○
Trefi neu fannau o ddiddordeb, mannau i aros
Adeilag eglwysig - Castell
Adfeilion - Heneb fegalithig - Ogof
Gerddi, parc - Mannau eraill o ddiddordeb
IRL: Caer - Croes Geltaidd - twr crwn
Panorama - Golygfan - Ffordd dygfeydd

Symbolau eraill
Lein gêbl ddiwydiannol
Mast telathrebu - Goleudy
Gorsaf bwer - Chwarel
Mwyngloddio - Gweithgarwch diwydiannol
Purfa - Clogwyn
Parc Coedwig Cenedlaethol - Parc Cenedlaethol

Comnarthaí ar phleanna bailte

Ionaid inspéise
Ionad inspéise agus
Ionad inspéise adhartha

Bóithre
Mótarbhealach, carrbhealach dúbailte le saintréithe mótarbhea
Acomhail mótarbhealaigh : iomlán - teoranta
Priomh-thrébhealach
Sráid: neamhoiriúnach do thrácht, ach í stáit speisialta
Sráid: coisithe
Carrchlós

Comharthaí Éagsúla
Aerfort
Leithead caighdeánach - Staisiún paisinéirí
Ionad eolais turasóireachta - Ospidéal
Gairdín, páirc, coill - Reilig
Staidiam
Galfchúrsa
Stáisiún traenach faoi thalamh
Príomhoifi g phoist le poste restante
Foirgneamh poiblí curtha in iúl le litir thagartha:
Músaem
Amharclann
Póitíní (ceanncheathrú)

Symbolau ar gynlluniau'r trefi

Golygfeydd
Man diddorol
Lle diddorol o addoliad

Ffyrdd
Traffordd, ffordd ddeuol
Cyfnewidfeyd : wedi'i chwblhau - cyfyngedig
Prif ffordd drwodd
Stryd : Anaddas i draffi g, cyfyngedig
Stryd: Cerddwr
Parc ceir

Arwyddion amrywiol
Maes awyr
Lled safonol - Gorsaf deithwyr
Canolfan croeso - Ysbyty
Gardd, parc, coedwig - Mynwent
Stadiwm
Cwrs golff
Gorsaf danddaearol
Prif swyddfa bost gyda poste restante
Adeilad cyhoeddus a ddynodir gan lythyren:
Amgueddfa
Theatr
Yr Heddlu (pencadlys)